CONSUL JOHN BEECROFT'S JOURNAL OF HIS MISSION TO DAHOMEY, 1850

Fontes Historiae Africanae/Sources of African History (FHA) is an international editing and publication project which was initiated in 1962 to organise a series of the sources of the history of sub-Saharan Africa. It is directed under the general auspices of the Union Académique Internationale and the general series editor Viera Vilhanova of the Slovakian Academy of Sciences. The British Academy established a British Committee in 1973 which published 10 volumes, and a new series in 1995, which to date has published 15. The FHA is committed to making African history as widely available as possible, and to that end is seeking to develop partnerships with African publishers to facilitate co-publication on the continent.

FONTES HISTORIAE AFRICANAE
SOURCES OF AFRICAN HISTORY
17

CONSUL JOHN BEECROFT'S JOURNAL OF HIS MISSION TO DAHOMEY, 1850

EDITED BY
ROBIN LAW

Published for THE BRITISH ACADEMY
by OXFORD UNIVERSITY PRESS

Oxford University Press, Great Clarendon Street, Oxford OX2 6DP

First edition published in 2019

British Library Cataloging in Publication Data
Data available

Library of Congress Cataloguing in Publication Data
Data available

Typeset by Amnet Systems
Printed in Great Britain by
TJ International Ltd, Padstow, Cornwall

ISBN 978-0-19-726653-3

Dedicated to the memory of
Gezo, King of Dahomey, whose voice
this volume attempts to recover

CONTENTS

ACKNOWLEDGEMENTS

My thanks to the National Archives for permission to reproduce this material, and to the British Academy for its support of the project. Malyn Newitt, Luis Nicolau Parés, Suzanne Schwarz and Phia Steyn read and commented upon draft versions of this Introduction, and Luis Nicolau Parés did likewise for the Endnote on the Dahomian 'Annual Customs'. Roquinaldo Ferreira, Luis Nicolau Parés and Silke Strickrodt provided material utilised in the annotation, while Amy Redgrave assisted in tracking and verifying references. Thanks also to Damien Bove, who prepared the maps.

MAPS

INTRODUCTION

This volume presents the text of the journal of John Beecroft, British Consul in western Africa, of a diplomatic mission to Gezo, King of Dahomey, in 1850, which is preserved in the National Archives at Kew.[1] This mission was part of a sustained effort by the British government to persuade Gezo to collaborate in the suppression of the trans-Atlantic slave trade, which extended over ten years (1847–56), followed by further representations addressed to his successor, King Glele, a few years later (1862–5).[2] Although the mission of 1850 was a failure, Beecroft's account of it is an invaluable source for the history of Dahomey, especially for the light which it throws on the role of the slave trade within the politics and economy of the kingdom, as well as its response to British pressure for the trade's abolition. This publication of Beecroft's text complements an earlier volume in the Fontes Historiae Africanae series which relates to a subsequent phase in these negotiations, comprising the journals and correspondence of Louis Fraser, who served as resident Vice-Consul to Dahomey in 1851–2.[3]

These negotiations, it should be stressed, are documented only from the British side: Dahomey, being a non-literate society, generated no written records of its own. Although letters were often written in the names of Dahomian kings, including several from Gezo and Glele in the course of their negotiations with the British, these were transcribed by foreign visitors and survive only in overseas archives. In Dahomey itself there is a rich corpus of oral traditions relating to the kingdom's history, but these include no recollection of the negotiations with the British on the slave trade, nor of the resultant confrontation between the two countries.[4] The Dahomian 'voice' on these issues can therefore only be recovered in so far as it was reported in the British sources.[5]

---

[1] The National Archives (hereafter TNA), FO84/816, ff. 154–229v.
[2] For an overview of these negotiations, see Law (1995a).
[3] Fraser (2012).
[4] See esp. Le Herissé (1911: 271–352), presenting an account by Agbidinikoun, a prince of the Dahomian royal family. This does refer to later treaties with Portugal (1885) and France (1890), which fell within the personal memory of the informant.
[5] A historical novel set in Dahomey under King Gezo, written in the 1930s, includes an episode recounting the reception of a British mission which is clearly inspired by that of 1850 (albeit chronologically displaced to the 1820s), but although this work is in general informed by a deep knowledge of Dahomian culture and traditions, its account of this mission does not seem to derive from traditional sources (Hazoumé 1978 [1938]: 345–88).

Beecroft's journal is not the only source for the mission of 1850. He was accompanied by a naval officer, Lieutenant F.E. Forbes, who also wrote a journal, likewise preserved in the National Archives.[6] Forbes' account is much better known than Beecroft's because it has been more readily accessible. His original journal was included in the 'Parliamentary Papers' printed to inform debates in the House of Commons the following year[7]; and Forbes elaborated it into a book, also published in 1851, which has been reprinted in modern times.[8] A recent collection of documents relating to Gezo's negotiations with the British, being drawn solely from the material in the Parliamentary Papers, includes Forbes' journal but not Beecroft's.[9] It is not clear why Beecroft's journal was not also selected for inclusion in the Parliamentary Papers, but it may have been because it is substantially longer than that of Forbes (around 53,000 words, as compared to 21,000), and much less well written and (as this editor is painfully aware) his manuscript is difficult to decipher. Furthermore, the available text of the journal was avowedly only preliminary—Beecroft having undertaken to produce a revised version, though he did not, in the event, do so.[10] The consequence has been that modern studies of the negotiations of 1850, and of Dahomian history more generally, have depended primarily on Forbes' evidence, with limited or no citation of Beecroft's journal.[11] This publication of the latter serves to redress this imbalance.

Beecroft's journal does not duplicate, but supplements and complements Forbes' version: not only does he give a fuller account, including incidents missed or omitted by Forbes, but their observations and interpretations of particular events which they both witnessed sometimes differ significantly. Detailed comparison between the two, which is a major concern of the editorial annotation offered in this edition, is not only essential to any attempt to establish 'what actually happened', but also offers an illuminating methodological exercise which throws light on the nature of European reportage of African societies more generally.

---

[6] TNA, FO84/827, ff. 234–81.

[7] House of Commons Parliamentary Papers (hereafter HCPP), *Correspondence Relating to the Slave Trade*, 1850/1, Class A, inclosure 2 in no. 220; also in *Papers Relative to the Reduction of Lagos* (1852), incl. 3 in no. 13.

[8] Forbes (1851) (reprinted, facsimile ed. 1966). Currently (2018) there appear to be no less than eight different facsimile reprint editions of this book available.

[9] Coates (2001). This is an abridged version of *Papers Relative to the Reduction of Lagos*, and includes a slightly abbreviated version of Forbes' Journal: 52–84.

[10] See p. xlvii.

[11] However, historians have often cited a brief account included in a letter from Beecroft to Viscount Palmerston, 22 July 1850, also printed in the Parliamentary Papers (and included in this volume, Appendix 3 'Supplementary Documents', doc. 8).

1 Beecroft and Forbes

John Beecroft (1790–1854), at the time of his mission to Dahomey in 1850, was a man of extensive African experience—over, as he himself noted, no less than 21 years[12]—though none hitherto specifically in Dahomey.[13] He had been resident since 1829 on the island of Fernando Po (nowadays called Bioko, and part of the modern state of Equatorial Guinea), which was legally a Spanish colony but had become the site of a British naval base and commercial settlement named Clarence (later Santa Isabel, and nowadays Malabo). When the British government officially abandoned this settlement in 1834, Beecroft became its de facto governor, and when Spanish authority was reasserted over the island in 1843 he was formally confirmed in this position, now as an officer of the Spanish Crown. He also engaged in trade with the West African mainland, in partnership with the Liverpool merchant Robert Jamieson, and he undertook voyages of exploration up the River Niger.[14] (His account of one of these voyages, in 1840, in the *Journal of the Royal Geographical Society*, appears to be his only published work.[15]) In 1849 he had been appointed British Consul for the Bights of Benin and Biafra, comprising (in terms of modern political geography) the West African coast from eastern Ghana to Equatorial Guinea, with instructions to mediate between British traders and the local African authorities, and to promote 'legal [i.e. non-slave] commerce', especially in agricultural produce, as a substitute for the slave trade.[16] His period as Consul (until his death in 1854) was marked by a willingness to interfere in local politics to advance the suppression of the slave trade, and British commercial interests more generally, by virtue of which he played a central role in the establishment of a British 'informal empire' over parts of the coast.[17] In particular, his promotion of British military intervention at Lagos, on the coast east of Dahomey, in 1851 (to depose the local king and impose a treaty for the abolition of the slave trade) can be seen as beginning the process which ultimately led to the creation of the British colony of Nigeria.[18]

---

[12] See Beecroft's Journal, p. 90.

[13] For Beecroft's earlier life, see Dike (1956a).

[14] He alludes to these explorations in his Journal, pp. 20, 91–2, 128.

[15] Beecroft (1841). Strictly, this is not Beecroft's own account, being mostly written in the third person, and evidently edited and reworked by someone else, probably Robert Jamieson, who is credited with having 'communicated' the text to the journal.

[16] HCPP, *Slave Trade*, 1849/50, Class B, no. 11: Viscount Palmerston to Consul Beecroft, 30 June 1849.

[17] Dike (1956b: 128–45).

[18] For the Lagos episode (and also some account of the Dahomian mission of 1850), see Lynn (1992).

Beecroft's co-envoy Frederick Edwyn Forbes (1819–1852) was a naval officer. At the time of the mission he was commanding the ship *Bonetta*, part of the British Navy's West African Squadron, which was engaged in patrols to intercept ships involved in the slave trade. Forbes had the advantage of previous Dahomian experience, although this was brief, comprising two short visits (about eight weeks in all) to the area in 1849/50.[19] Despite his relative youth (he was aged only 31 in 1850), he had already published two books, derived from his naval service, relating to China and to his experience in the anti-slaving squadron.[20] He had also submitted a paper to the Royal Geographical Society, reporting his discovery of a written script in use among the Vai people (of modern Liberia) in 1849.[21] His subsequent book on the Dahomian mission may therefore be presumed to have been envisaged from the outset, which should be borne in mind in evaluating his journal. Doubtless further volumes would have followed but for his untimely death in 1852.[22] His book on Dahomey, it should be noted, was not simply a work of disinterested reportage but had an explicit polemical purpose: to advocate a more aggressive policy towards the suppression of the slave trade through a total blockade of the African coast and military action onshore.[23]

How smoothly Beecroft and Forbes worked together on the mission is an interesting but obscure question. Their journals contain no hint of anything other than cordial cooperation, and Forbes included in his book an encomium on his fellow-envoy, praising his 'activity' and 'perseverance', and observing that 'As a fellow-labourer, although considerably my senior in years, he always took his share of the work; and as a companion, I would not wish a better.'[24] However, the numerous detailed discrepancies between their two accounts imply that they did not systematically compare notes on what they had seen and heard, suggesting at least a degree of distance between them. One particular instance of difference related to the praise-singers they observed performing at the Dahomian court, whom Beecroft termed

[19] In 4–29 October 1849 and 27 February–31 March 1850. His journals of these earlier visits can be found in TNA, FO84/785, ff. 479–94, and FO84/826, ff. 237–43; and were printed in HCPP, *Slave Trade*, 1849/50, Class B, incl. 9 in no. 9, and 1850/1, Class A, incl. 1 in no. 198; they were also incorporated into his book (Forbes 1851, i: 43–130).
[20] Forbes (1848; 1849).
[21] Forbes (1850): see also Forbes (1851, i: 135–218).
[22] In November 1851–March 1852 he undertook a second diplomatic mission, to Abeokuta, where he successfully negotiated a treaty for the abolition of the slave trade (5 January 1852), but he fell ill and died at sea on 25 March 1852. His dispatches from Abeokuta include substantial material on its history and geography, which it seems likely was intended as the basis of a further publication.
[23] See esp. the Appendix of 'Reflections on the Slave Trade and the means for its repression' (Forbes 1851, i: 131–55; and further remarks, ii: 158–60).
[24] Forbes (1851, ii: 205).

'minstrels', but Forbes called 'troubadours', explaining that this was 'the only appropriate names [*sic*] for them, they were not minstrels …'.[25] The issue is trivial, but perhaps it is not fanciful to see in it a reflection of disagreement in conversation between the two men. It is also suggestive that while in Dahomey they initially took their early morning walks together, but later more usually separately.[26]

Certainly, there is evidence of tension between the two on a subsequent occasion, in 1852, when Forbes was engaged in a second mission, to another African state, Abeokuta. He was reportedly furious when Beecroft sent a batch of military supplies, for transmission to the local authorities, to a British missionary resident there, the Reverend Henry Townsend, rather than to himself, and insisted that they should be handed over to him. Townsend commented that Forbes was 'jealous of his authority, & seemed to live and work for promotion, which made him disagreeable to those who might seem to him to be in the way of it, or who seemed to slight his position'.[27] Forbes' sensitivity about his own status is also suggested by his complaint against another missionary, the Reverend S.W. Koelle, for allegedly usurping the credit for the discovery of the Vai script.[28] It therefore seems plausible to infer that the differences between Beecroft and Forbes in their reportage of the 1850 mission reflected in part the tensions between them.

2 Dahomey

The kingdom of Dahomey[29] was located in what is nowadays the southern part of the Republic of Bénin (formerly the French colony of Dahomey which was named after the African kingdom),[30] its capital being the town of Abomey, about 100 km inland from the coast. It was one of the African states best known to Europeans in the eighteenth and nineteenth centuries, having the unique distinction that its history was the subject of a book published in

[25] Forbes' Journal, in Appendix 1, p. 158.
[26] From Beecroft's Journal, they walked together until mid-June, but generally separately thereafter.
[27] Church Missionary Society (CMS) Archives, University of Birmingham, C/A2/085, Rev. H. Townsend to CMS, 1 May 1852.
[28] Referring to the latter's report on the script, Koelle (1849). See Forbes (1851, i: 215), describing this as 'almost forgetting the pioneer, leaving it a matter of doubt to the reader, to whom the credit of the discovery belonged'. But in fact Koelle acknowledges Forbes' role in the very first sentence of his account.
[29] This spelling, used by Beecroft and Forbes, remains normal usage, at least in English, although a more accurate rendering of the name would be 'Danhomè'.
[30] The colony became an independent state in 1960, which was renamed Bénin in 1975. In this work, to avoid confusion, the name 'Dahomey' is applied only to the pre-colonial kingdom.

Britain as early as 1793.[31] The kingdom ceased to exist under French colonial rule, the last king being deposed in 1900,[32] but its surviving institutions and culture were documented in substantial works of anthropology,[33] and its pre-colonial history has attracted a fair amount of attention from modern academic historians from the 1960s onwards.[34] These earlier works, as well as my own research, have informed the interpretation and annotation of Beecroft's text offered in this edition.

Dahomey was a relatively recently founded state: Gezo (r. 1818–58), to whom the mission of 1850 was addressed, was remembered as only its ninth king, indicating that it was founded probably during the first half of the seventeenth century.[35] It had developed into a major military power, which dominated the surrounding region during the eighteenth and nineteenth centuries, conquering and absorbing several neighbouring states. In its official ideology, Dahomey lived in a permanent state of war, undertaking a military campaign every year during the main dry season (December to April).[36] In European perceptions it was notorious for its practice of human sacrifice, principally of captives taken in its wars, at public ceremonies called the 'Annual Customs',[37] and for its employment of female soldiers (whom Europeans inevitably dubbed 'Amazons') in its armed forces.[38] It was also an important supplier of slaves for the trans-Atlantic trade to the Americas, many of whom again were captives taken in Dahomey's wars. This trade yielded not only military supplies (guns and ammunition) and a range of luxury goods (especially cloth, tobacco and alcoholic spirits), but also cowry shells (imported ultimately from the Indian Ocean), which served as the local currency; as a consequence, the impact of overseas trade permeated throughout the domestic economy. The trade with Europeans was concentrated at the coastal town of Ouidah (spelled 'Whydah' in contemporary English usage), where the major European nations involved in the slave trade—Portugal, Britain and France—all maintained fortified trading posts.[39] Ouidah's role as the centre of European trade in Dahomey was reflected in the title of the

---

[31] Dalzel (1793).

[32] The kingship was, however, revived in the 1990s, so that there is nowadays again a King of Dahomey.

[33] Notably that of the French colonial administrator Auguste Le Herissé (1911).

[34] See esp. Akinjogbin (1967), Glélé (1974), Law (1991) and Bay (1998). For the nineteenth century, see also the unpublished theses by Ross (1967), Soumonni (1983) and Reid (1986).

[35] But the date conventionally given for the foundation of the kingdom, *c.*1625 (repeated by Forbes, Journal, pp. 174, 185), is merely a speculative estimate.

[36] For a list of Gezo's annual campaigns, according to Dahomian tradition, see Mouléro (1965).

[37] For Dahomey's reputation for human sacrifice, see Law (1985: 67–9).

[38] See Law (1993) and Alpern (1998).

[39] On Ouidah, see Law (2004b).

Dahomian Viceroy who administered it, the Yovogan or 'Chief of White Men', who figures prominently in Beecroft's journal.[40]

Gezo had come to the throne in 1818, by a *coup d'état*, deposing his elder brother Adandozan.[41] In Dahomian tradition, he is recalled as one of the kingdom's most successful rulers—'after [the founder] the one of our kings who did most for Dahomey'.[42] He is celebrated above all as a successful warrior, who in particular defeated the kingdom of Oyo to the north-east (in modern Nigeria), to which Dahomey had earlier been tributary, thereby securing his own kingdom's independence in 1823.[43] His reign also proved to be a significant period of transition in Dahomey's history, because the slave trade, which had been the mainstay of its external commerce, had now been outlawed, through its legal 'abolition' by the European and American nations involved, including Britain in 1807.[44] Initially, however, the slave trade from Dahomey, although now illegal—for the foreign purchasers of slaves, though not of course for the Dahomian sellers, under local law—continued to flourish, now directed mainly to Brazil and Cuba. The dominant figure in this illegal trade was a Brazilian merchant, Francisco Felix de Souza, who had assisted Gezo in his seizure of the throne in 1818, and was rewarded with appointment as the King's commercial agent at Ouidah, with the title of 'Chacha'.[45] Although this man had died in 1849, some of his sons—Isidoro (who succeeded to the office of Chacha), Antonio and Ignacio de Souza—remained prominent merchants, and are referred to in the records of the 1850 mission. However, the leading merchant in Dahomey (indeed, according to Forbes, 'the greatest slave-dealer in all Africa')[46] was now another Brazilian, Domingos José Martins (often rendered in British sources in a Spanish form, 'Domingo Martinez'), who also figures in the mission journals.[47] From the 1830s, there also developed a significant trade in palm oil (used mainly in the manufacture of soap), and by 1850, as Beecroft and Forbes noted, Martins and other Brazilian slave traders were also dealing extensively in oil, although

---

[40] Spelled by Beecroft in various forms, e.g. 'Avohgah', 'Eeahvoogau'; but he also frequently refers to him as the 'Caboceer [i.e. chief]' of Ouidah.

[41] Adandozan is not named in Beecroft's journal, which refers anonymously to 'the late king', but he was named by Forbes (who rendered the name as 'Adonooza', Journal, pp. 160–1).

[42] Le Herissé (1911: 318). For modern assessments of Gezo, see e.g. Adeyinka (1974) and Djivo (1977).

[43] Beecroft alludes to the Oyo war, p. 125, but gives no indication that he grasped its significance.

[44] On Gezo's policy towards this commercial transition, see Soumonni (1980; 1995) and Reid (1986).

[45] On de Souza, see Ross (1969) and Law (2004a).

[46] Forbes' Journal, p. 174.

[47] On Martins, see Ross (1965).

they generally regarded this as a supplement to rather than a substitute for the slave trade.[48]

3 The Anglo-Dahomian negotiations on the slave trade

Following the abolition of the slave trade in 1807, the British fort at Ouidah was judged no longer to have any commercial function, and was abandoned in 1812. However, British interest in Dahomey subsequently revived, initially through the development of the trade for palm oil (which was a significant raw material for British industry). The principal pioneer of this trade was Thomas Hutton, a merchant based at Cape Coast, the British headquarters on the Gold Coast (modern Ghana) to the west, who began trading along the coast to the east from the mid-1830s.[49] In 1838 Hutton reoccupied the Ouidah fort as a factory for the oil trade, though this occupation had no official sanction from the British government.[50]

Around the same time, the British government began to move towards a more interventionist policy in West Africa, as part of its campaign to suppress the illegal slave trade. This 'new African policy', as historians have called it,[51] sought to cut off the slave trade at its sources of supply within Africa, by the promotion of exports of agricultural produce as a substitute. This also implied seeking the active cooperation of African rulers and merchants: as the leading abolitionist Thomas Fowell Buxton put it, 'to make [the African] a confederate in the suppression of the slave trade'.[52] One aspect of this approach, which the British government took up from 1838 onwards, was the negotiation of treaties for the abolition of the slave trade with the rulers of African coastal states.[53]

Dahomey, as one of the places in Africa where the slave trade remained at a high level, inevitably became a major focus of this new policy. In 1841, an official inquiry into Britain's West African possessions recommended the reoccupation and restoration of the fort at Ouidah, among others, as a base for action against the slave trade, and this was endorsed by a Select Committee of the House of Commons in the following year, though nothing was done immediately to put this into effect.[54] British interest was reinforced by

---

[48] Law (2004b: 207–9).
[49] See Lynn (1997: 22) and Strickrodt (2015: 210–12).
[50] Law (2004b: 204–5).
[51] Gallagher (1950).
[52] Buxton (1840: 8).
[53] Dike (1956b: 81–96).
[54] HCPP, *Report from the Select Committee on the West Coast of Africa* (1842). See pp. iv–v of the Committee's Report; and also the earlier *Report of the Commissioner of Inquiry into the Western Coast of Africa*, 31 July 1841, included as Appendix 3 to the 1842 *Report* (see pp. 12, 15).

the account of a private visitor to Dahomey, the Reverend T.B. Freeman, head of the Methodist mission on the Gold Coast, in 1843, who reported that King Gezo was eager to revive relations with Britain, and in particular for the Ouidah fort to be officially reoccupied.[55] Freeman, indeed, was so impressed with Gezo's expressions of goodwill that he suggested that 'there would be but little difficulty in obtaining his co-operation in the suppression of the Slave-Trade', although there was nothing in Gezo's own reported statements which really warranted this optimism. The matter was discussed between the administration of the British possessions on the Gold Coast and the local naval commander, and two draft treaties for submission to Gezo were drawn up, one of 'amity and commerce', guaranteeing freedom of trade and protection for British merchants, and one whereby Gezo would 'abandon and prohibit' the slave trade in return for transitional compensation of goods to the value of £700 annually over seven years. However, the Colonial Office in London was sceptical about the King's alleged readiness to give up the slave trade, and no further action was taken.[56] The merchant Thomas Hutton also suggested an embassy to Dahomey to negotiate a treaty for the suppression of the slave trade in return for the development of trade in cotton, but again this was not taken up.[57]

In 1844 the Lieutenant-Governor of the Gold Coast, Henry Hill, did visit Ouidah, but this was on an unrelated matter—to seek compensation for a British subject (an African from the colony of Sierra Leone) who had been taken prisoner by Dahomian soldiers, and whose goods had been destroyed, while trading at Badagry, to the east, and, although Hill spoke to de Souza, he did not deal directly with the Dahomian authorities, and he does not seem to have raised the issue of the slave trade. Faced with the refusal of the Dahomians to pay compensation, Hill proposed the landing of an armed party at Ouidah to enforce it, but the local naval commander, to whom he applied for assistance, was unwilling to take such action (which would legally have constituted an act of war) without authorisation from the Admiralty, and again nothing came of this.[58]

Interest was revived by another private visitor to Dahomey, the Scottish explorer John Duncan (in the service of the Royal Geographical Society) in

---

[55] Freeman (1844: 260–4).

[56] TNA, CO96/2, George MacLean to Lord Stanley, 20 May 1843, inclosing Rev. T.B. Freeman to MacLean, 11 May 1843; Note by Stanley, 27 July 1843.

[57] TNA, CO96/3, Extract of letter from Hutton, undated, transmitted in Captain John Foote to Admiralty, 15 May 1843, incl. in Sydney Herbert (Admiralty) to Colonial Office, 9 Aug. 1843.

[58] TNA, CO96/4, Lt-Governor Hill to Stanley, 18 May and 11 Nov. 1844; CO96/6, Commander Jones to Hill, 6 Dec. 1844, incl. in Hill to Stanley, 26 Feb. 1845. A later account asserts that Hill in 1844 actually fired a cannon shot on Ouidah (Burton 1864, i: 103), but this seems to involve confusion with an earlier incident, involving a British warship engaged in anti-slaving operations, in 1840 (Law 2004b: 190–1).

1845, who again reported that Gezo wished for friendly relations with the British, including the reoccupation of the Ouidah fort, and this time (at least as subsequently represented by Duncan) explicitly stated that he was open to ending the slave trade: 'he should be ready and very glad to make any reasonable arrangement with the English Government for the abolition of slavery [*sic* = the slave trade], and the establishment of another trade'.[59] He also apologised for the treatment of the Sierra Leonian trader in the previous year, attributing his arrest to a 'mistake' on the part of the soldiers involved, and promised 'every protection' to future British visitors to Dahomey.[60] In 1847 an official mission to Gezo was finally organised, led by the Lieutenant-Governor of the Gold Coast, now William Winniett, who presented versions of the two draft treaties prepared earlier, although the compensation offered for giving up the slave trade was now reduced to $2,000 annually (equivalent to only about £417).[61] Gezo accepted the treaty of 'amity and commerce', which he 'signed' on 5 April 1847.[62] On the slave trade, however, his response was temporising: he claimed that he needed to consult his 'caboceers [chiefs]',[63] and asked that the British return in the following year to hear his decision.[64] Another official of the Gold Coast administration, Brodie Cruickshank, was duly sent back to Dahomey in 1848, only to find that Gezo's considered answer, after consultation with his caboceers, was essentially negative. Although still insisting that he desired friendly relations, including the reoccupation of the Ouidah fort, he maintained that the slave trade was so deeply embedded within Dahomian culture that it could only be abolished by a gradual process, over a period of years, and in any case the compensation offered was totally inadequate. He further suggested that the British should in the first instance stop the slave trade from neighbouring ports: 'he begs the Queen of England to put a stop to the Slave Trade everywhere else and allow him to continue it'.[65]

---

[59] Duncan (1847, ii: 267–71). But the letter which Gezo dictated to Duncan (see note 60) contains no such statement.
[60] TNA, CO96/8, King Gezo to Queen Victoria, incl. in Duncan to Stanley, Abomey, 1 July 1845.
[61] The dollar was officially valued at 4*s*. 2*d*. (50 *d*.).
[62] The text of this treaty is published in Crooks (1923: 310–12).
[63] The term 'caboceer', from Portuguese *cabeçeira* ('head', hence 'chief'), was in standard use at this time: although its application was vague, it implied the holding of formal political authority.
[64] TNA, CO96/11, Lt-Governor Winniett to Earl Grey, 12 May 1847, inclosing copies of draft treaties. See also the account by another member of this mission: Ridgway (1847).
[65] TNA, CO96/13, Winniett to Grey, 29 Nov. 1848, inclosing King Gezo to Queen Victoria, 3 Nov. 1848. Also HCPP, *Copy of Dispatches from the Lieutenant-Governor of the Gold Coast, Giving an Account of Missions to the King of Ashantee and Dohomey* [*sic*] (1849), incl. in no. 2: Report by B. Cruickshank, on his Mission to the King of Dahomey, 9 Nov. 1848 (cited hereafter as 'Cruickshank's Report').

Cruickshank nevertheless had the impression that Gezo might be won over if he could be convinced that he would receive a revenue sufficient to compensate for the loss of that from the slave trade. The British government also remained optimistic that he might be recruited as a partner in the abolitionist cause, and indeed seemed to be willing to go along with his suggestion of a gradualist approach to the issue. When Beecroft was appointed Consul in 1849, the area of his jurisdiction included Dahomey, so that the handling of relations with the latter now passed from the Colonial Office to the Foreign Office. At the same time, John Duncan (the explorer of 1845) was about to return to Dahomey, again in a private capacity (this time, on behalf of the Manchester Chamber of Commerce, to promote the cultivation of cotton there), and the government took the opportunity to appoint him as Vice-Consul to Dahomey. The instructions given to Duncan by the Foreign Secretary, Lord Palmerston, charged him with promoting 'legal commerce' as a substitute for the slave trade, but did not explicitly refer to the negotiation of a treaty for the abolition of the latter; a letter which Duncan was given to deliver to Gezo was likewise restricted to assuring him that 'legal commerce' would prove more profitable than the slave trade, without any mention of a treaty.[66]

Vice-Consul Duncan arrived in Dahomey in August 1849, taking up residence in the British fort at Ouidah, thereby meeting Gezo's wish for it to be officially reoccupied, and visited Gezo at his capital Abomey in September. The King welcomed the proposal for trade in cotton, and declared his willingness to give up the slave trade, 'so soon as he finds that by any other means he can raise sufficient revenue', though this formulation left open the question of whether (or how quickly) this proviso could be satisfied. He again undertook to consult his caboceers, and said that Duncan should return to hear his 'full answers' in the following year, at his Annual Customs.[67] Gezo had also expressed a desire to be visited by a British naval officer, and Lieutenant F.E. Forbes was selected for this task. The instructions given to Forbes by the local naval commander-in-chief, Commodore Fanshawe, now did raise explicitly the issue of a treaty for the abolition of the slave trade.[68] Forbes joined

---

[66] HCPP, *Slave Trade*, 1849/50, Class B, no. 1: Viscount Palmerston to John Duncan, 29 May 1849; incl. in no. 2: Palmerston to King Gezo, 29 May 1849.

[67] Ibid., no. 6, with incl. 1: Duncan to Palmerston, 22 Sept. 1849; King Gezo to Palmerston, 7 Sept. 1849 (the latter also included in this volume, Appendix 3, doc. 1).

[68] Ibid., incl. 2 in no. 9: Commodore Fanshawe to Lieutenant Forbes, 9 Sept. 1849. However, the letter given to Forbes to deliver to Gezo refers rather to a 'treaty of amity and commerce': ibid., incl. 3: Fanshawe to King Gezo, 10 Sept. 1849. Gezo had, in fact, already signed such a treaty in 1847, but perhaps Fanshawe was unaware of this.

Duncan in a second visit to Gezo in October 1849, but the King merely reiterated that he would give his answer at the Annual Customs.[69]

Duncan, however, had fallen ill during the mission, left Ouidah on 30 October 1849, and died shortly after, leaving the Vice-Consulate vacant. It was therefore decided that Beecroft himself should undertake the return mission to Gezo, together with Lieutenant Forbes: this was, in fact, Beecroft's first assignment in his new capacity as Consul. Beecroft, who was currently in Britain, received his instructions from Lord Palmerston in February 1850, prior to returning to Africa.[70] After some delay, due to the postponement of the Annual Customs, Beecroft and Forbes landed at Ouidah on 14 May 1850 and reached the capital Abomey on 26 May. They spent six weeks in Abomey (26 May to 6 July), before returning to Ouidah and re-embarking from there on 12 July. At their final interview with Gezo, on 4 July 1850, while he still insisted that he desired friendly relations with the British, and in particular wanted the vacant Vice-Consulate to be filled (if possible, he asked, by Lieutenant Forbes), he declared that he could not give up the slave trade 'at once', and again suggested that the British should close down the trade from neighbouring ports before he could consider agreeing to a treaty.[71]

It has been suggested that the failure of the 1850 mission was the personal fault of Beecroft, whose arrogant and aggressive attitude antagonised King Gezo.[72] The journals of Beecroft and Forbes do not really support this interpretation. Certainly, in the interview on 4 July, Gezo was visibly 'somewhat excited and annoyed' by Beecroft's refusal to consider even a limited continuation of the slave trade;[73] but this was due to the substance of the British position (which was of course dictated by the government in London) rather than Beecroft's manner of presenting it, and the interview ended amicably, with the King sharing a drink and a handshake with the envoys. The only significant show of aggression and bad temper on the part of the envoys (in which Forbes rather than Beecroft took the lead) was on a subsequent occasion, two days later, in connection with their demand for the release of a British subject held prisoner in Dahomey, and was addressed to subordinate officials rather than to the King personally.[74]

---

[69] King Gezo to Fanshawe, 18 Oct. 1849, in Appendix 3, doc. 2.

[70] Palmerston to Beecroft, 25 Feb. 1850, in Appendix 3, doc. 3.

[71] See the Journals of Beecroft and Forbes, pp. 150–1, 193–4; also King Gezo to Queen Victoria, 4 July 1850, in Appendix 3, doc. 7.

[72] Lynn (1992: 154).

[73] See Beecroft's Journal, p. 151. In his dispatch to Palmerston, he further stated that 'his countenance changed, and became a shade lighter' (Appendix 3, doc. 8, see p. 209). Forbes' account is more dramatic: '[his] countenance was almost blanched, his head down, his right hand rubbed his forehead while his veins swelled' and his voice was 'tremulous' (Journal, p. 194).

[74] Not recorded in Beecroft's journal, but in his dispatch (Appendix 3, doc. 8, pp. 210–11); see also Forbes' Journal, p. 195.

It is moreover clear that Gezo himself did not think that the negotiations had broken down: in the meeting of 4 July he expressed his desire that Beecroft should return to Dahomey in the following year at the next Annual Customs, and in February and again in April 1851 he sought to resume the negotiations, sending messages requesting that an officer should again come to Abomey.[75] In January 1852, he complained that Beecroft and Forbes, having come to witness his Customs, 'went away in the middle of them, and have not returned'; and in 1854 he claimed to be still 'anxiously waiting' for a reply to the message which he had sent through them.[76] Beecroft's assessment, however, in his report of the mission to Palmerston, was that further negotiation with Gezo was pointless, since 'it is too obvious that he has not the slightest desire to abandon the abominable [slave] Traffic', and that the only way to induce him to cooperate would be by a blockade of his port of Ouidah.[77] Palmerston wrote to Gezo in October 1850 to warn him that, since he had declined to make a treaty, the slave trade from Dahomey would now be suppressed by the British Navy without him receiving any compensation.[78]

The diplomatic path was not immediately abandoned, however, since a replacement Vice-Consul to Dahomey, Louis Fraser, was appointed in December 1850, and arrived belatedly to take up office at Ouidah in July 1851. But a visit by Fraser to Abomey in August/September did not go well. At his initial audience with Gezo, the latter appeared taken aback by the 'strong language' of Palmerston's letter, and deferred consideration of the British demand for the ending of the slave trade until 'another day', but a second meeting was taken up with other subjects without the issue of a treaty even being discussed. A letter dictated on Gezo's behalf reiterated his established line that the question of the slave trade should be left to be settled 'by and bye' rather than immediately, and after further ill-tempered exchanges Fraser walked out of the negotiations, leaving Abomey without being formally discharged by the King.[79] Report of this debacle reinforced Beecroft's conviction that 'whatever [Gezo] had to state relative to signing treaties was all twaddle', and that he would need to be coerced.[80] Palmerston had meanwhile already resolved that Dahomey should be blockaded, for which he sent

---

[75] HCPP, *Slave Trade*, 1851/2, Class A, incl. in no. 141: Lieutenant Dew to Capt. Adams, 27 Feb. 1851; George Prior, for King Gezo, to Queen Victoria, 26 April 1851, in Fraser (2012: 209).

[76] King Gezo to Queen Victoria, 12 Jan. 1852, in Fraser (2012: 228); HCPP, *Slave Trade*, 1854/5, Class B, incl. 1 in no. 23: King Gezo to Queen Victoria, 9 June 1854.

[77] Beecroft to Palmerston, 22 July 1850, in Appendix 3, doc. 8. Forbes likewise concluded that 'nothing but coercive methods' would secure a treaty (Journal, p. 195).

[78] Palmerston to King Gezo, 11 Oct. 1850, in Appendix 3, doc. 10.

[79] Fraser's Journal, 20 Aug., 6–7 Sept. 1851, in Fraser (2012: 73–4, 105–10); letter of Mehu (for King Gezo) to Queen Victoria, 7 Sept. 1851, ibid., 216–17.

[80] Beecroft to Palmerston, 4 Oct. 1851, ibid., 244–5.

instructions to the Admiralty in September 1851.[81] The blockade was duly instituted from 1 January 1852, under pressure of which Gezo did finally accept a treaty to abolish the slave trade, on 13 January 1852.[82] This, however, proved ineffective in practice, and slave exports from Dahomey continued into the 1860s. In the end, the cessation of the slave trade in Dahomey was due to the ending of demand in the Americas, rather than the conversion of the rulers of Dahomey.

4 The Annual Customs and the issue of compensation

In practice, negotiations with Gezo and his officials on the slave trade occupied relatively little of the time spent by Beecroft and Forbes in Abomey. Most of their journals comprise a detailed day-by-day description of the ceremonies of the Annual Customs.[83] Indeed, their principal value to historians arguably resides in these accounts of the Customs, which were a public expression of the ideology of the Dahomian monarchy, stressing its hereditary legitimacy, military prowess and the King's liberality in largesse to his subjects.[84] The presents which the King distributed comprised principally imported items—especially cowry shells, cloth and rum—and served to illustrate and emphasise the importance of European trade to the kingdom. Particular ceremonies witnessed by Beecroft and Forbes further dramatised the centrality of the slave trade in Dahomey, one enacting the unloading of cargo from a European ship, another an attack on a village with the taking of captives as slaves.[85]

The reason for this reportage, however, was not ethnographic interest, but because the Annual Customs, and more particularly their cost, were considered highly relevant to the issue of the abolition of the slave trade. The King's expenditure on the Annual Customs had become linked to the vexed question of the level of compensation which he might receive from the British government for giving up the slave trade. In the initial British discussions about the possibility of a treaty in 1843, as has been seen, the compensation to be offered had been set at £700 annually for seven years; but the treaty actually offered to Gezo by Lieutenant-Governor Winniett in 1847 reduced this to

---

[81] HCPP, *Papers Relative to the Reduction of Lagos*, no. 43, Palmerston to Admiralty, 27 Sept. 1851.

[82] For these negotiations, see Vice-Consul Fraser's journals and other documents, in Fraser (2012).

[83] For the schedule of ceremonies witnessed, see Endnote 1.

[84] On the Annual Customs, see Coquery-Vidrovitch (1964) and Nicolau Parés (2016, chapter 4, 181–235).

[85] On 31 May and 14 June 1850, respectively: see Beecroft's Journal, pp. 43, 103–5.

$2,000 (£417). In fact, the sum of $2,000 (equivalent to the selling price of only 25 slaves), was manifestly ludicrous if intended to represent the King's income from the slave trade. Winniett himself recognised that it was too low: although he acknowledged that he had 'no data' on the King's revenue from the slave trade, he thought that it must be 'considerably' more than $50,000 (£10,417) annually.[86] Gezo, in the following year, dismissed the offer of $2,000, observing that it 'would not pay his expenses for a week', and the Brazilian merchant Francisco Felix de Souza, presumably on the King's instructions, presented an estimate of royal income from the slave trade—based on 8,000 slaves exported annually, of which 3,000 were sold by the King, and including taxes levied on exports of slaves and on their transit to the coast, as well as the actual proceeds of slave sales—of no less than $300,000 (£62,500) annually.[87] This, however, was certainly an exaggeration: the figure represented gross receipts, with no account taken of costs, and in any case the number of slaves exported is unrealistically high, at least for the specific period of the late 1840s. Calculating the King's net return on slave sales, and reducing the volume of sales by half, would bring the sum down to something closer to $100,000.[88]

The draft of Palmerston's instructions to Beecroft in 1850 authorised him to offer up to £3,000 annually in compensation (while reducing the period of payment from seven to three years), although it is not clear whether this figure was in fact transmitted to Beecroft, since the version printed in the Parliamentary Papers merely left it to his discretion to 'make up with the Chief [i.e. the King of Dahomey] the best arrangement which you can on this head'.[89] Independently of this, Lieutenant Forbes had also suggested, in advance of the mission, that an annual subsidy of £3,000 would be sufficient to induce the King to give up the slave trade.[90] This was, in fact, the sum (which Beecroft equated with $15,000)[91] which was offered in the final meeting with Gezo on 4 July 1850.

[86] TNA, CO96/11, Winniett to Grey, 12 May 1847.
[87] Cruickshank's Report, 15–17.
[88] De Souza's estimate assumes that the King received the full sale price of slaves, $80 each, accounting for most ($240,000) of the total: but in fact he paid a bounty to his soldiers for each prisoner taken, which Beecroft was told was $10 (see p. 196), while the merchants who sold the slaves at the coast received a commission of $16 per head (Law 2004b: 145), reducing the King's net return to $54 per slave, or $162,000 for 3,000, which (with $60,000 in taxes), yields a revised total of $222,000. Note that Manning (1982: 48, 295, n.78), on the assumptions of only 2,500 slaves exported, a lower price of £15 ($72) per slave and a royal share of only 20%, suggests a gross royal revenue from the slave trade of only £8,000 ($38,400) annually.
[89] Palmerston to Beecroft, 25 Feb. 1850, in Appendix 3, doc. 3.
[90] HCPP, *Slave Trade*, 1850/1, Class A, incl. 1 in no. 198, Forbes to Fanshawe, 6 April 1850.
[91] This equivalence is based on a value of the dollar at 4s., rather than the official rate of 4s. 2d. For the varying valuation of the dollar on the West African coast, see Law (1994a).

The Annual Customs were crucial to this issue, because they represented a major, perhaps *the* major, item of royal expenditure. In his conversations with Duncan in 1845, Gezo had already put the cost of the Customs at the centre of his response to British demands for the abolition of the slave trade: 'for his own part he had no wish to maintain the Slave-Trade ... All he required was to have sufficient income to pay his officers and caboceers the usual quantity of cowries to present his people with, as is usual at the annual custom.' To Cruickshank in 1848, he likewise stressed the cost of the Customs: 'The state which he maintained was great ... the ceremonies and customs to be observed annually ... entailed upon him a vast outlay of money.'[92]

Gezo's demand that Vice-Consul Duncan should attend the Annual Customs of 1850 seems initially to have been intended to emphasise that he would be treated as a Dahomian official: as Duncan reported, Gezo told him that 'it will be necessary, holding office in his dominion, that I shall attend his annual Custom'. But after Duncan read to him Palmerston's letter claiming that 'legal' trade would be more profitable than the slave trade, Gezo remarked that 'when I [Duncan] attend his Custom, and see the quantity of money he pays to his people annually, I shall be better able to give an opinion on whether legitimate trade can be extended to afford a revenue equivalent'.[93] The detailed accounts of the Customs which Beecroft and Forbes recorded, including meticulous calculation of the amounts distributed in the royal largesse, were explicitly intended to provide a basis on which to assess the King's claims for compensation. Their journals, therefore, offer a mass of detailed material relevant to understanding the fiscal, as well as the political and religious, aspects of the operation of the Dahomian state.

In the event, however, the level of the King's expenditure quickly became an issue of disagreement between the British envoys and the Dahomians. After the first ceremony which Beecroft and Forbes witnessed, on 29 May, Dahomian officials submitted an estimate of the value of money and goods distributed by the King of 26,000 'heads' of cowries, the 'head' (2,000 cowries) being conventionally equivalent to the dollar; but Beecroft and Forbes calculated that the actual amount was less than $1,700.[94] The Dahomians subsequently moderated their claim to 32,000 heads for the entire Annual Customs, and 43,800 for a full year, including other ceremonies in the annual cycle; but Beecroft and Forbes claimed that only $12,115 had been expended at the Annual Customs, little more than one-third of the Dahomian

[92] Duncan (1847, ii: 267); Cruickshank's Report, 17.
[93] HCPP, *Slave Trade*, 1849/50, Class B, no. 6: Duncan to Palmerston, 22 Sept. 1849.
[94] See their Journals, pp. 32–3, 162.

estimate.[95] Forbes also made a less generous calculation (which was apparently not submitted to the King), allowing only $10,745 for the Annual Customs and $16,745 for the entire year.[96] These various estimates were conveniently close to the $15,000 offered as compensation, although, as has been seen, this figure had in fact been arrived at in advance, rather than being based on actual observation of the Customs.

At the final interview on 4 July 1850, Gezo did not directly challenge the figure of $15,000 for the proposed compensation: as Beecroft reported, he 'did not make any remark that it was a generous offer ... or otherwise'.[97] This was probably because the earlier discussions had already made it clear that there was no prospect of agreement on this issue. Gezo did, however, point out that ending the slave trade would undermine the ability of his senior officials and merchants to pay their taxes, as well as stop the revenue he received directly from it;[98] while on the following day his spokesmen drew attention to the fact that he incurred expense on military supplies, as well as on the Customs.[99] In February 1851, when seeking to revive the negotiations, Gezo took a different tack, declaring that 'it was his wish to stop the Slave Trade, but as all his revenue was derived from it he must have compensation', and requesting that an envoy should come to Abomey 'on revenue days to see the amount he received from the Slave Trade, so that [the Queen] may judge what she ought to give him to stop the Slave Trade'.[100] Presumably, having failed to impress Beecroft and Forbes with the scale of his expenditure at the Customs, he was now seeking an alternative, and hopefully more advantageous, basis for the calculation. But on this occasion, no envoy came, so the matter was not put to the test.

Palmerston had withdrawn the offer of compensation in his letter of October 1850, and this was reiterated in a letter from the commander-in-chief of the British Navy's West African Squadron, now Commodore Bruce, notifying Gezo of the blockade in December 1851; and no provision for compensation was included in the treaty which Gezo signed in January 1852.[101] It seems, however, that Gezo chose to regard the offer of compensation as still on the table and, although the sum offered in 1850 had been judged inadequate, he perhaps now felt it was better than nothing, and, in any case, the best he could expect. In 1855 he actually claimed that he had *agreed* to the

---

[95] See pp. 146–7, 190–2.
[96] See Appendix 2.
[97] Beecroft's Journal, p. 149.
[98] Forbes' Journal, p. 194 (it should be noted that this statement was not recorded by Beecroft).
[99] See pp. 153, 195.
[100] HCPP, *Slave Trade*, 1851/2, Class A, incl. 1 in no. 141: Lt Dew to Capt. Adams, 27 Feb. 1851.
[101] Commodore Bruce to King Gezo, 17 Dec. 1851, in Fraser (2012: 220–2).

proposal of Beecroft and Forbes that he should give up the slave trade in return for an annual compensation of 1,000 doubloons, referring imprecisely to their offer of $15,000:[102] 'he consented to it', but 'they took their leave of him, went away, and there has been nothing heard or seen of them since', and he maintained that he had subsequently accepted the treaty of 1852 on the understanding that 'Her Majesty promised to grant him every necessaries [*sic*] to meet the expense of his customs.' In a final message in 1856 he once more invoked 'the old and time honored customs of his ancestors', at which he was 'obliged to make large donations to his chiefs & people', to pay for which he recalled that 'a hope had been held out to him by Captain Forbes, that Her Majesty, on consideration of the sacrifice he was making in forgoing those pecuniary advantages [from the slave trade], would kindly make him some small return annually'. But, he claimed, 'he had waited year after year, to hear something from Her Majesty in reference to this subject, and had continued to suffer disappointment', so now again requested that the Queen might 'render him some little annual assistance of the kind he has mentioned'.[103] But this elicited no direct response from the British government, and no compensation was ever received.

5 Human sacrifice

Another feature of the Annual Customs which concerned the mission of 1850 was the human sacrifices which occurred in some of the ceremonies. The religious significance of these sacrifices related to the royal ancestor cult, being offered to the spirits of deceased kings of Dahomey. Beyond this, they were a demonstration of royal power, and more specifically of the king's exclusive right to take life, and also a celebration of Dahomian military successes, most of the victims being prisoners taken in Dahomey's wars.[104]

The grounds for British disapproval of human sacrifice require some comment, since they were not straightforward. It was not simply a matter of the brutality of the act. Indeed, given that public executions were still practised in Britain at this time, as a later British Consular envoy to Dahomey, Richard Burton, in 1863/4, conceded, 'A Dahomian visiting England but a few years ago would have witnessed customs almost quite as curious as those which

---

[102] More precisely, 1,000 doubloons = $16,000.
[103] HCPP, *Slave Trade*, 1855/6, Class B, incl. 1 in no. 15: Joseph Dawson to Consul Campbell, Ouidah, 29 Aug. 1855; Wesleyan Methodist Missionary Society Archives, School of Oriental and African Studies, London: Box 262, Rev. T.B. Freeman to Major Ord, Porto-Novo, 2 April 1856.
[104] For the relationship of human sacrifice to royal authority and militarism in Dahomey and elsewhere in West Africa, see Law (1985: 72–6).

raise our bile now.'[105] Nor does it appear that it was the supposed falsity of the religious beliefs which underlay the practice that attracted censure. In fact, the religious motivation tended to be discounted: Forbes, for example, claimed that the public sacrifices at the Annual Customs were not offered to any supernatural beings, but to 'the vitiated appetites of the soldiery'.[106] Rather, it seems that it was specifically the killing of prisoners of war which was condemned, since although this had been practised in Europe in earlier times, by the nineteenth century it was unambiguously considered contrary to the principles of international law.[107]

In the Anglo-Dahomian negotiations of the 1840s and 1850s, human sacrifice was not initially a central issue. The matter had been raised by private individuals: the trader Thomas Hutton, on a visit to King Gezo in 1839 or 1840, claimed to have told him that 'it was against [the Christian] God's law for one man to take away the life of another' (and moreover, that it would be more advantageous to the King to employ the victims in productive labour than to kill them);[108] while the missionary Freeman had apparently also expressed disapproval of human sacrifices in his interviews with Gezo in 1843.[109] But the issue was not taken up by the British government in the official negotiations initiated from 1847, nor was it included in the draft treaty offered to Gezo in 1847–8. Cruickshank, in 1848, did urge Gezo 'to lay aside the practice of human sacrifice, which was highly displeasing to the English people'; likewise, Forbes' instructions for his first visit to Gezo in 1849 included that he should, 'if opportunity is afforded … express to the King how contrary the practice of human sacrifice is to the principle of that [Christian] religion, and how gratifying it would be to … the Queen to know that the King had ordered it to be discontinued within his dominions'.[110] However, no provision for the abolition of human sacrifices was included in the draft

---

[105] Burton (1864, ii: 21).

[106] Forbes (1851, i: 32)—though he goes on to refer to other sacrifices offered to *vodun* (gods) and to deceased kings. Burton, who was an anthropologist as well as a British Consul, later still felt it necessary to refute the idea that human sacrifice in Dahomey was motivated by 'mere lust of blood', and to insist on its 'purely religious basis' (1864, ii: 19, 176).

[107] See e.g. the classic statement by the Swiss jurist Emer de Vattel (1797, Book III: ch. VIII, §149).

[108] HCPP, *Select Committee on the West Coast of Africa*, Minutes of Evidence, §10329, Evidence of W.M. Hutton, 22 July 1842.

[109] No mention of this is made in Freeman's own account (1844). But see TNA, CO96/8, King Gezo to Queen Victoria, incl. in Duncan to Stanley, 1 July 1845: '2 years ago Mr Freeman had called and had talked a great deal with him, and had spoken about sacrifices or beheading people at the Annual Customs'.

[110] Cruickshank's Report, 19; HCPP, *Slave Trade*, 1849/50, Class B, incl. 2 in no. 9: Fanshawe to Forbes, 9 Sept. 1849.

treaty presented to Gezo by Beecroft and Forbes in 1850, and it does not appear that the issue was raised in their final interview with him on 4 July.[111]

Nevertheless, the issue of human sacrifice arguably did play a key role in these negotiations, in relation to general perceptions of Gezo's policy and character. Gezo had sought to deflect British criticism of human sacrifice, first, by affecting to be personally sympathetic to the British position but constrained by the norms of his society. As he told Hutton in 1839/40, 'I would be glad to do as he wishes ... I think Englishmen are right, but ... I am king over this people whose customs I must observe ... I am but the creature of the system'; and the 1850 mission was likewise assured that 'Gezo ... has no delight in human sacrifices, and continues these awful scenes solely out of deference to ancient national customs.'[112]

At the same time, however, and somewhat contradictorily, Gezo claimed that he had, in fact, reduced the scale of human sacrifice, in deference to British susceptibilities, and more specifically that he had ceased to sacrifice prisoners of war. In a letter dictated to Duncan in 1845 he claimed that, since the urgings of Freeman two years earlier, he had sacrificed fewer victims and hoped 'gradually to abolish' the practice altogether, and in particular, asserted that four men whose decapitation Duncan had witnessed were guilty of 'murder', implying that the Dahomian sacrifices were comparable to the public executions carried out in Britain: 'the only Difference—you hang them with rope in England'.[113] Duncan, indeed, in his published account, referred to 'the abolition, in a great measure, of human sacrifices'.[114] Likewise, in talking to Cruickshank in 1848, Gezo claimed that 'since the conversations which he had with Mr Freeman, he had been content with very few sacrifices, and that these were criminals', implying that war captives were no longer killed. Forbes, on his first visit in 1849, also had the impression that 'the practice of human sacrifice is fast vanishing from the Kingdom of Dahomey'; indeed, in his interview with Gezo, Forbes actually thanked him 'for having so far reduced them in numbers'.[115]

Although the British at this point were not making the abolition of human sacrifices an explicit demand in their negotiations with Gezo, the latter's

---

[111] There is no mention of it in Beecroft's Journal, or in the original version of Forbes' Journal. In his book, Forbes does claim that they suggested that, in addition to Gezo renouncing the slave trade, 'in course of time, he could abolish those fearful sacrifices' (1851, ii: 187), but this was probably mere embroidery; possibly, in retrospect, Forbes thought that they *ought* to have raised the issue.

[112] HCPP, *Select Committee on the West Coast of Africa*, Minutes of Evidence, §10329, evidence of W.M. Hutton, 22 July 1842; Forbes (1851, ii: 32).

[113] TNA, CO96/8, King Gezo to Queen Victoria, incl. to Duncan to Stanley, 1 July 1845.

[114] Duncan (1847, ii: 305–6).

[115] Cruickshank's Report, 19; HCPP, *Slave Trade*, 1849/50, Class A, incl. 9 in no. 9: Forbes, Journal, 17–18 Oct. 1849.

claims to have reduced (or even effectively 'abolished') the practice were, it may be suggested, of critical significance in reinforcing the image which Gezo was seeking to project—of himself as a progressive monarch, with benign intentions, even if constrained by the limitations of the political and cultural situation in which he was placed. In effect, his liberal credentials on the issue of human sacrifice gave him moral capital, on which he could draw in trying to persuade the British to tolerate the continuation of slave-trading in the short term, on the assurance that he could be relied upon to deliver gradual reform over a longer timescale.

The mission of 1850, however, was decisive in discrediting the idea that human sacrifices in Dahomey had already been effectively abolished, and thereby Gezo's credibility as a reformer. Especially important were the only sacrifices which Beecroft and Forbes actually witnessed (and therefore described in detail in their journals), in a ceremony on 31 May 1850. What was shocking about these was perhaps less the number of victims (a comparatively modest 11), than the detailed brutality of the mode of their execution: they were thrown from a 12-foot high platform, before being beheaded and their bodies then abused. Even more critically, these victims were unambiguously not convicted criminals but prisoners of war from a recent campaign (against Atakpamé, to the north-west of Dahomey), and indeed (so it was believed) civilians rather than soldiers. As Forbes observed, 'There was not even the poor excuse that these men had committed a crime, or even borne arms against the Dahomans ... they were murdered, innocent men.'[116]

In contrast to the earlier negotiations, Commodore Bruce, in notifying King Gezo of the blockade of Dahomey in December 1851, cited as a reason for this not only his persistence in slave-trading, but also 'your abominable practice of murdering prisoners on public festivals and other occasions'.[117] A clause for the abolition of human sacrifices (and of the killing of prisoners of war) was included in the draft treaty presented to Gezo in January 1852, though in the event he refused to accept it.[118] It seems clear that it was the reports of the 1850 mission which had served to place human sacrifices at the centre of British concern. It is significant that Commodore Bruce, in an explanatory note on the blockade of Dahomey to Vice-Consul Fraser, emphasised that despite earlier representations on the matter, 'the only result was the murder of ten or eleven victims in the very presence of Her Majesty's

---

[116] Forbes (1851, ii: 42, 53).
[117] Commodore Bruce to King Gezo, 17 Dec. 1851, in Fraser (2012: 220–2).
[118] Draft treaty, in Fraser (2012: 225–7). The principal British envoy, Commander T.G. Forbes, acknowledged that he did not seriously expect Gezo to accept this clause, since abolition of human sacrifices 'can only be effected as civilization extends': T.G. Forbes to Commodore Bruce, 18 Jan. 1852 (ibid., 248).

Officers', referring to the sacrifices witnessed by Beecroft and Forbes on 31 May 1850.[119]

After the event, Gezo clearly understood the damage which this episode had done, and in 1853, when he was trying to revive diplomatic contacts with Britain, he even sent a message declaring that he 'would give up the practice of human sacrifices altogether, according to the recommendation of the English'.[120] What he meant by this is uncertain, but probably, again, that he would no longer sacrifice war captives, rather than that killings at the Customs would cease altogether. The British, in any case, did not respond to his message. Gezo's new policy, moreover, provoked internal opposition within Dahomey and was repudiated after his death in 1858 by his successor, King Glele.[121] Human sacrifice continued to be practised in Dahomey until the country's final conquest by the French in 1894.

6 Abeokuta

An additional issue between Dahomey and Britain, which had not previously figured in the negotiations between the two but was raised during the mission of 1850, related to Abeokuta, a large city 100 km east of Abomey (within modern Nigeria), which was the capital of the Egba people.[122] This had emerged as a significant military power in the 1830s, and had gained access to the Atlantic trade through the coastal port of Badagry, 90 km east of Ouidah (also within Nigeria).[123]

Abeokuta became a place of interest to the British government because of the settlement there, from 1838 onwards, of a number of 'Liberated Africans' (i.e. former slaves, freed from illegal slave ships arrested by the British Navy) from the British colony of Sierra Leone, who arrived via Badagry. Many of these had been converted to Christianity in Sierra Leone, and Abeokuta consequently became a target of British missionary activity, with the establishment of a Methodist mission in Badagry in 1842, followed by a Church Missionary Society (CMS) mission at Abeokuta itself in 1846. In addition to the residence there of numerous British subjects, Abeokuta also attracted British interest and favour because it became a significant supplier of palm oil, via the port of Badagry, where Thomas Hutton established a factory in

---

[119] Commodore Bruce to Vice-Consul Fraser, 6 Dec. 1851, in Fraser (2012: 219).
[120] HCPP, *Slave Trade*, 1853/4, Class A, no. 118: Rear-Admiral Bruce to Admiralty, 25 April 1853.
[121] See Law (1997b).
[122] See Biobaku (1957).
[123] For Badagry in this period, see Sorensen-Gilmour (1995; 1999).

1841.[124] The combination of its welcoming of Christian missionaries and taking up 'legitimate' trade in palm oil fostered a British misperception of Abeokuta (in supposed contrast to Dahomey) as committed to the abolitionist cause. Palmerston thus advised Beecroft in February 1850 that 'The people of Abbeokuta are said to feel a strong desire that the Slave Trade should be wholly abolished, and that legitimate traffic should be substituted for it.'[125]

Although Abeokuta's relations with Dahomey had initially been friendly, the two powers competed for influence in the area of Egbado, to the southwest of Abeokuta, which controlled the latter's access to Badagry.[126] The Dahomians also claimed authority over Badagry itself, although this was in practice tenuous and intermittent.[127] A first military clash between Dahomey and Abeokuta occurred in 1845, when the Dahomians attacked an Abeokuta force at Imoloju, inland from Badagry, but were beaten off.[128] In the aftermath, the possibility of a retaliatory attack on Abeokuta seems to have been raised in Dahomey, but in the event it was decided to direct the army elsewhere.[129] Again in 1848, the Dahomians actually proclaimed their intention to attack Abeokuta, but this was a feint to conceal their real target, the town of Okeodan, in Egbado, which was destroyed in January 1849.[130] Although Okeodan does not seem to have been formally allied to Abeokuta, the latter regarded this as an intrusion into its sphere of influence and an implicit threat to itself.[131] It responded by attacking towns in Egbado which were allied to Dahomey, including Ihunmbo, west of Okeodan (as was alluded to at the Annual Customs of 1850);[132] and later, in November 1850 (after Beecroft's mission), Igbeji, north of Okeodan.[133] Although British observers saw Abeokuta as an innocent victim of Dahomian aggression, the Dahomians cited these attacks to support their claim that it was in fact Abeokuta which was the aggressor.[134]

In October 1849 the CMS made representations to Lord Palmerston which, inter alia, alluded to the threat from Dahomey, referring to the recent

[124] Sorensen-Gilmour (1995: 60, 207).
[125] HCPP, *Slave Trade* 1849/50, Class B, no. 15: Palmerston to Beecroft, 25 Feb. 1850.
[126] Folayan (1972).
[127] Forbes (1851, i: 20); but see Sorensen-Gilmour (1995: 220–1, 229–30, 256–7, 264–5).
[128] Folayan (1972: 20–1).
[129] Viz. against Kenglo, in Mahi, to the north (attacked in 1846): Forbes' Journal, p. 177.
[130] Folayan (1972: 25).
[131] Forbes' Journal, p. 161 (also 1851, i: 21), implies that Abeokuta fought the Dahomians at Okeodan, but this seems to involve confusion with the earlier fighting in 1845.
[132] See Beecroft's Journal, p. 115.
[133] Folayan (1972: 22–3).
[134] See Forbes' Journal, p. 183; also Mehu (for King Gezo) to Queen Victoria, 7 Sept. 1851, in Fraser (2012: 216–17). It was later acknowledged that the Dahomian attack on Abeokuta in 1851 'cannot be considered as quite unprovoked': HCPP, *Slave Trade*, 1854/5, Class B, no. 47: Consul Campbell to Earl of Clarendon, Lagos, 15 Feb. 1855.

destruction of Okeodan and apprehensions that King Gezo was contemplating an attack on Abeokuta itself, and requested that the British government should send a mission to Dahomey to seek guarantees that Gezo would not molest the British subjects residing at Badagry and Abeokuta.[135] Palmerston's instructions for Beecroft's mission to Dahomey, therefore, included that he should warn Gezo that the people of Abeokuta were 'friends of England', and that the British government was bound to protect the British subjects living there and in Badagry and would therefore view any attack on either town 'with much concern and displeasure', and that he should seek to obtain a 'formal promise' from Gezo to abstain from such aggression.[136]

The Annual Customs of 1850 here again played a critical role in the development of this dispute. Ceremonies witnessed by Beecroft and Forbes on 11 June were accompanied by discussion of the target of the next Dahomian campaign, with many of the assembled military officers and courtiers urging that it should be Abeokuta, and this choice was affirmed at a ceremony of swearing loyalty for the coming campaign two days later.[137] In their final interview with Gezo on 4 July 1850, Beecroft raised the issue of Abeokuta, as instructed by Palmerston, stressing that it enjoyed British friendship. Gezo's response, however, was to reiterate his intention to attack it and to demand that the British subjects there should be evacuated.[138]

Following Beecroft's failed mission, in July 1850 Commodore Fanshawe wrote to Gezo warning him against attacking Abeokuta, because of the British subjects resident there, and stating that any injury to the latter would be considered an act of war and provoke a naval blockade of Dahomey.[139] Palmerston also, in his letter to Gezo in October 1850, urged that 'if you value the friendship of England you will abstain from any attack upon and any hostility against that town and people'—although this letter was not actually delivered to the King until August 1851.[140] The Dahomians had meanwhile proceeded to attack Abeokuta, on 3 March 1851, but were repulsed. This was not the end of the matter, however, since Vice-Consul Fraser, later in 1851, found that the Dahomians were discussing a possible second attack on

---

[135] HCPP, *Slave Trade*, 1849/50, Class B, incl. 1 in no. 14: Rev. H. Townsend to Secretary of the CMS, 17 Oct. 1849.
[136] This reference to Abeokuta was not, in fact, included in Palmerston's instructions for the mission to Dahomey, but (seemingly, as an afterthought) in separate instructions drafted at the same time for a mission to Abeokuta, which Beecroft was to undertake subsequently: Palmerston to Beecroft, 25 Feb. 1850, in Appendix 3, doc. 5.
[137] See Beecroft's Journal, pp. 93–6, 102.
[138] Ibid, p. 151.
[139] Fanshawe to King Gezo, 23 July 1850, in Appendix 3, doc. 9.
[140] Palmerston to King Gezo, 11 Oct. 1850, in Appendix 3, doc. 10.

Abeokuta in the next campaigning season (though no such attack in fact took place).[141]

It was the attack on Abeokuta, with its resident community of British subjects, that provided Palmerston with a plausible pretext to order the naval blockade of Dahomey (which was technically an act of war), since Gezo's refusal to accept a treaty for the abolition of the slave trade did not afford grounds for such action under international law.[142] The demand for peace with Abeokuta was therefore added to those for the abolition of the slave trade and human sacrifices in justification of the declaration of the blockade in December 1851.[143] In their negotiations for a treaty with Gezo in January 1852, the British tried to insert a clause requiring him to make peace with Abeokuta, but Gezo rejected this, suggesting that the British, rather than pre-judging the merits of the case and siding with Abeokuta, should have acted as mediators between the two parties.[144] The issue therefore remained unresolved. Recurrent reports of intended Dahomian attacks on Abeokuta continued to be a source of tension in relations with Britain through the 1850s and early 1860s, until Gezo's successor Glele did finally launch a second attack on the city (again unsuccessfully) in 1864.

7 The question of royal power

The mission of 1850 played a critical role in undermining British optimism about the prospects of agreement on the slave trade in a further respect— their understanding of the nature of the Dahomian polity. The inherited tradition of interpretation of Dahomian political organisation stressed the autocratic power of the king. The pioneer historian of Dahomey, Archibald Dalzel, in the 1790s, for example, had called it 'the most perfect despotism that exists, perhaps, on the face of this earth'.[145] In part, this perception reflected an uncritical interpretation of the rhetoric of Dahomian political discourse, which did indeed assert the absolute power of the king and represented the people of Dahomey as his 'slaves'.[146] This understanding implied that securing Dahomian cooperation in ending the slave trade was simply a matter of persuading the king, who, it was assumed, could readily implement

---

[141] Fraser (2012: 40, 100).

[142] For the legal issues, see Law (2010a).

[143] Commodore Bruce to King Gezo, 17 Dec. 1851, in Fraser (2012: 220–2).

[144] Commander T.G. Forbes to Commodore Bruce, 18 Jan. 1852, journal entry for 13 Jan. 1852, in Fraser (2012: 254); King Gezo to Queen Victoria, 12 Jan. 1852, ibid., 229.

[145] Dalzel (1793: vii). Cf. also M'Leod (1820: 37), 'a monarchy the most unlimited and uncontroled on the face of the earth'.

[146] Beecroft twice quotes expressions of this idiom (pp. 119, 130).

whatever he decided: Duncan, for example, opined that 'one word from him would be quite sufficient', since 'the King's power is absolute there, certainly'.[147]

The negotiations over the slave trade tended to challenge, and ultimately to undermine, this traditional perception. Gezo himself, in his dealings with the British before 1850, had consistently stressed the limitations of his position, claiming that any radical change of policy would provoke internal opposition. He told Hutton in 1839/40, for example, in relation to human sacrifice, that 'if I were not to give them these victims they would rebel and sacrifice me'; and likewise told Cruickshank in 1848 that 'The form of his government could not be suddenly changed without causing such a revolution as would deprive him of his throne, and precipitate his kingdom into a state of anarchy.'[148] Although reported in general terms, it seems evident that Gezo, in talking of the threat of 'revolution', had in mind the circumstances of his own accession to the throne, through the deposition of his predecessor Adandozan.[149]

Beecroft explicitly concluded, from his experience of the 1850 mission, that royal power in Dahomey had been exaggerated: 'I am perfectly satisfied that [the King] is under the control and opinion of several of his principal officers.'[150] Forbes likewise observed that the King could not act without the 'concurrence' of his 'ministers', and more particularly of the two senior of these, the Migan and the Mewu, who 'have, if united, actually more power' than the King, so that 'the monarch dare not enter into a treaty unless the miegan and the mayo coincide'.[151]

The reasons for this shift of attitude probably included the fact that, unlike earlier visitors, Beecroft and Forbes were aware of the deposition of Gezo's predecessor Adandozan, through allusions to it in songs which they heard sung at the Customs.[152] Forbes suggested that, if the King were to defy 'the will of the people' by refusing to undertake military campaigns or, more generally, to uphold 'ancient customs', he would be dethroned.[153] They may also have been influenced by discussions they had with Dahomian officials, including the Mewu, which demonstrated that they, as well as the King,

---

[147] HCPP, *Report of the Select Committee on the Slave Trade* (1848), Minutes of Evidence, §§3093, 3187, Evidence of John Duncan, 11 and 13 April 1848.

[148] HCPP, *Select Committee on the West Coast of Africa*, Minutes of Evidence, §10329, evidence of W.M. Hutton, 22 July 1842; Cruickshank's Report, 17.

[149] Especially since (at least in subsequent tradition) one of the reasons adduced to justify Adandozan's deposition was his alleged failure to offer the customary sacrifices to deceased kings (Le Herissé 1911: 116).

[150] Beecroft to Palmerston, 22 July 1850, in Appendix 3, doc. 8, p. 211.

[151] Forbes (1851, i: 82–3; ii: 62).

[152] Not explicit in Beecroft's Journal; but see Forbes' Journal, pp. 160–1, and Forbes (1851, ii: 23–5, 89).

[153] Forbes (1851, i: 133; ii: 17).

profited from and were committed to the slave trade: as Forbes observed, 'His Majesty's Ministers are one and all slave-dealers, and if the King was willing, he has not the power to treat.'[154]

Principally, however, their change of view seems to have been based on exchanges among courtiers (termed by Forbes 'debates')[155] which they witnessed during the Annual Customs. In particular, they reported a discussion on 11 June 1850 at which the main topic of 'debate' was the object of the next military campaign. Some of those who spoke urged that the previous campaign (against Atakpamé) had not been a comprehensive victory, and that it should be followed up, while others, as has been seen, proposed an attack on Abeokuta. Two days later, on 13 June, at the oath-taking ceremony for the forthcoming campaign, this dissensus had disappeared, with everybody demanding war against Abeokuta. Beecroft and Forbes were impressed at the freedom of speech exercised in the discussions on 11 June. Beecroft, in his journal for that day, reflected that 'The King does not appear to be the Despot as is currently reported'; while Forbes observed that 'In these public and open speeches alone is the King made aware of the state of the interior, and according to their tenor and requisition he acts.'[156]

A modern commentator has argued from this evidence that, in addition to their religious aspects, the Annual Customs 'served a political function similar to that of parliaments in Western countries', with debates in which anyone was free to challenge existing policy; and that the King, in announcing his decision, was expressing the 'final consensus' reached through this process of debate.[157] (Beecroft, it may be noted, also compared these proceedings to the debates in the British House of Commons, but with reference to their unruliness, with speakers being heckled and shouted down, rather than to their supposedly consultative character.[158]) This, however, is not wholly convincing. The 'debate' on 11 June was restricted to a small group of senior officials and (principally) military officers, who did not constitute any sort of representative body,[159] and was conducted within the royal palace rather than open to the public. Although speakers attacked each other, sometimes vehemently, nobody criticised or challenged the King: rather, they seem to be vying with each other in assertions of their loyalty to him. Moreover, the subject of 'debate' was very narrowly focused on the direction of the forthcoming military campaign, with no challenge to the general policy of military aggression

---

[154] HCPP, *Slave Trade*, 1850/1, incl. 1 in no. 220: Forbes to Fanshawe, 8 July 1850.

[155] Forbes (1851, ii: 86).

[156] Beecroft's Journal, p. 97; Forbes (1851, ii: 98–9).

[157] Yoder (1974).

[158] Beecroft's Journal, p. 99.

[159] In contrast to Yoder's reference to 'delegates from all regions of the country' representative of 'the entire Dahomean body politic' (1974: 419).

and no reference to the important matter of state currently facing the King—how to respond to the British demand for the ending of the slave trade.[160]

This is not to deny that such 'debates' played some political role, but they are perhaps better understood as a mechanism for generating support for the King's intended actions than for the determination of national policy. Forbes grasped that the central point of the proceedings was that the military officers 'asked' the King to choose a particular enemy for attack, and observed that 'the king professes never to make war on any country … until asked by his people thrice'.[161] This practice perhaps served to insulate the King from criticism should any campaign turn out badly, as that against Atakpamé had in fact done. But it seems likely that the 'consensus' ultimately reached was orchestrated by the King, rather than imposed upon him. However, what matters in the present context is the interpretation placed upon these proceedings by Beecroft and Forbes, and their inference was that the emphasis previously placed on the King's professed goodwill had been misplaced, as well as probably mistaken, because the King's personal inclinations were in the final analysis irrelevant, since he was constrained by his political position. From this perception it followed logically that Dahomian accession to British demands could be achieved only by coercion, rather than diplomacy.

8 Beecroft's and Forbes' accounts compared

The two accounts of Beecroft and Forbes are significantly different both in their general character and in their detail. Forbes is more reflective and analytical, offering a general account of Dahomey rather than contenting himself with a narration of what he saw and heard. This is especially so, unsurprisingly, in his published book, which includes two prefatory chapters on Dahomey's history and 'manners', appendices on its religion and fauna, and a vocabulary of the local language (Fon). But it is also to some degree true of his original journal, which, for example, explains, more explicitly than Beecroft's, the organisation of the Dahomian political and military hierarchy around the division between right and left (headed respectively by the Migan and the Mewu), and the appointment of female counterparts to male officials (termed their 'mothers'), chosen from among the women in the royal palace.[162] But, as

---

[160] Yoder seems implicitly to infer that support for war against Abeokuta, since it was allied with Britain, symbolised a more general defiance of British wishes, including over the slave trade. This, however, exaggerates the centrality of Abeokuta in Dahomian relations with Britain at this point: there is no indication that Beecroft and Forbes had even raised the issue with Gezo before their final meeting with him on 4 July 1850.

[161] Forbes' Journal, p. 177; Forbes (1851, i: 20–1).

[162] Forbes' Journal, p. 174.

was noted earlier, it seems likely that even Forbes' original journal was composed with a view to eventual publication. In contrast, there is no reason to believe that Beecroft intended his journal for publication.[163]

Forbes also shows more awareness of and engagement with earlier published accounts of Dahomey. Beecroft does observe that the political power, wealth and military resources of the Dahomian monarchy had been exaggerated, but does not cite any particular earlier sources.[164] Forbes in his journal specifically cites Cruickshank's report of his 1848 mission (though without actually naming him), and more explicitly Dalzel's earlier history, likewise to debunk their alleged exaggeration of the royal wealth.[165] In his book he cites several other published sources, in order to offer a sketch of Dahomian history but also to argue that the kingdom, although increasing in power, had remained 'unchanged in manners and habits' since it first came to European notice in the 1720s.[166] In this, however, his judgement was questionable, since his and Beecroft's evidence in 1850, in common with other accounts from this period, in fact indicates a much more prominent role for female officials within the political structure, as well as of the 'Amazon' army, and also a greater visibility at court of male members of the royal family (brothers of the king), than eighteenth-century sources had recorded.[167]

The more detailed differences between the accounts of Beecroft and Forbes of course to some extent reflect their different opportunities of observation. In particular, Beecroft was unwell, and unable to attend the ceremonies on 13 June, and learned about the day's proceedings only at second hand from Forbes; while contrariwise, on 19 June, Forbes was obliged by illness to retire at midday, so that for the subsequent proceedings we are dependent on Beecroft's testimony alone. However, even for those occasions when both were present, their accounts frequently differ.[168] It is not just that each records details missed or omitted by the other; they also frequently give different accounts, or at least different interpretations, of the same events. Even where they purport to record statements by the King (and other officers), their

---

[163] As was suggested (tentatively) by Lynn (1992: 164 n. 35) This was inferred from annotations to the journal which state that it was 'already in print' (or 'in type'): TNA, FO84/816, ff. 151v, 232v. But this was evidently incorrect, and presumably involves confusion with Forbes' journal, which was to be printed in the Parliamentary Papers.

[164] Beecroft's Journal, p. 97; Beecroft to Palmerston, 22 July 1850, in Appendix 3, doc. 8.

[165] Forbes' Journal, pp. 162, 165.

[166] Forbes (1851, i: 2–5); also reproducing the text of the earliest contemporary description of Dahomey (in 1724), (ibid., 181–95).

[167] On these changes, see Bay (1998: 177–8, 198–213).

[168] One curious and unexplained discrepancy relates to 23–27 June, when Forbes systematically dates events a day earlier than Beecroft; the matter is further complicated by the fact that in his published version Forbes moves events recorded in his original journal as occurring on 27–28 June, again, one day earlier.

accounts often differ, and sometimes more substantially than is attributable to abridgement or paraphrase. As an illustrative example, their different versions of what King Gezo said in their final meeting with him on 4 July 1850 are compared in Endnote 2.

In seeking to understand these discrepancies, it is helpful to consider the conditions under which their accounts were produced. First, it is clear that they were not composed as a running commentary on events as they were observed. In fact, it is explicitly noted at several points in Beecroft's journal that each day's proceedings were written up retrospectively, in the evening or the following morning. Since, however, it is impossible to believe that the mass of detail which Beecroft and Forbes recorded could have been held in their memories, it may be supposed that they took written notes on what they saw and heard at the time, which were then worked up into the final journals: as Consul Burton later explicitly observed, 'without the aid of writing it would be impossible to remember half the complications which occur'.[169] This assumption is supported by some instances where Beecroft appears to miscopy personal names—notably, those of Hwanjile, the mother of the earlier king Tegbesu, and of Agotime, mother of Gezo himself, given by Beecroft as 'Ah-wha-ge-see' and 'Sou-tee-mee', which must be errors for 'Ah-wha-ge-lee' and 'Gou-tee-mee', which only seems explicable if he was working from material already written down.[170] It would also account for some cases where Beecroft and Forbes attribute what are clearly versions of the same statement to different persons, this perhaps arising from confusion in the subsequent assembling of their notes when writing them up into the final journals. The existence of such notes would also explain Forbes' ability, in his published book, to include some additional material beyond what was in his original journal.[171]

Beyond this, the actual process whereby Beecroft and Forbes followed the ceremonies of the Customs, and more particularly the statements and discussions which accompanied them, requires detailed consideration. This raises the issue of the role of their African interpreters.

9 The process of translation

One of the seductive aspects of the journals of Beecroft and Forbes is that they appear to give access to a Dahomian 'voice', by extensively reporting what was said, sometimes ostensibly verbatim, by the King and other officials

---

[169] Burton (1864, i: 242).
[170] See pp. 119, 133.
[171] Examples may be found in his accounts of Gezo's statements on 4 July 1850, in Endnote 2.

and courtiers. In practice, of course, such statements are not recorded in their original language, Fon—with the very minor exception of a few fragments of songs which Forbes gives in his (very approximate) transcriptions of Fon.[172] More generally, they are recorded only as translated into English.

Beecroft himself, as a newcomer to Dahomey, can have had no prior knowledge of Fon, and Forbes gives no indication of having picked up any of the language during his previous brief visits. They therefore depended, for their communication with local people, on interpreters. Such interpreters were important, moreover, not only in translating actual verbal exchanges, but also in 'interpreting' what Beecroft and Forbes saw: for example, in the ceremonial processions which they witnessed, they could of course themselves observe the numbers of persons, their gender, clothing and what they carried—but to identify them as, for example, king's wives or persons from particular geographical regions etc., they must have depended on their interpreters.

Fortunately, there is quite a bit of information about those who served as interpreters for the various British visitors in this period.[173] Dahomian convention required the use of two interpreters, one for each party. Beecroft, in the interview with Gezo on 4 July 1850, referred to 'two interpreters, one on each side'; while Forbes, on his previous visit in 1849, likewise noted that a letter to the King was 'translated by both interpreters at the same moment, who often appeared to be correcting each other'.[174] The King of Dahomey's official interpreter for the English language was a man called Gnahoui, who was also a prominent merchant at Ouidah, trading in slaves.[175] On the English side, the principal local interpreter was a man called Madiki Lemon.[176] This man (who had also served Duncan and Forbes on their earlier visit to Abomey in 1849) was the grandson of a soldier who had served in the garrison of the British fort at Ouidah before its abandonment in 1812, and was recognised by the King as 'Governor' of the fort.[177] Both Madiki and Gnahoui, however, spoke only a form of 'pidgin' English, which therefore required to be 'translated' a second time into standard English to produce the texts with which we

---

[172] See Forbes' Journal, pp. 168, 176, 180.

[173] Law (2016).

[174] Beecroft's Journal, p. 148; HCPP, *Slave Trade*, 1849/50, incl. 9 in no. 9, Forbes to Fanshawe, 1 Nov. 1849, journal entry for 18 Oct. 1849.

[175] See Law (2016: 733–4): spelled 'Nawhey' by Beecroft, 'Narwhey' by Forbes.

[176] Forbes also refers to a third local interpreter, called Midjrokan ('Majelica', 'Magelika'), who was present at the final interview with Gezo on 4 July 1850, but explains that, although this man held the titular position of interpreter for the British fort at Ouidah, he was 'a bad interpreter' (1851, ii: 177). This man is not mentioned by Beecroft.

[177] Law (2010b). Beecroft spells his name 'Maduka', 'Maadaakee', etc., but more generally refers to him anonymously, as the 'interpreter' or 'deputy [*sic*] Governor'.

are generally presented—including reported statements by the King and the letters which British envoys and other visitors wrote on his behalf.[178]

Beecroft, however, also brought his own interpreter with him from Fernando Po, Thomas Richards.[179] This man had accompanied Beecroft on his exploratory voyages up the River Niger earlier, and subsequently also served on the expedition led by Dr W.B. Baikie to explore the Rivers Niger and Benue in 1854.[180] He was a former slave, who had been liberated from an illegal slave ship, after being enslaved in a Dahomian attack and sold into export through Dahomey.[181] His hometown was in Egbado, where the local language was Yoruba (also spoken in Oyo and Abeokuta).[182] Since he came from a frontier area, it is possible that he had grown up bilingual in Yoruba and Fon; alternatively, he may have picked up Fon during his period in captivity in Dahomey, before being sold at the coast. His knowledge of Yoruba was also of use in Dahomey, where many other Yoruba were held as slaves, from whom he could obtain information.[183] Forbes describes Richards as 'the most useful' of the mission's interpreters, but this may refer to his commitment to the abolitionist cause, being 'an undisguised abhorrer of the slave trade', rather than to his linguistic competence:[184] since he knew Fon only as a second language, his proficiency in it is not likely to have matched that of Gnahoui and Madiki Lemon, although it is of course possible that his English was better.

Mention should also be made of Joseph Peter Brown (called 'Peter Brown' by Beecroft), at this time employed by the merchant Thomas Hutton, who certainly spoke fluent and correct English and was also literate.[185] Brown was previously known to Beecroft, having been earlier employed as his servant, presumably on Fernando Po,[186] and his remarkable career had included serving on both of the major British exploratory expeditions up the River Niger, in 1832–4 and 1841–2.[187] Although he was from Cape Coast on the Gold Coast (where the local language was Fante), he had visited Ouidah several times before 1850 and spoke Fon, and he was to play a key role as interpreter

---

[178] For an exceptional example of a letter in 'pidgin' English, which presumably approximates to the interpreter Madiki's own words, see Mehu to Queen Victoria, 7 Sept. 1851, in Fraser (2012: 216–17).

[179] See Beecroft's Journal, p. 5.

[180] Baikie (1856: 29) and Crowther (1855: 8, 38–9). The Thomas Richards who was a prominent merchant in Clarence at this time (Lynn 1984) was perhaps the same person.

[181] Forbes (1851, ii: 176–7).

[182] Forbes names his hometown as 'Jena', i.e. Ijanna. However, it is clear that the town destroyed by the Dahomians was in fact Refurefu, nearby to the west, which had been settled by a group from Ijanna (of whom Richards was presumably one): see Forbes' Journal, p. 160, and n. 30.

[183] See Beecroft's Journal, pp. 127–8.

[184] Forbes (1851, ii: 177).

[185] See Law (2016: 734–8).

[186] Beecroft's Journal, p. 15.

[187] Beecroft alludes to Brown's service on the 1841–2 expedition, ibid., p. 86.

in the negotiation of the Anglo-Dahomian treaty of 1852.[188] However, when Brown had offered his services to Duncan and Forbes in 1849, Forbes had rejected him, on the grounds that he was allegedly acting as a 'spy' for the slave trader Domingos Martins.[189] This reflected a more general hostility on Forbes' part towards Hutton's agents in Ouidah, who he believed were over-friendly with the Brazilian slave traders and were indirectly supporting the slave trade by their willingness to deal with them. Brown was not employed by Beecroft and Forbes in 1850, but he did turn up at Abomey while they were there, on Hutton's account, and socialised with the mission, dining with Beecroft on two occasions and supplying him with information about Daho-mian affairs and the slave trade, although Beecroft regarded him as an unre-liable informant, given to exaggeration and self-aggrandisement.[190]

Interpretation was required not only between Fon (or Yoruba) and Eng-lish. The main language of Afro-European communication in Ouidah was Portuguese, reflecting the predominance of Brazilian merchants in the trade in slaves at this period. Portuguese was also spoken by at least some Daho-mian officials, including, notably, Gnahoui, who, despite his official status as English interpreter, according to Forbes actually spoke Portuguese better than English.[191] On a later occasion, in 1852, a letter in English was commu-nicated to King Gezo by being first translated into Portuguese (by a Portu-guese merchant who spoke English) and then from Portuguese into Fon (by Antonio de Souza).[192] No instances of such multilateral translation are men-tioned with regard to the 1850 mission, but Beecroft and Forbes spoke to the de Souzas and other Lusophone merchants at Ouidah, and also to Domingos Martins at Abomey.

Beecroft himself, however, did not speak Portuguese: in response to a later enquiry from the Foreign Office about his competence in foreign languages, he claimed to know only 'a little French' (and the limitations of his grasp of Portuguese are confirmed by his misrendering of the words 'El Rey', 'the King', as 'Le Rie').[193] Forbes' competence was only marginally better; he described himself as 'understanding but slightly Portuguese'.[194] On a visit to

---

[188] Commander T.G. Forbes to Commodore Bruce, 19 Jan. 1852, in Fraser (2012: 249).

[189] Forbes (1851, i: 53, 55): Brown is not named here, but his identity is clear from comparison with other sources.

[190] See Beecroft's Journal, pp. 86–7, 98–9, 101.

[191] Forbes (1851, ii: 175).

[192] Journal of Vice-Consul Fraser, 8 Jan. 1852, in Fraser (2012: 146). The Portuguese merchant who spoke English was Jacinto Joaquim Rodrigues, whom Beecroft met at Ouidah (see p. 5, this volume).

[193] TNA, FO2/7, Beecroft to Malmesbury, 28 June 1852—although it is surprising that Beecroft, despite his status as an officer of the Spanish Crown, knew no Spanish. For the misspelling see p. 24 this volume.

[194] Forbes (1851, i: 124)—but at least he got 'El Rey' right (Forbes' Journal, p. 156).

Isidoro de Souza at Ouidah, Beecroft and Forbes took Madiki Lemon as interpreter, which (since there is no evidence that the latter spoke Portuguese) suggests that Isidoro spoke in Fon, which Madiki translated into English.[195] Thomas Richards, however, did speak Portuguese, and was therefore able to report on a conversation among Portuguese-speaking merchants which he overheard.[196] So too did Peter Brown, who conveyed messages from Domingos Martins to Forbes and Beecroft.[197]

These issues of interpretation may have some bearing upon the discrepancies between Beecroft's and Forbes' accounts, especially with regard to their different rendition of reported statements. It is suggested that some of these differences may reflect the fact that they were using different interpreters— Forbes employing Madiki Lemon and Beecroft Thomas Richards. The hypothesis of the use of different interpreters is supported by the fact that on one occasion, when Forbes found a statement by King Gezo 'not loud enough to be heard', Beecroft was nevertheless able to register at least its gist, if not the actual words used.[198] That Forbes did not make use of Richards as interpreter is suggested by the fact that he got his name wrong, calling him 'John' rather than Thomas.[199] It is also suggestive that Forbes more systematically identifies persons speaking at the Customs by name, whereas Beecroft often says 'a man' or 'an Amazon', and that Forbes also gives the local names for several of the ceremonies observed which can readily be understood as Fon.[200] These differences are also explicable on the assumption that Forbes was using as interpreter Madiki Lemon, who (as a lifelong resident in Dahomey) would have been more familiar than Richards with the identities of Dahomian officials, as well as more fluent in Fon. This perhaps creates a presumption that, at least as regards the precise wording of reported statements, Forbes may be a more reliable witness than Beecroft.

At any rate, it seems plausible to suppose that some of the differences between Beecroft and Forbes in their reportage of Dahomians' statements arose from their use of different interpreters. A possible illustration of the problems which this might pose is provided by their final interview with King Gezo on 4 July, when Beecroft reports the King as saying that he could not employ his women in agricultural production because 'he did not wish to be laughed at by other nations'; whereas Forbes says this was because such work

---

[195] Beecroft's Journal, pp. 11–12.

[196] Ibid., p. 5.

[197] Forbes (1851, i: 92); Beecroft's Journal, p. 84. For Brown's knowledge of Portuguese, see Commander T.G. Forbes to Commodore Bruce, 18 Jan. 1852, in Fraser (2012: 249).

[198] Compare Beecroft's Journal, p. 96, and Forbes' Journal, p. 117.

[199] See his Journal, p. 192.

[200] See Endnote 1.

'would kill them'.[201] It seems conceivable that this arose from confusion between two similar-sounding Fon words—*kú*, meaning to die, and *kò*, meaning to laugh; this suggestion is strengthened by the fact that in Forbes' vocabulary of Fon these two words are transcribed identically, as 'koo'.[202]

10 The treatment of the text

Beecroft's journal exists in a single manuscript version, which is in his own handwriting. This is clearly, if not his original journal as written on the spot, at least a fair copy of it written soon afterwards: in transmitting it to the Foreign Office, Beecroft noted that he had taken 'two or three days' while at the island of Príncipe, en route back to Fernando Po, to 'prepare' the text, meaning presumably to copy and correct it.[203] It is poorly written in its grammar and spelling, with words sometimes omitted and punctuation frequently idiosyncratic (or altogether missing). Beecroft himself acknowledged that it had been written 'the greater part ... in a very hurried manner' and apologised for its 'grammatical errors', declaring his intention to 'amend' the duplicate copy of the text which he had retained when he had returned to Fernando Po.[204] But it does not seem that he did so: at least, there is no record of any such revised version having been transmitted to the Foreign Office, and if it ever existed it does not appear to have survived.

The present edition attempts an accurate transcription of the original text, with all its defects and idiosyncrasies. In cases where the reading is uncertain or conjectural, this is indicated by a question mark within square brackets. In the interests of comprehensibility, where words appear to have been omitted, the additional words (and, sometimes, punctuation marks) which seem to be required are likewise supplied within square brackets—and should, of course, be regarded as editorial suggestions, rather than necessarily accurately reflecting Beecroft's own intended meaning. All material within round brackets, in contrast, is in the original text.

The text is supported by relatively dense annotation, in order to assist evaluation of Beecroft's accuracy and to clarify allusions to matters which he does not explain fully or clearly (and which sometimes he may not have understood). Particular attention, as noted earlier, is paid to tracking (and, as far as is feasible, resolving) differences between the two accounts of Beecroft and Forbes. In addition, comparative, corroborative and illustrative material

[201] See Endnote 2.
[202] Forbes (1851, i: 239–40), giving 'koo' for 'die' and 'koo noo' for 'laugh' (i.e. *kò nŭ*, 'laugh at something').
[203] Beecroft to Palmerston, 22 July 1850, in Appendix 3, doc. 8, p. 211.
[204] Ibid., also Beecroft's Journal, p. 154.

is cited from the accounts of other European visitors to Dahomey in this period (of which the most informative is that of Consul Richard Burton in 1863/4), as well as from the substantial corpus of modern historical and anthropological literature relating to the kingdom. For the interpretation of words in Fon quoted by Beecroft and Forbes I have depended upon the dictionary by Fathers Basilio Segurola and Jean Rassinoux.[205] Endnotes 1 and 2 examine particular matters in further detail than is possible within the constraints of footnotes to the text.

This edition also includes, in three appendices, some supplementary documents intended to assist the interpretation, contextualisation and evaluation of Beecroft's journal, all of which are also to be found in the National Archives. Lieutenant Forbes' journal of the mission is provided in Appendix 1: although, as explained earlier, this text is already readily available, its inclusion here serves to facilitate the extensive cross-referencing which understanding and assessment of Beecroft's text requires. Appendix 2 provides a calculation by Forbes of royal expenditure on the Annual Customs, included in an appendix to his manuscript journal (but not printed in the Parliamentary Papers or included in his book). Appendix 3 includes various documents relating to the origins and outcome of the mission: letters from and to King Gezo; Palmerston's instructions to Beecroft, including the draft treaty which was presented to the King; and Beecroft's official dispatch giving a summary report of the mission shortly after its conclusion.

10.1 Note on spelling of names and titles

The spelling of words and names in Fon presents some difficulty. In the texts of the journals of Beecroft and Forbes, as presented in this edition, their own spellings have of course been retained, but in the annotation and other editorial contributions a more accurate and consistent approach seemed requisite. The problem is that the Fon language can be transcribed in a variety of ways. I have generally attempted a phonetically accurate version, albeit employing the standard Roman alphabet on grounds of familiarity, rather than the phonetic script (employed, for example, in the dictionary of Segurola and Rassinoux).[206] For proper names, on the other hand, it has seemed sensible to employ the forms in local current use, which generally adopt French spelling conventions: as, for example, the people 'Adja' and the town 'Agoué' (rather than 'Aja' and 'Agwe'); or the family names 'Gnahoui' and 'Quénum' (rather than 'Nyawi' and 'Hwenu'). For the titles of Dahomian officers (which are

---

[205] Segurola & Rassinoux (2000).
[206] So, for example, the guttural consonant is rendered by 'h' rather than 'x'.

actually much more commonly used in the journals than personal or family names) I have opted for a more phonetic version—for example, 'Mewu', rather than 'Méhou'. Difficulty arises in the not infrequent cases where titles appear no longer to survive in use today: here I have opted (where possible) to employ the spellings used by Richard Burton, since he made a more systematic effort than other European visitors to render the sound of Fon words accurately: thus, for example, the names (or titles) of senior female officers given by Beecroft as 'My-aho-paa' and 'Ah-pah-doo-noo-meh' (and variants) are taken to represent 'Mahaikpa' and 'Akpadume', and that of chief eunuch 'Too-noo-noo' is rendered as 'Tononun'.

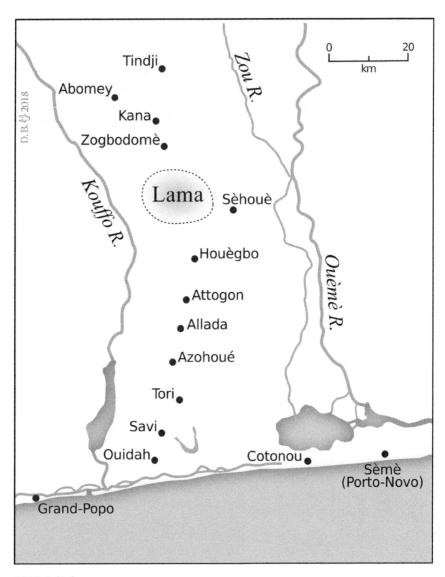

MAP 1 Dahomey

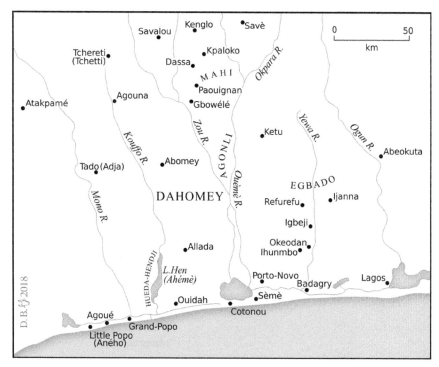

MAP 2 Dahomey and its Neighbours

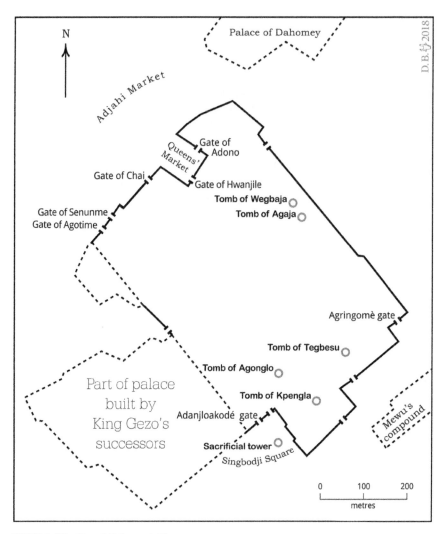

MAP 3 The Royal Palace at Abomey

Consul Beecroft's Journal

May 14th 1850

am fine w^r [= weather] surf moderate, daylight a suspicious vessel reported to be in sight in the offing[1] a signal from H.M.B. [= Her Majesty's Brig] Kingfisher for H.M. Steamer Phoenix[2] to weigh [anchor] and proceed in chase, half an hour steam was up & in chase, not more than half an hour elapsed strange sail signalized H.M.B. Ranger, Phoenix returned and passed within hail of Senior Officer,[3] and received orders to anchor close in shore for the accommodation of landing the Presents for the King of Dahomey and ourselves and Luggage &c shortly after we had anchored three canoes arrived alongside,[4] and I received a note from the Caboceer[5] stating that he had complied with my requisition as early as the beach would admit launching canoes. I received a kind note from Mr Hastie also agent for Mr Hutton[6] stating that he would send canoes, and render all the assistance in his power, to facilitate our landing at the same time with the Presents, 10.30 three canoes put of [= off] from the steamer for the Beach laden, three others on their way, at 11 o'clock I embarked accompanied by Capt Forbes in the Phoenix's Pinnace[7] for the Breakers,[8] Capt Harvey accompanied us in his Gig[9] to the back of the surf, under a salute of 20 Guns, instead of twenty six for Plenipotentiaries,[10] we shortly after embarked in a canoe of Mr Huttons, built in England, with our servants and luggage. she was a fine Buoyant vessel very high forward, well adapted for the Beach, we got forward near the Pilot, he very cautiously put her before the surf, with a show of Hats, and hands to Capt Harvey for his kindness, and attention & with his good wishes for a successful termination of our mission.

---

[1] I.e. one suspected of being a slave trader.

[2] The ship on which Beecroft had arrived.

[3] I.e. Senior Officer of the Bights Division of the British Navy's West African Squadron: in this case, Captain Henry Harvey, commanding the *Kingfisher*.

[4] Because of sandbars parallel to the coast and dangerous surf along the beach, European boats could not land at Ouidah, but depended on African canoes to communicate with the shore.

[5] I.e. of Ouidah, referring to the Yovogan.

[6] Thomas Hutton, who currently maintained a factory in the English fort at Ouidah; James Hastie had already been his agent there in 1849, when he had quarrelled with Forbes (see the latter's journal, p. 156). Hastie died at Ouidah, drowned while embarking or landing in a canoe, around the beginning of 1851 (Fraser 2012: 42).

[7] I.e. rowing boat.

[8] I.e. on the main sandbar.

[9] A small ship's boat.

[10] Artillery salutes were graduated according to the status of the person honoured: Beecroft and Forbes warranted 13 guns each in their capacity as envoys of Queen Victoria.

a canoe was capsized a few minutes before we reached the Beach, but fortunately no accidents beyond immersion, I took of my jacket and put on my swimming Belt, but we were fortunately landed without getting a foot wet, certainly the canoemen deserve good Praise for the good management of the canoe, we were received on the Beach by Mr Hastie, Monsieur Blanche[l]y, a French merchant,[11] and a younger son of the late De Souza's,[12] everything was landed safe with the exception of a chest of Guns, canoe was capsized well outside of the surf, so there was not the slightest chance of recovering it. it would of course soon be sand-warped.[13] we remained about an hour and a half on the Beach, until we had disposed of all the Presents and luggage, we then got into our Hammocks, with four bearers, and crossed the Lagoon, in parts it was above 4 feet deep,[14] a canoe certainly would be the most commodious plan,[15] we arrived at the English Fort about 2 o'clock. was received and welcomed by Mr Roberts, nephew to Mr Thomas Hutton,[16] a few old rusty Guns were fired as a salute. we immediately sent the silver Headed stick to the Caboceer, several of the Whydah gentlemen sent their sticks.[17] Captain Forbes and myself took a short walk in the vicinity of the Fort, and returned to dinner with Mr Hastie, and Roberts, retired to rest early in a very comfortable bed-room I presume recently occupied by Mr Hastie. midnight any quantity of vivid lightning

Wednesday May 15th

am cool and pleasant w[r]. arose early. 7 o'clock went to the Caboceer and paid our respects, and were very kindly received, he is remarkably stout, with rather a pleasing countenance, his feet and legs, small not in proportion to his body, he certainly looked seedy,[18] for he had been keeping it up all night, carouseing over their barbarous Custom the Fetish.[19]

---

[11] Agent of the French firm Régis of Marseille, which currently maintained a factory for the palm-oil trade in the French fort at Ouidah (Soumonni 1983): for his own recollections of Dahomey, see Blanchely (1891).

[12] I.e. Francisco Felix de Souza, who had died 8 May 1849, and whose position as 'Chacha' had now been inherited by his eldest son Isidoro de Souza; this 'younger son' was presumably one of the two brothers of Isidoro subsequently mentioned, Antonio and Ignacio.

[13] I.e. covered with sand.

[14] The lagoon runs parallel to the shore and has to be crossed in going to and from the town of Ouidah.

[15] Canoes were, in fact, used to cross the lagoon when the water was unusually deep, as by Vice-Consul Louis Fraser in 1851 (2012: 28–9).

[16] Roberts had been Hutton's agent at Ouidah also in 1845 and 1847 (Duncan 1847, i: 183–4; Ridgway 1847: 193).

[17] Personalised canes, used to identify the sender of a message ('by the way of cards', as Beecroft later remarks, p. 5).

[18] I.e. ill.

[19] Cf. below, p. 8, for further reference to 'fetish' dancing. The term 'fetish' (from Portuguese *feitiço*, 'artificial') was applied to various ritual objects and practices, as well as to gods (*vodun*).

after a short interview he wished me to inspect the Property left in his charge by the late Mr Duncan, belonging to Her Majesty's Government,[20] I found all in good condition, I ordered them to be repacked, and to allow them to accompany the other Presents for his Majesty, they had been left in his charge by Mr Aberdeen,[21] I took the opportunity to leave my Tent to be sent to Abomey to the King, after which we took our leave, and returned to the English Fort, and took Breakfast with Mr Roberts, Mr Hastie's duties called him to the beach early to ship palm oil, on board of the Jersey-Lass.[22] several sticks were presented this forenoon from different Portuguese residents here, by the way of cards.

I have not any opinion of their Political Kindness it is merely a cloak, it is too well known to myself that they dare not open their mouths personally to us. Nevertheless I know from very good authority, that is my own Interpreter Thomas Richards, that I brought with me from Fernando Po,[23] and sent him on shore in charge of the 1st canoe with the Presents, so he was on the Beach an hour before us, he can speak and understand Portuguese, he was near three or four of them on Beach, when the[y] saw Captain Forbes and myself in the canoe coming for the Beach, they prayed in Portuguese that the canoe might be capsized or swamped and we both drowned he told me this today not having time or convenience before, but the allwise God did not allow the Prayers of the wicked to prevail. Noon Ther[mometer] 84° wind westerly accompanied with fine dry weather, advised to dash[24] the Caboceer a sloutched [= slouched] Hat,[25] for which he was very grateful and overwhelming with his thanks. Phoenix underweigh[26] and in chase to the Eastwards pursuing a <u>Slaver</u>, I wish him luck,[27] this afternoon received a visit from Mr De Cinta, a Portuguese merchant from Madeira resident here for the last six years,[28] he has formerly dealt very heavily in the <u>awful traffic</u> of <u>Slaves</u>, at present he is extensively engaged in the Palm-Oil Trade, he is a most gentlemanly intelligent man in appearance and manner, he retired in half an hour.

---

[20] John Duncan, Vice-Consul at Ouidah, who had left his post in October 1849 (and died soon after).

[21] Henry Aberdeen, a botanist who had accompanied Duncan to Ouidah (O'Connor 2006: 332, 337–8); he had initially remained in Ouidah after Duncan's departure (see Forbes 1851, i: 97), but presumably left soon after.

[22] The *Jersey Lass* was again at Ouidah in December 1851 (Fraser 2012: 135).

[23] For this man, see Introduction, p. xliv.

[24] Coastal pidgin for (giving) a gift.

[25] I.e. one with its brim turned downwards.

[26] More correctly, 'under way', i.e. moving.

[27] The successful capture of this ship was reported on the next day (p. 9).

[28] Cf. HCPP, *Slave Trade*, 1849/50, Class B, incl. 10 in no. 9, Lieutenant Forbes to Commodore Fanshawe, 5 Nov. 1849, 'Jacinta'; Forbes (1851, i: 92), 'Tacinta [= Jacinta] de Rodriguez': i.e. Jacinto Joaquim Rodrigues, a leading merchant of Ouidah (Law 2004b: 199).

Capt Forbes and myself deemed it prudent to form our own mess,[29] having two Bed-rooms and a small sitting room, instead of the Hall being appropriated to our use rather than encroach on Mr Roberts, or Mr Hastie's privacy, besides the trouble and expense. I communicated the same to Mr Roberts, so the affair was mutually and amicably arranged.

After dinner we took a walk through the Town into the country, it is a complete <u>Prairie</u> as far as the [eye] can discern, and really very Picturesque, Hedges, and Ditches are only wanted to fancy yourself in England on a summers evening, sky, serene & clear, and pleasantly cool, a breeze sweeping without interruption over the immense plain, on our way home passed the mansion of the late De Souza, it is a ponderous mass without any appearance, open in front and walled in the rear, with a massy grass thatch, I presume it must harbor any quantity of vermin.[30] Ignatio's is apparently more neatly laid out and walled completely round. Antonio de Souza's is a small neat two Story House, I believe neatly furnished.[31] all these seen on our way from the plain to the English Fort.[32] I have not as yet seen the late Mr Duncans Cotton Plantation, I am sadly afraid he was very much too sanguine on his success of cultivating cotton in Africa.[33] We reached the fort at sunset. Capt Forbes and myself spent the evening agreeably conferring on our mission. retired to rest at 10 o'clock. Ther 81°. midnight dry w[r] but sultry.

Thursday, May 16th

I arose at 5 o'clock. Ther 74°. washed and shaved in readiness to receive our friend the Vice-Roy[34] as he promised to pay us a visit early, but we were disappointed, he had been carouseing all night, and required sleep when he ought to be have been on his legs, I am extremely sorry that Mr Hutton, has thought fit to take the greater part of the useful community belonging to English

[29] I.e. to eat separately.

[30] The main de Souza house was now occupied by Francisco Felix de Souza's eldest son (and successor to his office of Chacha), Isidoro. Forbes described it as 'a large ill-built erection of no particular form' (1851, i: 105–6).

[31] Ignacio and Antonio de Souza, younger brothers of Isidoro and also prominent traders.

[32] Beecroft's walk in 'the plain' was evidently to the west of Ouidah: Antonio's house was in Zomaï quarter, at the western end of the town; Isidoro occupied the main de Souza compound, in Brazil quarter, further east, south-west of the English fort; and Ignacio lived at Kindji, closer to the fort (Law 2004b: 215).

[33] Duncan had been commissioned by the Manchester Chamber of Commerce to promote cotton cultivation in Dahomey (Ratcliffe 1982: 92, 95–6). Soon after his arrival at Ouidah he reported that he had planted 'a quantity of cotton seeds sent me from Manchester', and subsequently that he had 'a number of men' engaged in planting further cotton seeds obtained from the King at Abomey, (HCPP, *Slave Trade*, 1849/50, Class B, nos 4, 7: Vice-Consul Duncan to Viscount Palmerston, 7 Aug. and 22 Sept. 1849).

[34] I.e. the Yovogan.

Town,[35] with him to Badagry,[36] they have been absent about six weeks, it appears rather mysterious, I trust there is not any sinister motive to annoy, still I have a better opinion of Mr Hutton, but it is very annoying, as we are in want of people to send the King's Presents on to Abomey. There are only a few Hammock bearers here, Noon all the Presents were removed from the Fort to the Caboceers, he having received orders from his Majesty to leave Whydah for the Customs at Abomey on the 20th Inst[ant][37] this afternoon we waited on Monsieur Casse and Blanchely at the French Fort,[38] and were very kindly received, showed us through the whole Factory, it is well adapted for trading purposes, with large <u>Vats</u> for storing palm oil, they will have a great quantity left after dispatching the Barque Bon Pere she will be completed in a day or two having 300 Tons.

we had previously applied to Mr Hutton for a supply of cowries for the mission, they not having any we were necessitated to purchase from Monsieur Casse at 21 dollars per cwt [= hundredweight] a high price[39] I ordered two casks,[40] and thirty pieces of different sorts of cloth, for use at Abomey We returned at 4 o'clock to the English Fort. We met a Brazillian named Jose dos Cento, who came to Whydah a poor man, but has become rich, from his own direct energies, and perseverance, he ships a great quantity of Palm oil, as well as a little in the Slave Trade when a fair opportunity offers, on that point he does not speculate much,[41] I am glad to be encouraged to state that the legitimate [trade] is beginning to Bud, competition has become so great that it has so far enhanced the value of Palm Oil from 2 dollars for a measure of 19 Gallons to six dollars for the same,[42] so it is too obvious, that could the

---

[35] I.e. the quarter of Ouidah centred on the English fort, and largely occupied by persons attached to it (whose indigenous name is Sogbadji).
[36] On the coast, 90 km east of Ouidah (in modern Nigeria), where Hutton also currently had a factory.
[37] I.e. the 'Annual Customs', subsequently witnessed by Beecroft, between 29 May and 22 June.
[38] Esprit-Cases, who had arrived to succeed Blanchely as agent of Régis.
[39] The 'head' of 2,000 cowries, which was conventionally equated with the dollar, had a weight of 5 lbs, so $21 for 1 'hundredweight' (112 lbs) is close to this nominal value; but perhaps Beecroft expected to get them at cost price.
[40] The weight is subsequently given as 909 lbs (1,014, minus 105 for the weight of the casks, pp. 8, 10), i.e. about 8 cwt: at $21 per cwt, this would have cost $168. The mission subsequently obtained further cowries from a British naval vessel much more cheaply: see Forbes' Journal, p. 156.
[41] Cf. Forbes (1851, i: 114), who met this man earlier in 1850, and gives his name as 'Don José dos Santos': i.e. José Francisco dos Santos, a Brazilian merchant settled in Ouidah (Law 2004b: 192–3). Forbes gives a slightly different assessment of his involvement in the slave trade: 'having once embarked in the slave trade he is still a gambler, and his speculations often bring him in a loser'.
[42] Earlier in 1850, Forbes reported a rise from $3 to $7 per measure since 1844: Journal, 6 April 1850, in HCPP, *Slave Trade* 1850/1, Class A, incl. 3 in no. 198.

abominable [i.e. slave] traffic be crushed legitimate trade would soon outsway the odium.[43]

Whydah has many drawbacks, the distance it has to be rolled to the Beach, for shipment, at a risk,[44] these are obstacles not to be easily surmounted, but it only requires the energies & mind of the purchasers to obviate, in a great measure, a moiety of these difficulties and commence a new plan, if the other [trade] was finished the Path would be made perceptible.

Received from the French Fort 1014 lbs of cowries and the 30 pieces of cloth ordered.

After dinner I took a walk accompanied by Capt Forbes and Mr Roberts, round the Fort, on our way we came upon the Fetish peoples performances their superstitious fooleries and rogueries, we were detained a short time, as they belonged to English Town, looking at their distortions, and gesticulations, going round the circle, Keeping time to their rude music of country Drums,[45] and Horns,[46] there were a great number of lookers on with us en passant,[47] at last an aged Lady and three or four more of Grey haired venerables, Old Gents heads of the Fetish, came up and paid their respects to us, we were then in a measure obliged according to the Custom of the Country to acknowledge the same and give them a small present of rum, particularly being Englishmen and strangers, for which they overwhelmed us with thanks and e[n]comiums, shortly after Capt Forbes and myself left and prolonged our walk a short distance into the country, the Path we had chosen appeared a very impoverished soil, Iron stone, and mica, saw several gigantic Bombax Trees, taken possession of by the Fetish and walled in,[48] the country as far as the eye can discern is level, with a Park like appearance, we returned at sunset. on our arrival at the Fort found a messenger from Badagry with letters from Mr Hutton stating that he had remained at Porto Novo, on his way here,[49] the

[43] I have not found 'outsway' in any dictionary, though Beecroft may have been thinking of 'oversway', to overrule; the intended meaning seems to be 'overcome the prejudice', i.e. against 'legitimate' trade.

[44] I.e. palm oil, in barrels, which were rolled along the path to the beach (Law 2004b: 214).

[45] 'country', i.e. locally made.

[46] See also Forbes (1851, ii: 4). From Forbes' description, this was probably a festival for Dangbe, the leading *vodun* (deity) of Ouidah, who was incarnated in snakes (royal pythons) maintained at his shrine (see Law 2004b, 94).

[47] 'in passing' (French).

[48] The silk-cotton or kapok tree (*ceiba pentandra*), called in Fon *huntin*, and regarded as a *vodun*. Forbes, earlier in 1850, noted 'the fetish tree, a huge cotton giant', on the Abomey road (1851, i: 125).

[49] The name 'Porto-Novo' was applied to a coastal village, 55 km east of Ouidah, and by extension to the kingdom to which it originally belonged, Dahomey's south-eastern neighbour, whose indigenous name was Hogbonu (see Videgla 1999). The modern city of 'Porto-Novo' (now the capital of the Republic of Bénin), 10 km inland, is the former capital of the kingdom,

messenger was one of their own people, he of course accosted Mr Roberts in a very friendly manner, it did not seem pleasing to Mr Hastie. Capt Forbes and myself left and retired to our own domicile and talked over other matters more serious connected with our mission we retired to rest at 9 o'clock this day ends with very fine w^r. reported that a very small schooner of 35 Tons [was] taken by Phoenix belonging to a Black man named José liveing at Aghwey.[50]

Friday, May 17th

am dull cloudy w^r at daylight Capt Forbes accompanied me two or three miles into the Country and returned about 7 o'clock when it was announced that the Caboceer intended, waiting upon us, accordingly we were hurried at our Breakfast; for we had scarcely begun when himself and mob were heard in the distance with their ding-dong music, he was mounted on an ass[51] with a white umbrella an emblem of Peace, with a Host of rabble in his rear, he entered the Hall and shook us kindly by the hand he took a seat only for a few minutes during which he informed me that he intended to leave for Abomey on the 20th in the evening I then told him that we should leave the day following, he then left as he had a number of calls to make, we escorted him outside of the Gates, he bid us good bye, until we meet in Abomey.

Sent of or rather Paid ten women 15 strings each[52] to leave this afternoon with 20 Kegs of rum. Mr Casse from the French Fort returned our call[,] shortly after his entrée Antonio De Souza and Jose dos Cinta, called to pay

---

while the coastal village is nowadays known by its indigenous name, Sèmè. At this period, confusingly, the coastal village of 'Porto-Novo' (which was currently the main base of the Brazilian merchant Domingos José Martins) was controlled by Dahomey, rather than by the king of 'Porto-Novo' (see Fraser 2012: 152). Beecroft's references to 'Porto-Novo' seem all to relate to the coastal village.

[50] Agoué, on the coast 50 km west of Ouidah. Cf. Forbes (1851, i: 102), referring to 'José Almeida', said to have 'almost a monopoly' of the slave trade at Agoué, but elsewhere he gives the name as 'Joachim Almeida' (HCPP, *Slave Trade*, 1850–1, Class A, incl. 3 in no. 1098: Forbes to Fanshawe, 6 April 1850): i.e. Joaquim d'Almeida, an African-born former slave, who was the leading Brazilian slave trader at Agoué in the 1850s (Strickrodt 2015: 200–1). The ship captured was the *St Antonio Vincedor*, taken off Porto-Novo on 15 May 1850: see HCPP, *Slave Trade*, 1851/2, Class A, incl. in no. 147: List of Vessels Captured or Detained by H.M. Squadron on the West Coast of Africa, for being engaged in the Slave Trade, 1 March 1850–28 Feb. 1851 (but this ship is not included in the Trans-Atlantic Slave Trade Database (hereafter, TASTD)).

[51] Later, at Abomey, the Yovogan was seen riding a pony (p. 30). Duncan in 1845 found that he owned both 'a very fine donkey' and 'a small pony' (1847, i: 119).

[52] I.e. strings of cowries: a string (conventionally equated with an English penny) contained 40 shells. The women were employed as porters, for whom the daily wage was 120 cowries, or 3 strings (Forbes 1851, i: 122), so 15 strings represented payment for 5 days.

their respects, ere the latter was well seated Monsieur Casse commenced an attack, rebuking Antonio de Souza, for not lending him canoes, he said he could assist Englishmen, and not French men. I was rather astonished for it was uncalled for as Antonio was our guest[,] on the part of Monsieur Casse, I was rather provoked he saw that, and got up to leave Capt Forbes handed him the acot [= account] on a scrip the weight of the cowries, deducting the Tare for the Casks,[53] which was less 105 lbs than his account rendered, he said he had merely sent the gross weight.

We were necessitated to order four cases of claret 1 case of Gin 1 case of Lique[u]rs, for use at Abomey he left immediately. Antonio De Souza fancied that he paid me a great compliment, when he stated that I was very like his Father De Souza, Cha-Cha for Whydah, Antonio himself has rather a forbidding countenance, he is very full eyed[54] with a large scar in his underlip he did not remain long after <u>Casse</u> left. After we had got rid of our guests Forbes, myself and deputy Governor of the Fort,[55] commenced and paid the <u>cowries,</u> for the conveyance of the King's Presents, and to pack our own stores, and comforts, which amounted in all to seventeen packages, took a late dinner after which a short walk outside of the Town passed a large Fetish Place belonging to Ah-jaa-vee, he is as report say immensely wealthy a Blackman, full of folly and superstition as the story goes his Father left him the property,[56] we reached the Fort at 7 o'clock during the evening a Portuguese gentleman called on us and smoked a cigar as a matter of course, he left about 8.20, when we had a short conference relative to the impolitic proceedings of the Senior Officer C[aptain] Harvey ordering a Target to be made of the small schooner prize to the Phoenix,[57] knowing us to be on the Beach, aggravating and tantalizing their fellows on shore, without a speck of the smallest atom of use.

Gift to the Caboceer four pieces of cloth a musical box, Nawhey[58]— 1 piece of cloth.

Midnight fine pleasant dry w^r.

---

[53] I.e. the allowance made for their weight.

[54] I.e. having large eyes.

[55] I.e. Madiki Lemon (see Introduction, p. xliii). Forbes calls him 'commandant [of the fort] for the King of Dahomey' (1851, i: 54), but evidently Beecroft regarded Hutton's agent Hastie as the 'governor', and Madiki as his subordinate.

[56] Cf. Forbes (1851, i: 113), who gives the name as 'Ahjovee': i.e. Adjovi, one of the leading indigenous merchants of Ouidah, his 'fetish place' being the sacred grove of Kpase, the legendary founder of Ouidah, north-east of the town (Law 2004b: 175).

[57] I.e. it was destroyed by cannon fire.

[58] Gnahoui, the king's English interpreter and also a leading Ouidah merchant (see Introduction, p. xliii).

Saturday, May 18th

am fine w[r],[59] daylight Captain Forbes accompanied me in a walk along the Abomey road about three miles until we came to a swamp,[60] on our approach the miasmata[61] ascended similar to the smoke of a small village in the valley, in the distance, we approached it and found the dense fog to be about twelve to fifteen feet from the surface, at that season there was water about two feet deep, we returned a great number of Fetish houses on this path in and near the Town, one large one a Levee[62] was assembled groups prostrated on the ground round the exterior,[63] the interior full of the Fetish men at a Palaver[64] we arrived at the Fort at 7.30.

took breakfast, after which we dispatched our stores and provissions, and other necessaries, Paid the carriers 205 strings of cowries. Sent our sticks to Isadore's[65] and Antonio's messenger returned and stated they would receive us at 11 o'clock. H.M.B. Ranger has anchored off here, it is only a few days since she was in sight off here, her station is off Ahgway and <u>Po Poo</u>,[66] no appearance of the Gladiator. 11 o'clock we left the Fort accompanied by the Deputy Governor to call on Isadore De Souza, we were ushered into a square-yard, found all doors closed, a Negro I presume the porter ran and knelt on the steps, and wrapped [= rapped] very cautiously with his knuckles at the lower part of the door, a female voice answered from within, and opened the door, he told her Englishmen sought admittance, she very abruptly shut it and walked of, shortly after she made her appearance and handed out chairs, and commenced to sweep the Hall, she evidently intended us to sit there until she made or put her master's house in order to receive us, We were necessi-tated to inform our Interpreter[67] that we did not intend to remain in the <u>sun</u>. She had skimmed a Palm leaf over the floor we were permitted to make our entrée we stalked about the room for ten minutes when <u>Isadore de Souza</u> made his appearance and shook hands, this man is now sold to the King of Dahomey for life, he dare not leave at his <u>Peril</u>, he desired us to be seated, he

---

[59] In the MS this day's entry begins with a misplaced version of the beginning of that for the previous day, omitted here.

[60] Called by Burton 'the Agbana water' (1864, i: 130–1), nowadays 'Agbananou'.

[61] I.e. fumes.

[62] I.e. a morning reception.

[63] This was probably the sacred *huntin* (silk-cotton) tree at the northern exit from the town (cf. note 48), under whose shade 'fetish meetings' were held (Burton 1864, i: 125).

[64] West African coastal pidgin for a discussion or dispute (Portuguese *palavra*, 'word').

[65] Isidoro de Souza, eldest son of Francisco Felix de Souza and successor to his office of 'Chacha'.

[66] There were two coastal towns called 'Popo'—Little Popo (modern Aného), west of Agoué (in modern Togo), and Great Popo (Grand-Popo) to the east (in Bénin): the two are distinguished in Forbes' Journal, p. 193. References to 'Popo' in Beecroft's journal seem to relate to the former, which was currently the more important commercially: see Strickrodt (2015: 198–202, 210–15).

[67] I.e. the 'Deputy Governor', Madiki Lemon.

is a sulky looking fellow, heavy and sluggish in his manner, introduced ourselves waiting on him as the Cha-Cha and to thank him very kindly for his
timely assistance in sending of canoes to land the Presents for the King of
Dahomey he said he was very glad to see my face at <u>Whydah</u>, he said that he
had been informed that I had come purposely to visit Abomey, I replied in the
affirmative that it was our intention, he enquired when we were due to leave,
I told him that it was our intention to leave on Tuesday, he said that he fully
intended to leave on the same day.

he introduced wine, and we took a glass each the Customs was next introduced, he talked quite familiarly about cutting of heads &c &c[68] he said the
late King was a great Tyrant, that he used to torture them by taking of a
member at a time, and of his opening them and taking out their hearts, and
salting the inside and sewing them up again,[69] he stated that the present King
was a good humane man, nevertheless he will take of about two hundred and
fifty heads,[70] at the same time grinning and stating that that he had better sell
them here,[71] he then began to verge on rather an unpleasant topic, [I] thought
it advisable to rise and wish him a good morning, he is evidently a sulky fellow, I should not like to cross his path, we next called on Antonio his Brother,
we were very kindly received, him and me played a Game at Bagatelle,[72]
smoked a cigar and took a glass of sherry, his House is small but very neatly
fitted, he remarked several times my striking likeness to his Father, he said he
had mentioned it to his mother, and he expressed a wish that I would call on
her, I told him that we were going to call on Jose Centa's where we met a very
gentlemanly person, who spoke very good English, I was informed afterwards
that he was from Hamburgh,[73] we took a glass of wine and made a short stay,
we then returned to Antonio's and was introduced to his mother, she was
reclining on a couch, an immense mass about twenty stones, she was not able
to walk her daughter was present rather good looking a <u>mustee</u>,[74] they were
very much gratified that I condescended to call to see them, I was so much like
the old <u>Cha-Cha</u>. I think she must be a similar mass to Daniel Lambert,[75]

---

[68] Referring to human sacrifices at the 'Annual Customs'.

[69] I.e. Adandozan, deposed in 1818. Local traditions refer to his cruelty, although not to the
specific outrages mentioned here (e.g. Le Herissé 1911: 313–14).

[70] The number sacrificed in 1850 seems to have been significantly less (see Endnote 1).

[71] Forbes elaborates, saying that Isidoro claimed that the sacrifices 'were entirely the fault of the
British government, in keeping up the blockade', implying that slaves who could not be exported
were sacrificed (1851, i: 6).

[72] A form of billiards. An earlier visitor noted that the de Souza premises in Zomaï included a
billiard room (Ridgway 1847: 196).

[73] Perhaps Lorenz Diedrichsen, a Hamburg trader active at Ouidah (Newbury 1961: 40, 57).

[74] I.e. of racially mixed descent: strictly, a 'mustee' was a person of one-eighth black ancestry
(having one black great-grandparent).

[75] Lived 1770–1809, reputed to be the heaviest ever person on record (weighing 50 stones/700 lbs
at his death).

took a glass of liqueur and wished them good morning on our arrival at the Fort a large fire broke out a little from it and destroyed several Houses Capt Forbes and myself visited the spot, they succeeded in stopping its progress by unroofing the Houses to leeward, the poor people were in a great state of consternation & excitement water had to be brought some distance and only in large country Pots[76] returned home and dined 5 o'clock took a walk over a Prairie of some extent and returned to the Fort at 6.30 Mr Roberts spent part of the evening retired to rest at 10 o'clock. Midnight fine cool w^r.

Sunday, May 19th

daylight fine dry w^r we took a walk as far as the swamp, it is about five miles there and back we returned at 7.30 the dews are very heavy at this season of the year, as long as they continue dry weather may be anticipated to continue. Count Nawhey[77] called to pay his respects &c &c At noon had the very great pleasure to see Her majesty's Steamer Gladiator anchor off this Port with a large Brazillian ensign flying at the fore, it is possible she may have captured the <u>Palmeiro</u> that shipped from Po Poo on the 5th or 6th inst 758 slaves,[78] if so the Captain will be very coolly received by Capt Adams[79] after firing on the Rangers Boats.

Noon fine w^r with steady westerly winds.

5 o'clock went according to invite to dine with Antonio De Souza, we reached his mansion in due time, he marched us of to his brother Ignatio he is a stout yellow man very like his Brother Isadore but a rather more pleasing expression of countenance, the House and yard is large and capacious, and has once been a splendid house but it now appears to be Poverty stricken without any Furniture inside, several of the outer buildings are in a dilapidated state there is a Grape vine in the house yard, everything goes to show the remains of once a splendid habitation, we sat down to dinner shaded by large Trees in the outer yard, ten in number including three youngsters intelligent boys with fine countenances and prominent eyes, we had a very good dinner, in due time the Queen's health was proposed and drank I returned thanks and proposed the Queen of Portugal,[80] Forbes proposed the Emperor of Brazils after which I proposed the King of Dahomey, my health and Capt Forbes was drank, their manners are rude with the best intentions during the latter part Capt Casse and Blanche[l]y made their appearance, accompanied

[76] Fires were a recurrent problem in Ouidah and other urban centres (Law 2004b: 79–80).
[77] The title 'Count' given to Gnahoui (only by Beecroft) is not explained, but presumably alludes to his high status within Dahomian officialdom.
[78] This ship does not in fact seem to have been captured (and is not included in TASTD).
[79] Commander of the *Gladiator*.
[80] Although Francisco Felix de Souza was born in Brazil, which had been independent of Portugal since 1822, he had continued to assert his Portuguese nationality (Law 2004a: 195–6).

by an old French Gentleman,[81] their visit was really very short, so I presume they were rather taken by nonplus[82] at meeting us they left at the same time apologizing for having intruded. Antonio introduced rather an odd question: he enquired if he could not become a British subject, I told him it is possible by paying a round sum for his naturalization he could then claim British Protection and Privileges, I am at a loss and cannot for one moment come to any conclusions [about] his motive for such enquiries,[83] after which he dipped into another matter and began to read a Loanda Gazette[84] relative to the capture of the Gallianna by Cyclops,[85] all that can be said, it was a very indelicate proceeding, at such a time and in such a place I found it high time to be moving of we left at 8 o'clock and arrived at the <u>Fort</u> and spent an hour or two with Roberts and Hastie. Captain Casse and his party paid us a second visit, it was to request a favor from me, that was to sign a certificate that the Barque Bon Pere sailed from this Port clear of disease, no medical officer on board or on shore, I told him that if the Captain gave me a certificate signed by himself, to that effect, I would back it as no medics in the land, they left shortly afterwards, we retired to rest at 10 o'clock,

Midnight fine dry w[r].

Monday, May 20th

daylight H.M. Steamer Phoenix anchored off this Port four vessels of war, and it is likely that they are shipping 700 slaves at Po Poo. it is an extraordinary fact that H.M.B. Ranger has been off and on here for the last week, all the Whydah Gents left here for the place of shipment,[86] well knowing that it was solus[87] without a solitary cruiser, so they have a very good chance of success.

---

[81] Not identified.

[82] I.e. a state of perplexity.

[83] Likewise, in 1851, Antonio told Vice-Consul Fraser that he 'wishes to be put under British protection' (Fraser 2012: 139). His motive was probably to seek protection against the Dahomian authorities.

[84] I.e. the *Boletim Oficial do Governo Geral da Provincia de Angola*, also known as the *Gazeta de Loanda*, the official newspaper of the Portuguese colonial authorities in Angola, published from 1845 (my thanks for this information to Roquinaldo Ferreira).

[85] The *Galliana* was a ship owned by Antonio de Souza, which was arrested on suspicion of slave trading in 1849, but released due to lack of evidence: see HCPP, *Slave Trade*, 1849–50, Class A, no. 98. In 1851 Vice-Consul Fraser found Antonio aggrieved that he had not received the compensation paid for this false arrest, which had been appropriated by the Portuguese government (Fraser 2012: 32).

[86] Merchants based in Ouidah often sent slaves for embarkation at Little Popo (and other places along the coast to both west and east), in order to evade the attentions of the British Navy (Law 2004b: 192–3; Strickrodt 2015: 198–203).

[87] 'alone' (Latin), hence, unattended.

I received a short kind note from Capt Adams, Phoenix [is] of for Fernando Po and Ascension, Capt Forbes wrote a kind note to Capt Adams, 3.30 the Gladiator was underweigh from the westward, received from her two casks of cowries, it was an unfortunate affair for the Kingfisher's Gig to be anchored so near the back of the surf, her grappling[88] giving way they had not room to get an oar to bear, so she was swamped, with six men and a midshipman, fortunately no loss or injury, they were assisted by Kroo-men on the Beach,[89] and sent up to the Fort, got a change of garments from Capt Forbes, Mr Hutton arrived from <u>Porto Nova</u>, also Peter Brown formerly an old servant of mine some years ago.[90]

I was up rather too a late hour talking over different matters relative to our mission. Midnight, apparently fine.

Tuesday, May 21st

am thick cloudy w[r] daylight squally appearances to the eastward, ended with showers of rain, no wind, busily employed packing up, great difficulty to get carriers patience is really a great blessing and very necessary, after great palavering and a world of trouble, we got clear of the Fort at 5.15 pm with a salute from their honeycombed guns, Mr Thomas Hutton and his suite, set us outside of the Fort and wished us success on our mission, we stopped for a few minutes at the Caboceers his man in charge came out and saluted us and threw dirt on his head[91] and wished us a pleasant journey, after which we got into our Hammocks, for a short distance merely to keep the bearers together until we got outside of the Town, then we got out and walked, to the swamp, we got in to cross it after which we walked to the village called <u>Sah-vee</u>,[92] at 7.30 just there I encountered the fellow with my bed apparently going to take a sleep he said it was too heavy however we got him set of again we got into our Hammocks, and proceeded about 8 o'clock we crossed another swamp[93] protected partially by Limbs of Trees laid transversely:[94] rather awkward travelling in the dark Hammock bearers stumbled several times, we arrived at the

---

[88] I.e. grapnel, a small anchor.

[89] Kru, an ethnic group in what is today Liberia: Kru sailors were commonly employed on British naval and merchant vessels at this period.

[90] For this man (now employed by Hutton), see Introduction, pp. xliv–xlv.

[91] This was a standard accompaniment of prostration (cf. e.g. Burton 1864, i: 260–1).

[92] Savi, 8 km north of Ouidah.

[93] Called by Burton (1864, i: 143–5) 'the Nyin-sin swamp', nowadays 'lagune de Toho'.

[94] Cf. Freeman (1844: 251), 'a rude bridge … [made] by placing a number of stout bantlings, each about eight feet long, one above the other, until the top ones were sufficiently high above the mud and water to obtain a dry footing'; Burton (1864, i: 144), 'a corduroy road, rudely made with rugged tree trunks'.

village of <u>Toree</u>,[95] at 9 o'clock, it is rather an extraordinary built place, it had been market day, we met great numbers returning to <u>Whydah</u>, we were lodged comfortably in a house belonging to Nahwey built of switch [= swish] and mud,[96] had a cup of Tea and a few Boiled Eggs, fortunately my Bed made its appearance in the interim, but not any Boxes, had not any clothes had they been required for a change, hung my Hammock in a sort of verandah, but I slept very little, it being too small, the remainder [*sc.* of the night?] fine dry cool and pleasant w[r]. the fellows were well tired they did not make much clamour with their Tongues, their olfractories [= olfactories] sounded like Bugles, and Horns.[97]

Wednesday, May 22nd

daylight fine w[r] 6.30 we started on our journey, I walked until 8 o'clock when I got into my Hammock, passed through a small village[98] it was market day, rested about ten minutes to take some refreshment such [as] a Glass of ale, and a Biscuit, we arrived at <u>Ah-laa-daa</u>[99] at 10 o'clock, it is a straggling place, it was market day, it was rather thronged with people en route to Abomey we took a short walk as far as the Palace Gates,[100] and in the square we encountered the large cases for the King of Dahomey, they had been four days from Whydah[101] we returned to our quarters changed our linen &c., received a gift from the head woman of the <u>Harem</u>[102] of a jar of water, and a calabash of palm oil chop,[103] sent her a small present in return, the Host of our mansion sent a gift of a jar of <u>Peto</u> country Beer,[104] and a calabash of country chop. after which we took a seat under an orange Tree to regale ourselves with a little Breeze and look around us amongst the country Bumpkins, it was a motley group. it was amusing to hear their jok[e]s passed

---

[95] Tori, 9 km north of Savi.

[96] 'Swish and mud' is pleonastic, since the former in fact refers to mud (mixed with straw) used as a building material (see Forbes (1851), i: 128).

[97] I.e. noses: referring to snoring.

[98] From comparison with other sources, this was Azohouè, 10 km north of Tori (e.g. Forbes 1851, i: 56, 'Azohwee').

[99] Allada, 19 km north of Tori.

[100] The 'palace' at Allada was not, at this period, a normal royal residence, being occupied by the king only 'occasionally' (Freeman 1844: 252). Duncan described it as a 'king's house built for the accommodation of white men' (1847, i: 207), though Beecroft and Forbes do not seem to have stayed in it.

[101] See p. 10.

[102] I.e. of the women occupying the 'palace'.

[103] Pidgin for 'food'.

[104] The term 'peto' (more commonly spelled 'pito') is not the local (Fon) word for beer (which is *ahàn*), but a coastal pidgin term.

on each other, we lost the marrow through the Interpreter,[105] some little fellows with eagerness were watching the decline of a cigar, expecting the gratification of a smoke from the last half inch, others with their mantles open to receive a piece of orange, or any other thing that a white man could take they were ready to devour any part you gave them, in the heat of the day you will always find a Group lounging under the shade of those large Trees, about the market place & square. after dinner in the cool Capt Forbes accompanied me round the Palace walls, it is about two miles, in a dilapidated state in places, sunset a great quantity of vivid lightning which continued[,] about midnight a great clamour, and din, Beating of Drums, and firing of Guns, on enquiry we found that it was Isadore de Souza, the Cha-Cha entering the Town.

Thursday, May 23rd

am thunder and lightning, 2 o'clock a severe Tornado, with torrents of rain, we were aroused by it sweeping through the roof & taking possession of our tenement, I believe that I was somewhat better of than Captain Forbes, for he got completely drenched, indeed most of our people were exposed, it continued until after daylight, when it cleared away, and became fine, nevertheless it was very damp underfoot, I went outside on the [omission?] found all on the move, Ignatio De Souza came up and shook hands, complained about his nights fare, I returned took a cup of Tea and an Egg, and then got fairly started on our journey about 7.50[,] the White Mans Caboceer Ignatio[106] took the lead Drums, Gongs and Guns, we followed in the rear being fairly eclipsed, by the number of his retinue, I went in my Hammock for a short distance, then got out and walked to a small village called Dun-noo[107] where we arrived at 10 o'clock, we rested about 10 minutes, when we started I got into my Hammock, until we reached Oga-goo[108] walked to Asso-whey I got into my Hammock to Wheeboo[109] where we reached at 11.45 waited about a quarter of an hour for Nawhey's appearance to determine upon the road the long or short one to Abomey there is more difficulty in crossing by the short route, we had no desire to be stuck fast and get fever, so we decided to take the long

---

[105] Presumably 'marrow' in the sense of 'essence'.

[106] Ignacio had been given the rank of 'Caboceer' (Forbes, *Journal*, pp. 155–6), but the term 'White Man's Caboceer' translates the title Yovogan, which was a distinct office.

[107] Donou, a short distance north of Allada.

[108] Apparently miscopied: other sources (including Forbes (1851, i: 60), on his first journey in 1849) refer here to 'Atooogo' (and variants), which is identifiable as the modern village of Attogon, 6 km north of Allada.

[109] Assihoui, a short distance north of Attogon , and Houègbo, 22 km north of Allada.

route it is only a few hours,[110] we arrived at Haa-gaa-gan[111] about 2 o'clock[112] Ignatio had arrived some time before us, and taken his quarters, he of course gave them up, only fair being the only quarters appropriated for white strangers, I believe he went and took his quarters up with Count Nawhey, we were five hours walking it is full eighteen miles, we passed several patches cleared and cultivated, and great numbers of Palm Trees, but I did [not?] encounter any cotton Trees, but it is not cultivated the abominable wars keeps the country desolate it is awful to look upon the waste of a fine country, Ignatio had a great many followers about 150. he had a great quantity of rum. 5 o'clock he sent a messenger to ask us if we would take a cup of coffee

we of course accepted his kind offer, it was shortly after sent all silver, it might have been a little ostentation on his part to display his wealth, nevertheless it was very kind, this is a small filthy Town and in a dilapidated state, we retired to rest early.

Friday, May 24th

I was awoke by the noise of Drums and Horns, of course I concluded it must be about 4 o'clock so of course I got up and aroused Cook, and the servants, it was moonlight but very near setting got my bed packed up then got a light and looked at my watch and found it to be only 2.30, so there we were for two hours and half to wait for day light, however Ignatio and his gang started about 3 o'clock Capt Forbes had the laugh on me for he did [not] attempt to rise until we got a light and then it was too early, so I amused myself by smoking a cigar until 5 o'clock had the fire alight and kettle boiled, took a cup of coffee, and started of our carriers, we got fairly started at 6.30 I walked to the first water[113] where we arrived at 8.30 it is a ravine about 15 feet deep the water was not more than fifteen inches, in places sandy bottom, it was in motion trending to the southward, Capt Forbes had a wash and a shower Bath. the greater part of the carriers, and Hammock Bearers, dabbled in it we remained and took a little refreshment and started again at 9.30 and proceeded very comfortably until 10.30 when we came to the identical swamp, light blue clay and mud halfway up the thigh the water was of a milky colour, I think it is not

---

[110] The short route was across the marshy area called the Lama; the longer route (also taken by Duncan and Forbes in October 1849), skirting the eastern edge of the Lama, added 20 miles to the journey (Forbes 1851, i: 60).

[111] Not identified: Duncan and Forbes in 1849 travelled via Sèhouè, 15 km north-east of Houègbo (Forbes 1851, i: 62: 'Sequeh').

[112] This should perhaps be '5 o'clock', since Beecroft goes on to say that the journey took five hours.

[113] I.e. of the Lama: as Forbes noted in 1849, the route taken 'did not altogether clear the swamp, but passed several soft patches' (1851, i: 62).

at its worst so bad as report says, it is not 100 yards this part, we got through it with a trifle of staggering to and fro without any accident, 11.30 we arrived at another hole similar to the last but if anything deeper, in places, shortly after we arrived at a small village, and rested for half an hour, after which we crossed three more Pools of the same sort, and arrived at 2 o' clock at the market place called <u>Zoh-bo-doo-mee</u>[114] Ignatio was on the start for <u>Canna</u>[115] after amusing ourselves here about an hour we were conducted about a mile into the country to reside for the night in a neat African Farm House, belonging to Nawhey's Brother, it was a beautiful situation surrounded with well cultivated Farms, in a splendid level country, in the distance a great number of noble majestic Trees with a very tempting fruit suspended to their lofty branches [similar] in appearance to a rich Burgundy Pear with rather a more Brilliant red, or rather resembles the rips[?] and Pippins, its country name is <u>Daa-see</u>.[116] I had a very comfortable sleeping room given me, before dark we walked to two or three of the Farm Houses, they are neat and comfortable, ground clean and in good condition, returned and had a very refreshing supper and a cigar, Nawhey had his quarters here also, retired to rest at 9 o'clock after a fatiguing day of 9 hours and walking half the way, I slept soundly until 4 o'clock, I looked out it was a delightful morning, the night was cool and pleasant what a delightful country and soil if this Despot could be satisfied to conquer and make them Tributary leaving them quiet in their country what a land of bliss he would have, and trade, instead of devastating it by rapine fire and death.

Saturday, May 25th

daylight Ther 74° a fine and pleasant morning we commenced our journey at 5.30 for <u>Canna-Minna,</u>[117] I travelled about eight miles over a delightful, and beautiful country, passed great numbers of people on the road, returning from the market to their homes in the vicinity, we arrived at the Town at 7.30 it is an extensive place laid out in the most satisfactory way, large Farms and sufficient space for a free circulation of air all round, passing the farms on our route I saw but few labourers in the field, I presume the Country Custom

---

[114] Zogbodomè, 29 km north of Houègbo by the direct route across the Lama (and 25 km north-west of Sèhouè).

[115] Kana, 7 km north of Zogbodomè.

[116] Probably the 'ackee', or 'false cashew' (*Blighia sapida*), but the Fon name for this is *lisé* (cf. Burton 1864, i: 78). 'Pippins' are a type of apple, with reddish colouring. 'Rips and pippins' makes no obvious sense, unless a corruption of 'Ribston pippins', the name of a particular variety: this would require that Beecroft misheard the term, presumably in conversation with Forbes.

[117] An alternative name for Kana, nowadays obsolete.

must be in some measure the cause, for all that pay Tribute money must attend and present it to the King,[118] there is a large Palace and two minor ones here built by the former Kings,[119] large Guard Houses outside of the walls, for his soldiers, on his annual visit,[120] the walls must be miles round, the country fine and level as far as the eye can scan, the road from here to Abomey is wide, you can drive two or three carriages abreast,[121] after breakfast we went outside and took a seat under a shady Tree called the milk Tree from a white matter that oozes out.[122] Capt Forbes had taken a Navel seat[123] elevated about seven feet in its forks of three large limbs, reading Sam Slick.[124] opposite side to me was a gang of Loungers who were discussing Politicks, about their last Ah-taapam war,[125] buying water, and other eatables, made from Indian meal and Palm oil, in round balls, at times I strolled round amongst the mob, discovered several Houssa, Youribaa and Bornou people[126] one or two recollected the Ethiope's visit to Rabbaa and Laddee,[127] I was prevented from asking any further questions through my Interpreter from there been [= being] called away.[128]

I went and took my seat as usual a small Fetish Girl came and went down on her Knees before me and looked me very steadfastly in the face, she was decorated all over with beads I soon found that she was soliciting from me a

---

[118] Beecroft also refers subsequently to the payment of 'yearly tribute money' at the Customs (p. 75). No such payments were recorded during the ceremonies which Beecroft witnessed: Forbes explains that the tribute was conveyed into the palace 'under cover' (1851, ii: 173).

[119] Forbes (1851, i: 64) states there were four palaces; a modern survey also identified four palaces at Kana built down to Gezo's reign (Monroe 2014: 160–5).

[120] The King resided at Kana early in the year, when the army returned from its annual campaign, before proceeding to Abomey to celebrate the Annual Customs there (Forbes 1851, i: 17).

[121] Several European visitors commented on the width of this road: e.g. Fraser in 1851 compared it to Portland Place, a street in central London noted for its great width (2012: 60).

[122] The African milk tree (*Euphorbia trigona*).

[123] Meaning presumably, one at the central point.

[124] *The Clockmaker, or the Sayings & Doings of Samuel Slick of Slicksville*, by Thomas Chandler Haliburton, satirical sketches published in 3 vols, 1836–40.

[125] Atakpamé, north-west of Dahomey (in modern Togo), which had been attacked in the most recent Dahomian campaign, earlier in 1850.

[126] I.e. Hausa, Yoruba, Borno. The term 'Yoruba' is nowadays used to refer to a broad linguistic group, centred in what is today south-west Nigeria, but extending westward into Bénin and also including Atakpamé in Togo; but originally it had a more restricted application, to the kingdom of Oyo (north-east of Dahomey) and neighbouring groups under its control or influence (Law 1977a: 4–5). Hausa and Borno are further north-east again, in what is today northern Nigeria. It is not clear who these people were, but (since some of them had met Beecroft earlier, outside Dahomey) perhaps visiting merchants.

[127] Beecroft made two voyages up the River Niger in the steamship *Ethiope*, in 1840 and 1845, reaching Raba, the capital of Nupe, on both occasions; the reference here is probably to 1845, when he also visited Lade, downriver from Raba (cf. p. 128).

[128] Presumably referring to Thomas Richards, who had accompanied Beecroft on his voyages up the Niger and whose first language was Yoruba.

few cowries, I gave her ten, after which she clapped her hands and looked up in my face with a solemn and pensive air, she was bountiful in her thanks, and left, she was in the distance with her eye on Captain Forbes, he was out of her fastidious reach, I left for a short time, and when I returned I found she had retired, shortly afterwards tinkling of small Bells was heard, the Loungers dispersed for a short time, I sat still, and enquired the reason, seeing above 50 women with country Pots on their heads marching Indian file, I was informed they were the Kings wives, and it is a strict <u>Law</u> that man is forbid to look on them at his Peril so that accounted for the dispersion of the Tree Loungers, turning their backs on them, until they had past.[129]

during my stay a Pig was killed cut up and boiled sold to passers by, and others, shortly afterwards a market was established with everything to eat in a small way for the passengers that were expected to arrive before dark, there was every little country refreshment for strangers, they were aware that the Cha-Cha was expected, with his Party to attend the Abomey Customs[,] in due time he made his appearance it strongly points out their industrious habits, they were all women,[130] Cha-Cha's Drums, wind instruments, making an awful clamour, with the firing of Guns. Ignatio met his brother, and saluted him they came and shook us kindly by the hand, after which we took a short walk, of a mile we reached one of the King's Palaces, it is not near so large as the Palace at Ah-laadaa, every path of the country here has a beautiful appearance, it is more like a Park than [any] other description I can give of it, it shows that the seat of war is kept far away from the Dahomeian's they appear to place every confidence in this Despot's Protection, but I shall be better able to judge after seeing his Customs, we returned at sunset, the small market that had been got up for the accommodation of the new arrivals was not removed until some time of the dark during my walk my mind was fully occupied with the beauties of nature, I could fancy myself in any place but in Africa, the serene quiet about the country Farms, but to revert back to the horrible and abominable practices of the Dahomeian Nation, weaned you immediately from these country blindnesses, during our walk from the Palace Gates, we stopped to look at two men employed making Cotton, and Grass Clothes,[131] they are very fine and made with sword, instead of the shuttle,[132] it

---

[129] European visitors regularly referred to this requirement to give way to the king's wives, which was considered a major inconvenience: cf. e.g. Duncan (1847, i: 257–8), Forbes (1851, i: 25) and Burton (1864, i: 191–2).

[130] European observers consistently reported that retail trade in markets in Dahomey was dominated by women (Law 1995b: 202–3).

[131] So-called 'grass' cloths were actually woven from fibres of the leaves of the raffia palm: Picton & Mack (1979: 32–7).

[132] Referring to the vertical loom, for which a wooden 'sword' is used to press down the threads (i.e. replacing a comb, rather than the shuttle): (Picton & Mack 1979: 71, 89).

will be a slow process the former to the latter shortly after our return the Kings messenger arrived with his stick to Cha-Cha.

Our messenger arrived with my Ring and Capt Forbes stick[133] with the Kings compliments that he will be most happy to see us and welcome us to Abomey, I was expecting a great noise and clamour from the two parties of Cha-Cha, and Ignatio, but the fact was they were too much fatigued to take their nocturnal Promenades, we returned to rest at 9 o'clock. Midnight cool pleasant weather outside. African Travellers, ought to know that African Houses are not calculated for the comforts of a European.

Sunday, May 26th

am fine and pleasant w[r] daylight prepared for our entrance into the City of Abomey got fairly started at 6 o'clock on a splendid road, sufficiently broad to drive 14 abreast ornamented on each side here and there with large majestic Trees, towering over the heads of quantities of the beautiful Palm Trees interspersed under their lofty Protection [= protecting?] branches Corn Plantations tastefully cleared and laid out in ridges, it was quite a Novel sight to see all the carriers making the best of their way possible with all on their heads, according to age and strength trotting along Hammocks in the centre, gave all together a grotesque appearance. I walked accompanied by Captain Forbes, until 7.30 half an hour we would be at the entrance of this great Democrats City,[134] Abomey the Capital of Dahomey, just at the spot I got into my Hammock was a large Shea Butter Tree, but none of the nuts are ripe at present,[135] we passed the first temporary entrance[136] and came upon numbers of Fetish Houses neatly built of red clay and sand, all in the vicinity clean, and neat, beautifully ornamented with Trees, interspersed amongst those idols of superstition, about 8 o'clock we came to the grand entrance, a wall about 50 yards east and west, with a Gate near each end, the left is the King's entrance only shut with wickets, a ditch and a temporary bridge of pieces of wood about 18 feet long and 6 in diameter laid close to pass in at the Gate it is of a

---

[133] These had evidently been sent to the King earlier, to announce their arrival at Kana.

[134] Evidently ironic, since elsewhere Beecroft refers to Gezo as 'the Despot'.

[135] The shea (or *karité*) tree (*Vitellaria paradoxa*), from the nuts of which shea butter is made, used in Dahomey as a skin lotion and for other medicinal purposes. Beecroft later bought some shea butter at Abomey (see p. 128). There was considerable British interest in the commercial potential of shea butter at this time: the abolitionist propagandist Fowell Buxton suggested that it could be 'appropriated to the same uses with the palm-oil', including the manufacture of soap (1840: 321–2).

[136] Abomey was surrounded by a defensive moat (called *agbŏ*, whence the name Abomey, i.e. *agbŏmè*, 'within the moat'), entrance being by bridges through walled gates (Randsborg & Merkyte 2009, i: 41–8, also 40, fig. 4.8).

very rude construction[137] a few yards on to the left of the entrance are 17 pieces of ordinance of various calibres used for saluting we proceeded two or three hundred yards farther when we halted under a large Tree and got out of our Hammocks, we were met by Nawhey who conducted us inside of a court yard to Dress, we had just completed our toilet in the open air and sprinkled a little Eau de Cologne over my Bald pate to keep it cool under the ordeal of an African sun for five or six hours, in an Iron bound dress, and cocked Hat; at that time the din of drums, and Horns were heard in the distance, I went outside of my dressing apartment under the Big Tree where there was a refreshing westerly Breeze, shortly after Ignatio Caboceer for white man arrived, with about 150 followers, 75 armed and the others carriers, he approached and saluted us, and shook hands, 9 o'clock Isadore the Cha-Cha of <u>Whydah</u> arrived, I presume the only difference in numbers were the rude musicians on Isadore de Souza's side, they commenced dancing, and singing, complimentary extempore songs to their masters &c &c Cha-Cha came up to us but we were prevented shaking hands there was a faint [= feint] made on his part, but I cannot account why it was not completed, nevertheless he appeared displeased, and of course did not exactly know his position, with us and the King. he ought to have made himself easy on that point, being a King's officer. I believe they fully expected to head the Procession, from our position to the Palace.[138] There was [a] full rigged Schooner about 40 feet long on wheels,[139] with the Union Jack flying at the Fore, French Ensign at the Peak, she was a present from Cha-Cha some years ago,[140] she was to proceed the Procession, 10 o'clock I began to feel a vacuum in my stomach, as there was no sign of any movement I sent my steward to the mayogaus house[141] to bring a bottle of Hock,[142] and some Biscuits. The arrival of these Portuguese and their followers, was not correspondent with their display of Banners, and umbrellas of silk variegated and scalloped ornaments round the edges, there was a great display of ostentation, their dress was plain excepting small Gold laced velvet caps just stuck on the crown of the head, rings, Chains gold watches, & appendages, but several of their family were in dressing Gowns of common printed Calico. The King's stick was presented to him before it came

---

[137] This was the south-eastern gate of the city, subsequently referred to as the 'Kana Gate': illustrated in Forbes (1851, i: opp. 69).

[138] Beecroft may have misunderstood the issue, since Dahomian etiquette placed persons in reverse order of rank (e.g. Burton (1864, i: 41, 208), 'the junior ranks preceded', 'juniors first').

[139] Forbes' Journal (p. 157) says 'about 28 feet' (but in his book (1851, ii: 8), 'about twenty feet').

[140] I.e. from the first Chacha, Francisco Felix de Souza (as specified by Forbes, 'the late Char Char').

[141] More usually in the shorter form 'Mayo' (the suffix -gǎn meaning 'chief'). Beecroft subsequently alternates between the two spellings: i.e. Mewu (or Mehu, Meu), the title of one of the two senior 'chiefs' in Dahomey, the other being the Migan.

[142] German white wine.

to us, they were then sure of precedence I took a Tumbler of Hock, and a Biscuit, at last Nawhey ordered a movement he conducted us in the front near the full rigged Schooner, we advanced about 100 yards to a large Tree, under its shadow we halted, the little vessel was wheeled on, Cha-Cha and his tribe were moving on in succession after her, the vessel abreast of myself and Capt Forbes, they were rather to their discomfiture, arrested in their progress, and seated on our left.[143] The Caboceers were approaching in procession, but when near us they advanced double quick, for we were surrounded by five or six hundred people, in full uniform not much protection from the sun's rays, about noon: Ther 120° [*sic*] The first Caboceer came up went round us three times, firing of muskets, then came up and saluted the Cha-Cha and Ignatio, which were in the center as they had politically placed them, so all the Caboceers performed the same evolutions, excepting one that came up and saluted, myself and Forbes, first for which he was rebuked by the Mayogau and the Caboceer for Whydah, after they had completed their performances, then commenced the Grand Procession, Schooner named Viva le Rie Dahomey[144] in front, Cha Cha pushing on very anxious to be next the vessel but of course he was stopped until my Hammock and Capt Forbes and all our suite were in rear of the vessel, the others in our rear, the Procession moved slowly on half an hour had elapsed we arrived at the Grand Square[145] where there stood a circular Golgotha[146] 25 feet high the Posts supporting the roof about 8 feet apart decorated with 8 or 10 skulls in each 16 compartments made about 140 skulls,[147] besides 30 which ornamented the steps to the entrance of this Golgotha, we were trotted round the square three times in our Hammocks saluting the King as we passed him under the Porch at the entrance to the Palace,[148] the square is about 700 yards round, music, shouting, firing of Guns, and all sorts of din and clamour, the third round stopped short at the Porch, got out of our Hammocks, Caboceers & Mayo down in the dust, on their bellies, the

---

[143] By Dahomian convention, the right side took precedence over the left.

[144] Forbes (1851, ii: 8), has, more plausibly, 'Gézo Rey de Daomée'.

[145] Adjoining the royal palace, to the south, nowadays called 'Place Singbodji'.

[146] The name of the place of the crucifixion of Jesus, thought to mean 'place of a skull'. Forbes called this structure 'the Palaver House' (Journal, p. 157), and described it (in his book (Forbes 1851, ii: 10)) as 'a small octangular building'. This seems to be the *vizun* or 'tower of sacrifices' recalled by Le Herissé (1911: 180).

[147] Forbes gives the number as precisely 148 skulls; he understood that they were from the previous year's campaign against Okeodan.

[148] Beecroft generally refers to a single main palace, but Forbes to two distinct (but adjoining) palaces, called 'Agrim-gomeh' and 'Dange-lah-cordeh', i.e. Agringomè and Adanjloakodé (1851, i: 69). These were strictly the names of different gates of the palace (Burton 1864, ii: 239–40), but it seems that 'Agringomè' was applied more generally to the north-eastern part of the palace, built by earlier kings, while 'Adanjloakodé' was the southern portion, associated with Gezo and his father Agonglo (r. 1789–97).

King was resting on a silk blue cushion, with a rich white flowered satin robe ornamented with coloured velvet thrown over his person, they crawled on their bellies near His Majestys presence, when they arose, we advanced, I first saluted the King[,] Forbes and our party, Cha-Cha and Caboceers next, we were seated on our chairs in the center of the Grand entrance, ChaCha & Caboceers were near his person after a few compliments enquiring after Her Majesty's welfare &c and taking about a Thimble full of Gin, we were seated again, no person is allowed to look on him when he drinks, shouting, and firing of guns, a handkerchief is held before his face,[149] Cha-Cha talked a few minutes in a whispering tone, of course he could not Politically do otherwise, so of course we rose to take our leave with his permission, the King accompanied us into the square, took his leave of the Cha-Cha, he conducted us about 100 yards then took leave, at the same time asked our Names, he said he would see us again in a day or two, we were conducted to our Domicile it belonged to the Prime Minister[150] a very comfortable African house two Bed rooms and a sitting room, only fault it is on the ground floor, it has a good Kitchen and yard. I was well tired and in a profuse perspiration, the sun was very oppressive in the middle of the day, it was now three o'clock, we took dinner in the cool of the evening, took a short walk, and retired to rest at an early hour.

Monday, May 27th

daylight fine wʳ Ther 75° 6 o'clock Kings stick arrived with his compliments to enquire after our wellbeing, after which sticks from the whole of the King's ministers were presented,[151] as well [as] from Cha Cha and his brothers, returned the compliment by sending ours it is an awful Tax on rum,[152] system of dram drinking, employed until nearly 2 o'clock writing my Journal, then dressed to go to the <u>Mayogau's Levee</u>, in compliance with his kind invitation,[153] accordingly we went to the Palace Square, opposite the Palace we were

---

[149] This practice was regularly described by visitors to Abomey: cf. e.g. Duncan (1847, i: 222), (Forbes 1851, i: 28–9), Fraser (2012: 65) and Burton (1864, i: 244–5).

[150] Forbes says the Mewu (Journal, p. 157). The term 'Prime Minister' was also applied to the Mewu e.g. by Duncan (1847, i: 217), but Forbes used it for a different official, the Migan (Forbes 1851, i: 81ff.). In fact, the Migan was senior in rank to the Mewu, although the latter was more prominent in dealings with Europeans.

[151] Beecroft and Forbes use the term 'ministers' to distinguish a group of officials of higher status than the generality of 'caboceers': this corresponds to the Dahomian term *gbonugan*, 'great chiefs', said to have been seven in number, including the Migan, Mewu and Yovogan (Le Herissé 1911: 37).

[152] Meaning presumably that they were expected to give rum to their visitors.

[153] Forbes explains that several 'ministers' held levees at one or other of the palace gates.

introduced to him and seated on his right, after saluting the Grand Vizier[154] shortly after Cha-Cha and his party arrived and seated on his left, he paid his respects to us and shook hands, a minstrel was then as in the days of yore, taking the highest seats in the House, singing Praises aloud to the people around,[155] a short time intervened when a host of the King's sisters made their appearance, and took their seats as near our noble host as convenient, we were next to him I must acknowledge I was rather astonished to see so many of the royal family assemble to drink rum, after they had addressed our noble host the minstrels, Father and son, sung the King's Praises aloud, after the father's performance the son commenced and sung to the Group of the royal family, the lad pleased them better than his Father could do, they remained about an hour, when they arose to depart, they were very fairly dressed, some amongst them very stout, & rather aged, Mayo-gau had frequently to draw on his Exchequer for rum, in various sized Bottles, Case Bottles[156] to Eau de Cologne D[itt]° there were about fifty of the King's sisters & daughters they had rather a disputed contest with each other, some received Gifts of ½ Pints others of ½ Gallon Case Bottles, the issue lasted full half an hour, before they could finally get clear of the multitude of lookers on, it was rather a degrading sight to see so many of the royal family scrambling for rum.

I can assure my readers that their eyes were rivetted on the unfortunate case that contained the rum, they harangued each other on the profligacy of their proceedings after the ardent speech they had cautiously provided themselves with empty Bottles, so as to start and return the Prime Minister his vial or Bottle directly, some of his daughters were well looking, but staid, some had vests on with real and moc[k] Coral, real Popoo Beads,[157] others silver Bracelets, and chains with small silver crosses attached to them. The Minstrel and his son were singing Praises aloud to their King, and the Dahomian nation, having beaten <u>Aa-taa-Pam</u> nation, there were two sets of musicians, and round the circle about one hundred country Umbrella's, several of the Caboceers came and saluted the <u>Grand Vizier</u> and ourselves, Mee-gau[158] a very stout man came there, and saluted us and the Cha-Cha, the umbrellas

---

[154] Although the wording might suggest this is a separate person, this title also seems to refer to the Mewu. Forbes in his book (though not in his original journal) also applies the term 'Grand Vizier' to the Mewu (1851, i: 22, 81ff.).

[155] Forbes used the term 'troubadours', rather than 'minstrels' (cf. Introduction, pp. xvi–xvii): the Fon term is *hanjitó*, 'singer' (cf. Burton (1864, i: 212): 'ahanjito').

[156] I.e. square bottles, for fitting into a case.

[157] A type of blue glass beads (also called 'aggrey' or 'akori'). Forbes explains that they were so-called because 'dug up inland of Popoe' (1851, i: 28). They were probably in fact manufactured in the Yoruba city of Ife (in modern Nigeria), those dug up elsewhere being recovered from old graves (Euba 1982).

[158] Migan, the highest-ranking 'minister' after the King.

are made after the same plan as the Chinese,[159] we took our leave about 4 o'clock, and on our way called on the <u>Avoh-gah's Levee</u>,[160] took a Glass of Lemonade and proceeded to our quarters, and dined I retired to rest early an hour or so afterwards the Mayo-gau called to see us, he was too late I was fast asleep, he would not allow them to awake me, he left his message that the <u>King</u> desired to see us early on the morrow.

Midnight fine dry w^r

Tuesday, May 28th

daylight fine dry pleasant w^r Ther 75° arose early, and took an early Breakfast, 8 o'clock dressed in readiness for His Majesty's messenger, we left exactly at 8 o'clock shortly after arrived at the Palace Square, where we were seated under a shady Tree, to be gazed at by all the little boys for an hour, it was 9 o'clock when we entered the dusty Palace, we were again arrested at the inner part not longer than ten minutes, when we were ordered to follow the <u>Mayo-gau</u> and <u>Avoo-gah</u>, the moment the light of His Majesty's countenance shone on them, they fell to the ground, and kissed the earth, threw dust over their heads, crawled on their bellies near the King, meanwhile we were standing in the rear uncovered,[161] they rose to their feet we then advanced to the King, who came to receive us and cordially shook hands, and snapped fingers, we then took our seats, our Interpreter on the left, and Richards on my right,[162] he handed him my Letter I wrote him on board HM B. Kingfisher, previous to my departure for Fernando Po, acquainting His Majesty of my appointment as Consul and of my having presents, also of my intentions to be at Whydah before the 15th of May to accompany Capt Forbes, on his mission to Abomey[163] after which statement I rose and handed him the Queens Letter,[164] he put it to his forehead broke the seal and handed it to me to read, it was read in sentences and interpreted when we came to the Foreign Slave Trade, it was told him of course he appeared to have anticipated it, he expressed anxiety about the Fort at <u>Whydah</u>, wishing to know if the Government intends sending out, any person to take charge of it,[165] he then enquired if Capt Forbes were going to remain at Whydah or going to England, that if he did

---

[159] Forbes (1851, i: 72) refers to umbrellas 'ornamented like those of the Chinese'. In China, he had observed that officials had a 'state umbrella of crimson silk, trimmed with vermilion or yellow' (1848: 260).

[160] I.e. Yovogan. Beecroft subsequently also spells this 'Eeah voo gau'.

[161] I.e. bare-headed—Europeans being required to remove their hats when meeting the king.

[162] The first interpreter was evidently Madiki Lemon.

[163] This letter has not been traced in TNA.

[164] I.e. Viscount Palmerston to King Gezo, 25 Feb. 1850 (Appendix 3, doc. 3).

[165] I.e. to replace the deceased John Duncan as Vice-Consul.

not he expressed a wish that I would remain, I then informed him that my
Consulship extended from Cape St Paul to Cape St John's[166] I then told him
that I believed it to be the intention of Government to send out some person
in due time,[167] I then told him that Fernando Po was my head quarters, that if
necessary, I would visit Abomey annually and at any other period if required,
but he had not the most distant idea of the Geographical Position of any
place beyond <u>Badagry,</u> or <u>Lagos,</u> & Porto Novo to the eastward,[168] Whydah,
Ahgway, & Popoo to the westward, we were obliged to refer back to the Letter the sentence of the Treaty for the suppression of the Foreign Slave Trade
and to explain fully to him that we were invested with full power from the
Queen of England, to make that Book,[169] that he was not requested to give up
a large revenue without a subsidy, he then said you have come to see my
Annual Customs, we told him that we had and after we had seen them we
would be better able to confer or talk our Palaver on the Treaty, or Book,[170]
The Caboceer of Whydah remarked that we were always Palavering about the
Slave-Trade, the King told them plainly that they understood our mission,
that they [had] six weeks, to think it over in their minds, and heads, and [he?]
hoped that they would do so, and give it the consideration it deserved, he then
communicated that he had finished the <u>Canna</u> Custom, <u>Fetish</u>,[171] and it would
take six weeks to finish the Custom he was just now going to commence,[172] so
it would be full that time ere we could leave, he said all the Customs would not
be finished under five or six months,[173] but he did not desire us to stop that
time, he was anxious that we should be present at the watering of the ground
of his Ancestors,[174] it would be six weeks then we could go, he referred to a

---

[166] Cape St Paul (in modern south-eastern Ghana) was conventionally considered the western
limit of the Bight of Benin; Cape St John (in modern Equatorial Guinea) was the south-eastern
limit of the Bight of Biafra.

[167] Beecroft had been involved in discussions at the Foreign Office about the appointment of a
new Vice-Consul while in England earlier in 1850: the man selected, Louis Fraser, finally arrived
in Ouidah in July 1851.

[168] Lagos, 150 km east of Ouidah (in modern Nigeria).

[169] The word 'book' (Fon *wĕmà*) refers to any sort of written document, here the proposed treaty.

[170] More specifically, they would be able to assess the level of compensation to be offered (as
Forbes says more explicitly: Journal, p. 159).

[171] The Custom at Kana was performed on the return of the Dahomian army from war, and
immediately prior to the main Annual Customs at Abomey (see p. 146). The term 'fetish' applied
to this Custom alludes to the fact that sacrifices were offered to *vodun* (gods), rather than (as in
the main Customs) to the deceased kings (Forbes 1851, i: 32); an earlier account states that the
Kana Custom involved oracular consultations (Brue 1845: 59).

[172] The Customs in fact concluded on 22 June, i.e. only 3½ weeks (25 days) later: perhaps Gezo
was counting in Dahomian 'weeks' of 4 days?

[173] Cf. p. 145, where it is said that the sequence of Customs would conclude in December (so
actually taking six to seven months).

[174] Translating the Fon idiom *sìn kòn ny'àyĭ*, 'pouring water on the earth', which refers generally
to religious libations and also serves as a euphemism for human sacrifices: see Nicolau Parés

Vice Consul, and was anxious to know if Capt Forbes could not remain as that at Whydah, he was again told that he was going to England, directly after his mission, we again begged leave to instil into his mind the Power we were invested with from the Queen of England, to make a Treaty or Book, we reminded him, that Winniett, Cruickshanks [*sic* = Cruickshank], Freeman, Duncan and Forbes had visited him on the same Palaver,[175] but they were not invested with the same Powers as we were to make a Treaty that our mouth was all same the Queens,[176] I then told him that I had brought him all the Presents he sent a demand to England for by Capt Forbes,[177] that they should all be sent on our return home to the house, he then said that he would be ready after the Customs to listen to our proposal. The Caboceer of Whydah appeared to be the only one present that had any inclination to become a stop Gap.[178] If our Interpreters are right and state true the King's reply, to the Caboceer, that there was more money to be made by the Palm oil, than the Slave Trade. I really doubt that the King would acknowledge and make openly such a statement.[179] Our conference ended, he accompanied us a short distance from the Palace, to the Square, shook hands and left us, I am to state that our interviews have been so far encouraging, there is a glimmer of a Star in the East,[180] on our arrival at our domicile set them to work to unpack the presents, set the clocks, and musical Boxes, agoing, gave them in charge to the Mayogau, Avygah, & Nawhey, they sent them to the Palace, after which we took a walk as far as Dahomey,[181] walked round the Palace, then to the

---

(2016: 217–35). Here, the reference is to sacrifices offered for deceased kings and royal mothers in the latter part of the Annual Customs (7–22 June). The Fon term is reproduced only once by Beecroft, as 'see-qua-ah-hee' (p. 107), but systematically by Forbes (as 'see-que-ah-ee' etc.).

[175] Referring to the missions undertaken by Winniett (accompanied by the missionary Freeman) in 1847, Cruickshank in 1848, and two visits to Gezo by Vice-Consul Duncan (the second with Forbes) in 1849.

[176] A literal translation of the Fon idiom employed to convey the term 'plenipotentiaries' (cf. Forbes' Journal, pp. 192–3).

[177] See HCPP, *Slave Trade*, 1849–50, Class B, incl. 2 in no. 9, Forbes to Fanshawe, 9 Nov. 1849, transmitting the King's request for presents: these included guns, clocks, hour-glasses, hats, silk, rope, musical boxes, chairs and sweet wines.

[178] 'Stopgap' normally means a temporary substitute, but here it seems to mean an obstacle.

[179] The wording is misleading, since no such statement by the King was reported earlier. Forbes' account (1851, ii: 18–19) makes clear that it was the English party who said that 'the palm oil trade, if cultivated would in a very few years, be far more lucrative than the slave traffic': presumably, it was thought that Gezo had implicitly endorsed this view by his recommendation to his chiefs to give the English proposal 'the consideration it deserved'.

[180] I.e. of hope: the allusion is, of course, to the Bible, Matthew 2:2.

[181] I.e. the original royal palace, to the north of the main palace, which Beecroft visited on 11 June (p. 92). The name 'Dahomey' was originally applied to this palace, and by extension to the kingdom.

Ah-gee-ah market place,[182] saw the monument of stones, brought from the
Maa-hee country,[183] individually a stone each there must be several hundred
Tons, it is about 20 feet high a sacred monument, we approached the sacred
Pile, and very innocently broke a few pieces of different sorts of Granite of a
superior quality particularly the Black hard Scotch Granite, but we were not
allowed, to take any part of it without the King's permission, so we very
quickly gave up our Prizes, and extended our walk to Dec-can,[184] and looked
at the Palace the King built about two years ago and named it Coomassee,
after the capital of Ashantee,[185] it is tastefully laid out, with an Avenue of
large Trees, in its front and nearly up to the Bee-con market,[186] did not see
anything particular in it to sell, beyond common country commodities,[187] on
our way we encountered all the Caboceers, with all their rude Pomp, and
Parade, they had all been visiting the market, we were in the midst of the
motley group, with their large country umbrellas, Avygah of Whydah on his
small Pony[188] saluted us as we passed on, a line of matt Huts opposite the
Palace wall for the accommodation of strangers, from other parts of his
dominions, a strong Tornado would sweep them all away like chaff before
the wind, as soon as we arrived we took dinner, after which Capt Forbes and
myself had a short conference on the Vyhe language[189] and relative to the

---

[182] Subsequently spelled more correctly, 'Ah-gah-hee' (and 'Ah-jah-hee' by Forbes): i.e. Adjahi,
north-west of the main palace. This is nowadays no longer a marketplace, the area having been
built over.

[183] Mahi, north-east of Dahomey. According to Burton, this monument related to the conquest
of the Mahi town of Kenglo, in 1846 (1864, ii: 170); but Forbes, who described it on his first visit
to Abomey in 1849, understood that it 'commemorate[d] the subjugation of Anagoo' (1851, i:
85), i.e. Anago, a name applied to the Yoruba (see note 229). The French merchant Blanchely,
who saw the monument later in 1850, links it to a war against a country which had obstructed
John Duncan's passage from Dahomey to the north in 1845 (1891: 563–4), which is consistent
with the identification with Kenglo (cf. p. 62), but might also apply to the Yoruba town of Dassa,
west of Mahi (see King Gezo to Viscount Palmerston, 7 Sept. 1849, in Appendix 3, doc. 1,
p. 201).

[184] Presumably this should be 'Bee-con', as subsequently in this paragraph.

[185] Kumasi, the capital of Asante, in modern Ghana. Beecroft subsequently says that this palace
was built in 1845, i.e. five years earlier (p. 54); but in fact, it already existed in 1843, when it was
described as 'the King's new palace' (Freeman 1844: 266).

[186] Gbèkon, the southern suburb of Abomey, outside the city moat, in which the Kumasi palace
was situated. The market here (still today the principal market of Abomey) is called Houndjro
('Hungooloo' in Forbes, Journal, p. 173).

[187] The implied absence of European-imported goods is noteworthy, but Forbes in 1849 reported
that 'foreign as well as native goods' were sold in the markets (HCPP, *Slave Trade*, 1849–50, Class
B, incl. 9 in no. 9, journal entry for 18 Oct. 1849), while Fraser in 1851 saw flints, tobacco and
snuff on sale in the Adjahi market (2012: 77).

[188] One of several references to horses in the processions. For horses in Dahomey, where they were
few in number and ridden only on ceremonial occasions, see Law (1980a: 22).

[189] Vai, an ethnic group in what is today Liberia, which Forbes had visited in 1849, when he
discovered a local written script in use there (see Introduction, p. xvi).

Interpretation of the King's letter and his reply[190] all insist that it was right confidently knowing that we are empowered to make a Treaty, with His Majesty on the spot, without any further references, unless it is necessary to make any additional alterations as to the amount for a subsidy or remuneration then it will have to be sent to England to be ratified should the British Government deem fit it will soon be replied to retired to rest at 10 o'clock dull cloudy w^r

midnight dull unpleasant w^r

Wednesday 29th May

daylight cloudy cool morning arose at 5 o'clock shaved, washed, and dressed in readiness for the King's messenger. The King's stick came and others as usual it is an awful tax on rum, 7.30 the King's messenger arrived and we left for the Palace, we reached the square and took a seat under the spreading branches of a large Tree, for a short time, when we were ushered into the Palace yard, we were very quietly seated, when we were escorted by Mayo-gau, Nawhey, Avo-gah, and others to the entrance of the same Chamber we held the conference in yesterday, we saluted the old Lady called Ah hyaa-paa,[191] after which we took our seats, she was privileged to talk with the gentlemen, she brought a small silver watch that Captain Forbes had sent to the King, as a Present, she was at a loss to find out its intricacies of regulating, and winding up, he unfortunately broke the Glass, the old Lady gave it up immediately for a new glass to put in [there?] not [being?] watch-makers in Abomey, she next introduced the clocks she brought them in all positions, I shewed her the winding, striking and regulating the hands, and the Position that they should always be in, I moved the hands and struck the hours round, and set them by my own watch, after which she introduced spirits and water, shortly after we left to join His Majesty, it was about 9 o'clock, we entered a square yard at the rear of the Palace, the King was seated on an elevated cushion, under a Canopy of various coloured country umbrellas, a great number of calabashes of skulls, and Fetish ornaments on his right hand, also Groups of women and

---

[190] By 'the King's letter' is meant that written by Palmerston *to* the King.

[191] 'Maehaepah' in Forbes (Journal, p. 159): Beecroft himself later spells this name 'My aho-paa', 'My-haa-paa', etc.; while Burton gives the form 'Mahaikpa' (1864, i: 249). Beecroft later calls her 'head of the Amazons' (p. 67), but this perhaps means of the women inside the palace, rather than of the female army. Forbes in his journal calls her the female 'Grand Vizier' (p. 159), and in his book identifies her as the 'coadjutor' or female counterpart of the Tononun, or chief eunuch (1851, ii: 123). For the system of the 'doubling' of senior male officials by female equivalents within the palace (termed their 'mothers'), see Bay (1998: 239–41). However, the interpretation of the Mahaikpa as the female Tononun is implicitly rejected by Bay, who regards her simply as the head of the king's female messengers (ibid., 219).

men right and left under a Canopy of country umbrellas exactly similar to the Chinese made ones, the Group of women were about 2000 & 28 minstrels taking the highest seat in the square, sang aloud Praises to Gezo and his people, I presume the other groups to be about 3000 men with 28 minstrels, after saluting His Majesty we were placed in our chairs directly opposite him behind the Caboceers, right and left, <u>Poo-voo-soo</u> Captain of a Band of Blunderbuss men,[192] performing antics, and mountebank tricks before the King[193] he came up and accosted us, with your <u>Servant Sir</u>, he had a small band of music, also a boy about eight or nine years of age his son, dancing and going through the same antics &c as his Father, men soldiers commenced and sang his Praises aloud, of his warlike spirit and despotic sway, mentioning the last victory of Ah taa Pam war, the River Volta,[194] a place of great Trade with <u>Popoo</u>,[195] this was all their themes; a second party performed the same, then Gifts were brought and distributed amongst them

28 men 28 heads of cowries [each]	784 heads or dollars[196]
4 small Baskets of cowries	24 d°
1 case of rum and 4 cotton Hkfs [= handkerchiefs]	

Amazons again commenced singing in the same strain, as the men

28 women 28 heads of cowries	784 d°
4 small baskets of d°	24
1 case of rum 4 cotton Hkfs	dollars <u>1616</u>[197]

shortly afterwards Cha-Cha and his body Politic arrived after saluting the King he passed to us and I shook hands, the mayo-gau placed him on our right, but somewhat in our rear, he appeared to be pleased and gratified, after this a great many women singing Praises it commenced to rain, we were removed to a shed, and remained there until 2 o'clock when it became fair and we left for our domicile, Nawhey stating that he would come in the evening and report Progress, accordingly he called about 5 o'clock with a tribe of followers,[198] he commenced his calculations, and endeavoured to throw dirt in our eyes,[199] by stating that all the cowries given away today

---

[192] Spelled by Forbes 'Pohvehsoo'; and 'Kpo-fen-'su' by Burton (1864, ii: 35). A blunderbuss is a wide-bored musket, firing several shots simultaneously.

[193] As Beecroft later notes (p. 56), this officer was also 'a sort of court fool'.

[194] It is not clear why the Volta, which is 80 km to the west of Atakpamé, should be mentioned in this context. Perhaps this is an error for the River Mono (named later, p. 94), 25 km east of Atakpamé.

[195] Atakpamé was linked commercially to Little Popo at the coast via the navigable River Mono (Strickrodt 2015: 62, 219).

[196] The 'head' of 2,000 cowries, conventionally equated with the silver dollar.

[197] This is the total of the cowries only and does not include the value of the rum or handkerchiefs. Forbes (p. 162) gives different details and a total of $1,698.

[198] Forbes says that he was accompanied by the Mewu and the Yovogan.

[199] I.e. deceive us.

amounted to 26,000 [i.e. heads] however we proved to him from our own accounts that he was dreaming, or he must think us to be fools, he finished his conference there and then, without uttering a whisper on the matter and bid us good night; We retired early to rest.

Midnight dry w[r]

Thursday, 30th May

<u>Programme of the King of Dahomey's performances in the Palace Yard</u>
I arose early as usual and prepared myself to attend when the King deemed fit to send his messenger, took an early Breakfast. King's stick made its appearance, and others were brought as customary, we sent ours in return[.] 7.30 the messenger arrived to announce the King's pleasure, We left immediately arrived at the square and remained shor[t] time under our favourite Tree, when the Mayo-gau and <u>Dag-bah</u>[200] escorted us to the Gates of [the Palace?] the first [thing?] that met my eye, at the entrance was a pool of Blood, a great quantity must have been absorbed for the awful sacrifice was committed before midnight,[201] we were very unnecessarily cautioned not to step in the blood, we entered and found a large Tent erected about 35 feet high with all the rude country devices were [*sic*] described[202] and Groups on the sides, and front were squatted, the Caboceers were all in their gayest dresses, we saluted the Throne and were seated directly in front of it.

1st Captain for soldiers approached and performed several evolutions, his crawling on his back, and belly then gave a few somersets [= somersaults].

2[ndly] Cha-Cha or rather Isadore de Souza arrives and takes his seat with his followers on our right.

3rd King arrives clashing of Drums & shouts of Praise, rise and salute him sends a Table and sets out refreshments

4th Caboceers (58) rise and walk before the Tent in Procession[203] Ignatio was ordered to join they were all in full dress, with short swords kneels and salutes His Majesty according to custom, they then rise and disperse to their seats

5th Procession of military officers (30) performed as above silver Bracelets, and ornaments

---

[200] Dagba, the personal name of the Yovogan.

[201] Beecroft subsequently saw six newly severed heads in Singbodji Square (p. 40).

[202] I.e. depicted.

[203] For the following procession, cf. Forbes' list, in the 'Appendix' to his MS journal, in TNA, FO84/827, ff. 285–9v; also Forbes (1851, ii: 213–24).

6th Procession (28 men) privileged to salute His Majesty, standing, for certain fetes [= feats] performed by their ancestors, among themselves[204]

7th Eunuchs saluted His Majesty.[205]

after which His Majesty walks from under his Tent to where we are seated, shook hands and enquired kindly after our welfare took a Thimblefull of Gin. a shout and 6 muskets fired[,] the handkerchief removed from before him he advised us to remove a little to the right should it rain we would get awful wet being in a hollow, he then left us, and went to the Cha-Cha and his suite, performing the same ceremony, and returned to the Tent. a salute of Blunderbusses by women soldiers

5 Mallams[206] salute the King standing[207]

a very stout Amazon takes up a large Blunderbuss and fires it of.

50 soldiers dressed in Blue Baft Coats or rather Frocks with a red piece sewed on the back cut in shape of a musket & white linen caps.

20 Band of Amazons salute the King with Blunderbusses, receive rum.

14 Africans who had bought their freedom at the Brazils,[208] approach and salute the King standing[209] waving their Handkerchiefs over their heads, & crying Viva Viva Le Rey de Dahomey

100 procession of men soldiers march of to the Ah-gee-ah market as centrys [= sentries].

20 women Caboceers arrived, after which follows a Procession of women carrying all sorts to the market and return with them merely a vast display.[210]

6 Amazons in front well dressed.

8 Band with Horns

2 carrying cowries.

---

[204] Forbes, in the MS version of his list, identifies those who were excused from prostrating as 'Kings stick bearers', i.e. his messengers, who carried ornamented canes (called *makpo* in Fon, '*récades*' in French, to authenticate their status: see Adandé (1962)); he explains that they were exempt from prostration by virtue of carrying these canes, before which others were required to prostrate (Forbes 1851, i: 25).

[205] Eunuchs were employed in the royal palace: for their functions, see Bay (1998: 113–14). Vice-Consul Fraser in 1851 was told that the King had about 100 eunuchs, but this was probably an exaggeration (2012: 98): the largest number seen by Beecroft together on any one occasion was 30 (p. 37).

[206] I.e. Muslim clerics (Hausa *mallam*, from Arabic *mu'alim*). Forbes (1851, ii: 214) says 16 mallams, specifically 'from Haussa'. European visitors regularly reported meeting Muslims from the interior at Abomey (for other references, see Law 1986).

[207] But Forbes says that they 'prostrated and kissed the dust', which made him doubt whether they were really Muslims.

[208] I.e. African-born ex-slaves who, after obtaining their freedom, had returned to Africa: there was a substantial community of these in Ouidah (Law 2004b: 179–82).

[209] The Brazilians were excused from prostration because they were considered 'white men'.

[210] As Forbes observes, the ceremony was 'a public display of the monarch's wealth' (1851, ii: 36).

2 with wands, a Truck[211] with a Banner with various rude devices.

9 Banners   14 with long horns

18 with wooden clubs covered with scarlet

a Caboceer Amazon with a large axe

90 Carriers of Jars of rum covered with white Baft

130 " Cowries—20 Caboceer women

30 Amazons   with sticks

32   "   "   swords

22   "   "   muskets

2 Glass chandeliers, and ornaments of different sorts of the country

25 carrying silver ornaments

30 soldiers armed

12 musicians

16 Kings sisters

30 a Band of Privileged Ladies[212]

50 a Group of the Kings musicians

20 a Group of children

12 Amazon soldiers armed

2   "   blunderbusses

5   "   Long Danes[213]

24   "   Grass clothes white head dresses

8 men with blunderbusses

2 women

46   "   white baft

8   "   Hats

47   "   Pipes

8   "   rolls Tobacco[214]

16   "   Callabash of Beef

11   "   Blunderbusses

1   "   Bows and arrows

30 soldiers armed

8 Dwarfs

14 soldiers armed

12 Band of musicians

---

[211] I.e. a wheeled carriage. Beecroft subsequently refers to several other wheeled vehicles exhibited during the ceremonies, including some of local manufacture. On wheeled vehicles in Dahomey, where they were drawn by people rather than by animals and were used exclusively for ceremonial rather than utilitarian purposes, see Law (1980b: 252–3).

[212] Forbes, in his MS list, says 'female stick bearers in hats': they correspond to the male officials excused from prostration seen earlier (see note 204).

[213] I.e. 'Dane guns', long-barrelled muskets.

[214] Brazilian tobacco was sold in 'rolls', with a standard weight of 80 lbs.

30 soldiers armed

60 Amazons Elephant Guards,[215] Drums & skulls.

30 soldiers armed

30 women   "   12 Band of music a large Drum ornamented with skulls a wooden Horse on trucks and a stool on him

12 Gong women

30 soldiers a Horse 12 Band of music

30 D°· armed

30 D°   "

12 D°   "

20 D° 12 a Band of music

30 soldiers a Horse

12 music a carriage country made

30 soldiers armed 2 Ladies with Parasols

16 silver ornaments

19 wash Basins

7 D°   D°

10 small ornaments Toby Philpots[216] &ca

12 mahogany Boxes

8 Liquor cases

12 children in a group

Imitation in wood of a Hill that the Town of Kangaaroo stood upon when he conquered it[217]

1220 carriers of calabashes of cowries 2 and 3 heads in each

200 wooden Bowls 2 heads each

18   "   "

14   "   "

110 carriers of cloth

10   "   pouches

<u>10</u>   "   Kegs of rum

1582

12 men in small canoes & baskets awfully pinioned and gagged carried on mens heads to the market and back dressed in white Baft and a coloured Handkerchief tied around their heads. they are to be sacrificed.[218]

---

[215] Forbes says 'elephant destroyers' (1851, ii: 218): this refers to two regiments of Amazons who were employed in hunting elephants (ibid., i: 157–9). Forbes also calls them 'bush rangers' (e.g. Journal, p. 177): the Fon term was *gbètó*, i.e. 'hunters' (Burton 1864, ii: 49).

[216] Ceramic jugs in the form of an old man.

[217] Kenglo, in Mahi, which Gezo had conquered in 1846.

[218] On the following day the number of prospective sacrificial victims paraded was 14 (though only 11 were actually killed). It is odd that both here and in describing the actual sacrifice,

1 Large Kings Drum ornamented with 12 skulls

1 small D° ” ” ” d° ”

2 Ponies 2 sheep 1 ram

1 Large Circular Box full of cloth

Kings Bathing Tub. Chinese Pagod[a] of silver

2 large cannesters [= canisters] 4 feet high for sugar. 2 setts of rocket Tubes

2 Large Stools King takes on his war excursion

5 stools accompanied by a Group of women that are not allowed to speak to w[h]ether [by] man or woman excepting the King,[219] well dressed with silver ornaments, round the head silver wristlets, striped satin dresses, or rather flowing robes, silver scymeters [= scimitars][220] with quantities of coral & Popoo Beads.

3 Silver Tea Pots 13 Callabashes contents unknown

Sing praises aloud for twenty minutes and saluting him with their muskets above their heads in both hands. 200 women soldiers.

8 women.

16 D° 12 Band of music

10 Fetish women and children

1 country made carriage

33 silver ornaments, 15 white Glass bottles

1 silver scymitar 13 Blue Bottles

1 D° Basket 50 Large Jugs

42 ornaments mantle Piece	1 chandelier
50 chambers [= chamber pots]	2 Trunks
1 Wash stand	1 Long Tin Box
2 Banners	1 Toilet case

30 soldiers armed 4 stools, 4 Flags 2 Boxes of skulls

30 Kings family & sons	30 Eunuchs
30 Mallams wives	12 Band of women
12 Band of music	12 D° D°
1 Callabash of skulls	30 soldiers armed
30 a group of singing women	
30 a Group of Youriba women[221]	

Beecroft omits an 'alligator' (i.e. crocodile) and a cat which Forbes observed among the victims (Journal, pp. 164, 166).

[219] This suggests the category of privileged royal wives called Kposi, 'Wives of the Leopard', whom 'no one was permitted to speak to' (Bay 1998: 242). The Kposi were also seen in procession on 3 June (see note 317).

[220] I.e. curved swords.

[221] Forbes says 'from the Lefflefoo province' (1851, ii: 221), i.e. Refurefu, in Egbado, south-east of Dahomey, whose conquest by Dahomey is mentioned by Beecroft subsequently (pp. 72, 98).

30 a D° of Kaangaaroo[222]   D°   5 Kings head wives with
                                      umbrellas
30 Dancing women   30 soldiers armed
12 Band of music   12 Band of music
King sent us a country Pot of rum as a Gift ornamented with Beads
1 Bayonet   30 with the Kings mother[223]
40 soldiers   30 soldiers & skulls
2 skulls   12 Band of music
1 Banner
30 in this group Kings Grandmother[224] and family silver ornamented stick
with ornaments of the same
12 Band of music   5 Banners
                                     2 stools
30 soldiers   5 Boxes
12 Band of music   1 Banner
30 Grandchildren   1 stool
6 Banners   30 soldiers
30 soldiers   1 skull
12 Band of music   30 Band of music
30 soldiers
30 Kings family Agella Adonna[225]
1 stool
12 Band of music

Forbes notes that the different groups of women 'each perform[ed] the peculiar dance of their country' (1851, ii: 39).

[222] Forbes says 'from the Taffla provinces' (1851, ii: 221), but this name is otherwise unattested and not identifiable.

[223] Later named as Agotime (p. 133, with note 604). Forbes describes this woman more precisely as 'the lady holding the title of royal mother' (1851, ii: 221). This alludes to the office of Kpojito, 'the one who bore the Leopard [i.e. the king]', conventionally translated as 'Queen Mother' (Bay 1998: 71–2), who was not necessarily the king's biological mother, but might be another woman appointed to the role. In fact, the original Agotime was already dead by October 1849, if Forbes correctly understood a ceremony which he says was 'in memory of [Gezo's] mother' (1851, i: 84). The successors to deceased Kpojito (and some other offices) assumed their personal names and identities, as well as their titles, a practice referred to by anthropologists as 'positional succession' (Bay 1998: 38–9).

[224] Later named as Senunme (see p. 129, with note 591): i.e. the Kpojito of Gezo's father Agonglo. Beecroft notes later (p. 65) that the king's actual grandmother had died 'some years' earlier, the woman so-called in 1850 being 'adopted'.

[225] Forbes, in his MS list, refers here to the titular 'mothers' of the kings 'Tohcohdohnoh' and 'Agahjahdoossoo', i.e. Dakodonu, the first king of Dahomey, and Agaja Dosu, the fourth king (died 1740). The names 'Agella' and 'Adanna' represent Hwanjile and Adono, which Beecroft later gives in the forms 'Ah-wha-ge-lee' and 'Ah-doo-noo' (pp. 113, 119). In fact, however, Forbes was in error about Hwanjile, who was the Kpojito of Tegbesu, the fifth king (1740–1774), rather than of Dakodonu (Bay 1998: 91–6).

30 dancing men named Abu'da daa[226]

12 Band of music	6 Banners
1 Banner	6 Tails Horse[227]
12 Band of music	12 Band of music
1 Banner	30 Kaagaaroo people
12 Band of music	6 Banners
30 soldiers	5 shields & skulls
6 Banners	12 skulls
30 soldiers	30 soldiers
1 Cuirass	12 Band of music
12 Band of music	
2 Union Jacks	
12 Band of music	
30 Kings household,	

7 Kings cast of[f] wives[228] ornamented with silver Bracelets, and armlets, danced before the King, with the Brass shields, and skulls, in their hands, music and singing Praises aloud, they were taken from the Ahnagoo people the head of these women was at the Capture of them.[229] King sent us a little refreshment of spirits[230] and water in a Cruet stand of crimson Bottles they looked very gay stand was silver our Interpreter from Whydah[231] insisted that the mustard Pot was the Tumbler to drink from however we made it answer the purpose.

Shortly afterwards King paid us a visit from the Tent and was very courteous indeed, and hoped that we were not incommoded by the rain, he showed us the plan of attack of the Town of Kaagaaroo it was in Brass, he was much pleased with it it was in the shape of a shoe with a very high instep, half way was the wall of their defence and the Gate, the Town was on the high peak of the instep, he attacked them at the walls and entrance, and succeeded and

---

[226] Not identified, but the second element might represent *dada*, 'father', a title applied to the king (i.e. 'the king's *abu*').

[227] Horse-tails were commonly used in West Africa as fly whisks (Law 1980a: 169). Burton later understood that they were the 'distinguishing mark' of the court singers and drummers (1864, i: 212).

[228] Forbes says 'mothers by the King' (1851, ii: 222).

[229] Cf. later reference to 'the Ah-naa-goo war' (p. 111). On the term 'Anago' (in modern Fon usage, more commonly 'Nago'), see Law (1997a): it is nowadays used as a synonym of 'Yoruba' in its general linguistic sense, but in the accounts of Beecroft and Forbes seems to mean specifically the western Yoruba, immediately neighbouring Dahomey, while 'Yoruba' usually refers specifically to Oyo—though the application of these names was in practice overlapping rather than clearly distinct. Duncan in 1845 heard of a war waged against the Anago 'about six years ago', i.e. *c.*1839 (1847, i: 266–7), but there were wars against more than one 'Anago' group in the 1830s, including Refurefu, in Egbado (p. 72) and Savè, north-east of Dahomey (p. 108).

[230] Forbes says 'wine' (1851, ii: 223).

[231] I.e. Madiki Lemon (as distinct from Thomas Richards, the interpreter from Fernando Po).

beat them, he then told us that he would not trouble us any more to day, as it had been so wet, but early in the morning he should expect us at the market to throw away Cowries, so we shook hands and took our leave, and returned to our quarters as I passed the Golgotha in the Palace square I noticed six fresh skulls that had been taken of last night, we returned home quite satisfied of the Kings Plan. About 1000 dollars were distributed today[232] about ½ a dollar a man we left about 3 o'clock.

Friday 31st May

I arose at 4 o'clock and prepared to be ready for the King's messenger at daylight. 5.30 took a light Breakfast, and was prepared to depart for the market,[233] to be an eyewitness of the munificent benevolence of this great Despot. sent for our Interpreters, and desired them to send to the Grand Vizier, and to acquaint him that we were ready to go to the market, they are so slow that we were at a loss to give them an Impetus, for they are famous for Procrastination, without [= unless?] self reigns predominant, several messengers arrived stating that the King had left the Palace, we were there wasting our time sauntering about the yard, waiting for the messenger from Mayo-gau, we at last made a start and joined the Procession, a short distance from our own house, King at the head in his Hammock, on our arrival at the Grandstand[234] the King sent us a case Bottle of rum, there were several thousands congregated, awaiting the arrival of His Majesty they were in Groups of several hundreds, belonging to the King, his Brothers, and sons, Mayo-gau, Mee-gau, Dag-bah or Caboceer of Whydah & Cambaa-dee's[235] people all dressed in a common Grass cloth wrapped, also each a Bag of the same material to deposit, their cloth, and cowries, gained at the scramble. the King had entered the Grand stand and was on the Platform looking over the Breastwork, with a white cotton night cap on a velvet waistcoat and a wrapper. Amidst the shouts and loud acclamations, of the multitude, we took our seats under a large Tree, a few yards from the Grand entrance, the Groups went round the square three times, all the head men of each party carried on mens shoulders, clapping their hands and singing aloud the Kings Praises, they all halted abreast the Grand stand, the King in his velvet vest and white night cap, looked somewhat ridiculous being such a great Potentate in his own opinion, and that of his people, he harangued the people, they then came forward in Parties head men mounted on other mens shoulders, 1st the Kings

---

[232] Forbes (Journal, p. 164) says $800 in cowries, plus rum.
[233] I.e. again the Adjahi market, as Forbes explicitly states.
[234] Forbes says 'a huge raised platform'.
[235] Later identified as the 'king's treasurer' (p. 48); spelled 'Camboodee' by Forbes, 'Kangbode' by Burton (1864, i: 229) 'Kanbodé' in recent tradition (Glélé 1974: 146).

2nd his Brothers, 3rd sons, 4th Mayogaus, 5th Mee-gaus, 6th Viceroy of Whydah, 7th Cambaadees that was all. they were all awaiting anxiously the commencement of this novel but unpleasing scene. I have ommitted [*sic*] to mention that the Blacksmith of Abomey his Party his name is Ni-gou An-hi-gou, the King made a short speech, they yelled, and shouted then commenced the scene, strings of cowries now and then a solitary head of cowries, with about 15 pieces or parts of white Baft, it was not ad libitum,[236] half an hour then there was a respite. Mayogau and the Caboceer or Eeah voo gau of Whydah came and conducted us to the Grand entrance, we ascended about 12 feet and upon a Platform covered with dry grass, and a Breastwork of four feet round it, covered with oil cloth, and a variety of other cloths, round it were fourteen large umbrellas for the accommodation of those that were privileged to look over the Breast-work, some of the umbrellas ornamented with small Dutch looking glasses, on each scallop of the curtain round those umbrella's, they had a very gaudy appearance particularly when the suns rays struck them, a number of Banners als[o?] planted around. we were seated some distance in the rear for a short time, we were very anxious to see the scramble, and told the Mayo-gau that we were, in a malposition, that they better had left us outside, they then removed us to the breast work and planted us near a Flag staff with the union jack flying on it, I looked round on all the Property there deposited on the Plat-form and presented to our view, at the highest calculation there could not be more than 3000 heads of cowries, and I presume not more than three or four hundred pieces of common cloth, the King was planted in the left wing, then he commenced to throw away strings and heads of cowries, cloth, country cloth, and white baft, were thrown sans ceremonie[237] amongst the mass, all being anxious to have a good position it was awful the fighting and scrambling amongst a mass of 3000 people. headmen mounted on the shoulders of others and supported by two others making the best of their way through the mass as close as if they were wedged in particularly at the part where the King was stationed, whoever got hold of it first was beset, and beat in awful manner until he relinquished the prize the strong walked upon the Heads and shoulders of the weak, to the part, [where] they saw the most articles thrown, the Perfume from them was anything but grateful,[238] it was similar to a foggy mist from a swamp, it was really calamitous, to look at,[239] the Gong went for silence, The King then harangued them, on their attacking each other in that fearful manner and the strong man,

---

[236] 'at will' (Latin), i.e. unlimited.

[237] 'without ceremony' (French).

[238] I.e. acceptable, refreshing.

[239] Similar ceremonies of throwing cowries to be fought over by the attendant crowd were witnessed (at different points in the ceremonial cycle) by Fraser in 1851 (2012: 104) and by Burton in 1864 (ii: 3–5).

overpowering the weak, and walking him down, he said the first that got possession it was not to be taken from him, cloth, or cowries, and he requested them not to do so, that the person who got first hold was not to be pounced upon by a mob to take it from him, during this 53 of the King's women, passed with jars of water on their heads.[240]

Gift to 30 soldiers	a piece of white Baft each.		
D° to Headmen of Abomey 50.	10 heads of cowries and 4 pieces of cloth.		
Maa-hee country 50 men	10 heads	4 pie[ces] cloth	1 Bottle of rum
Ag-goo-nah people[241] 40 D°	10 D°	4 D°	1 B[ottle] of rum
20 Ashantee D°[242]	6 heads	1 pie of cloth	1 D°
16 Eyeo's[243]	4 D°	1 D°	" D°
2 Headmen	1 D° each	1 Pie Cloth each 1 B of rum each	
1 Head Mallam[244]	1 Do	1 Pie white Baft	
30 soldiers			30 pieces white Baft
50 men—	10 heads of cowries		4 D° cloth
40 D°	10 D° " D°		4 D° D°
20 D°	6 D° " D°		1 D° D°
16 D°	4 D° " D°		1 D° D°
2 D°	2 D° " D°		2 D° D°
1 D°	1 Do " D°		1 D° D°
	33	rum	5B 4B

King sent us a Gift of a Basketful of Bannanas,
King's fool[?] 7 Banners, surmounted with 7 skulls,
1 head of cowries— 10 heads 4 pie[ces] King's present to us
½ D° 4 Gunners, 15 D° to 30 headmen of the Town of Abomey
1½ 25

8.30 I retired under the Umbrella's and took a little Breakfast, shortly afterwards the King sent for us, we went with our suites, Cha-Cha or Isadore De Souza accompanied us, with his gang—we were ushered into his presence

---

[240] For the following, cf. the list in the 'Appendix' to Forbes' journal, TNA, FO84/827, ff. 289v–90; also in Forbes (1851, ii: 227–9).

[241] Agouna, north-west of Dahomey, which had been conquered by Kpengla, the sixth king of Dahomey (reigned 1774–89) (Le Herissé 1911: 307; Dalzel 1793: 175–8, 'Agoonah'). But Forbes here has 'Ahgonee', i.e. Agonli, who are a different people, situated east of Dahomey (1851, ii: 228).

[242] Forbes, in his MS list, says these were 'followers of Ashantee Ambassador'. Beecroft subsequently mentions the presence of an Asante ambassador in Abomey (p. 82).

[243] Oyo, north-east of Dahomey.

[244] Presumably, the Imam of the Abomey mosque: the existence of a mosque in Abomey was noted by Forbes (1851, i: 33).

and [he] shook hands, with us, and desired us to follow him we went to the end of the Grand stand there was a small Tent erected he recommended us to sit under it, it being closed in we found it too hot. so we preferred standing outside, so I took my stand next to the King, and Forbes next to me, Cha-Cha and his [party] next, it was amusing to see the King of Kings at Childs' play he was busily employed looking at, and giving orders about discharging the small schooner, into a small Boat on wheels, a Negro with an oar imitating steering. she carried 4 Kegs of rum 2½ Gallons each, 4 rolls of Tobacco, a few pieces of cloth and about 20 heads of cowries, she made four trips the schooner was discharged, distributed to each of us Cowries to throw to the mass, it was really childish, for a man of the King's apparent Knowledge, and sense to be playing such tomfooleries, he gave away to different parties there on the spot about 120 heads of cowries, he clapped me on the shoulder and said he was tired and intimated that we might go and rest for a while, it was then 11.30 we took a little refreshment, during which time he was preparing, for the awful ceremony, of murder, and blood, about 12 o'clock I saw the unfortunate wretches, that passed us yesterday at the Kings yard to the market and back brought up upon the Platform and placed in Indian file along the Breastwork,[245] four men in the centre, they were captured by the women soldiers, some were in Baskets, others in small canoes, tied and secured as you would a Turkey to roast, with a piece of wood in each of their mouths as a Gagg fastened behind, the back part of the neck, their Bodies covered with a piece of white Baft, and a new Handkerchief round their heads, whilst we were talking over this awful and melancholy affair that was just about to take place, Captain Forbes asked Madukaa our Interpreter[246] if he thought the King, would spare any of these unfortunate victims, his reply was yes,[247] [Forbes said?] then I will release two at 100 dollars a head Nawhey was sent for, he was dispatched to the[248] King to enquire into this affair of mercy, in less than fifteen minutes he returned, to say the King, desired to see us, we went he took me to the Breast-work and showed and pointed out the place, where this bloody and awful deed was going to be performed, he asked if we wished to see it, I shook me [= my] head and said No! then came the Point about the saved ones, he did not hesitate in the least,[249] he said Forbes, might

---

[245] Forbes (Journal, p. 166), gives a total of 14 victims exhibited, as compared with 12 paraded on the previous day.

[246] I.e. Madiki Lemon, later spelled 'Maa-du-Kaa', 'Maa-daa-kee' etc.

[247] It is likely that the King had anticipated the request: when Hutton attended the Customs in 1839/40, Gezo ordered one of the prospective (eight) victims to be spared, as a goodwill gesture (HCPP, *Select Committee on the West Coast of Africa*, Minutes of Evidence, §10329, Evidence of W.M. Hutton, 22 July 1842).

[248] In MS the words 'to the' repeated.

[249] Forbes, in contrast, says 'after a little hesitation' (Journal, p. 166).

look and see which he would choose, he told him the first, and last one, they were brought I chose the second one, so the awful crisis for those unfortunate[s] being postponed I trust for wiser ends, he asked us again if we had any desire to see them pitched over a fall of 12 feet on their heads, we again said no! and retired, to our seats, he harangued the people for half an hour, on the merits of the case, as taken in war from their enemies[250] the people outside cried for their blood, Gongs went then a loud shout, with music, the unfortunates were all placed in file, with one end of the canoe, or Basket, on the Breast-work, the other supported on a mans head, the cloth, and handkerchief were removed, and they were pitched over one after the other, the King saw four and retired, to his seat, [the] four last pitched over by his <u>Amazons</u>, they having been captured by them,[251] I believe Ignatio, and Antonio De Souza remained and looked on during the whole tragedy,[252] Isadore had better feelings he remained near us, after this awful scene we left the place, with the Mayo and E-ah-voo-gau we saw the blood of the unfortunate victims each of them were in a Basket pointed [out] to us by the Mayo I told him that I looked on them with sorrow, the mass outside were nearly all armed with large Bludgeons, we were told that after their heads were taken of the Bodies were dragged some distance to a Pit, all the way they beat the body to a perfect mummy[253] with their large sticks, then threw them into a Pit, [I asked?] what good or evil, could they derive from such a barbarous practice, the Caboceer [*sc.* of Whydah] merely smiled, we parted and got into our Hammocks, and arrived in time to save a severe wetting from a violent shower of rain.

The Present of 10 heads of cowries, the King had given us, Nawhey commenced to share out sans ceremonie, a head for Mayo, Caboceer, himself and Boys. Capt Forbes remonstrated with him, for attempting to touch them, in that way, without first asking us, we told him that we would ask Mayo, and the Caboceer, he then acknowledged his fault and left the 8 [*sic*] heads, and very submissively took his leave, we then set to work to write the remarks and occurrences of the day, one that I have not the slightest desire to see performed again, dined at 6 o'clock, but it was sour[?] for we been [= being] obliged to take so much deleterious of solids, & drinkables, that I could not relish [it] I took a short walk and retired early to rest the evening was cool and pleasant.

---

[250] The victims were captives from the recent war against Atakpamé, as Forbes explicitly notes.
[251] As Beecroft later indicates (p. 72), a total of 11 men were sacrificed.
[252] Antonio de Souza had initially remained at Ouidah when his brothers left for Abomey (Forbes, Journal, p. 157), but had evidently joined them there subsequently.
[253] I.e. to a pulp.

Saturday, 1st June

am heavy rain, daylight it cleared away and became fine, Ther 71° cool w^r I took a short walk before breakfast, the road was clean from the heavy rain, having taken of[f] the surface, thousands had travelled the same road yesterday, to and from the despots Great festival I walked towards the scene of blood, but not having a desire to see the spot I returned to Breakfast, met Nawhey he was not in a good humour, Forbes had gone to take a walk without his usual escort, as customary, I told him that I had two of the hammock bearers with me, he asked me if I wished to see his head taken of, the custom is that a boy of his or the Mayo's should always follow the white-man, the Palaver would not come to us, but after we had taken our departure, they would be punished by fine, or otherwise, for they are responsible to the King for our safety, they have often tried to persuade us, that it was not healthy to walk early in the morning, I was obliged to tell them that we knew better than they did what was most condusive to our health, and our own welfare, the morning was by far the pleasantest part of the day particularly in Africa, sticks received and sent as usual, Domingo Martins sent his card, and stick, to C[aptain] Forbes,[254] 8 o'clock Ther 74° Richards my Interpreter, per chance encountered a relation of his, a Youriba man, slave to the King,[255] 11.30 a messenger arrived and announced that the King was ready to go to the market, we left and arrived at the scene of blood at 12 o'clock, found the Grand stand of yesterday's performances had totally disappeared, all was perfectly clear, and a large Tent of Country umbrellas erected, for the reception of the King, they were erected under the branches of several large Trees, we seated our selves near the spot, to await the Kings arrival, soldiers flocking to the ground, Caboceers and retainers.

30 minutes P.M. King arrives and takes his seat under the Union Jack umbrella, Tent[,] sent for us to join him, we were placed near him on his right, shortly afterwards Domingo Martins arrived in a handsome Hammock, and Bearers, neatly dressed, a red Band round their Caps, with his Initials on them, a small Negro boy in livery Blue with red facings, he was most graciously received by His Majesty, and placed a short distance in our rear, Cha-Cha and his Party were on the left.

Procession of Caboceers with Banners and Umbrellas marched round the Square three times in files of 10—amounting to 3308

Banner men	50
Musicians	360
Bow and arrowmen	<u>40</u>

---

[254] Domingos José Martins, the Brazilian merchant, who had arrived from Ouidah.
[255] Richards was from Ijanna, in Egbado.

	3758
Procession of Amazons performed the same as the men	<u>3000</u>
	6758

Men ornamented with long Grass advanced firing and
carrying a Union Jack   20

Son of the King of Ashantee[256] advanced and saluted
the King said to be Tributary[257]   40 retainers

The men soldiers marched in slow time twice, third time quick step and halted before the King

Amazon soldiers did the same and halted in the rear.

Caboceers performed the same evolutions and halted in the rear.

They all having walked round the first time a slow pace in review in files from 8 to 20 gave us an opportunity to count the whole of them.

King sent his aide de camp to give orders to the General of the Men soldiers, to advance slowly to the attack, and open fire, they performed the evolutions very well.

They then advanced up at quick step, firing well, separating into skirmishing parties, the aide de camp ordered the General to cease firing, and draw his troops up before the King, the Standard of Dahomey on the head of a Boy, which is a Leopard with a snake twisted round the body of the Leopard,[258] it was in front of the Troops.

King rises and goes in front of his men soldiers, music and praises, aloud he takes a musket and fires it [the] second flashed in the Pan,[259] His Majesty went on one Knee and fired with an aim, twice rose and made an attempt to dance, fired again then advanced a few yards, looking earnestly at some one in ambush, then fires, loud acclamations, his soldiers appeared to be delighted, they all sung aloud his Praises none like Gezo their King, tinkling of Bells, with their muskets raised above their heads, he enters the Tent the multitude rise to receive him, he shakes hands with us, Domingo Martins and the Cha-Cha, a volley of muskets is fired the soldiers retire in order to the rear.

---

[256] Later named as 'Ah-jaa-ba' (p. 81): he was presummably in the company of the Asante ambassador who is mentioned later (p. 82).

[257] Forbes says that Gezo had 'declared Ashantee subjugated', and had named his suburban palace 'Kumasi', after the Asante capital, in commemoration of this (1851, ii: 89). This 'declaration', however, was evidently an empty boast: for discussion see Law (1994b: 161–2).

[258] Forbes (Journal, p. 167) says 'a leopard killing a snake'. The leopard (or 'tiger') was regularly described as the national 'fetish' of Dahomey (or sometimes, that of the king specifically): this refers to Agasu, the totemic ancestor of the royal family, who was reputedly a male leopard who impregnated a human princess (Nicolau Parés 2016: 168–80).

[259] I.e. misfired.

The Snake is the Fetish of Whydah.[260]

King issues orders to his aidedecamp for the Amazon Troops to advance they accordingly advanced at slow march firing performing exactly the same evolutions as the men, equal if not better, the attack was performed by the Amazons with much more uniformity than the men. half an hour skirmishing they were then drawn up before the King's Tent chaunting [= chanting] His Majesty's Praises aloud, officers advance and invite His Majesty to honor them with his presence, same as he had performed in presence of his men soldiers, His Majesty rose his vanity being on the stretch, and advanced to their front, they rejoiced, and were actually in e[c]stacies he performed nearly the same evolutions as he had already done before his men soldiers, he then retired to his Tent, amidst the shouts of Joy, and acclamations of his people, music and firing for ten minutes, His Majesty presents them with a Gift of two cases of rum. They salute the King aloud & present before the people the Gift from His Majesty for the three men we ransomed yesterday, viz.

1 roll of Brazillian Tobacco

1 Keg of rum

20 Heads of cowries

2 Bags of D[o261]

They then commenced and sung Praises aloud to the [*sic*] Isadore or Cha Cha of Whydah and Domingo Martins stating that the latter made them a Gift of as under viz.

10 muskets

10 Kegs of rum

20 Kegs of Powder &c for the AhtaaPam war,[262] ends with firing, and shouts of Praise retire in order and ground Arms.

60 of the Kings soldiers advance and fire a salute for Domingo, and the Cha-Cha with a loud shout and retire in order.[263]

A small Troop of the King's soldiers advance firing[.] Fetish men with all their awful emblems of superstition, and <u>Gods</u> of <u>Baal</u>,[264] sing and dance before His Majesty a few minutes and those Devils have such an effect on his Majesty's weakness, that he goes out of the Tent, and joins in the performance of those Fetish people and took into his hand dancing at the same time their

---

[260] I.e. Dangbe, the royal python (cf. note 46). This comment presumably relates to the snake depicted in conflict with the leopard on the standard mentioned earlier: perhaps the emblem alluded to the Dahomian conquest of Ouidah (in 1727).

[261] A bag of cowries contained 20,000, i.e. 10 heads: this is probably a gloss on the preceding entry, rather than a separate gift.

[262] Forbes gives the Fon text of this song (Journal, p. 168).

[263] For this day's parades, cf. the Appendix to Forbes' journal, in TNA, FO84/827, ff.290–v, also reproduced in part in Forbes (1851, ii: 224–7).

[264] Baal is a name given in the Old Testament for the god of the Canaanites: hence by extension, any 'false' god.

calabashes of congealed blood, he performed the ceremony of lying his hands [on] it,[265] then gives it to the High Priest of the Fetish,[266] retires to the Tent, Gift of three small Bottles of rum, the Fetish then retires.

King's Brother salutes him, and retires with a little rum, it is odd they [i.e. the King's brothers] are all poor, I presume it is his policy to keep them so, they are prevented from being inclined to commit any rash acts.

Banners a Union Jack Blunderbussmen advance firing covered with long Cane Grass, accompanied by a Troop of musketeers, decorated in the same stile [= style].

Officers of the Troops advance and salute His Majesty by firing, and retiring in order.

Officers of Blunderbuss men and Clubsmen advance and fire and salutes the King and retire in order

Agooney people conquered and now his troops[267] advance firing a salute to the King, retire in order

Aidedecamp running to and fro ordering the Caboceers to advance.

Officers firing	—	8 Caboceers advance firing
		3 D° ” ”
		1 D° ” ”
		1 D° ” ”
		2 D° ” ”
		1 D° ” ”

Cambaa-dee King's Treasurer advance with his people firing advance to the Tent firing ceases and sing aloud Praises to the King, the General address the King in front of 50 of his Troops, with white scarfs, over their necks hanging in front the King asked them the reason they were not all in the same dress, his reply was that he was short of 80 scarfs, I did not hear the Kings reply, they again sing his Praises aloud, retire in the rear and ground arms.

Caboceer Gin-ah-gee 1 umbrella advance firing and salute the King

Caboceer Gee-bee-tee 1 D° advance firing a salute to the King retires in order

Caboceer Keh-Kee-maa 1 Umbrella, advance firing a salute to His Majesty and retires in order

---

[265] Forbes says that he poured rum on it (Journal, p. 168).

[266] Perhaps referring to the Agasunon, or priest of Agasu, identified by Burton later as 'the highest fetisheer' or 'chief fetisheer' of Dahomey, analogous to the Archbishop of Canterbury (1864, i: 262, 352–3).

[267] Agonli, east of Dahomey. Cf. the later allusion (p. 56) to this conquest as having occurred 'a few years past'; Burton later described the Agonli as 'tributary' to Dahomey (1864, ii: 231). The wording indicates that these were war captives, now incorporated into the Dahomian army. Dahomian tradition recalls that persons from Agonli formed a distinct unit of the army, who served as porters rather than combatants (Le Herissé 1911: 70), but Beecroft clearly understood them to be fighting men.

Caboceer Eh-du-oh 1 umbrella salute the King and retire in order

Caboceer Ah-ting-ge-ree[268] 1 D°   salute the King and retire in order

6 mallams in Blue Baft dresses belonging to the Eyo country sing Praises aloud before the King and his people, and retire in order

2 Caboceers 2 Umbrellas Boo-Kaa & Nun-haa salute the King by firing and retire in order

King's son Yaa-Koo-hoo and minister So-goo[269] salute His Majesty

King delivers a short address stating that we do not see all his Troops a great number are guarding the frontiers, against the enemy he did not state the number that were so employed[270]

Ah-laa-geea Kings head Drummer salutes his Master allowed to carry an Umbrella, retires in order

Cam-baa-dee advances and Prostrates himself before His Majesty, and rubs dirt on his head face, and arms

Appeh 1 Umbrella[271]

Caboceer Fo-goo-pah 2 Umbrellas   ) salutes the King firing retires

D° To-Koo-noo   2 D°   ) in good order

3 o'clock Cam-baa-dee's people advance a second time, and salute His Majesty by throwing dirt on their heads, & faces, rubbing their arms with it rise and shout aloud 'Gezo', their King, with their muskets uplifted above their heads, retire & ground arms.

6 Umbrellas, Banners 4 Union Jacks, Poo-so-ooh one of the Chief Generals,[272] advances firing and music, he approaches the King with two wooden Images, in his hand a club, and a skull in a Basket, he makes a great number of gesticulations, that signified that he would rather die himself, than the King's person should be injured, he returns to his people and takes a Bullocks head of Brass, dances and presents it before the King, he brings a third in a black painted case a Fetish ornamented with cowries, he is full of superstition and aged, great confidence in his own Powers as a warrior, he was quite

---

[268] Perhaps miscopied, cf. 'Tin-gaa-vee' subsequently (p. 116, and see also note 548).

[269] Forbes, in the MS version of his list, has 'Saugan', i.e. Sogan (lit. 'horse chief'), the title of an official who supervised the activities of royal slaves outside the palace, including the plantations which supplied its provisions, who was one of the seven *gbonugan daho*, or 'great chiefs' (Le Herissé 1911: 37, 42–3). A subsequent reference indicates that the Sogan also had military functions (p. 120, 'Soo-gaa-saa'): these perhaps related to provisioning the army in the field (Bay 1998: 114).

[270] Forbes (Journal, p. 169), counted 6,800 soldiers in the review, and opined that 'perhaps an equal number' were posted 'on the frontiers', comprising a standing army of 'no more than 14,000'; this would be supplemented in wartime by local levies, but the army sent to war would number no more than 20,000, leaving 8,000 to guard the capital and frontiers.

[271] Cf. 'Akpi', described as one of one of the 'warriors and worthies of the King' (Burton 1864, i: 312, n.).

[272] Posu, title of the second-in-command of the army and commander of the left wing in battle.

satisfied with his own Powers and that he was all right and a great man, sing, dance, and retire in order.

Ag-gow's people, 7 umbrellas not able to be present in person, being sick, he is the General that takes charge of the Kings person when he goes to war,[273] firing of Guns, dancing, singing and music, retire in order and ground arms.

Caboceer—	1 Umbrella—	Oh-gen-hoo		
D°—	1 D°—	Ah-do-maa-doo		
D°—	1 D°—	Gen-ah-hoo		
D°—	3 D°—	Ya-go-boo-oh		
D°—	1 D°—	Ya-fun-peh		
D°—	1 D°—	daa-foo-Koo		
D°—	1 D°—	daa-nah-Gao		
D°—	1 D°—	Hing-gan	Banner	1 Union Jack
D°—	1 D°—	Boh-Peh[274]	”	D° ”
D°—	1 D°—	Mah-too-noo		
D°—	1 D°—	Faoh-nee		
D°—	1 D°—	Noo-dee-feree[275]		Union Jack 2 shields
D°—	1 D°—	Ah-chee-see[276]		
D°—	1 D°—	Na-pee-veeh	King's Brother	
D°—	3 D°—	Ah-buu-paa	” ”	1 B. of rum
D°—	2 D°—	Ah va kee-voh		
D°—	1 D°—	Soo-tee-tong		
D°—	1 D°—	Too-fah, King's Brother[277]	Horns	
D°—	1 D°—	Ah son yong[278]	2 shields	
D°—	2 D°—	Toh-ka-nee-pee Jah[279]		
D°—	1 D°—	Gaa eh-goo		

[273] Gau, commander-in-chief of the army and commander of the right wing. The Gau was absent and reported sick throughout the Customs (see also pp. 110, 120, 123). Forbes thought that this was a cover for the fact that he had been killed in the recent Atakpamé war (Journal, p. 186).

[274] I.e. Bokpè: identified by Forbes (1851, i: 73), as 'the governor of the capital', i.e. of Abomey.

[275] Identified by Forbes as the 'Caboceer' of the Brazil quarter of Ouidah (1851, i: 105, 'Gnodefereh'): i.e. Noudofinin, the name of a family in Ouidah who claim descent from a royal official (Law 2004b: 104).

[276] Probably miscopied: Forbes here has 'A-che-lee' (1851, ii: 225), i.e. Hechili, who is mentioned by Beecroft himself later (p. 77).

[277] Tofa. This man had in fact died in the 1820s (Le Herissé 1911: 328–9); the man referred to here is evidently someone who had succeeded to his position and name—another instance of 'positional succession' (cf. note 223).

[278] Cf. 'Assoyon' in Burton (1864, i: 312).

[279] Forbes, 'Toh-koo-noo-vee-joh' (1851, ii: 225): cf. 'Tokonon-vissau', 'Tokunon-fisan' in Burton (1864, i: 313, n.; ii: 126, n.).

D°— 13 D°— Ah-la-loo-de-Cun-jah, head man and manager of the King's Household[280] four of his sons in the Troop, they address their Father with firing music, dance and sing Praises, receive a Gift of rum, and retire in order and ground arms.

Caboceer—	I Umbrella—	Ah-Koo-Koo-yee
D°—	1 D°—	Foh-san-boo
D°—	1 D°—	Kaa Kee nee haa
D°—	1 D°—	Ah-ga-see-pee-gah
D°—	1 D°—	Oh maa a-nee King's Brother

Maa-daa-hoo King's Eldest son[281] advances with his Troop, music, and firing, he advances kneels and salutes, his Father, the others did the same dance and sing, music and firing, retired in order and grounded arms.

1 Large white umbrella with them others salute the King firing and music.
1 umbrella 5 men firing & salute the King

1 D° " "	Too-vee-saa	King's Brother	
1 D° Caboceer	Mee vaa deeh		
1 D° "	Ah-Kin-nee-veh		
1 D° "	Ap-ah-hoo	King's Brother	
1 D° "	Oh-ah-too		
1 D° "	Goo-doo		
1 D° "	Ah-do-Koo-noo	King's B[rother][282]	1 Union Jack
1 D° "	Toh-poo[283]		
1 D° "	Ah-Zong	ornamented with a Bullock's head,	

attached to it a Brass chain, danced, and fired Guns, music and singing Praises aloud, before the King retired in order

3 Umbrellas Too-maa-tee King's Brother,[284] fired muskets, saluted the King & danced and sung, Gift of a Bottle of rum retired

---

[280] Not otherwise recorded. The official in overall charge of the palace had the title Ajaho, which Beecroft lists on a later occasion (p. 77): possibly the name given here was the Ajaho's personal name.

[281] Forbes, in his MS, has 'Bah doh hong', while Beecroft later spells the name 'Baa-da-hoo' etc.: i.e. Badahun, later (1858–89) King Glele. He was not strictly Gezo's 'eldest son', but his designated heir apparent, the Fon term for which, *vì dáhó*, literally 'great son', refers to seniority of status, rather than age (Bay 1998: 85).

[282] Adukonu (Bay 1998: 172).

[283] I.e. Tokpo. But there were several persons with this name or title: Forbes lists 'Toh-poo' as one of the King's traders at Ouidah (1851, i: 111), that is, Tokpo, the name of one of the merchant families there (Law 2004b: 115); Tokpo was also the title of a senior official of the capital (one of the seven 'great chiefs'), described as 'minister of agriculture' (Le Herissé 1911: 37, 43); Burton later refers to a 'Tokpau', who was a 'war chief' (1864, i: 313). Note that Beecroft appears to list two persons called Tokpo in the ceremonies on 7 June (pp. 78, 83).

[284] Tometin (Bay 1998: 172). This man held the title of Mewu, as a royal counterpart to the substantive official so called (ibid., 177–8). Neither Beecroft nor Forbes shows any awareness of

Fetish men with their mummeries crying aloud that they had Power to cause his enemies to sleep, awful superstition a Gift of a Bottle of rum and retire.

Gan-seh, King's Brother[285] advances and salutes the King, music and dancing, he retired backwards from his presence to his own people, fired a volley and retired in order to the rear

Eh-vah-nah-hee saluted the King by firing and music singing and dancing retires in order to the rear.

So-too-goo King's Brother performed the same ceremony

5 mallams to the late King,[286] advances and salutes Gezo they were received on their Knees, presented a small Gift of rum, and retired, I was not aware that the Priests were obligated to bend the Knee to Royalty[,] at Rabaa they were exempted.[287]

Ignatio de Souza Caboceer for white man advances with music and firing, he approached his Majesty with a slow and diffident step, not pleased with his position, arrives at the Tent his people perform a few evolutions, King rises and leaves the Tent, and takes him by the hand, and beckons the Cha-Cha to join them but he grins, and declines, Ignatio and his people dance, King retires to the Tent and took his seat, fired a volley of musketry and retired to the rear, Ignatio takes his seat amongst his family a gang of slave dealers.

Caboceer of Whydah—appears in the distance, music, singing and dancing, accompanied with volleys of musketry, he approaches the Tent in a very submissive position on his Belly, then rises to his Knees with his head still in the earth, He then approaches the King in a very crouching manner with his present of

> 2 Bottles of Gin
> 2 D°   of rum
> 2 D°   of wine

He then retires throwing any quantity of dirt on his head, face and arms.

King sent us a Gift of two Baskets of new corn

Mee-gou['s] people in the distance advancing firing, music, and dancing, 2 Boys advance to the Tent blowing Horns, the party arrives and performs several evolutions, 5 Boys dressed in Blue white striped frocks to below the Knees with white Caps over their Ears, with red cloth ornaments, they are the garments to be worn by the unfortunate creatures to be next

---

this 'doubling' of royal with commoner officials, although it was explicitly described later by Burton (1864, i: 209, 221–5).

[285] Ganse, who was the royal counterpart to the Migan (Bay 1998: 172, 177–8).

[286] Forbes says six mallams 'from Eyeo [Oyo]'.

[287] Beecroft had visited Raba, in Nupe, in 1840 and 1845. But his comment does not take account of the fact that Nupe was under Muslim rule.

sacrificed,[288] music, singing, and dancing, fire a volley and retire to the rear, 5 umbrellas.

Kings undertaker[289] approaches His Majesty and salutes him, as Customary a Gift of a Bottle of rum and retires.

Mayo-Gau next in the distance, with a large band of soldiers about 300 Banners flying—music, dancing and singing, with volleys of musketry, the Mayo approaches the Tent as sprightly as a young man hands the King's stool to one of his staff, and retires with music and dancing to his former position, advances again in haste, going through the same ceremony with any quantity of dust, he approaches His Majesty, as his Grand Vizier on his Knees with his head in the dust, he receives a Gift of a case Bottle of rum, he then approaches the King in a very solemn manner, and presents his Gift in a Basket, it was not opened so I did not know its contents, after which two of his people appeared before the Tent, with a Bag of crimson satin full of cowries, about 10 heads, or 10 dollars and 3 Hkfs[?] of the same sort as the Bag, he harangued his people for about ten minutes, on this splendid Gift from His Majesty, the old sycophant began and sung Praises to the King aloud for this enormous Gift after which his party retired in order to the rear.

After which we took our leave of His Majesty. Domingo Martins [did so] at the same time, we walked home accompanied by Nawhey on our arrival we presented him with one of the Baskets of corn. A Glass of sweet wine, he then took his leave we dined at 6 o'clock after which we talked over the affairs of the day and retired at 9.30 a fine cool evening.

Sunday 2nd June

I arose at 5 o'clock, a fine cool pleasant morning Ther 75°. Captain Forbes accompanied me as usual on our morning walk, down the Canna-Minna road, and returned by the Bee-con road, on our way we passed on our right a group of about forty squatted in the middle of a Grass Field their black pates only in sight, chaunting[,] they are Mayo-Gaus people, they come out there to practice quietly, to get their vocal powers in tune and have their Extempore songs by heart before they are called to perform before the King, he would be highly displeased did he know they had been practising publicly before the people, previous to their performance before him, so it is too obvious it is the

---

[288] Presumably, to be killed overnight on 2/3 June: Forbes' Journal records seeing the decapitated heads of six [*sic*] victims in Singbodji Square on the morning of 3 June (p. 169).

[289] Forbes, in his MS list, explains: 'when a man of distinction dies this man takes a country cloth from the King to bury him in'.

sole reason why they seek out an obscure place to practice in, we walked on and passed the Palace he built in 1845 and named it after the Capital of Ashantee Coomassee,[290] we passed on through the delightful avenue of Trees, receiving a cool grateful Breeze, under the shadow of their lofty Branches, we stopped at the <u>Bee-con</u> market Place we were accosted by Ah-hoo-pee King's Brother[291] and a Caboceer[292] they shook us very cordially by the hand, and made anxious enquiries as to our comforts and well being, I presume they were on their way from their country seats, to Town residence to dress for the King's <u>Levee</u>, we arrived at our Palace at 7.30 sticks had been presented and ours sent accordingly, rum must vanish under such ordeals, an appearance to save it is very unpleasing in sight of these stick Bearers, it appears it has become a custom, as such a <u>Law</u>. sat down and took Breakfast at 8.20 after which read a Chapter in my Bible then wrote part of my Journal, until 5 o'clock took a late dinner and retired to bed at 9 o'clock

Midnight fine w[r]

Programme Monday 3rd June

Daylight fine w[r] we took an early Breakfast[,] 7 o'clock left for Palace arrived at the Square 7.35 entered the Court Yard,[293] and saluted the Throne, the King had not arrived.

The liberated Africans from Brazils entered and saluted the Throne, with Viva le Rei de Dahomey three times, Head of the Blunderbuss Troop came up[294] with his music and followers, painted about his face with chalk round his Eyebrows, nose, and mouth, he was a grotesque figure, he had 2 Drums, and 8 or 9 followers, his son a small boy about 9 or 10 years of age, imitating his Fathers actions, and evolutions, Caboceer Ah-sin-yong, we met yesterday on our walk round by Coommassee and the Bee-con market, he came up and saluted us, he was well dressed, yellow, red, and white, striped satin and silk Frock, a quantity of Bead ornaments, around his neck, such as local, and Popoo, beads.

10 men of the Kings household Kneels before the Tent with Horses Tails in their hands, waving them, and singing Praises to their King,

7 Gong-gong-men[295] singing and beating their Gongs round in front of the Tent.

---

[290] See note 185.
[291] Spelled 'Har-o-pay' by Fraser (2012: 63), 'Ahopwe' by Burton (1864, ii: 126, n.): i.e. Ahokpè, who was the son of King Agonglo by an Afro-European woman (Law 2004b: 164–5).
[292] Named later (below, this page) as 'Ah-sin-yong'.
[293] I.e. of the palace: cf. Forbes, Journal, p. 169, 'the Court of the Palace of Dangelahcordeh'.
[294] I.e. Kpofensu (see p. 32).
[295] Fon *gàngàn* (reduplicated from *gàn*, 'iron'), 'gong'.

8 o'clock Cha Cha and his party arrived and saluted the Throne.

6 Fetish men arrived with Iron rods, ornamented heads covered with white Baft.

Table set with refreshments, but not any thing that I would drink although we had to go through the form with His Majesty.

8.30 His Majesty arrives, dressed in a splendid satin robe, car[e]lessly thrown over his shoulders a slouched Hat, Gold rim, broad Gold Band, with crown ornaments of Gold, and gold Tassels. 9 Amazons armed, saluted with music and firing of Guns, he entered the Tent Guards retire

3 Eunuchs arrive and salute His Majesty

8 men on their Knees throwing dirt on their heads, three times, empty a jar of water and rub it on the Ground, and retire, their watering of the Grave of his ancestors[296]

Caboceers all rise in full dress, Mayogau, Mee-Gon ah [*sic*], Dagbah, Caboceer of Whydah, in rich scarlet velvet cloaks, each a silver plate on the left side of their heads, Gyanuseh, King's eldest Brother[297] in front, walk in Procession three times before the Tent, 24 in white dresses and 31 in common, after which they all Kneeled and Kissed the earth, and threw dirt over their heads three times, rise and return to their seats.[298]

A Gift from His Majesty of a Callabash of Oranges return our thanks.

Cam-baa-dies people rise and Parade before the Tent three times, 21 with muskets, two followers, named Too-moo-gee & Gam-qua-gee they are all officers, Kneel and Kiss the earth, and throw dirt on their heads, rise and retire, receive a Gift of a 4 Gallon demi-John of rum.

14 Eunuchs, Chief in a scarlet cloak salute the King and retire.

9 o'clock Domingo Martin's enters and salutes the King, pays his respects to the Cha-Cha, and shook hands with us, and took a seat near us, he was very condescending handing cigars shortly after he had been seated.

10 of the Kings umbrella bearers.

2 Dwarfs, Guard 25 soldiers 6 Band of music

40 King's stick Bearers, all salute him by Kissing the earth, and throwing dirt on their heads, singing and music, a Gift of 1½ Gallons of rum, and retire.

30 Kings Family, his Brothers, and their sons, salute the King by Kissing the earth three times, a Gift of 8 Bottles of rum, for royalty and retire.

---

[296] See note 174. Here, referring literally to a libation of water, rather than metaphorically to the blood of human sacrifices.

[297] Presumably, this is again Ganse (cf. p. 52).

[298] For the following procession, cf. TNA, FO84/827, ff. 290v–8v; Forbes (1851, ii: 229–42).

10 mallams, salute the King on their Knees, clapped their hands, three times then cover their faces the same, and put their right hands on their left Breasts. A Gift of one head of cowries that is 1 Dollar

a Gift to the		Mayo-gou of	80 heads of cowries			
a	" "	" Mee-gou "	80	"	"	D°
a	" "	" Hoo-opoo "	20	"	"	D°
a	" "	" Poo-vo-soo "	20	"	"	D°
			200			

Kiss the ground three times and throw dirt on their heads and retired.

200 Ah-goo-nee people enter and fire a salute with musquetoons,[299] and 3 small Brass pieces [i.e. cannon], 1lb mounted on wooden carriages, after which a salute was fired from the Battery outside the Palace yard, music, singing, and dancing, these troops have been captured a few years past.

50 women soldiers fire 48 rounds from the same pieces, afterwards music, and singing, they then each take a piece and run to the entrance of the Tent, and display their strength of arm, and agility of body, by holding the musquetoon in one hand above their heads, as a salute to his Majesty, a Gift of 10 heads of cowries a loud shout and retire.

a Gift to Poo-vo-soo Captain of the Blunderbussmen a silver Tea Pot full of rum, he Kisses the earth, and covers himself with dirt empties the vessel and returns it, he is a sort of court fool he is privileged

Cha-Cha rises and advances before the King and salutes him, he has permission to retire with his people he being indisposed, a Gift of a large Bottle of rum.

Caboceers of the Amazons advance and salute the King, well dressed with coral & Popoo beads round their necks also a number of silver ornaments, crosses & Bracelets, and armlets of silver, music, singing and dancing for half an hour & retire.

20 minstrels perform before His Majesty singing his Praises aloud a Gift of a Case bottle of rum and retire.

10 o'clock the King leaves the Tent, and walks to our stand, salutes us and Domingo, and shook us by the hand, looks at our remark Books, he asked Domingo if he could write English, and if we were friends, to the latter he replied in the affirmative, he then took our Caps and examined them thinking they were velvet, he took a small glass of spirits, a shout and musketry. He then retired to the Tent.

Officers of the Amazon Troops, salute His Majesty they are elegantly dressed, retire without music or Guns.

Maa-hee women salute with musquetoons, and Blunderbusses, returned by the big Guns outside, they dance and sing, and walk in Procession, after

---

[299] I.e. short-barrelled muskets.

which they salute the King by holding the arms they had fired in one hand above their heads, and retire.

6 women well dressed with whips in their hands
8 Horn performers
3 women with wands in their hands
20 musicians, music and dancing
60 followers
9 Banners, 7 Long Horns
6 musicians of different sorts of rude country instruments
18 men a Hoe each. 1 Scymitar
2 women—with Beads ornaments
66 D°— country Pots   Plain
17 D°— D°   ”   ornamented with beads
9 D°— D°   ”   large   D°   ”   D°
8   ”   Baskets small country
9   ”   D°   large   D°
34 ”   Blue and red   Jars
25 ”   D°   ”   Jars
7   ”   Green   D°
17 ”   Yellow   D°
10 ”   red   D°
1   ”   D° [*sic*] 4 heads of cowries
34 ”   ornamented country Baskets
31 ”   D°   D°   D°
13 ”   D°   D°   D°
19   white Hats
68 ”   sticks red wrapped
16 ”   D°   blue   D°
12 ”   wands white   D°
2   ”   dressed in variegated colours
2   ”   carrying Images
2   ”   dogs
2   ”   sheep
3   ”   wooden Images,
19 ”   Toby Philpot Jugs
20 ”   wearing cottage Bonnets and wrappers and bead ornaments
13 ”   with Brooms in their hands
36 ”   D° muskets wearing red caps
8   ”   Pots ornamented with cowries
12 ”   with Black Hats and 8 retainers
37 ”   with an assortment of cloth on their heads
2   ”   Glass chandeliers

7   "   with assorted ornaments
1   "   silver ostrich 2 eggs made at Abomey from dollars[300] by a man
               that was, sitting near us his father was a Brazillian
12   "   music in the rear
8   "   silver ornaments
30   "   singers
11   "   Horns and callabashes with cowries, ornamented with Pease
               [= peas] or small pebbles to make a din
6   "   Baskets of common cloth
1   "   night stool Gilt
1   "   callabash
8   "   with muskets
4   "   "   Brass Trumpets
1   "   Head woman under a scarlet umbrella, with a gilt ornament
               Lady not visible
40   "   in a Group music, Horns, and Drums
16   "   Guards. sing dance and salute His Majesty move on in
               Procession
2 women bearing   Callabashes contents unknown
2 D°—   "   Blunderbusses
5 D°—   "   Hats
4 D°—   "   D°   scarlet
7 D°—   dressed in white
9 D°—   D°—   fantastically
300 D°— bearing on their heads, small Baskets on wooden Plates
55 D°—   bearing Blue Bottles
50 D°—   D°—   white D°
2 D°—   ponderous in size salute the King
3 children followers
30 men   "
6 Banners ornamented with skulls
2 men   Bearing the King's stools
30   "   armed with Blunderbusses
8   "   Bearers King's washing Tub or rather Bathing
22   "   Guards and retainers
1 woman Sedan Chair[301] ornamented with crimson, and gold
6   "   Guards
10   "   Bearers
10   "   musicians

---

[300] Imported silver dollars were melted down or beaten to make jewellery (Law 1994a: 60).
[301] A seat carried on poles by two persons.

3	"	Banners
8		a Box on wheels
4	"	Guards
2	"	Ostriches, one with a canopy[302]
1	"	Big drum
10	"	with a Landau[303]
8	"	Guards
2	"	Banners
6	"	a Green Box on wheels
22	"	followers
10	"	Band of music
8	"	Carrying a large silver ornament
13	"	followers
10	"	Band of music
40	"	a large Bed-stead hung with red damask
5	"	Guards
16	"	2 Horses, 2 sheep
4	"	1 large white umbrella ornamented with jaw-Bones[304]
4		Banners
12		followers
6		1 large Drum ornamented with skulls
14		Guards
15		Bearers, I small Box, 1 Large & 1 small dresser ornamented with 12 skulls each
10		Band of music
8		Blunderbussmen
5		Guards with muskets
12		D° 1 woman under two silk umbrellas said to be Kings family
6		a Wooden Horse on wheels
5		Guards
2		Umbrellas
10		Band of music
4		Banners
4		2 Large Tin canisters for sugar
20		a Family Coach[305]

[302] Ostriches were not, of course, native to Dahomey, but imported from the interior, presumably as a curiosity. For Gezo's interest in exotic animals, cf. a report in 1826 that he had sent messengers to Yauri, on the River Niger, in an unsuccessful attempt to obtain a camel (Clapperton 1829: 80).
[303] I.e. a four-wheeled carriage.
[304] Forbes adds 'from the Eyeo [= Oyo] war' (1851, ii: 234).
[305] I.e. a large closed carriage.

15	Guards
2	Dwarfs
12	Blunderbusses
16	with muskets
2	Banners
12 men	1 native sofa
12 "	Guards
6 "	a wooden Horse on wheels
20 women	1 Carriage
6 Dº—	Scarlet Flags
25 Dº—	Guards
4 Dº—	Brass Drums
3 Dº—	Tambours[306]
12 Dº—	2 country drums
5 men	Drum makers well dressed in various robes,

wands in their hands with white cloth over the upper ends

40 women in Procession drawing a carriage followed by 4 war stools, Banners

10 Dº	
10 Dº	followers
1 Dº	under a large Umbrella
26 Dº	armed as her escort, she is the overlooker and

superintendant of markets, as Tax gathererer[307]

40 Dº	2 large Drums ornamented with skulls
6 Dº	2 small Brass pieces
6 Dº	Band of music
20 Dº	Guards
20 men	with Blunderbusses

Procession commences with

8 children	
12 women 1 Box	
20 Dº—	Guards, it infers that it [= the preceding box] is

rather valuable, followed

6 Bearers	by an old Chair out of fashion, a Chair with a

wooden Bird on it richly ornamented

20 men	Guards

---

[306] A type of drum (shallow and single-skinned). Forbes has 'tambourines'.

[307] Forbes describes this woman only as a 'head wife' (1851, ii: 236). Beecroft's description of her function is odd, since no other source suggests that any royal woman played such a role. However, the reference may be to a small market on the north-west side of the palace, called the 'Queens' Market', where food and handicrafts produced by the women inside the palace were sold (Bay 1998: 212; Randsborg & Merkyte 2009, ii: 54).

6	"	a Gilt Chair
8	"	a Gig[308]
6	"	a Glass Coach[309] made at Abomey
16	"	as Guards
5	"	Banners
6	"	2nd country Glass Coach
6	"	Gongs
6	"	Guards
12	"	a Family Coach
2	"	Guards
16	"	followers, 2 richly dressed in scarlet and Gold,

several other followers and King's wives magnificently dressed, with white caps followed by

4	"	Brass drums made at Abomey
6	"	1 Sedan chair
100	"	Guards well dressed
21 women		white Parasols satin
1		D° Brown silk
1		D° Blue velvet
6		a wooden warrior on wheels.
12		Two wooden Horses mounted made at Abomey

by one of the King's family[310]

Procession

1 man	with umbrella
1 D°—	one Banner
10 D°—	Followers
6 D°—	a wine cooler on Trucks
10 D°—	Followers
2 children	dressed
3 women followed by	
10 D°—	with different sorts of ornaments
16 D°—	4 Gallon Case Bottles in Callabashes on their heads
10 D°—	Basins
10 D°—	D° full of worsted scarfs for trade
1 D°—	silver ornament
5 D°—	white basins

---

[308] I.e. a light two-wheeled carriage.

[309] I.e. one with glazed windows.

[310] But Forbes says '2 wooden mounted horses on wheels (English)'—presumably it was the wheels which were English-made (1851, ii: 237).

13 D°—	Boxes with pieces of silk laid on them, all colours, and qualities
2 D°—	with ornaments
1 D°—	Gilt vase
1 D°—	a Brass Pan, in it a handsome worked Basket
8 D°—	a large Ottoman,[311] made of Skins tanned
1 D°—	a very large country Hat, as large as a common umbrella
1 D°—	a Hammock, a symbol of the Town of Kan-gaa-

roo that the King declared war against and conquered for ill treating the late Mr Duncan, and impeding his Progress,[312] the King I believe is a Prisoner at Abomey,[313] it is made of wood. this said Hammock

Next Procession

3 women	Three stools
3 D°—	D° Callabashes
3 D°—	Large European Umbrellas
2 D°—	Small d°. d°
5 D°—	Large Callabashes
2 D°—	Baskets contents unknown followed by

12 children very tastefully dressed

2 woman with a very large Broadbrimmed Hat

4 D°—   with Helmets richly Gilt with silver armlets, upper robes white, with rich coloured silk, and satin, white, scarfs, tipped with scarlet fringe, Gold Ear rings, and a number of silver ornaments, white Plumes on their Hats, similar to those worn in the days of King Charles,[314] richly ornamented with silver, and Gold, the same sort were worn in Henrys days[315] they had in their dress quite a Theatrical appearance and certainly would not have disgraced Drury Lane, or Covent Garden,[316] for their dresses were magnificent without being gaudy. they are the wives of his Majesty's Private Bed-Chamber,[317] they sung Praises to the King, and shouted in loud acclamations that they would fight for him to the death, none can fight equal to

---

[311] I.e. a cushioned chair.

[312] Duncan had been refused entry into Kenglo in 1845 (see his account, 1847, ii: 61–2, 'Koglo').

[313] Forbes, in the MS version of his 'Appendix', lists the 'King of Kanjaroo' among recipients of royal bounty on 31 May.

[314] Forbes (1851, ii: 238) specifies that this means Charles II (r. 1660–85).

[315] Presumably King Henry VIII (r. 1509–47).

[316] I.e. the theatre district of London.

[317] Forbes (who says six women) calls them 'the Paussee', explained as the king's 'principal wives' (1851, ii: 238), i.e. Kposi, 'Wives of the Leopard', whose precise status and functions are unclear (see Bay 1998: 241–4).

them, the senior had on a rich Gilt sword. the Procession passed on followed by,

9 women	silver ornaments
4 D°—	D° Baskets
7 D°—	Basins
6 D°—	Coloured Basins
8 D°—	Glass ornaments

a Procession advances, and salutes the King; it appears that it an Old
Custom for a woman of the Kings Harem, to be adopted mother to strangers,
that may visit Abomey, Cook and send them chop, during their stay, a Gift is
expected,[318] our English mother I have not as yet seen her,[319] but she sends a
fair quantity of Country Chop, Corn ground and made into a consistency of
Hasty Pudding called Dab-a-Dab being so like in shape to them,[320] also palm
oil chop, but not for the stomach of Europeans, at the head of this Procession
was Domingo Martins adopted Abomey mother, after they again salutes the
King, she makes Known to Domingo through his Interpreter that she is going
to address herself to him, he arose and went and stood opposite to her, she
then commenced and sung his Praises aloud, and thanked him for the under-
mentioned, viz.

10 muskets

10 Kegs of Powder

10 Kegs of rum, that was given them for their use at the late Ah-taa-Pam
war, for his Guns and Powder did good execution in assisting to beat them
at that war, after which a small silver salver is sent with spirits, and water,
The King drinks his health. Troop of Amazons, also, huzza, and musketry
he then drinks the Kings, and the Ladies [health], thanks them for their
compliments, and retires to his seat, The senior held either a Gold or Brass
stick in her hand, [the one] next to her a cane beautifully mounted with silver, another had splendid sword, scabbard silver mounted, they were all
superbly dressed

30 singing women

200 The Group altogether, all this show once a year has been gathering for
the last 150 years, but I am well informed that he does not parade all his
worth every Custom it is Totally on account of our presence, to endeavour as

---

[318] For this practice, see Bay (1998: 241).

[319] This 'English mother' is named by Forbes as 'Eeawae', i.e. Yawe (Journal, pp. 170 etc.); she did
appear in the ceremonies of 13 June, which Beecroft did not witness (ibid., p. 178).

[320] 'Hasty pudding' is made of flour stirred into boiling water or milk. 'Dab-a-dab' was made
from ground maize or Guinea corn, boiled in water until thick and moulded into cakes (Burton
1864, i: 136, n.). The term is not Fon, but from coastal pidgin: the Fon term is *amiwó*. The phrase
'so like in shape to them' is obscure, but from a subsequent passage (p. 88) seems to allude to the
'Dab-a-dab Hills', north-east of Dahomey.

far as possible to throw sand in our eyes, he has had the Plunder of all the nations about him, that he has conquered. the Procession passed on to the market Place for some display before his people.[321]

230 [in total]

Procession

Advances and salutes the King in front of the Tent

8 women	I Large Dahomian Chair or stool
1 do	white silk or satin umbrella
12 do	1 Box covered with scarlet cloth, on Trucks, said to contain silver
26 do	with long ornaments, covered with variegated cloth
1 do	silver scymitar
1 Do	silver ornaments
1 do	Box—Do
3 do	Glass ornaments
6 do	Do Do
30 do	various sorts of ornaments country &c
10 do	Glass water Bottles
17 do	water coolers
56 do	Chamber pots
2 do	Glass Bottles containing wine
52 do	White Glass water Bottles
51 do	Blue do do do
76 do	Large Blue Case Bottles 2 3 & 4 Gallons each
22 women	White Jars
50 do	Coloured do
1 do	Handsome Callabash
11 do	Glass Shades, large size
1 do	Extra large
3 do	Trunks
2 do	wash stools
1 do	Handsome easy chair
1 do	Toilet and Glass Mahogany

Procession

Advances, Too-noo-noos the Eunuch his mother,[322] at the Head

---

[321] As Forbes notes (Journal, p. 169) this day's ceremonies represented a repetition of the Custom of displaying the king's wealth, in the Adjahi market, as performed on 30 May.

[322] Later explained as 'the head eunuch' (p. 94); spelled 'To-no-nun' by Burton (1864, i: 227–9). The term 'mother' here refers to female counterparts of officials, appointed from among the women of the royal palace. As noted (note 191), the female Tononun may be identical with Mahaikpa, who is mentioned by name by Beecroft on several other occasions.

1 Brass Kettle with a skull, of an African King, 2 shields, 1 stool, with skulls, the shields, were ornamented with skulls, 1 Large Umbrella 3 Banners, she was dressed magnificently with a silver Helmet, commenced to sing Praises to the King, after which she commenced upon Domingo, in a similar strain to the one sung by his adopted mother, Domingo rises and goes in front and salutes her.

10 women in superb white dresses, 1 callabash with skulls, 1 red Box on wheels

10 Band of music

10 women followers

3 women dancing with Tails attached to their waists giving them a circular motion as they danced

30 D°   music and followers

Procession

24 women of Whydah advance and salute the King and sing Praises aloud.

3 D° Guards they pass on and proceed to the market

Procession

60 women of the Youribaa nation perform the same ceremony as the last and pass on to the market

Procession

50 women of To-too[323] advance with music and salute the King, with singing and dancing, after which they proceed on to the market

Procession

40 virgins with 9 umbrellas belonging to the Kings household

10 Band of Music advance and salute the King, dancing and singing Praises in honour of his deeds in arms and conquering his enemies, they pass on to the market

Procession 1 Banner 3 men armed, 2 Bayonets on Poles, salute the King and pass on.

Procession

1 Banner, King's Grandmother, mother and all the other branches of the Elders of His Majesty's family, the greater part all adopted,[324] his Grandmother died some years [ago], advance and Kiss the ground sing his Praises aloud, a Gift of one case bottle of rum, pass on to the market according to custom, followed by

2 women Umbrella Bearers, 2 country Pots with skulls, a Chain ornamented with D°, 4 Brass Pans full of skulls

---

[323] Forbes says 'of Kato' (1851, ii: 241; but in the MS version 'Kabo'): i.e. Ketu, a Yoruba kingdom to the east of Dahomey. Forbes understood that Ketu was subject to Dahomey, not through conquest but having 'voluntarily submitted' (1851, i: 20).

[324] Cf. notes 223–4.

2 covered Pans, d°, 1 Brass Kettle a skull and about 60 followers altogether

Procession

1 Banner, 60 virgins in white wrappers, an elder of the King's family of course adopted dressed in rich scarlet velvet cloth, with a skull, crimson cap silver ornaments, also a silver mounted stick

25 women Guards

12 d°   Band of Music singing Praises and dancing pass on to the market.

Procession

1 Banner, 1 Umbrella, advance his Grandfathers adopted wives,[325] salute the King, by singing, and dancing, Praising His Majesty's munificence silver Head dresses, pass on to the market

followers—2 Pots of skulls, 2 stools ornamented with Pans of skulls

Guard 5 women

Band 6

20 other followers

Procession

King's family Grandfathers widows, 1 umbrella, 1 Pan of skulls

Guards 5

Music 4

30 followers, sing Praises and pass on to the market

Procession

1 Banner, and 4 musicians, 4 singing women with Horses Tails in their hands, Group dancing, and singing as usual, music in the center

Gift of a Case Bottle of rum, pass on to the market.

Guards 30 women

Procession

2 o'clock, 4 Banners, 2 umbrellas, 1 man dressed in a Black Cloak, 6 in red damask wrappers, conical caps of various colours, singing and dancing, they passed on[,] Group [*sic*]

30 men I could not glean who the man was in the Black coast so singular to the rest

Procession

30 women with Blue Tunics, and short swords, 5 Banners, 3 drums, called Ah-na-baa-duu,[326] 2 were of Brass and 1 copper, country made dance and sing, salute the King and pass on to the market

---

[325] Gezo's grandfather was King Kpengla (r. 1774–89).

[326] Fon term not identified, but the first element may be *nà*, 'princess'.

Procession
40 men   2 callabashes with skulls, 2 skulls ornamented with cowries, men in red caps and silver ornaments, 10 stepped out and formed a figure with their heads close together for five minutes holding their muskets in the left hand, after which they commenced dancing, and singing, 2 Black ornaments of wood with red striped Kilts, Guards moving and keeping time, King's Gift a Jar of rum ornamented with beads of various colours, and qualities, the[y] salute the King aloud and pass on to the market.

Procession
10 Houssa people advance and salute the King and sing his Praises, to the King, and Cha-Cha de Souza, pass on to the market.

Procession
a Band of singing women, two with half a head of silver on their heads left side, singing Praises and dancing pass on to the market.

20 in the Group

4 o'clock His Majesty sent us 3 Bottles of rum in a white wash-Basin, return our thanks

Procession
6 skull Banners, 4 Brass Shields with a skull on the centre of each, 7 of the Kings cast of wives or rather pensioners, sing and dance with the shields in their hands, they were superbly dressed named Kang-yans-hell.[327] 12 small scarlet Flags, upon small staffs borne by Boys, 10 men with Horse Tails in their hands, waving them to the King, several of the Kings wives singing Praises to His Majesty harping upon the late De Souza's proceedings, towards the King, stating that through his interest he got Englishmen to bring what the King desired, she retired, another came out of the group and called upon EKoo-poo-hoo, the King's Brother and told him to come forward and listen, she sung at some length, occupied nearly an hour the Praises and e[n]comiums on his character and courage in war, he returned thanks, he received one head of cowries, it was presented to him by an old Lady, head of the Amazons, and confident [= confidante] to His Majesty her name is My ah-paa,[328] she harangued the group of women on her Knees, requesting them to sing to please their King, she retires, another sings a silvery note 2 heads are presented in the same manner as the first, requested to sing on, another stands up a Jenny Lind,[329] 4 heads are presented, and requested to sing on, her Tongue became more oily and sweet in the Kings ears, that he is constrained to send out 10 heads, 1 Keg of rum, 2 jars of rum, ornamented with Beads and cowries, they then commence in reality and sing his Praises aloud with a

---

[327] Not identified.
[328] I.e. Mahaikpa (cf. note 191).
[329] A famous opera singer (1820–1887), known as 'the Swedish nightingale'.

Chorus, They then call the King's sons and sisters, also his daughters, about 40 in number, The head of this regiment of Amazons address the Group on the munificent Present the King had given them, the[y] then presented them with a jar of the rum, they Kissed the ground and thanked her, rise and retire, King sent us a Gift of Gouruu[?] Nutts,[330] in a silver cup, for which we thanked his Majesty.

A Group advance to the Tent singing and calling aloud for His Majesty, to show himself before them he came out from the Tent, and danced a few steps before his chosen people, and retired amidst the thanks, and applauses of his people, with a volley of musketry, they drank to the King's health in skulls of their enemies, they are privileged to wear them in front, they sing & dance and present their muskets, spring a constables rattle[331] and retire from the ground, they were all well dressed and accoutred
200 of them.

Procession
20 women with Bows, and arrows, advance and salute the King, sing and dance for a short time, and pass on to the market, the first Procession was returned from there, passed the Tent, and went to their quarters, returned in a short time in Procession and saluted His Majesty and retired from the ground.

Procession
30 women belonging to his pensioned wives approached His Majesty and saluted him, with clapping of hands, and gesticulations of their bodies, singing and dancing, passed on the market
Band of music 9.

Procession
80 a regiment of Amazons or rather a Troop, or company, in front three silver Plated shields, officers with silver ornaments, in the shape of a Coronet on their heads, saluted the King by dancing, and singing his Praises, passed on to the market.

Procession
180 Elephant Guard advance and salute the King and sing aloud his Praises, dance and perform a number of evolutions, they were well dressed and accoutred, with white caps, the Elephant on them with Blue cloth, received a Gift of 3 Heads of cowries, 1 Large case Bottle of rum, passed on to the market.

---

[330] Reading uncertain, but probably referring to kola, *goro* in Hausa (cf. 'gooroo' in Beecroft (1841: 188)).

[331] In England, a policeman's rattle was used to raise an alarm: it is not clear whether this is used here literally or metaphorically.

Procession

20 men brought the Plan of the Town and situation of Kan-gaa-roo also 5 musquetoons, for our inspection, the Plan is made from a junk[332] of wood, at first sight in the distance it would be taken for stone,[333] it is a very good imitation, I presume of the place and its position, it would have been passed of as a stone only [= except for] our close inspection.

The Musquetoons are old excepting two and they are fitted for Percussion, which they have a dislike for, they would rather have Flints,[334] they requested us to make a memo of them, the King was anxious to have a number sent and all with Flints, we retired to our seats, a short time after we received a Gift of a Basket of Oranges, from His Majesty, we thanked him. My-haa-paa the aged Lady made her appearance from the Tent, the Mayo-gau was called, they met each other on their Knees, the conference was short, we were beckoned to, also Domingo Martins, we went from our seats, and were conducted into the King's presence, He shook each of us by the hand, and then began to show and point out to us the dilapidated state of his Tent, and enquired if he could not have one from England, I replied everything were to be got in that quarter, he then invited us to look at a large wooden sofa, of a very common structure, he expressed a wish for a new one, he then declined saying any more on that matter, he requested that we would call in the morning and take the dimensions of the Tent, and sofa, His Majesty then accompanied us outside of the Palace, to the center of the Square, he then stopped short and said that he was going to see his men soldiers receive some rum, had we any desire to accompany him, we declined, he said after which he intended to go to the market, to distribute cowries, and victuals, he wished us to accompany him, he said he would send a messenger when he wished us to come, we shook hands, and walked home, under the escort of an old Grey headed Eunuch, it was 6 o'clock when we reached our domicile, we had just time to swallow our dinner, when the messenger arrived, to state that His Majesty had left the Palace for the market, I accordingly put on a great Coat that I used to wear in England, and followed Count Nawhey, and our Interpreters, to our Hammocks, I was not in the smallest way conversant with the King's motives for going in the dark, to visit this scene of blood, as for his statement of going to throw away cowries, it was all Fudge, and a perfect Farce.

However we got into our Hammocks, and was soon at the main load [= road], when we were near the masses that were moving in regular Procession,

---

[332] I.e. lump.

[333] In fact, Forbes in the MS version of his 'Appendix' refers to 'the imitation Kanjaroo stone'.

[334] Vice-Consul Fraser in 1851 also recorded the Dahomian preference for flintlocks (2012: 65). Percussion caps (which had been introduced in the British army in 1839) were evidently still a novelty in Dahomey.

but it is only presumption, for it was too dark to see any distance except from the flash of musketry fired at intervals, we were arrested for a few minutes, to allow His Majesty's Hammock to pass in front, after which we moved into the Procession, amidst the din of all sorts of rude music, Guns, and the clamour of tongues, it was certainly a strange spectacle, it was conducted with order, and regularity, it speaks volumes, for such a well arranged system of order amongst a Barbarous people, it was certainly romantic being a fine star-light night, added to such a magical scene, we arrived at the Golgotha, they had formed a reception plan since yesterday we took our seats under a large Tree, directly opposite to us was the Cha-Cha he had a Lantern but not another glimmer was to be seen, only from the heavens, we remained seated about two minutes, when we moved on slowly, and dimly, into the receiving Court, we were seated but it was difficult to difine [=divine?] where, a Table was placed, and a Callabash with a great quantity of Country Chop, placed before us, but it was soon removed, and about 2 or 3 heads of Cowries, were sent by His Majesty as a Gift to each, they were taken possession of by the Mayo-gau, who said he would take care of them until tomorrow, shortly afterwards we were moved of the Palaver was done, His Majesty in front, we were in the rear, he went direct to the Palace, and we arrived at our Palace at 9 o'clock, having been two hours in performing this farce, it is all a cheat to throw sand in our eyes if possible, we were not more than half an hour at the market, I was pretty well tired of that day's ribaldry and Tomfoolery. Richardson['s] show of wild Beasts &c was of more value, and worth,[335] certainly it was a novel sight. I retired to rest at 10 o'clock night cool and pleasant, accompanied with dry w[r]

Tuesday 4th June

daylight cool pleasant w[r] Ther 75°, as usual went to take our usual walk down the Canna road, and returned by Bee-con and the Coommassee Palace, we passed through the Palace Square at 7 o'clock on our way from there to our own quarters we stumbled on the Mayogau, mounted on his Poney, with Banners, Band, and armed followers, we stopped, he dismounted, and joined us and unhesitatingly said we must go with him to the Palace, to measure the Tent, at the same time a messenger arrived that had been dispatched by him to our house, of course not finding us there, he was on his way to his master when we joined, we told [him] that our arrangements when we left the King last evening was 9 o'clock directly after Breakfast, that we could not enter to defile the King's Palace with this garb on unshaven, and

---

[335] Evidently alluding to the 'menageries' exhibiting wild animals which were popular in England at this period; however, 'Richardson's Show' was the name of a travelling theatre.

unwashed, he must allow us to go and dress we would return in half an hour, so he very reluctantly yielded, the fact is he is too old between seventy, and eighty, odd to state by the time I had commenced to shave a messenger arrived to tell us that the King wanted us, I told him to go and tell the Mayo, that I should not leave until I was thoroughly ready, as I had just delivered this another fellow arrived with the same tale, however he remained and left with us at 8.30 we were soon at the Palace Square, when we were seated under our old shady Tree, whilst we were sitting a body of armed Amazons came from the Palace, being the wives of the King we were obliged to give way, and move from our position, to let them pass, we could not look on them, after all the hurrys we were seated a full hour before we were admitted within the Palace, on our entrée the first thing that presented itself were 400 Basket of cowries on each side, which amounted to 800 heads which were to pay his men soldiers, we then went under the Tent, and measured its diameter 45 feet height 35 feet it is an old fashioned one it has a wooden frame, and covered with country cloth, over it a red Baize cover, and Painted with most awful devices cows heads, men cutting of heads &c &c &c they pestered us for half an hour about these awful devices that it must be exactly the same on the one ordered to be sent out, we told them that Captain Forbes has a sketch of it, they stated that the King is very anxious that it should be at Dahomey, at Abomey, by the or before the commencement of the next yearly Customs, the next in the demand was an old fashioned wooden sofa, Dimensions 9 feet by 4 feet wide common height, after all this we were anxious to leave not having had any Breakfast it was then 10.30 and had been obliged to inhale not the most agreeable perfume on an empty stomach. Patience is a great virtue in the interior of Africa, particularly at <u>Abomey</u>, they appraized His Majesty that we had done and were ready to leave he sent his compliments, stating that he was so busily engaged that prevented him from waiting on us, but we must take something before we leave, spirits and water were introduced, we tasted and drank the King's health, after a great deal of Procrastination, we got out of the Palace the Mayogau had a great desire for us to remain to see the soldiers paid, we told him that we had already counted the heads intended to be paid unless they only intended to pay part of them away no more was said we left at 11 o'clock and returned home and took Breakfast after which commenced writing my <u>Journal</u>, continued at it until 5 o'clock when it was communicated that the Mayogau was coming to pay us a visit, he at last arrived with the three saved ones, from an awful and ignominious death,[336] and were [omission?] and unfettered[,] no longer in the Bonds of slavery, the small canoe and two Baskets that they were each

[336] I.e. the three prospective victims for sacrifice on 31 May, who had been redeemed by Beecroft and Forbes (see pp. 43–4).

manacled in, accompanied them, they were eyewitnesses to eleven of their comrades or friends that were launched of to a fall of 12 or 14 feet on their heads previous to decapitation, I have mentioned it fully on the day the awful performance took place, the one I have is emaciated he has had a severe attack of dysentery and reduced to a skeleton, he informed us that it was from fright, thinking continually of the awful death that awaited him, the other two are more robust, and in good health, Capt Forbes administered medicine that he had brought with him from <u>Bonnetta</u> with directions to use it, we gave them a wrapper each, and Capt Forbes gave the sick man a Pair of Flannel Trousers, we expected of course that they were going to be placed at once under our charge, but the old Mayogau threw obstacles in the way stating that they were afraid they might run away as their country was not a long distance from Abomey, after due consideration we considered it as well as long as they were well fed, and comfortable, in conditions [= on condition] that they were shown to us every morning early, the matter was then concluded that it was likely they would be as comfortable as being here for we had very limited accommodation.

I handed over to Mayo my one hundred dollars [337] after a long Palaver about counting them they at last decided them right, and they were handed over to the King's messenger.

Mayogau took a Glass of Cordial and left, after which we dined, walked for an hour before our own premises, talking over the Politicks of the Dahomeians, as far as we could possibly dive into them. 8 o'clock we returned to the Grand Viziers Palace, chatted and smoked a cigar until 10 o'clock when we retired to rest.

Midnight fine dry w[r]

[Wednesday][338] 5th June

Daylight fine cool pleasant w[r] Ther 70° 5.30 Capt Forbes accompanied me on our usual walk, down the <u>Canna Minna</u> road about 200 yards from the Gates are Plantations two 32 Pounder cannonades [= carronades],[339] under umbrella Grass Tents, they had certainly escaped my eye hitherto, a mile further on the road is a small village on the right hand side of the Youribaa nation called <u>Laf-la-foo</u> that he [= Gezo] conquered, so he Planted a new Town of that nation in the Dahomeian nation[340] if he did so with all instead of murdering

[337] In payment for redemption of one of the 'saved ones'.

[338] MS gives 'Thursday'.

[339] I.e. short-barrelled, large-calibred cannon.

[340] Cf. Forbes (1851, i: 31, 68), who gives the name as 'Leffle-foo' (and describes it as a 'province of Anagoo'); Burton (1864, i: 286), 'Leflefun'. The destruction of this town is also recalled in Dahomian tradition (Le Herissé 1911: 323–4: 'Lèfou-Lèfou'), and is said to have occurred in

and selling, he would soon become a great man and make the Dahomeians a very great nation, he has a large Fetish house on upper side of the Laf-la-foo village, they have a fine Farm of Palm Trees, and corn, we walked on below the Bee-con road to a large Shea Butter Tree and returned direct by the same road and arrived at our domicile at 7.20 they brought the saved, the sick man appeared fresh & better, he received another dose of medicine and a Cup of Tea, they then returned to their lodgings, 8.30 took Breakfast, after which I commenced to write as usual my Journal, Noon the King's Brother named [blank] he is a piece of a mechanic,[341] he carved out the two Horses and several other figures in wood they are exceedingly well executed, gave him a Gift of 1 Scarf, J.B. [= John Beecroft] a piece of Cotton Print C.F. [= Captain Forbes] we took a Glass of wine he saw clearly that we were fully intent on what we were about, he very wisely said you are to[o] busily engaged, to be disturbed, if you will allow me I will take my leave, and call another day, to see when we were likely to be more at leisure, he very Politically took his leave. I continued my Journal until 5 o'clock, I then considered that all work and no play made Jack a dull boy; Capt Forbes had started of solus for a walk I strolled into the road under the shade of the large Tree when our Hammock-men and other Loungers, of the lazy part of the community were deeply engaged at different gambling Games, two or three more industrious than the rest with the Distaff and Bobbin spinning cotton, for making the small hand cast Netts,[342] Captain Forbes returned and we dined, Count Nawhey paid us a visit and informed us that the Kings women were going early in the morning to wash[343] that we must not go to walk,

we remonstrated and told him that we were not Prisoners, that it was unequivocally necessary for our health to take a walk in the morning, we could take an opposite direction to the King's wives, or women, we had not the least desire to look on their beautiful countenances, of the King's Harem, so we gained our point so the Palaver was set,[344] we continued our walk outside of the Prison walls, up and down the road with our body guard about us like Turkey Buzzards, and a fellow in the rear playing a Jews Harp, one of the late

---

1836/7 (according to the list of Gezo's campaigns given by Mouléro (1965: 52–3)): i.e. Refurefu, a town in Egbado (Law 1977a: 276–7). It is noteworthy that Beecroft here (as elsewhere: see pp. 37, 45 and notes 221, 255) classifies the Egbado as 'Yoruba', whereas Forbes (again, as elsewhere, see note 545) regards them as 'Anago'. This may reflect their use of different interpreters (see Introduction, p. xlvi), with Beecroft's interpreter Thomas Richards following the usage of British missionaries (derived from Sierra Leone), but Madiki Lemon giving Forbes the local usage in Dahomey.
[341] Forbes names the King's 'artisan brother' as 'Sohsar' (Journal, p. 163).
[342] I.e. fishing-nets.
[343] I.e. to the water source at Dido, north of Abomey, described by Beecroft later (p. 88).
[344] I.e. settled.

Mr Duncans retainers he accompanied him to the Kaa-ga-roo country he played very well on the Instrument[345] 7.30 returned to our domicile, and talked over different Topics until 10 o'clock then retired to rest.

Thursday 6th June

daylight fine cool w[r] Ther 75° 5.30 went out on our usual walk, went out at the Canna Gate, turned to the left on the Thing-gee road,[346] we went along the edge of the ditch of the Town from the Gate for half a mile when it turns abruptly to the NE, it is filled with <u>Prickly Acacia</u>, we kept on the road and left the ditch, about a mile farther on the right is a small Palace, belonging to the King,[347] I am informed that he has a very extensive one at Thin-gee about 20 miles from Abomey,[348] which he frequently visits one of our hammock bearers was sent by the <u>Ahygogan</u> [= Ahyvogan, i.e. Yovogan] of Whydah as a messenger to the King to report Mr Duncans death[,] on his arrival at Abomey, the King was at Tingee [*sic*] so he had of course to proceed there to report his unfortunate errand,[349] for which he said the King appeared to be much hurt, we walked for an hour on the road, and returned, there is very little cultivation going on to what is needed here, a great quantity of waste country, we arrived at 7.15 The saved were there the sick man much improved, gave him a dose of Quinine and wine, the other two said they did not eat Pork, or rather swines flesh, they belonged to the mallams or Priests,[350] they then returned to their quarters, we took our Breakfast, after which all the Brazillian liberated Africans, called to pay their respects, twelve of them, Houssa, Youribaa and <u>Bornouese</u>,[351] they told us that they came [i.e. to Dahomey] with an intention to go to their country and wished to land [at] Ahgway, or Badagry, but they were not allowed, they were obliged to land at <u>Whydah</u>, and lost the greater part of their Property, on landing and never got any

---

[345] A 'Jew's harp' is a small lyre-shaped instrument with a single metal tongue, played against the teeth. Duncan in 1845 played a Jew's harp before the King (1847, i: 254–5), and Forbes noted that in 1849 Duncan met at Abomey 'several old friends' whom he had taught to play the instrument (1851, i: 87).

[346] Tindji, 15 km north-east of Abomey.

[347] Not identified: no such palace is indicated on the maps in Monroe (2014: 131, 155, figs 4.8, 5.5).

[348] Cf. Monroe (2014: 126–7).

[349] In October 1849 Gezo said that he was about to go to Tindji, 'to make a custom to the memory of his mother' (Forbes 1851, i: 84). Tindji is said to have been the hometown of Gezo's mother Agotime (Bay 1998: 178).

[350] I.e. they were Muslims.

[351] Referring to their original homes, prior to their enslavement and transportation to Brazil. Descendants of Brazilian repatriates in Ouidah still recall their ancestors' African origins; they are mostly Yoruba but also include persons from Hausa and Borno (Law 2004b: 181).

redress, one aged man in particular had been in thraldom 56 years in the Brazils, he paid for his freedom 500 dollars, and 250 for his wife, they have been here about 14 years,[352] they brought a fair quantity of comforts with them, but unfortunately the[y] lost the greater part of them, but of course they could not get any redress, they were not allowed to Travel through the King of Dahomey's dominions, to their own country, so they are practically slaves at the present moment, for they cannot move without the King's permission, not even to Porto-Novo, along the Beach, they are obliged to visit Abomey at the Annual Custom, and produce Presents, and yearly Tribute money, I presume they will not leave [Abomey] before the Avyogah returns to Whydah, they received a Glass of Claret each and took their leave, sent of a messenger to Whydah, for romals,[353] &c, <u>Paper</u>, employed until 5 o'clock writing, Peter Brown arrived he called to pay his respects, he was asked to dine, he spent the Evening, and left at 8 o'clock, during which he communicated that he was going to England for what end or purpose he is at a loss to define[354] I asked him a plain question if he could inform me how many Tons of Palm Oil Domingo shipped from Porto Novo last year all he could make of it was 800 Tons same quantity from Whydah.[355] I have heard it reported that he actually cleared 80,000 dollars last year by Palm Oil.[356] Retired to rest at 10 o'clock.

Midnight cool dry w^r

Friday 7th June

We started as usual at 5.30 to take our morning walk, we went out at the Canna Gate, and turned to the left along the ditch of the Town, it is planted

---

[352] I.e. since *c*.1836: the re-emigration of ex-slaves from Brazil to Africa on a large scale began in the aftermath of the slave rebellion in Bahia, in north-east Brazil, in 1835 (ibid., 179).

[353] More usually spelled 'romaul', a sort of cotton cloth, originally made in India but also imitated in England.

[354] Brown apparently did visit England during 1850/1, but was back at Ouidah by October 1851 (Law 2016: 737).

[355] Martins' main base was at Porto-Novo, but he also had an establishment at Ouidah (Law 2004b: 201).

[356] Forbes had given this figure earlier in 1850: HCPP, *Slave Trade*, 1850/1, Class A, incl. 3 in no. 198: Forbes to Fanshawe, 6 April 1850. Forbes' account of a conversation with Martins on 10 June (Journal, p. 174) includes a statement by the latter (not reported by Beecroft) that he had made $70,000 by the palm-oil trade in the previous year (which is changed to $80,000 in the published version, see Forbes (1851, ii: 85)). On the assumption of a profit rate of 20 per cent (for which, see Law 2004b: 228), and a price for oil of $100 per ton, these figures would imply that Martins was turning over between 3,500–4,000 tons annually. Brown's figure of 1,600 tons seems more plausible. Note that in the following year, 1851, Martins' trade was estimated at over $200,000 annually, evidently gross, which would indicate around 2,000 tons (Fraser 2012: 30).

with prickly <u>acacia</u> we followed the road until, we reached the Caboceer of Whydah's Country House it is a beautiful country and a well cultivated farm, it has a Forest of Palm Trees about it, it is inherited by his brother after he was appointed Caboceer of Whydah, he is called Duc-co-cou,[357] a man has to be very circumspect under such a despot, he degrades and exalts at will, 6.30 we returned towards the Town, and arrived at our quarters at 7.15, found our saved ones waiting our arrival, found the sick man improved gave him Quinine, and wine,

A messenger arrived at 9.30 from the King we left and came to an interior Court at 10 o'clock,[358] 2 skulls ornamented the Gate Posts on each side, advanced & saluted the King, singing men in his procession.

3 Tombs covered with Grass, they were circular and ornamented for the occassion with silver ornaments, on their Tops. [359] we were seated directly opposite to the King to the right of the Fetish Gang, in the center[,] I was seated in the rear the Kings Crier, address the King a few sentences, Groups round the Court yard and country Umbrella's, The singing women had white bands round their heads, one of them had a baby in her arms, one dressed like a Harlequin,[360] with an old Shakoo,[361] and feather, they dance and shout then go on their Knees, and sing Praises aloud.

Kings sisters salute the King, by Kissing the ground, and throwing any quantity of dirt on their heads, and arms.

---

[357] Cf. Duncan (1847, ii: 259) and Forbes (1851, ii: 72–3). These name the place as 'Doko', 'Dehkon' (i.e. Dokon), while Duncan names the Yovogan's brother as 'Awassoo [= Awesu]', so perhaps 'Du-co-cou' is a confusion with the name of the place.

[358] Forbes (Journal, p. 171) says that this was in the Adanjloakodé section of the palace.

[359] Forbes here does not refer explicitly to 'tombs' but to '3 small tents', but he states (in his original journal, though not in the published version (1851, ii: 73–4)) that this was the first day of the 'Sequeahee', or 'earth-watering' custom, implying that sacrifices were offered to one or more of the deceased kings (presumably, as on subsequent occasions, in the evening, after the English party had left). References here and elsewhere to 'tombs' (or in Forbes, 'mausoleums') may relate not to the actual tombs (*adohó*) of the kings, but to buildings called *jèhó*, which contained only wrought metal commemorative altars called *asén* (Monroe 2014: 184–7). The 'silver ornaments' mentioned here (and subsequently) were probably a particular form of *asén* placed on roofs of *jèhó* (Bay 2008: 48, 51). Note that Forbes says that only the central one of the three buildings was topped by such an 'ornament', which perhaps suggests that only one king was involved in this day's rites. The identity of the king (or kings) honoured is uncertain. Burton's account of 'watering' ceremonies conducted by King Glele in 1864 (albeit at a different point in the ceremonial cycle) indicates that these began with rites for his father Gezo, at the latter's Kumasi palace (1864, ii: 167): possibly, therefore, these initial rites on 7 June 1850 were performed for Gezo's father Agonglo. However, they did not take place at Agonglo's suburban palace (which was in Gbèkon quarter, on the south of Abomey), but in the main palace.

[360] A pantomime character, whose costume was of variegated colours.

[361] Shako, a cylindrical military hat.

Mie-gaus people is called, a Gift of   6 heads[362]

May[o]-gau	D° " D°	D° "	6 D°		
Caboceer of Whydah	D°		6 D°		

1 Banner 2 very old Union Jack in rags

Ah-Qua-noo[363]	6	heads of Cowries		
Ah-joo-noo[364]	6	D° of D°		Palm oil Trader Whydah[365]
Que-jah	6	D°		Whydah
Quo-do-noo	6	D°	D°	
Nawhey	6	D°	D°	
	30			
Ah-che lee	4	D°	D°	English Fort Caboceer[366]
Ah-hee bah ne me	4	D°	D°	
Ah-sah-noo	4	heads of cowries		
Ah-do-moo-hun-soo	4	D° "	D°	
Eh-ah-hoo-ca na	2	D° "	D°	
Tom-hoo-tee [= Tometin]	2	D° "	D°	
Gan-sah [= Ganse]	2	D° "	D°	King's Brother
Too-koo-alaa-daa	2	D° "	D°	
Boo-ge-le-noo	2	D° "	D°	
Too-fah [= Tofa]	2	D° "	D°	King's Brother
Ah-jaa hoo[367]	2	D° "	D°	Abomey
Ah-ba-se-phaa	2	D° "	D°	Abomey
Buuge-foo	2	D° "	D°	English Town[368]
Buu jah-too-noo	2	D° "	D°	
Mah-nee	3	D° "	D°	

[362] For this list, see Forbes' Appendix, in TNA, FO84/827, ff. 289–302v; Forbes (1851, ii: 243–6). Forbes says (in the MS version) that it includes 'almost every name above the common attending the customs'.

[363] Quénum (also spelled 'Houénou), which is the name of a prominent merchant family of Ouidah, the person in 1850 being the founder of the family, Azanmado Quénum (Law 2004b: 176–7). The five names beginning with Quénum are those of the principal Dahomian merchants at Ouidah, those following being Adjovi, Codjia, Hodonou, and Gnahoui (see ibid., 201–2).

[364] Evidently miscopied: Forbes has 'Ah-joh-vee' (1851, ii: 243), i.e. Adjovi.

[365] Forbes earlier noted that Adjovi possessed 'a very extensive palm-oil plantation' at Ouidah (ibid., i: 115–16).

[366] I.e. the official who oversaw (and collected taxes from) the English fort at Ouidah. Cf. Forbes, Journal, p. 160, spelling the name as 'Heechelee'; Fraser (2012: 81), 'Ar-chil-lee': i.e. Hechili, the name of a Ouidah family descended from a Dahomian official (Law 2004b: 104).

[367] Ajaho, the title of the superintendent of the king's servants inside the palace, who was one of the seven 'great chiefs' (Le Herissé 1911: 37, 42).

[368] I.e. of Ouidah (cf. pp. 6–7).

Ah-voo-loo-Koo	2	D°	"	D°	Portuguese Town[369]
Juu-ah	2	D°	"	D°	Whydah
Too-su-pah-sah	2	D°	"	D°	
Ah-dee-de-noo	2	D°	"	D°	
Noo-de-fee-nie [= Noudofinin]	2	D°	"	D°	
Gac-sah	2	D°	"	D°	
Ah-si-voh	2	D°	"	D°	
Qui-tee-see	2	D°	"	D°	Whydah
Soo-gau [= Sogan]	2	D°	"	D°	
Boo-be-a-be-too	2	D°	"	D°	
Nee-pee-hong	2	D°	"	D°	King's Brother[370]
Ah-hoo-Pee [= Ahokpè]	2	D°	"	D°	
Soo-gom	3	D°	"	D°	
Ah-poo-na-paa	2	D°	"	D°	Whydah
Ah-buu-Ka-noo	2	D°	"	D°	
Si-wan-ah-hoo	2	D°	"	D°	
Ah-quo-gong[371]	2	D°	"	D°	
So-soo-so-too	2	D°	"	D°	
Ah-go-doo	2	D°	"	D°	
Ah-ting-baa	2	D°	"	D°	
Hoo-gang	2	D°	"	D°	
Tah-poh[372]	2	D°	"	D°	
Koo-sah	2	D°	"	D°	
To-goo	2	D°	"	D°	
Yo-go-bo-lo-Koo	2	D°	"	D°	
Ah-go-so-too	2	D°	"	D°	
A-deh-ma-noo	2	D°	"	D°	
Boo-Kong[373]	2	D°	"	D° ∘	
Ba-caa-swa[374]	2	D°	"	D°	
Ah-baa-hoo	2	D°	"	D°	
Ba-Ka-do-doo[375]	2	D°	"	D°	

[369] I.e. the quarter of Ouidah associated with the Portuguese fort (also called Docomè).

[370] Cf. 'Enekpehun', given as the name of a brother of Gezo by Burton (1864, ii: 126, n.). This seems to be a variant spelling of 'Linpehoun', which appears later in Beecroft's journal as 'Laa-pee-hoo', etc.

[371] Forbes has 'A-poh-loh-gau' (1851, ii: 243), which suggests Aplogan, the title of the provincial governor of Allada, who was counted among the seven 'great chiefs' (Le Herissé 1911: 37, 44).

[372] Forbes has 'Tok poh', i.e. Tokpo: cf. note 283.

[373] Forbes, 'Boh Kon' (1851, ii: 244), perhaps *buko*, 'diviner,' a priest of Fa, the *vodun* of divination.

[374] Ibid., 'Boh Koh soo ah', perhaps *buko* + a personal name.

[375] Ibid., 'Boh Koh da dah', perhaps *buko Dada*, 'the king's diviner'.

Ah-he-la-puu	2	Dº	”	Dº	
Coo-oh-pa-laa	2	Dº	”	Dº	
Soo-po-vee	2	Dº	”	Dº	
Ah-daa-ye-ree	2	Dº	”	Dº	
Ah-hoo-noo	2	Dº	”	Dº	
Sa-ba-dag-ba-hoo	2	Dº	”	Dº	
Sa-paa-doo-noo	2	Dº	”	Dº	
Maa-ah-vee	2	Dº	”	Dº	
Ah-daa-see-gaa	2	Dº	”	Dº	woman
Oh-caa-mo-noo	2	Dº	”	Dº	
Baa-Kaa-jaak-tee	2	Dº	”	Dº	
Ba-ah-baa	2	Dº	”	Dº	
Du-ja-ah	2	Dº	”	Dº	
Ah-noo-ah-noo	2	Dº	”	Dº	
Ha-naa-noo	2	Dº	”	Dº	
Ba-da-see-cha-cha[376]	2	Dº	”	Dº	
Che-che	2	Dº	”	Dº	
Voo-do-ng-hoo[377]	2	Dº	”	Dº	
To-Koo-vee-so[378]	2	Dº	”	Dº	
Ah-ja-wa-nee	2	Dº	”	Dº	
Ah-da-fan-coo	2	Dº	”	Dº	
Ah-che-lee-vee[379]	2	Dº	”	Dº	
Ah-hoo-too	2	Dº	”	Dº	
Ta-vee-saa[380]	2	Dº	”	Dº	
Ah-hoo-vee[381]	2	Dº	”	Dº	
Ah-hoo-pah	2	Dº	”	Dº	
Sam-baa-die	2	Dº	”	Dº	
Kaa-saa-bah	2	Dº	”	Dº	
Oh-faa-noo	2	Dº	”	Dº	
La-ha-coo-baa	2	Dº	”	Dº	
Ah-daa-wee-dee	2	Dº	”	Dº	
Uh-bang-waa	2	Dº	”	Dº	
Eh-an-dee	2	Dº	”	Dº	
Chaa-ma-noo	2	Dº	”	Dº	

[376] Presumably, 'Chacha's Badeesee'.
[377] Perhaps *vodunno*, 'priest'?
[378] Forbes, 'Toh koo noo veh soo' (1851, ii: 244); cf. note 279.
[379] I.e. Hechili-vi, 'Little Hechili' (or 'Hechili junior').
[380] Tavisa is remembered as the title of an official concerned with the levying of a tax on palm-oil production (Le Herissé 1911: 86).
[381] Perhaps *ahovi*, 'prince': but Forbes has 'ah-oh-see', which might be *ahosi*, 'king's wife' (1851, ii: 244).

Dig-nee-voo	2	D°	,,	D°
Ka-tag boo hee	2	D°	,,	D°
Joh-oh-nee-gee	2	D°	,,	D°
Haa-gee-ma-coo	2	D°	,,	D°
Taa-see	2	D°	,,	D°
Maa-bon-doo	2	D°	,,	D°
Baa-taa-Ke-see	2	D°	,,	D°
Mah-eh-see	2	D°	,,	D°
So-man-gee	2	D°	,,	D°
Poo-suu-pah[382]	2	D°	,,	D°
Taa-paa	2	D°	,,	D°
Haa-nuu-mee	2	D°	,,	D°
Ah-qua-que	2	D°	,,	D°
Jun-qua-ne	2	D°	,,	D°
Hung-Baa-gee[383]	2	D°	,,	D°
Hee-dee-gee	2	D°	,,	D°
Ah-dang-boo-see	2	D°	,,	D°
Waa-ah-ta	2	D°	,,	D°
Zah-Kaa-nee[384]	2	D°	,,	D°
Ah-hoo-ma-see	2	D°	,,	D°
Ah-lo-do-fo-no-Koo K[ing's] B[rother][385]				
	2	D°	,,	D°
Baa-da-hoo [= Badahun]	2	D°	,,	D°
Ah-bo-Ko-sar	2	D°	,,	D°
Poo-goo	2	D°	,,	D°
Poh-bah	2	D°	,,	D°
Ag-goo-se-vou-sou	2	D°	,,	D°
Voo-dose-gee-hoo	2	D°	,,	D°
Voo-daa[386]	2	D°	,,	D°
Vo-no-er-gaa	2	D°	,,	D°
Ah-vah-he-hee	2	D°	,,	D°
Vo-do-noo-ah-puu-nee[387]	2	D°	,,	D°

[382] Possibly 'Fosupo', deputy to the female Posu (Burton 1864, i: 224).

[383] I.e. Houngbadji, later identified as a female military officer (p. 111).

[384] Perhaps 'Zokhenu', deputy to the female Gau (Burton 1864, i: 222).

[385] Forbes here has 'Ah-boh-loh-poh-noo-gan' (1851, ii: 244), and elsewhere 'Ahlohlohpohnokou', described as 'next to', i.e. deputy/assistant to the Posu (Journal, p. 186): cf. 'Alo-lokpo-nun-gan', mentioned as a brother of Gezo by Burton (1864, i: 313, n.; ii: 126, n.); and also 'Alodokponugan', given later as the title of 'the senior brother of the reigning king, who served as titular head of ... the royal family' (Bay 1998: 300; Le Herissé 1911: 183).

[386] Cf. Burton (1864, ii: 126, n.), 'Voda, brother to the present king [Glele]', i.e. a son of Gezo.

[387] The first element seems to be *vodunno*, 'priest'; 'ah-puu-nee' is perhaps a personal name.

Wu-maa-hoo	2	Dº	”	Dº	
Bu-too-paa-soo	2	Dº	”	Dº	
Maa-voo-dee	2	Dº	”	Dº	
Ah-gen-na-ga[388]	2	Dº	”	Dº	
Ah-to-ah-noo	2	Dº	”	Dº	
Ah-huu-gan	2	Dº	”	Dº	
Ah-jaa-baa	2	Dº	”	Dº	Prince of Ashantee
Baa-daa-tie	2	Dº	”	Dº	woman
Noo-no-voh	2	Dº	”	Dº	King's son[389]
Bah-kon-see	2	Dº	”	Dº	
Sah-ah-vaa	2	Dº	”	Dº	
Ah-jaa-caa-la	2	Dº	”	Dº	
Ah-waa-sog-bah	2	Dº	”	Dº	
Ah-bo-va-nah	2	Dº	”	Dº	
Gee-wah-naa-nan	2	Dº	”	Dº	
Zaa-ha-Kaa	2	Dº	”	Dº	
Ah-foo-pin-Kaa	2	Dº	”	Dº	
Dou-hoo-noo	2	Dº	”	Dº	
Ah-eh-jah	2	Dº	”	Dº	
Ye-ah-voo	2	Dº	”	Dº	
Ah-paa-see	2	Dº	”	Dº	
Do-soo-la-gee	2	Dº	”	Dº	
Tah-nee	2	Dº	”	Dº	
To-saa-noo	2	Dº	”	Dº	
Ba-daa-nee	2	Dº	”	Dº	
Zoo-hoo-see	2	Dº	”	Dº	
Ah-da-eh-see	2	Dº	”	Dº	
Ah-taa-chee	2	Dº	”	Dº	
Ah-dan-eh-fau	6	Dº	”	Dº	
Too-so-de-noo-bee-vee	4	Dº	”	Dº	
Maa-du-Kaa [= Madiki]	4	Dº	”	Dº	Interpreter
Hoo-tong-gee[390]	2	Dº	”	Dº	
Boo-gan-nee	2	Dº	”	Dº	

[388] Forbes here has 'Ah-doh-ne-jeh' (1851, ii: 245), which suggests 'Adanejan', a nephew of Gezo, who in 1863/4 was serving as the royal counterpart to the Migan and was a 'favourite at court' (Burton 1864, i: 221), recalled in tradition as Adandejan (Bay 1998: 249–50).

[389] Cf. 'Nonnovo', said to be Gezo's eldest daughter, but reportedly 'a woman passing as a man' (Burton 1864, ii: 126, n.).

[390] Cf. Forbes, Journal, p. 163, 'Hatongee, the silver smith'; Burton (1864, ii: 34), 'Hun-to-ji, or King's silversmith': i.e. Hountondji, the family name of the blacksmiths of Abomey (Bay 1998: 191–2).

The People belonging to Doo-Koo[391]	6 heads
Ah-loo-Pee[392]	6 heads
Suu-gang	6 heads
Kings Brothers	6 heads
Ah-baa-goo-doo mee	2½ D°
Ambassador from Ashantee Oh-coo-coo[393]	<u>6 D°</u>
Oh-maa-se-pah-dee	2 heads
Bah-loo-cuu	2 D°
Ah-Zoo	1 D°
Gah-ah-mah	2 D°
Doo-sah-pah	2 D°
Ah-caa-loo-go	2 D°
Pee-daa-pa-taa	2 D°
Dee-goo-loo-gee	2 D°
Ah-poh-toh	2 D°
Maa-tou-soo	2 D°
Boo-Koo-cha-paa[394]	2 D°
Ah-tang	2 D°
Ah-do-maa	2 D°
Ah-la-qua-Koo	2 D°
Ah-maa-soo[395]	2 D°
Yah-whe nee	2 D°
Eunuchs	2 D°
Do-goo-koo-soo	3 D°
Ah-maa-gee	3 D°
Pee-daa	2 D°
Pah-nee-gan's people[396]	2 D°
Cam-baa-die [= Kanbode]	6 D°
To-noo-noo Eunuch	4 D°

---

[391] I.e. Dokon, the location of the estate of the Yovogan's brother (cf. p. 76, with note 357). The MS version of Forbes' Appendix here has 'Eeavoogons Brother', the printed version (1851, ii: 245), 'People from Dekkon'.

[392] I.e. Alokpè: subsequently identified as a military officer (p. 146).

[393] I.e. the Akan name Kwaku (given to sons born on a Wednesday); this man is called by Forbes 'Coco Santee', presumably 'Kwaku Asante' (1851, ii: 245). For diplomatic relations between Dahomey and Asante in this period, see Law (1994a: 161–2).

[394] Again, perhaps *buko*, 'diviner' + a personal name; Forbes has 'Boh-ko-che-ah-peh' (1851, ii: 245), which suggests Tchiakpè, the name of a family in Ouidah (Law 2004b: 21, 69).

[395] Forbes has 'Ah moo soo', i.e. Amusu, a common Fon personal name.

[396] *Kpanlingán* is the name of a sort of gong, but it is also used as a title for a royal praise-singer, who uses this instrument (Glélé 1974: 112–13).

Kah-so-peh[397]	4 D°
Taow-pooh[398]	3 D°
To-noo-gan	2 D°
Ahbooo-ge-pee	2 D°
Ah-mu-na-suu paa	2 D°
Haah-dee	1 D°
Go-goo	1 D°
La-gaa-groo	1 D°
Ka-gee-nee-Koo	1½ D°
Ah-Paa-doo	1 D°
Hong-see-noo	1 D°
Bah-whee pah[399]	1 D°
De Souza or Cha-Cha and the rest	5 D°

Brazillian liberated Africans who bought their own freedom

	6	Viva Viva Le Rie de Dahomy
Bah-gaa-dee the Mahee King	3	Tributary[400]
58 Caboceers	6 heads	
Ah-puu-eh-peh	3 D°	
Du-mah-goo-loo-gee[401]	3 D°	
Drummers	3 D°	
Poo-voo-soo's [people]	1	
Court fool	1 Head	
Ah-poo the court crier	2 D°	
May[o] receives	80 D° to give amongst a number	

that were absent and would meet in his Yard, as stated by himself, and Nawhey

Band of music	12 heads
Caboceer [*sc.* of Ouidah?]	a Bottle of rum & 1 head

sings and invites the King to come in the midst, he complys, dances, salutes us and retires

Ah-baa-Jah Poueh a Band of music

several in scarlet wrappers ornamented with small Horns, on their heads

---

[397] Perhaps miscopied for 'Kah-oo-peh', as Forbes has 'Koao-peh' (1851, ii: 246), probably the same as the 'Cou-pah' later described as 'store-keeper to the King' (p. 148).

[398] 'To-oo-poh' in Forbes, i.e. Tokpo (cf. note 283).

[399] Forbes here has 'Mee-ah-wee-pah', i.e. Mahaikpa.

[400] Gbaguidi, the title or dynastic name of the kings of Savalou, north-west of Mahi: cf. 'Bagadee' in Duncan (1847, ii: 224). Duncan, who visited Savalou in 1845, confirms that it was subject to Dahomey: strictly, it was a distinct country from Mahi, but its king exercised authority over part of the Mahi country (ibid., 229–30).

[401] Identified by Forbes as 'king of Pangweeah' (1851, ii: 246), i.e. Paouignan, in Mahi; also visited and described by Duncan, who noted its recent 'subjection' to Dahomey (1847, ii: 17–26, 'Paweea').

7 Guards, 10 with Horses Tails in their hands, skulls in a Brass Calla-bashes, sing aloud, His Majesty's praises, receive a case Bottle of rum and retire, all the cowries, that were to be distributed, had been given, so we were tired out by the continual tirade of singing, and dancing the same time

Sent Nawhey to ask permission to depart the rest of Cha-Cha's party appeared more anxious than ourselves to depart, we were allowed to leave, went and saluted the King, and left, accompanied by Domingo, and Ignatio de Souza, we took leave of each other, in the Grand Square, Domingo Martins, told us that he expected to leave in a day or two for Whydah, that he would [call?] on us previous to his departure, when we arrived at our quarters it was 3 o'clock, being early, we made up our minds to go to the Market being the first time that we had had opportunity, since our arrival, for it is held every fourth day,[402] there are petty ones every day, we had to send to inform the King, our Whydah Interpreter, said it would be advisable to do so else some person would tell him that they had seen us, at the Ah-jaa-hee Market, he might be displeased, as we left the Court yard, previous to all the singing Parties, finishing their songs of Praise.

it was all right we proceeded to the place, it was rather late, a great number had left, their commodities were in very small lots, it is extensive the ground, I did not see any fine country cloths, or Grass Cloths, I bought a few small articles of country manufacture, not seeing any fine grass or other cloths, I postponed purchasing any, for that day.

It was a novel sight to see Peter Brown a Black Cape Coast man, in our front in a Hammock,[403] and our two Interpreters in our rear with each of our Umbrellas over their Pates, it was amusing the market people enjoyed it, see-ing two white men without either, it was I dare say considered by the commu-nity ridiculous, for our Interpreters were ashamed and struck their umbrellas, I took two or three turns through the market, and purchased some cotton as a specimen, to send to Manchester,[404] but, I did not see any quantity, all that I got was half a head of cowries, I had not an opportunity of weighing it, Peter Brown had sent his Hammock on, he joined us and said that Domingo Martins, had authorized him to state, that whatever we might require, during our stay at Abomey and Whydah, if it was in his store, that it was at our ser-vice, that on his arrival at <u>Whydah</u>, he would give his principal orders to that effect, we told him to thank him, and should we be in want we should avail ourselves of his Kind offer, if necessary, after dinner we walked in front of

---

[402] The major markets in Abomey, with those of Kana and Zogbodomè, followed a four-day cycle, with Adjahi on the first and Houndjro on the second day (Burton 1864, i: 335, n.).

[403] Brown was allowed to use a hammock because he was considered a 'white man' (Law 2016: 741).

[404] The Manchester Chamber of Commerce had corresponded with Beecroft earlier in 1850 about the promotion of cotton cultivation in West Africa (Ratcliffe 1982: 92).

our Hammock until 8 o'clock, entered and discussed matters of the day, and retired at 10 o'clock. Thermometer at noon today 84° at sunset 78° rather higher than it usually has been.

Saturday 8th June

I arose at the usual hour 5 o'clock, Ther 75°, 5.30 started for a walk down the Canna Road, and returned by <u>Bee-Kon</u>, of course passed the Coommassee Palace, and cast an eye at the market,[405] it was too early, there were but few articles at that early hour 7 o'clock we were several times arrested on our walk by the tinkling of small Bells warning us of the approach of the King's Wives, we wheeled round, and showed our backs until they were passed, on our route home we met Poo-voo-soo with a stick in his hand the head of it bandaged, carefully with a piece of country cloth, he was white washed round his eyes, and mouth, which gave him rather an odd appearance, the same person is frequently mentioned in my Journal, he accosted us in bad English your servant (Sir) we asked him to allow us to see his stick, he instantly complied and took of the wrapper, it was a Copper Image, and a skull with it, of the same, we asked him who it was symbolical of, he said it was a Caboceer named [blank] of one of the Maa-hee Provinces, taken by the late King's Father, and beheaded,[406] he said it was in his Keeping, after which we took our leave and arrived at our mansion, at 7.15 our saved ones were waiting our arrival, administered medicine to the sick man, gave them their Provissions, they then returned to their quarters, Mr Peter Brown called on us, we entered into a dialogue about Ah taa pam, it is too obvious by all that can be gleaned, it has not had a successful issue, for he [= the King] lost 150 and captured about 230, so says report, it must have been an exp[en]sive war, and as[?] so without any Profit. In the mean time a messenger arrived said to be from the King to state that he is going to hold a (Levee) in his inner Court to day, I strongly suspect that it is not the case that the old <u>Mayo-gau</u> has only had a pleasant dream, it was at last decided that it would be safe for us to see the market, they are famous Procrastinators 11.30 we left and reached it at 12 o'clock, it was very much thronged we went round it several times, that is in the vicinity where the stands are for the sale of country cloth &c &c, purchased several [h]andsome specimens of Brass and Iron manufactures, returned home at 2 o'clock on our way purchased ½ a dollars worth of cotton I laid out 13¾ dollars, in cowries, I wrote until 5 o'clock, after dinner Mr Brown called on us and reported the news of the day, he stated that the

---

[405] I.e. Houndjro market.
[406] I.e. King Agonglo: Dahomian tradition recalls that he defeated and killed Adjognon, king of the Mahi town of Gbowélé (Le Herissé 1911: 310–11).

Cha-Cha had received a Letter from Whydah, stating the capture of a fine <u>Brig</u> by H.M. Steamer Gladiator they did not know a word about it until the 4th inst. she was captured the 28 Ultimo[407] and the Crew not landed for nearly a week,[408] I believe Cha-Cha is embarked in the matter it will be unpleasant intelligence, Mr Peter Brown remained rather long and late he became tedious, it was 10 o'clock then I was obliged to give him a strong hint that we always made it a point of retiring mostly at 9 o'clock, he made some mystical assertions, Carr of the late Niger Expedition Governor of the Model Farm, he stated that the canoe threw overboard a quantity of the manillas[409] Composition [= comprising?] their own Property to receive Mr <u>Carr</u>'s Property, it is too obvious their intentions after such a proceeding, he ought not to have been allowed to have entered the Canoe, it is a strange report:[410] we retired at 10.30 to rest

Midnight fine w[r]

Sunday, 9th June

daylight fine dry w[r] 5 o'clock Ther 76° 5.30 started on our morning walk Brown accompanied us, we walked about three miles down the Canna Road, to a large Shea Butter Tree, and arrived back at our quarters at 7.15 as usual our saved ones were there, the sick man improving gave them Victuals, and they returned to their quarters, after cooling myself after my morning walk, I had a tepid wash and then took a light Breakfast, read a chapter in my Bible, then I was obliged to write my Journal, 11.30 Mr Brown called and informed us that the whole of the De Souza's and Domingo Martin, had gone to the King to hold a Conference, various inferences was and may be drawn, reports say that Isadore de Souza, is in debt to Domingo 42000 dollars, and that Ignatio and Antonio have gone to prove the debt,[411] and that he [= Isidoro] owes the King on his Fathers account, a great amount 100,000 dollars,[412] if it is the case, they knowing too well our errand, it is then too obvious their motive, only to prove that if the abominable traffic is abolished, they have not

---

[407] The *Bom Fim*, captured on 25 [*sic*] May 1850: HCPP 1851/2, *Slave Trade*, Class A, incl. in no. 147: List of Vessels Captured or Detained ... 1 March 1850–28 Feb. 1851 (not included in TASTD, though this does include an earlier voyage by the same ship, no. 4594).

[408] Crews of slave ships arrested by the British Navy were sometimes put ashore.

[409] I.e. bracelets, of copper, which served as currency in the Niger Delta.

[410] Alfred Carr was the prospective manager of the cotton plantation established at Lokoja on the Niger by the British expedition of 1841, but went missing and was presumed to have been murdered on the lower Niger in November 1841, Brown being a witness of the circumstances of his disappearance (Allen & Thompson 1848, ii: 150, n.).

[411] I.e. to verify it.

[412] Duncan in 1849 heard that at his death de Souza was in debt to the King for $80,000: HCPP, *Slave Trade*, 1849–50, Class B, no. 7: Duncan, Whydah, 22 Sept. 1849.

the means of liquidating their debts, however it remains for a more decisive explanation, as our information is only fabulous and imaginary[.] Pm a Partial shower of rain, 2.30 it cleared away and became a very fine day. Ther 78 at 2.30. 4.30 gave up waiting for the day, took a short walk to the Canna Gate and back, on my way a quarrel ensued with a gang of wool gatherers, all women, several young ones but one in particular, an elder, was determined to have a fight and when remonstrated with by the lookers on and passers by, she still persisted in spite of all reason and sensible advices she said she was a slave and did not fear death.

two men then interfered and took her by force, and carried her away for some distance I retired home, Capt Forbes soon after made his appearance, and we dined at 5 o'clock, after which Brown called, and stated that Domingo had but just left the Palace[.] in the evening in the course of Conversation, Domingo was several times mentioned of his promise through him [= Brown] to wait on us on a certain day, and that we had neither seen nor heard anything of him, and that I entirely laid the blame on Brown, and that I had formed my opinion on the matter altogether, I then told him that it appeared only in one light, that he Domingo never intended to call, and that I strongly believed Mr Brown's statement to be fallacious, and unprincipled,[413] I gave him a severe cathecising [= catechizing],[414] and rebuke, and he endeavoured in the most abject way to clear him self, but I would not admit of it, so he left, and we retired to rest at 10 o'clock. a fine dry evening.

Midnight fine dry w[r]

Monday 10th June

daylight cloudy with fresh Breezes westerly no umbrella's from the Mayo-gau according to promise to protect us from the Sun's rays, for he professes equal affection for us, and says he hopes to see us again, 6 o'clock took a cup of coffee, after which a messenger arrived with the King's stick, to enquire after our welfare, and stated that the King wanted to see us to day, now this was the first time that a messenger had been sent from the King in that novel way, during which the Umbrella's made their appearance, Maa-daa-kee, and Nawhey, were sent for to communicate with the messenger and the Mayo-gau to ascertain the fact on this important matter several peas and cous,[415] and in the interim Nawhey brought in two coats to try for six dollars, each, we took them to be settled on our return, at last it was decided that we might start and return by three or four o'clock, to see the King, it was 7 o'clock when we

---

[413] But in fact, Martins did call on the English party the next day (see p. 91).

[414] I.e. cross-questioning.

[415] Perhaps 'Ps & Qs', referring to rules of propriety.

started, we arrived in sight of the Hills at 8.15[416] fully expecting, by the accounts given to have two or three hours going, so much for their knowledge of distances, the description they had given me was an extraordinary one, our Interpreter had accompanied Mr Thomas Hutton of Cape Coast to the same place,[417] I enquired of him the appearance of the place he said it was a large Hole, and high mountains in the rear, The Hill we stood on overlooked a beautiful valley, with conical, and undulating Hills, and beyond about 40 miles beyond in the distance Hills, and two or three flat ones like table land, they are named by the Dahomeians Dab a Dab Hills[418] a consistency they make from corn &c by that name and in the shape of those two Hills,[419] we sat down on a large stone of conglomerate, and Iron, and took a hearty Breakfast of part of a Guinea fowl and a Bottle of Ale, between us, after which we descended into the valley, and walked about a mile to a swamp. a great number of people were passing backwards, and forwards, for water, we bought a Pot for our own use, and left on the Hill the greater part of the Hammock Bearers. The recevoirs [= reservoirs] are merely Holes dug into the swamp,[420] we returned on our way back we passed the ruins of a Farm and House, beset with Palm Trees, it belongs to the Kings Brother he formerly resided altogether [*sic*], but since the King anointed him a Caboceer, he is obliged to live at Abomey,[421] his son is left in charge it is in an awful dilapidated state, I really thought to have found a well, by the description, an enemy coming upon them from that quarter might very readily, cut off their supplies of water, it might be awfully acted upon by poisoning the Holes, we ascended the Hill again at 9 o'clock, and on our way picked up a number of specimens of chalk, Iron stone, and Granite, it was rather unfortunate that

---

[416] Referring to a high point to north-west of Abomey, with a view of hills in the distance, which Duncan and Forbes had visited in October 1849 (Forbes 1851, i: 71; ii: 82).

[417] This was probably during Hutton's visit to Gezo in 1839/40, when he reported seeing 'beyond Abomey, northwards, land of a hilly character': HCPP, *Select Committee on the Slave Trade*, Minutes of Evidence, §10329, evidence of W.M. Hutton, 22 July 1842.

[418] Duncan had reported this as the name of a group of hills which he observed in the distance to the east during his journey through the Mahi country in 1845 (1847, ii: 38), referring presumably to the hills of Savè, 100 km north-east of Abomey. However, the hills now seen by Beecroft and Forbes were evidently those of the Mahi country itself, the nearest of which, Gbowélé, is about 55 km from Abomey: either they misapplied the name 'Dab-a-dab', or it was used generically of hills of this shape. The valley between is that of the River Zou, which formed the boundary between Dahomey and Mahi.

[419] For the corn cakes called 'dab-a-dab' see p. 63. The wording is awkward, seeming to say that the cakes were named after the hills, whereas the reverse is the case.

[420] The main water source for the royal palace at Abomey, named by Burton (1864, ii: 236, 241) as 'Diddo', i.e. Dido (or Didonou). Forbes refers to 'deep pits' (1851, i: 72). Beecroft and Forbes provide the earliest documentation of such man-made 'caves' (or *souterrains*) in the Abomey area, which have recently attracted archaeological study (Randsborg & Merkyte 2009, i: 60–97).

[421] It is not clear which of the many brothers of Gezo mentioned by Beecroft and Forbes this was.

the weather was dull and cloudy, not clear as usual, but I presume from our position to the Hills in the distance it must be between 35 and 40 miles, across the valley our elevation is about 120 feet, as I scanned my eye over it, I could only discover two or three farms in the distance, it is not more than 5 miles from <u>Abomey</u>, the features of the country is completely changed, from a Plain to an undulating country, as far as the eye can discern, our Interpreter's idea of the Kong mountains,[422] is vague and erroneous, he said they were in the smoke beyond, or rather the clouds, I told him the distance was too great under any atmosphere to see the distance they must be of, but he cannot have the smallest idea of a mountain, never having seen one, there are two or three pretty conical Hills in the valley, beautiful situations[,] it was once thickly populated and of course richly cultivated, and interspersed with numerous villages, years ago in the present King's Grandfather's day, they were Hostile to each other, and he being the stronger devastated it and so it has remained as we now see it,[423] took a little refreshment and started on our Hammocks, at 10 o'clock, and arrived at the Palace Square in an hour and ten minutes so it is not more than five miles. The King was holding a <u>Levée</u> to pass <u>Domingo</u>,[424] with his women soldiers, he was polite enough not to allow us to pass, without the compliments of the morning, although we were in dishabille[425] after a good walk, we would much rather have declined appearing in our morning dress, at the King's Levee of his choice Amazons, however no excuse would be allowed, so we entered the Square, of his Troops, and saluted His Majesty he asked in a jocular manner, if we had not brought him some Breakfast from the country we had been visiting, we told him it had gone on before us, but on our arrival at our quarters we would send him some part, in

---

[422] This name was at this period applied by Europeans to a mountain range which was wrongly thought to extend throughout the interior of West Africa (Bassett & Porter 1991). Duncan had earlier used it to refer to the hilly country of Mahi (1847, i: 272, etc.).

[423] This reference to devastation presumably relates to the Mahi country, beyond the River Zou. Gezo's grandfather, King Kpengla, is credited by a contemporary source with a campaign against the Mahi, who were 'routed with great slaughter' and the country 'ravaged' (Dalzel 1793: 165–6). But there were also subsequent wars. Kpengla's successor Agonglo fought successfully against the Mahi, destroying the town of Gbowélé (see note 406; cf. also Akinjogbin 1967: 180–1). Duncan in 1845 found the site of the town of Gbowélé, on the summit of the hill, deserted and still strewn with bones from its destruction by the Dahomians, but implied that this had occurred more recently, the current Dahomian governor of the area having been appointed after its surrender (1847, ii: 9–14). An earlier contemporary report refers to Dahomey's recent conquest of some 'districts' of Mahi, which might be the campaign referred to by Duncan (Robertson 1819: 268–9): from the date, this must have occurred under Agonglo's successor Adandozan (1797–1818), but it is not recalled in Dahomian tradition, which insists that Adandozan's campaigns were uniformly unsuccessful, in order to justify his deposition by Gezo (Le Herissé 1911: 312).

[424] I.e. give permission to leave.

[425] I.e. informally dressed (French *déshabillé*).

the mean time he sent spirits, and water, and took a little with us, a shout and firing of muskets, he again reminded us that a friend going out early in the morning, to the country, should not forget to send his friend a part (a metaphor), after which he invited us to remain and see the performance, we excused ourselves and asked him to allow us to go to our quarters and dress &c that we would do ourselves the honour to return in half an hour Domingo Martin was there <u>solus</u>. Troops of women soldiers advancing and singing his Praises aloud, for Guns, Powder, and Rum, he sent as a present before they went to the last war.

We returned home and changed our habille and returned to the Palace Square with our retinue bearing as under

5 Kegs of rum 2 large case Bottles of Gin and 2 Bottles of Cordials.

We encountered the King in the square I presume he had been dismissing Domingos Martins for he was in the midst of a Party of his male soldiers advancing to the ground we saluted him and he shook hands, I told him that I had brought him a small present from the place I had visited this morning, in sight of Dab-a Dab Hills, he smiled and conducted us to a seat, Amazon Troops withdrew, a select party of the men, and two boys, came on the ground amongst them was one of the King's sons they commenced to sing and dance accompanied by a Band of music, I have not seen before any African dances so well performed, it was quite Theatrical, it would not have disgraced Drury Lane, or Covent Garden, They were officers excepting the two boys.

It continued two hours, the figures[426] were numerous during the time, every fresh sequence two leaders of the party advanced to the musicians, and sung the tune, it was very pleasing to the ear, their attitudes were graceful and well performed, very much different to most African dances that I have seen, and it is not a few during Twenty one years, every now and then they struck up a vocal chorus to the tune, they frequently were stopped and the two leaders advanced to correct the music, for they danced particularly to tune.

An Amazon rose and said they must finish their dance quick, for they had occupied the ground too long already, that they wished to perform, their performance was ended in about fifteen minutes after the Amazons speech, the two boys advanced to the musicians, and sung a tune from them to play for the finale.

King sent us a Gift of a small Basin of Palm nutts, two small case bottles of rum, the men advanced near to the King, his son desired leave to enquire after his Fathers health The King told them to turn round and pay their respects to the Whitemen, there were only Forbes and myself, they advanced

[426] I.e. dance patterns.

we rose to receive them, went through the compliments of a salute, and gave them a small case Bottle of rum, they then presented it before the King, he told them to accept it, they then thanked us most respectfully and retired to drink it.

A Band of women rose and saluted His Majesty, and sung a short chaunt and retired.

A second Band of ten women, and two little Girls, got up and commenced to perform the same figures as the men, appearance of a squall and rain, King invited us to take a Glass of spirits, he gave us permission to leave[,] a few drops of rain, on our way, after our arrival a heavy shower. The King expects to see us as he passes our door at 6 o'clock, he made his appearance shortly after the time,[427] we went outside.

Men soldiers in front, next the Caboceers, then His Majesty in his Hammock, he stopped a minute abreast of us, and sent a case Bottle of rum, then followed the Amazon's and Caboceers, then his empty Hammock, when it is their privilege to be in front he goes in it and visavisa [= vice versa] they presented with the same as if the King had been there, then followed the Cam-baa-dee and his band of followers it rained until 7.30 when it cleared away and became fine, we returned: inside[,] after which we had an unexpected visitor <u>Domingo Martin</u>, called to pay his respects before his departure for Whydah, in the morning, he remained an hour took a glass or two of wine, and smoked a cigar, and talked over his Palm-Oil trade in a familiar manner unasked, at Porto Novo he was not diffident in communicating the quantity of Palm oil he had shipped on board of the ship <u>Foame</u> [= *Foam*], Wood master, 90,000 gallons in 30 days, that was good work, from an open beach exposed to the sea breeze and the fetch of the whole Atlantic, it was at the rate of 10 Tons per diem,[428] his Hammock Bearers were in the next yard, they thought he had remained a good time and as it was getting late, they communicated their desire by the drum, he did not appear to take any notice of it, at last the headman came and told him that it was time to go, of course they were not his own people they belonged to the King, he resided at the house of the head Hammockman, so he is similar to ourselves partially a Prisoner before he left he very Kindly, made us an offer of any thing he had, that we might stand in need of, he asked me if it was my intention to remain at Whydah, I told him the extent of my Consular duties he said I had to[o] much to perform he asked if I had ever resided at Benin,[429] of course I told him that I had visited it twice and went by its Creeks into the <u>Quorra</u> or

---

[427] On his way to the Dahomey palace, where the next day's rites were performed.

[428] One ton of palm oil = 320 gallons.

[429] The kingdom of Benin (in modern Nigeria).

Niger in 1840,[430] he told me that Lagos was Tributary to Benin,[431] so our conference ended it was 9 o'clock, we escorted him to the outer yard, shook hands and left him, it rained and was a very unpleasant night I omitted to remark after our return from the Kings this afternoon Nawhey entered the yard with several men bearing Callabashes of different articles, Capt Forbes said in a jocular way Nawhey never mind the Bullocks leave them outside, never dreaming for a moment that there were any, to our utter astonishment in stalked two Black Bullocks as a Gift from the King, a large Callabash of corn flour, and a Pot of Palm oil each. 10 o'clock we retired to eat rainy unpleasant w[r].

Tuesday 11th June

am dull cloudy w[r] daylight inclinable to rain, the saved called early this morning and got their wants supplied, took an early Breakfast, at 7 o'clock to be in readiness for the Kings messenger to go to the <u>Dahomey Palace</u>, The King never moves but the hearts of his people accompany him, after all the bustle, and confusion, it was 10 o'clock, before we got started, and arrived at the Palace of Dah[432] at 10.22 groups were sitting, here and there, und[er] their country Umbrellas, we saluted the King, and took our seats, amongst the motley group, on our left were three Circular Tombs, roofed in, with conical roofs, with silver ornaments on each top,[433] round them and in front a great number of skulls, and Bones, of the Human frame, in great quantities, the names of the Tombs are Cen-lee[?][434] four Images covered with, country cloths, and guarded by groups of twelve in number, with umbrellas, and Fly

---

[430] Kwara, a common local name for the Niger. For this voyage, see Beecroft (1841).

[431] Lagos was originally a colony of Benin and was still nominally subject to it, although effectively independent, at this time (Smith 1978: 6).

[432] As Forbes notes here (Journal, p. 174), the name 'Dahomey' is said to commemorate Dan, a local ruler who was killed by Dakodonu, the founder and first king of Dahomey.

[433] Forbes' Journal (p. 174) identifies these tombs as those of 'Tahcohdohnoh and his successors' (which becomes 'Tah-coodoono and his family' in his book: Forbes (1851, ii: 87, 92)): i.e. Dakodonu. Skertchly in 1871 identified three tombs in the Dahomey palace as those of Dakodonu, Aho (= Wegbaja) and Akaba, the first three kings of Dahomey (1874: 392–3), while Blanchely in 1848 also refers to three tombs in a separate palace (evidently Dahomey), as those of 'Daho [= Dako, i.e. Dakodonu]', 'Kaka Demenanou [= Wegbaja]' and 'Akaba Huine Tounébététon' (1891: 547). Wegbaja's tomb was in fact in the Agringomè section of the main palace (Le Herissé 1911: 288, n. 2), the structure seen in the Dahomey palace being presumably a *jèhó*, or commemorative shrine, rather than his actual burial place (cf. note 359).

[434] Perhaps a misunderstanding, since no term resembling this referring to a tomb is identifiable in Fon. However, *zènlí* is the name of a sort of pot played as a drum, by striking its mouth with a fan, which is used specifically in funeral rites. (My thanks for this suggestion to Luis Nicolau Parés.)

Clappers, they are the unfortunate beings intended for the sacrifice, this evening, at the watering of the Tombs of his ancestors.

singing men in the Kings presence, an Amazon rise, and address the assemblage [= assembly],[435] relative to the Aa-taa-Pam war, stating that they sent and invited, the Dahomeians to come to war, they applied to the King, & he gave them orders to go and destroy it, Poo-vo-soo entered and saluted us, he was disfigured with chalk, as on former occasions, it was astonishing the number of Turkey Buzzards, planted on the roof of the Palace, and in the yard, I counted 200, instinct must have drawn them there, to await the deeds of darkness, and blood, they advance in Bands, or parties, the Amazon Troops, to state their positions and the effect they had in that position, at the war, if any were found deficient, they are heavily fined.

King passed or paid a Drum or Band 20 heads.

11 o'clock Cha-Cha enters, and salutes His Majesty.

Callabashes of skulls, before and near the King.

An Amazon rises and speak,[436] that they wish to ask the Mayo-gau, to request His Majesty to order them to go to Ah-gaa-ah,[437] others asked to go and attack Abbeokutta,[438] others say that they requested the King, to send messengers to those countries, that harbour the Ah-taa-Pam people, that they must immediately give them up to the King of Dahomey, else he must declare, or rather make war, on those countries,[439] another Amazon gets on her feet, and announces, publickly, that she is in debt for the stores of Provissions, she purchased to carry for her use at the Ah-taa-Pam war, she is very anxious to go and endeavour to get Cowries, to liquidate her debt, others get up and state, that they are ready, and willing, to go to any part His Majesty may please to order, a metaphor from the same, a Dog is strong in his Jaw, and breaks Bones, we will do the same to the place, the King may please to send them.

14 Amazons in loose Vestures, appear[440] and several other followers, speak, and corroborate the above statement,

Mayo-gau, state that if there are any parties dissatisfied with the conduct of any other party, and do not wish it to see[?] come[?] [= to see it come?]

---

[435] Named by Forbes (*Journal*, p. 175) as 'Ahpahdoonoomee', i.e. Akpadume (cf. p. 96, note 461, below).

[436] Again, named by Forbes as Akpadume.

[437] The Adja people, whose capital was the town of Tado, west of Dahomey and south-east of Atakpamé (also within modern Togo). Forbes' account makes explicit that Adja was targeted because people from Atakpamé had taken refuge there.

[438] For the background to the Dahomian conflict with Abeokuta, see Introduction, pp. xxxiv–xxxv.

[439] I.e. Adja, as Forbes makes explicit (*Journal*, p. 175).

[440] Forbes says '*demoiselles du pavé*', i.e. prostitutes: cf. also p. 131 and note 599.

before the Public, he would advise them to confer with Too-no-noo, the head Eunuch, so as to enable him to lay it before the King.

Mayo-gau again states that there are 80 men soldiers, that have disgraced themselves, at the late war.[441]

They arise and chaunt, desiring the King to send them to attack the Ah-taa-Pam's again.

Several state and corroborate, merely what the last sung, comparing revenge to Black soup, in good estimation in the country of Dahomey, they name it sweet,[442] if he would allow them the A-gow or general is ready, to take her women Troops immediately.[443]

Another Amazon states,[444] that it is all true, but it is not necessary to have so [much] palaver about it.

A man soldier rises and say, that the King has given to the River Moo-naa[445] human sacrifices, Bullocks, Goats, Fowls, and Cowries, fully believing that the River God, would preserve them in their war against the Ah-taa-Pams, that the Great Fetish of the River, promised to give their enemies into their hands.

A second say, would they not like to go and attack the Baa-ah's, or the Abbeokutians[446] no reply.

Egg-boo sah[447] say that they should have interrupted the former speaker on the last war,[448] for the King is well acquainted how the Ah-taa-pam people escaped, and who the faulters [*sic*] are, they must go and route [= rout] them out wherever they may have gone, and that it ought to be put in force directly, what he has dared to state are his own sentiments, and that he has not any more to say on the matter, that he always was and is ready to obey His Kings mandate, that this is the time, and season to speak,[449] that if any of his actions,

---

[441] Later identified as the soldiers of 'Saa-paa-see' whose case was discussed at the end of this day's proceedings (p. 98).

[442] Forbes does not mention soup or revenge here, but says rather that the male soldiers said that 'the Amazons are "sweet mouthed"'.

[443] Here referring to the female Gau, the officers of the 'Amazons' bearing the same titles as those of the male army.

[444] Named by Forbes as 'Passo', i.e. Posu, here the female officer of this title, who seems in fact to have been Akpadume (see note 582).

[445] The Mono, east of Atakpamé.

[446] I.e. the Egba, the people whose capital was Abeokuta. Forbes gives this differently: 'If we are not able to go to Bah, we should say so and let some other party go.'

[447] Spelled subsequently 'Egboo-za', 'Eg-boo-sah' (and 'Ekbohsah' by Forbes), and described as 'head of Kings Family Troop' (p. 115) and 'King's brother' (p. 126); also mentioned by Duncan in 1845 as 'Egboza', described as 'commander-in-chief of all the King's army', meaning presumably of the King's personal bodyguard, rather than of the whole army (1847, i: 239).

[448] From comparison with Forbes' version ('to interfere in a palaver is not right'), this should perhaps be 'should *not* have interrupted'.

[449] Forbes has 'Is this a day on which to find fault?'

had been considered wrong the King would have displaced him, that his mother lives in the Palace,[450] and is fully acquainted with his nature and disposition.

An Amazon,[451] states, that she wishes to state a metaphor about <u>Baa-ah</u>, the people are compared to a Cat-Fish, called Ah-paa-taa-pee, they sting the Kings, people,[452] a great shout to put her down.

Another rises and supports her by a simile, a person making his own living, is not to blame for approaching the King.[453]

Mayo-gau [says] that a man that takes a late supper is not able to rise early in the morning.

His Majesty replies that such a man is lazy, and indolent and of no use, to himself nor his master, he further remarks that when he leaves his Palace in the morning, not any person Knows, when he will return, or where he resides,[454]

The King's Drum-maker[455] say that wherever the people go the Amazons must follow.[456] they were six days at Ah-taa-Pam,[457] and some would have liked to have assumed the Kings place.[458]

Ah-go-gee-sah say a man that sends a crier round the Town, gets a ready sale, for his articles.[459]

Soh-we-luu-ji-sah, Huu-maa-hee names of the King's Drum-makers.

Isadore de Souza left at 2.30 pm.

All their Theme for the next war, is they desire permission from their King to attack Baa-ah.

a man say that they must not go to attack that place, with their cloths over their shoulders,[460] he was interrupted by the people.

---

[450] Referring to his female counterpart, rather than his biological mother.

[451] Again, named by Forbes as Akpadume.

[452] Forbes (who spells this 'pah tah seh heh') says only that it 'has a natural protection'. There may be some confusion here, since Fon *akpatá* means 'tortoise' (or 'turtle').

[453] Forbes says 'if ... one gives a part to the King'.

[454] Forbes has 'If one leave a country ... he is not likely to return in open day, he will return in the night.'

[455] Named by Forbes as 'Hoomahhee'.

[456] Forbes has this the other way round: 'If the King's daughters [= female soldiers] go to war, the King's sons [= male soldiers] will go also.'

[457] Forbes adds 'without seeing anybody', i.e. they ran away on the Dahomians' approach.

[458] I.e. of the King of Atakpamé.

[459] Forbes describes this intervention as a song in which 'all' joined, and gives the text in Fon, which he explains as alluding to the Atakpamé having 'challenged' the Dahomians to war (Journal, p. 176).

[460] Forbes has the opposite, 'we can go to war with our clothes on', glossed as meaning 'no preparation'.

Pah-do-noo-mee, an Amazon,[461] say that she is ready to speak to the men, face to face, no reply.

2nd Amazon say[462] that she was chosen by the King, to go to Ah-taa-Paam, she is equally ready to go to Baa-ah.[463]

Huu-maa-hee say that if Pah-da-noo-mee goes that his party must follow, she told him to [keep] silence[,] that Drummers, were not the A-gow or General, to talk in that manner, for 40 drummers were sufficient to take to war.

3rd woman say that when she goes to war, her eye is not on any one place, but all over the camp,[464] so should the A-gow's, she would always be awake, as the second in command,[465] she is anxious that when war palaver is in discussion, she must speak, the Ah-taa-Pams, cannot point their feet towards Abomey, for their feet, and legs, will swell, that they die, one by one[466] that if they were to beg the King to make Peace, she is one that would not agree to it.

A man soldier say that he is within the Palace walls, to make this statement, that when he goes to the Baa-ah war, he will do an exploit, the King will hear of, he is interrupted and put down.

A woman[467] speaks to exalt the Troop, before the King, and say that his Amazon soldiers, are the main road, he has to walk on to Victory.[468]

It is rather Keen cutting for the men.

The King Politically interferes, and changes the subject, distant from war, he addresses himself to the Mayo-gau, after a short discussion to clean the roads, in and about Abomey.[469]

His Majesty dismiss this Party, they smother themselves with dust, with loud acclamations. a soldier states that formerly before they went to war, they bought corn from the Commissarial department, at Ah-ja-ah but now they

---

[461] Spelled subsequently 'Ah-pah-doo-noo-meh' (as also by Forbes) and 'Ah-pah-doo-meh'; also mentioned by Duncan in 1845, who spells the name 'Apadomey' (1847, ii: 277), and subsequently by Burton, who gives it as 'Akpadume' (1864, i: 224 etc.). Later identified by Beecroft (p. 126) as the female Gau, but seemingly in error (see note 582).

[462] Forbes attributes this statement also to Akpadume.

[463] Forbes gives this differently, 'If the King decides against the Attahpahms we can have Bah also', implying that they could attack both, rather than choosing between them.

[464] Forbes again differs: 'In time of peace, my eyes are everywhere, in war concentrated into one focus.'

[465] The syntax is ambiguous, but the 'she' who would remain awake is presumably the Gau, rather than the speaker: the description of her as 'second in command' is odd, since the Gau was in fact the commander-in-chief, but perhaps is regarded here as 'second' to the Migan, who was the Gau's civil counterpart and superior.

[466] Forbes attributes this statement to 'Hoomahhee' (Journal, p. 177)

[467] Again, named by Forbes as Akpadume.

[468] Forbes: 'the Amazons are the King's sandals'.

[469] Forbes found this statement 'not loud enough to be heard'.

have not any good place in reserve,[470] it appears that he infers, that the war had done harm, by destroying Towns, and cities into ruinous heaps, instead of making them Tributary, he has several [tributaries] nevertheless in the Maa-hee country.[471]

Another rise and state that many thing in the market is very high, to what they were formerly 1 Goat and Sheep 3 dollars, Fowls 20 & 22 strings of cowries, each[,] nearly half a dollar.[472]

The King does not appear to be the Despot as is currently reported, else at the Customs it is a privilege, he distributes Gifts of cloth, in strips[473] in 6 Bags, 1 roll of Tobacco, and one broad rimmed Hat, the right [i.e. to these gifts] is disputed by another soldier, head of a Troop,[474] and [he] states that he has done Fetes at the Kaan-gaa-roo war, he cut of a King's head, the other has not distinguished himself, in any war, equal to that,[475] it appeared that it was an old custom to have those Cavils, and disputes, for he had seized the cloth in the Presence of the King,[476] however after half an hours clamour the matter was overruled by the King and the other party seized the cloth and

---

[470] Forbes attributes this discussion of food supplies to 'two of the King's brothers', named in the published version as Ahokpè and Linpehoun (1851, ii: 102).

[471] Duncan, travelling through Mahi in 1845, found that it had recently been conquered by Dahomey and the local population left in place as tributaries. The Mahi were not, however, as Beecroft seems here to imply, the only recently conquered people who had been made tributary: others included the Agonli (p. 48, note 267).

[472] Forbes attributes this intervention to Houngbadji (p. 177). A dollar = 50 strings. Compare prices given earlier by Forbes: at Allada, 8 fowls for $1 (i.e. 250 cowries/just over 6 strings per fowl) and at Ouidah, 200 cowries (= 5 strings) for a chicken, 2,500 cowries (= $1.25) for a goat, 5,000 (= $2.50) for a sheep (1851, i: 55, 110). This complaint of rising prices may reflect a depreciation of the value of cowries which was beginning at this time (Law 1994a).

[473] Cloth in Dahomey (as elsewhere in West Africa) was often woven in narrow strips.

[474] This relates to the party of 80 soldiers earlier reported to have 'disgraced themselves' in the Atakpamé war, whose commander is later named as 'Sah-paa-see'. Forbes names the officer who disputed their right as Houngbadji. Forbes refers to this discussion as 'a sort of trial' (Journal, p. 175), and in his book to the 'King's Court of Justice' (1851, ii: 86), which seems to exaggerate the formality of the proceedings.

[475] The syntax is opaque, but from what follows later in this paragraph, the person who claimed to have beheaded an enemy king is 'Saa-paa-see' and 'the other' is Houngbadji: Forbes attributes this statement not to 'Saa-paa-see' himself but to the Amazon 'mothers' of the accused party, who now intervened to defend them (Journal, p. 177). Further confusion arises from the contradiction between this passage, identifying the decapitated king as that of Kenglo, and that later in the same paragraph which refers to the king of Refurefu: Forbes' version names the latter.

[476] Here 'he' is presumably Houngbadji, although if so the male pronoun is an error, since this person is elsewhere identified as a female officer. It should be noted that the Fon language does not distinguish gender grammatically, which is a potential cause of confusion in the process of translation.

walked of with loud acclamations of joy.[477] Sah-paa-see was the name of the man that claimed this Gift,[478] because he decapitated the King of Laa-af-laa-foo, stating that the other had not killed a King in war.

Band of music	6 heads of cowries
Singer a case Bottle of rum	

The same party returned after depositing their Gift and receive a quantity of Chop or Provissions.

Too-noo-noo Kings head Eunuch	1 head of cow[ries]
1 Bottle of rum for his small band	
King's Brother	2 heads D°
” ” children	2 Bottles of rum

His Majesty drinks, acclamations, and firing of muskets, dance & sing

Band of music	2 heads
” ” Gongs	1 D°
” ” Music	<u>2 D°</u>
	14

a heavy shower of rain[,] remove our position under the escort of the Mayo-gau and the Caboceer of Whydah, to the outer Porch the rush was too much, I was partly carried through the Gate way, after we took our position, the Hammock men had an arduous task, to keep us out of the pressure of the mob, passing in and out, with and for their Gifts, half an hour elapsed, when the rain ceased we got permission to leave.

Gift of 2 case Bottles of rum & 1 Basket of cassava.

Gift of 7 heads of cowries given during our stay in the Porch.

we returned home, P. Brown accompanied us, out of the court yard.

After dinner I straggled to Browns quarters, it is a perfect labyrinth, the various Houses, yards &c narrow and small, the houses, he has a small family with him, we commenced a dialogue on the Slave Trade, gleaned some rather useful information, although he is a slippery fellow.

He said what he was going to state, was received from a man deeply interested in the Slave Trade, at Lagos, he has stated that the only sure, and final means, to put a stop to the abominable traffic is to route them out of Lagos, and fix the right heir on the Throne, which is at present at Bagdagry [= Badagry], and enter into a Treaty with him for the suppression of the Foreign Slave Trade,[479] it would have an effect on the King of Dahomey, before any

---

[477] I.e. the cloth was restored to the original recipient, whose 'disgrace' was by implication revoked.

[478] Spelled by Forbes 'Tehpehseh'—clearly one or other of these versions is a miscopying.

[479] The king of Lagos, Akitoye, had been deposed in favour of his nephew Kosoko and exiled in 1845. He was now at Badagry and seeking the British government's assistance for his restoration, in return for accepting the abolition of the slave trade (Smith 1978: 19). Brown's unnamed informant was almost certainly Domingos Martins, who had traded at Lagos during his first

other plan that can be devised, should he decline making a Treaty, under any circumstances, I trust that the time is not far distant ere they will carry that plan into execution.[480]

Caboceer of Whydah pays a Tribute of 500 dollars annually,[481] Mayo-gau pays so much a head for each slave he takes in war,[482] and cannot dispose of them without the Kings permission, but still; I have my doubts as to the truth of that statement,[483] The speeches made to day was similar to hard debates, in our House of Commons, for an harangue or speech from any one, that was not satisfactory, was immediately put down by the people, The Amazon Troop appear to carry the sway for they speak very freely before a ruler of such Despotic sway, more is said than in the presence of Monarchy,[484] retired to rest at 10 o'clock damp unpleasant w^r to be seated six or seven hours on the damp ground, chairs of course but your feet is the main point.

Wednesday 12th June

Daylight dull damp w^r went to take our usual morning walk, down the Canna road, and returned at 7.15[,] after Breakfast paid our Hammock bearers, and

---

period of residence in Africa in 1835–44 (which included the beginning of Akitoye's reign), but found himself excluded on his return in 1846 and settled instead at Porto-Novo. Martins had supported an unsuccessful attempt by Akitoye to recover his throne in 1847 (Ross 1965: 80). He had suggested that the British should intervene to reinstate him in January 1849 (United Kingdom Hydrographic Office, OD9A, F. Struvé, 'Report on the Results Obtained by the Expedition ... to Survey and Explore the Coast Lagoon between the River Benin to the Eastward and the River Volta to the Westward, in the Bight of Benin, West Africa; the Present Portion of the Survey Having Extended from Whydah to Adjudo [1848–9]', 11–12: my thanks for this reference to Silke Strickrodt), and again expressed support for this plan in 1851 (HCPP, *Papers Relative to the Reduction of Lagos*, incl. 2 in no. 39, Rev. C.A. Gollmer to Beecroft, 21 Feb. 1851). It may be noted that Martins' role in soliciting the British intervention at Lagos is not mentioned in modern academic analyses (Smith 1978; Lynn 1992).

[480] This passage is of interest in suggesting that Beecroft was beginning to think of intervention at Lagos even before the failure of the Dahomian mission, in qualification of the argument of Lynn (1992), that this policy was a reaction to his failure in Dahomey. Cf. also p. 145.

[481] Referring to the tax paid at the Annual Customs (cf. p. 20). By comparison, the Migan is said to have paid 2,000 heads (Forbes 1851, i: 75), the trader Quénum $3,500 (Blanchely 1891: 576). On taxes paid by caboceers and traders, see also Forbes' Journal, p. 194.

[482] This does not mean that the Mewu did not also pay 'tribute', since he is named by Forbes later among those paying both 'duties [on trade] and presents [= annual tax]' to the King (ibid.). An earlier reported statement by King Gezo clarifies that the 'duty' was paid by all 'the caboceers' (not the Mewu alone), and only 'when [slaves were] sold' (Duncan 1847, ii: 264). The export duty on slaves was $5 per head (Cruickshank's Report, 16).

[483] Despite Beecroft's scepticism, Dahomian tradition confirms that royal permission was required for the sale of war captives, who were technically received as gifts from the king (Le Herissé 1911: 52).

[484] Perhaps a word is missing—e.g. 'more than [usual] in the presence of Monarchy'?

others, 10 men, and 20 women carriers, after which I availed myself of the opportunity to write.

At noon King's Brother named [blank] called on us, he produced a large country cloth for sale, but the price he asked was enormous, it would not be easy to guess the amount fancy 59 dollars nearly, 13 £s sterling,[485] he must have deemed us perfectly unacquainted with the value of such articles, he must himself be a mercenary piece of royalty, he took a Glass of wine and retired, shortly after a man and a woman called, they both spoke English, and told us they were liberated Africans from <u>Sieirleon</u>, had been residents of Whydah for the last ten years, [486] the woman came to complain that her husband was a Prisoner in the Kings yard,[487] I requested her to state the circumstances of the case she states that on his arrival at Whydah from <u>Sieirleon</u> he was consumptive,[488] the Caboceer recommended him to a country Doctor, he failed in doing him any good, for several years, after a time he was recommended to go to Ah-tah-pam, which it appears he did and got cured of his disease, after being there a year, he was returning from there to Whydah, and was picked up by the Kings Troops [i.e. of the King of Dahomey], that were at the war, he must have known that the war had been declared by the Ah-taa-pams, sending to inform the Dahomeians they were ready, he ought to have left their country at once, ere the enemy occupied all the Paths for he is a subject of the King of Dahomey, he might treat him as a spy, being taken in or near the enemy's camp leads to suspicion, after which I strongly advised her to keep her own secrets, that I would be better able to treat with the King on that matter after I had introduced my own affairs of the mission we were on. she then retired she speaks English very well[489] Mr Brown sent us a present of a few Limes and a Tin of mock Turtle, he was of course invited to dine and take part of it at 5 o'clock he called I went out across the road with him, to look at a particular Cotton Tree, in the yard where he lodged, it is different to the generality, a spreading Tree with a red flower, and green seeds, whilst talking, Too-no-noo the Eunuch, and a few of his retinue made his appearance, and requested to speak to Brown, they of course left me and went inside of his domicile, I walked across the road to our own premises, the interview was short the Eunuch soon left and Posted[490] of[f,] he [= Brown] returned and found me, and

---

[485] At the official value of the dollar, at 4*s*. 2*d*. (50*d*.) sterling, $59 = £12 5*s*. 10*d*.

[486] I.e. Sierra Leone, referring to the British colony, where slaves freed from illegal slave ships were resettled. There was a small community of Sierra Leonians in Ouidah at this time (Law 2004b: 182–3). Freeman, at the beginning of 1843, likewise reported that they had arrived two or three years earlier (1844: 242).

[487] Named later as John McCarthy (see p. 152).

[488] Forbes (Journal, p. 177), refers to 'hooping cough'.

[489] On McCarthy's case, see further pp. 152–4.

[490] I.e. hurried.

said the King had sent for him in private not through the Mayo-gau, Peter laid great stress on the word Private, a few minutes had hardly elapsed, when a messenger arrived from the Mayo, for Brown's attendance, at the Mayo's mansion he left I then told him 5 o'clock was the dinner hour, we waited until 5.30 when he came, he said that he had excused himself by telling him he was going to dine with us, that he would call after dinner, in the dusk of the evening, at and after dinner his Theme was the Private messenger, he even went as far as to state that his adopted mother at the Mee-gau's was about to commence to build him a house for his own special use, when he visits Abomey, it is not to cost him a penny, now it is all fudge, and nonsense, he left us at 7 o'clock, to go to the Meegau, we retired at 9 o'clock to rest. w^r clear and dry.

Thursday 13th

Arose at daylight morning fine and pleasant we walked out of the Canna Gate, and took the left for, Duucan,[491] 6.30 we returned it looked very thick and lowering to the Eastward, it began [to] rise and look awfully black, we walk quick to endeavour to reach a place of shelter before it struck us, however, I very soon saw we were in for a complete drenching, I commenced to run it was no use it struck me on the Back a strong wind and rain in torrents, I very soon felt the sudden chill when precipitation was checked it took us three quarters of an hour to walk home, I immediately changed everything and rubbed my body with Brandy and water, and took a dose of Quinine, I did not expect to be called upon to go to the King to day, directly after Breakfast a messenger came to desire we would be in readiness to go the Market to see the preparations making for the morrows shamfight, I felt symptoms of ague, nevertheless I dressed to go, but we were detained two hours during which time my symptoms increased, so I was obliged to decline my visit Capt Forbes went (solus) I took a second dose of Quinine, and laid down had a slight attack of the cold stage, indeed it passed of with a very slight attack, I got up at 4 o'clock but felt very seedy. Capt Forbes returned at 5.30 during the afternoon a shower of rain, The King very kindly accommodated Forbes near him under a matt, to secure him from getting wet; he states that he was Kept partially dry, from information the whole affair today were the Amazons, spouting, and singing, Metaphorically about their victories,[492] Ah taa Pam was not mentioned,[493] as they had conquered them and destroyed their

---

[491] I.e. Dokon (cf. p. 76, with note 357).

[492] Forbes describes this ceremony as 'the Amazons swearing to be faithful next War' (Journal, p. 177).

[493] I.e. as a possible target. This is confirmed by Forbes' original journal, but in his book he interpolated a speech by one officer stating that 'the Attahpahms must be exterminated first' (1851, ii: 109).

Town, they left them for the Present, it cannot be of long duration for one or other of them must burst forth in Praises of their Great and mighty King.

The greater part of their theme was for the King to allow them to go to attack <u>Baa-ah</u> or <u>Abb[e]okutta</u> I presume Baa-ah is a large [place?] near the latter place[494] their songs were that they had conquered all the petty nations, that there were only two Great nations remaining in this part and that it was impossible for two Rams to feed out of the same stall their Horns must get entangled so two great nations cannot exist near each other.[495]

They then sung aloud if the King would allow them to go to war with Baa-ah, if they could not conquer it, they prayed that the God of thunder, would destroy them all,[496] it is too obvious that they are fully bent and determined on the downfall of <u>Abbeokutta</u>, but Baa-ah is the Theme of their Metaphorical songs, and expressions. The Great King made a speech not overburthened with wisdom, it was that if a man send a dog into the Bush in chase that if he returned without his Prize its head ought to be the forfeit and thrown to the Turkey Buzzards.

That if they went to attack Baa-ah and was not successful they were perfectly acquainted what they must expect will befall them, and them that escaped and returned would not go unpunished, this was nearly the purport of their days performance, with the exception of music, and dancing.

Another extraordinary piece of superstition attached to their Category of Fetishes is that the Blue Po Poo Bead is the excrement of a particular snake, that no person can look on and live[497]—went to rest at 8.20, dry and clear.

Midnight fine w^r

Friday 14th June

am cloudy dull w^r arose at daylight, after a refreshing nights rest, felt much better, decided to go to the great to do to day, at a shamfight

8.30 arrived at the ground,[498]

10 o'clock the whole of the Caboceers, with Banners, and music, arrived on the ground Ignatio about the centre of the Caboceers.

King's Troops, Banners, and music

---

[494] Beecroft here seems not to grasp that 'Egba' and 'Abeokuta' in fact referred to the same place.
[495] Not reported by Forbes at this point, but on 22 June he quotes a similar idiom, 'two rams cannot drink out of the same calabash' (Journal, p. 188).
[496] I.e. they swore an oath by the *vodun* (god) of thunder, So (also called Hevioso). Forbes gives the text of this oath in Fon (p. 180).
[497] This was alluded to in songs sung on this occasion, recorded by Forbes (p. 179): the reference is to the *vodun* Dan Aïdohuedo, identified with the rainbow, who was represented as a snake (Burton 1864, ii: 148; Le Herissé 1911: 118–19).
[498] I.e. Adjahi market.

2 Union jacks

King arrives on the ground dressed in a Country Cloth, saluted by his male Troops, firing, dancing, and singing.

Caboceers and ministers, salute the King.

Ignatio took a seat on my left.

we were on the right of the King, Cha-Cha on the left, Kings Brother approach him with implements of agriculture, for repair, request that he will give orders in the proper quarter that they may put in order.

Mayo-gau was called and ordered to find the Blacksmith, which was done, immediately.

11.15 50 woman soldiers advance, the chief addresses the King, and states that there is a large Tree, which requires to be cut down, they pass on and place Patrols and look out parties.

2000 advance, the chief salutes the King, they wear the white caps, with a blue alligator in cloth, as ornaments, given on Mr Cruickshanks visit from Cape Coast.

A Maa-hee man a Crier behind us, aloud, oh King of Kings,[499] and a shout that war is coming, from the people placed inside the stockade, Fetish people pass the King[,] Kings mule,[500] and Guard, with all the paraphernalia of the Commissariat.

100 women a reserve Guard.

Mayo address and salutes the King, upon matters of the Patrols, they are moved of to another position.

Too noo-noo the head Eunuch, rebukes the Mayo-gau on account of his stool Bearers being in a dirty state not fit to come before the King.

The Procession march past in Regiments, a crier in the rear calling the people to come and see for themselves war is coming.

Report to the King that the Troops are all on the ground.

An Amazon belonging to the Caboceer of Whydah speaks,[501] en passant, and states that she is always ready for war, that at any time she is wanted and do not come forward must punish her.

Third time round, King tells them that they must now go to war.

King remarked that the crier is a Maa-hee slave, they have the Gift of the mouth.

King Jokes with his people around him.

Hah-qua-dee, speak and say they are ready for the word.

---

[499] Forbes (on an earlier occasion) gives this phrase in Fon (Journal, p. 177).

[500] Forbes here refers to the King's 'horse' (p. 181). Mules were uncommon in West Africa (Law 1980a: 46–7), but there are other references to them in Dahomey, including in Freeman (1844: 256).

[501] Forbes says the Yovogan's 'mother', i.e. his female counterpart.

A reconnoitring party comes up, and holds a conference, King coughs, a shout and Knocking of Gongs.

King orders a party to go on the road to look out for stragglers.

They send a few Prisoners, a man incognito belonging to the enemy, they make use of his information for the attack.

The King leaves the Tent to reconnoitre the sto[c]kade, we moved from under the Umbrellas to see the commencement of the great Sham-Fight, Bands of Troops moveing here and there,

Patrols at different parts of the Paths.

King goes round the Stokade, under white umbrella, a few small parties running to and fro.

King enters the Stokade a Gun is fired the Town is taken, we moved on to the left to have a fair view, all that I can see was a Grass fence,

The King entering and returning from the Village, a rush from it to endeavour to escape a sally of Troops, after them.

a regular Slave Hunt, instead of a sham fight as I had expected, it was all over[,] Prisoners all marched in, one between two, before the Tent, King takes a body of Troops, behind the Stokade, where they quietly leave their muskets, then they come in front and kneel down for ten minutes close to each other, a Band in the Rear, fire over their heads, they jump up with the Palm branches in their hands, and of course walk it down, pick up their arms, and form,[502] now they have only to destroy the Town, we entered under the Tent, and left the King to amuse himself, pulling down a few grass Huts, &c &c under the fire of a few muskets, Prisoners escorted in, a number with small Bundles of Grass under their arms, as an imitation of heads cut of, I counted about 250 with those Bundles on their heads, and under their arms,

New mode of warfare, the stokade, and Town, is taken after the war, and Prisoners are sent in, the Stokade is 100 feet in length from Palm Branches stuck in the ground, with others longitudinally at the top, and bottresses [= buttresses], to support them.

Daa-maa-dag-bee accosts the Throne and ministers, and states that she has taken a Prisoner, and that when she goes to the next war, she will forfeit her head, if she has not a Prisoner.

Others marching past, with imitation of heads in Bundles, of grass, it only goes to show the barbarity of the Custom,

The King buys all from two to five heads of Cowries.[503]

---

[502] I.e. draw up in formation.

[503] Captives taken in war were appropriated by the King, who paid their captors for them: cf. Cruickshank's Report, 16, which gives the bounty paid as 'a couple of dollars [i.e. heads] for each captive'. But a higher figure, of $10 per slave, was given to Beecroft later (p. 146).

Four men came up with a slave each, belonging to separate regiments, and enquire after the King's health.

Gaa-doo-noo-me arrives and salutes the Tent, Agow Commander in Chief of the women soldiers[504]

2.30 King arrives opposite his Tent, Troops muster around him, he addresses a small group, making signs here and there, apparently correcting some of their movements, enters the Tent and shakes us by the hand, and said he had returned from the war, he had just got seated when it was announced, that a snake was in the Tree on his left, a musket was fired, in a minute the fellow was down and produced the snake in his hand, with the head just exposed, it had a long wound about the center of its body, as if from a Cutlass, on enquiring who it was that shot it, we were informed it was the Kings son, we complimented the King on the able mark of this son, he only stated that it was a slave of his.

a supposed return of the enemy, greater part of the Amazon Troops, on their Knees ready for a sally forth, firing in the distance, orders given they all sally forth, and surround them, the mass moving so fast shook the Earth near the Tent, they were hid from our view by the quantity of dust, [which] they got up by the movement, They return with the King of the Country and a number of Prisoners, also the Queen of the Country in his rear, salute the King, en passant, 3.30 a squall with rain, permitted us to retire to a house in the vicinity, belonging to the Cam-baa-dee. We were there a short time when the Lord of the Mansion, arrived and said that the King, desired to see us, but as he [= we?] had been pleased to honor his Home with our presence we must take something before we leave, so he accordingly introduced a dram of Gin, we of course tasted with him, after which we left for the Tent, when we reached his [= the King's] presence, He presented us a quantity of country chop, which we thanked him for, and as it was likely to rain, he left it optional to ourselves, to go or stay, we chose the former, he gave us the rest of the Programme for the day, that was that he had only to pass a number of the Caboceers, and then to proceed to Ah-grin-goo-mee,[505] that he would see us again tomorrow, we took our usual parting glass, he left us outside of the Tent, and we made the best of our way home, it commenced a partial shower of rain, Nawhey was our escort, we came to a part where several of the King's wives were passing, from the Sham Fight, we were rivetted until they

---

[504] Also mentioned by Duncan in 1845, as 'Godthimay', described as 'commander of one of his Majesty's female regiments' (1847, i: 248); spelled 'Gounémé' by the French officer Vallon in 1856 (1860/1, i: 338; ii: 348), 'Gundeme' by Burton (1864, i: 221, etc.). Vallon and Burton identify her as the female Migan, rather than the Gau; and Beecroft himself subsequently names a different person, Hetungan, as the female Gau (p. 120). Since the Migan was the civil counterpart (and superior) of the Gau, the confusion is understandable.

[505] Agringomè, the north-east gate of the palace.

had past on, and obliged to be Kept in the rear, at a snails pace, had it rained in torrents, we should have been obliged to have gone through the ordeal, so much for slavery, and despotic sway, we did not get into our Hammocks, until our arrival in the Palace Square, we arrived at our quarters just in time to escape a heavy shower of rain, followed by twelve Baskets of different sorts of country chop, it continued to rain heavy with distant thunder, for some time, when it partially cleared away a great din of music outside of our door, upon enquiry we found that the King intended to pass, we went out and found a mob, congregated, with country [*sic*] a number of country umbrellas, of all sorts, and classes, also several soldiers, Capt Forbes took a fellows musket, and tried the Lock, he told the soldier that it would not go of, fancying the Pan cover too loose, the fellow seized it and charged it in a minute, drew his short sword, and placed it between the Teeth, went on one Knee, and fired, then ran as fast as he could as if after his enemy, for some distance, then returned for which he received a Gift of a Pint of rum, after which he retired, and drank it or deposited in a vial of his own, returned and performed with great agility a country dance, he was an active muscular fellow, Peter Brown was present, he took the musket and performed several manoeuvres, with great agility, and satisfaction, presenting arms &c &c,[506] after which it commenced to rain, we went inside, 7 o'clock the King passed in Procession we went out and saluted him he sent us a case Bottle of rum, and passed on we returned & retired to rest at 9 o'clock, it was clear and starlight.

Saturday 15 June

Programme

am rainy unpleasant w^r daylight continued rain, a greater number of sticks this morning than usual, on account its being rainy to guzzle rum.

10 o'clock the Mayo-gau paid us a visit, and apologized for the reason of our being called to[o] early having to wait generally an hour on the damp ground, before we entered the Palace, that for the future the King's messenger shall arrive first, before you are sent for, at 11 o'clock we left for the Palace, and arrived at the inner court at 11.15 and saluted the King, Band & Banners.[507]

4 Union Jacks, with singers

---

[506] In the Niger Expedition in the 1830s, it was noted that Brown had earlier served as 'an Adjutant in the Cape Coast militia', so was able to train other members of the expedition in the handling of firearms (Laird & Oldfield 1837, ii: 280).

[507] This was in the Agringomè section of the palace, as Forbes' journal makes explicit (Journal, p. 182).

On our arrival they were rather complimentary to us as Englishmen, that our visits were looked on as advantageous, to the King, and that it was good to be friends.

To the left of the King, were Horns and skulls, and other implements of Barbarism sprinkled with the blood of sacrifices.

Hay roofs in front, right and left, for the accommodation of the community assembled, behind us were three Conical Tombs roofed in ornamented with skulls, and human Bones,[508] interior were victims to be sacrificed in the evening,[509] Guards and attendance [*sic*] at each

Another party of singers, chaunting the Praises of the Whydah Traders.

Caboceers and followers, acknowledged the compliment, by presenting themselves, before the King, and throwing dust on their heads, & Bodies.

Improvements going on in this court yard.

Fetish men and ornaments on our left.

Thee-noo Head Trader of Whydah,[510] he has an immense head, and neck, sung Praises to the King, calling him their only protector

Kings sister on his right.

a Crier anon[511] Cries, oh King of Kings, see-qua-ah-hee arrive[512] the liberated, Africans, from Brazil salute the King as usual.

Singing against the Youribaa nation,[513] and invite the King to honor them with his presence without the Tent

King replys that he has heard all their Praises for his Father with the sacrifices.

Poo-voo-soo makes his appearance disguised as usual, but of course he is a favourite, and privileged.

Peter Brown arrives and takes his seat on our left.

---

[508] Forbes says that the rites of this day were in memory of Agaja, the fourth king of Dahomey. Skertchly in 1871 describes a single building ('a long barn') which he understood to contain the 'ashes [*sic*]' of Agaja and the three following kings, Tegbesu, Kpengla and Agonglo (1874: 398–400). In fact, the actual tombs of these four kings are at separate locations within the palace (see Map 3), so that what Skertchly saw was more probably a symbolic *jĕhò* (cf. note 359). The three 'tombs' seen by Beecroft on this occasion may have been shrines for Agaja, Tegbesu and Kpengla (Gezo's father Agonglo having perhaps been already honoured earlier, on 7 June: see note 359).

[509] These sacrifices are not mentioned by Forbes.

[510] Probably miscopied, presumably representing Quénum (cf. p. 77, with note 363). 'Head Trader' is probably a translation of the title *ahisigan* ('chief merchant'), applied to Quénum and other leading merchants of Ouidah (Law 2004b: 202, 250–1).

[511] I.e. at once.

[512] I.e. the ceremony of *sìn kòn ny'àyĭ*, 'watering the earth' (cf. note 174).

[513] Here referring to Abeokuta—although commonly this was regarded as a 'separate nation' from the 'Yoruba' (i.e. Oyo), as is noted by Forbes, Journal, p. 161.

King calls the Agow of his Amazons,[514] and says aloud, that a person ought not to take food before he first washes his hands.

minstrels sing for the women, that the Custom will soon be over, then they make ready for war.

The Head Amazons speech, say that they are always ready to comply with the Kings orders.

a man in the multitude bawls aloud, if the King is displeased they must not perplex him but endeavour to please him.

Two maidens present themselves each with a Glass of Spirits, two men are called, they present the Gift as a token, or pledge of their being intended to be given unto them to wife, as a Gift from the King, laughter they prostrated themselves, after taking the contents of the glass, and throw dust on their heads, names of men Ah-chee-lee & Ah-koo-too[515]

Band a Gift of 14 heads of cowries.

A man presented himself[516] and says he wishes to speak to the King, he is told that he cannot be admitted, he insists[,] he is taken away by force a scuffle ensures, he bawls out to his King, he is carried of, shortly afterwards he again makes his appearance, with his own party, a sham scuffle is got up but at last he is allowed to succeed, they take him on their shoulders and prostrate him before the King, he did not speak but merely threw dust on his head.

King appears under a Black velvet umbrella trimmed with Gold lace he had on a robe of rich worked silk, he held in his hand the skull of Ah-coo-choo-nee on a distaff to spin cotton, he was taken at Sha-bee,[517] a crier calls out the names of the different countries, he has conquered and made Tributary, to Dahomey, a great number of skulls, in front and on the left of entrance of the Tent, King retires sends us 2 callabashes of chop, and 1 Pot of Peto or country Beer.

Band of singers 5 heads 1 Bottle of rum.

---

[514] Comparison with Forbes' Journal (p. 182) indicates that this refers to Akpadume—though the identification of her as the Gau seems to be an error (see note 582).

[515] Burton gives 'Akutu' as the name of a female officer, 'captainess of King Gezo's life-guards' (1864, ii: 252), but Beecroft's 'Ah-koo-too' was clearly male. Possibly there were both male and female officers of this name?

[516] Forbes says 'one of the royal nephews'.

[517] Forbes has 'Kohcharnee, king of Anagoo'. Sabe ('Savè' on modern maps) is a Yoruba (= Anago) town, north-east of Dahomey, whose destruction by Gezo is recalled in later Dahomian tradition, which gives the name of its defeated king as 'Ekotchoni' (Dunglas 1957–8, ii: 67–9): i.e. Ikosoni, who was not actually king but *balogun* (war chief) of Sabe, and its de facto ruler during an interregnum (Palau Marti 1992: 193–201). Duncan earlier heard the story of a king of 'Annagoo' who, with two other kings (including that of Oyo) had threatened to make Gezo's head 'a balance to a distaff' but were defeated and suffered this fate themselves, but did not name the Anago ruler (1847, ii: 41–2). The Sabe king's head attached to a distaff was depicted on the wall of Gezo's palace (Waterlot 1926: plate XIVA).

1.30 showers of rain, singers commence a short chaunt that the King and his family God has preserved, they will live long, and have every enjoyment.

A Gift of 2 Bottles of rum.

A calabash of Goats, Fowls &c &c for chop.

I Head of cowries

music and dancing King leaves the Tent and waits on us, shook hands and took a Glass of Gin, a shout with muskets fired he said he did not wish to detain us in the rain too long. likely to get fever, we were perfectly aware of that, and, I am only astonished that we have escaped it, the Caboceer of Whydah passed us out and shook hands, we just arrived home in time to escape a heavy shower, of rain, [we] mean to depend on the Caboceer, and Nawhey's account of Gifts after our departure the remainder of the day unpleasant we went to bed early.

Sunday 16 June

am dull wʳ daylight inclinable to rain. Ther 75° messenger arrived, from the Mayo, left at 10 o'clock and arrived at the Palace at 10.30 saluted the King[.] at all the Courts hay roofs, from 50, 60 or 100 yards, all thrown out from the wall for the accommodation of the King's family &c &c he always sit in the Porch, at the entrance to the inner yard.[518]

King's dress to day sky Blue figured satin sandals & silver clasps.

Band of singing men.

Skulls and Banners.

silver Horns on their heads as ornaments, the Theme of their songs was that Saa-ah God, gives the Power,[519] I enquired particularly if it was their Fetish, the Interpreter, said no it [i.e. their fetish] is named Paugh,[520] they must have a slight knowledge of an omnipotent [god],

---

[518] Forbes' Journal (p. 182) says that this was again in the Agringomè section of the palace. Although Beecroft does not mention tombs here, he later refers to human sacrifices which were to be offered in the evening; Forbes in his book (though not in his original journal) says that this day's rites were again 'watering the graves' of King Agaja (1851, ii: 131). However, it seems likely that they also applied to his successors, thus concluding the rites for the kings, before attention shifted to their 'mothers' (Kpojito), from the following day.

[519] Forbes (on a different occasion) gives the form 'Seh' (Journal, p. 189), which is explained in his book as 'the supreme and invisible god' (1851, i: 171). The term *sé* in fact refers to spirits generically (including e.g. an individual person's soul), but it is also used of the supreme/creator god, especially in the form Ségbó, 'Great Spirit'.

[520] *Kpò*, 'leopard', referring to Agasu, the ancestor of the Dahomian royal family, who was worshipped as a *vodun* (cf. note 258).

same display of skulls as yesterday, particularly Ah-gee-nae-coo as a distaff for spinning cotton.[521]

His Majesty is addressed today Paugh, Tiger[522] Phraseology, singing.

11.45 refreshments of spirits and water, no wine so of course it serves the Turkey Buzzards that beset us, and are about us

The Brazillian freemen arrived as usual Viva Viva le Rie de Dahomey.

Ignatio De Souza arrives and takes his seat at a distance the familiarity has blown over to the dab-dab Hills, and take root there, the old Proverb too much [familiarity] breeds contempt.

Noon a soldier advances with his musket goes on his Knees and commences an oration sans ceremonie, singers wanted to stop him, however he persisted, he did not care he had something to communicate to the King at last the Mayo-gau interfered and ordered him to desist, and wait that he should be heard.

The singers continued it was about the Houssa nation making fine cloth, they must go there and get some for the King, to wear,[523] they are desired to cut their song short.

The man soldier say that the A-gow, and Mee-gau are not present both being sick he then commences on the dilapidated state of the Palace walls, and appears to attach all the blame on the Mayo-gau, and the sick absentees, the matter did not please the old Prime Minister, however he went on [to] state that Mayo-gau and Caboceer of Whydah, would have to cut of a head each tonight, that there were two more, four altogether to be sacrificed, the Caboceer's feelings are not so blood thirsty , as the old devil the Mayo-gau, he pays fifteen strings to a wretch to perform the awful ceremony, but the old fellow rather than pay the sum of 15d̲. performs the awful deed himself, it cannot be to save the 1s/3d he must have some strong Political motive relative to his own family connected with his duties, as the Mayo-gau, because he could get as many miscreants for 15 strings each as he pleased, it appears to be a thirst, they have imbibed from their continued murderous warfare.

King speaks but so low as not to be heard.

---

[521] Recalled in later Dahomian tradition as a Yoruba general defeated and killed by Gezo at Kpaloko in the Mahi country, probably in 1832/3 (Skertchly (1874: 326): 'Ge-nah-Koh'; Le Herissé (1911: 320–2): 'Adjinakou'; for the date, cf. Mouléro (1965: 53)): i.e. Ajinaku (a nickname, meaning 'Elephant'), who was an ally of Ikosoni of Sabe, mentioned on the previous day, p. 108 (Palau Marti 1992: 196–7).

[522] The king was commonly addressed and referred to as Kpò, 'Leopard', alluding to his descent from Agasu.

[523] The Hausa city of Kano was a major centre of cotton cloth production. Heinrich Barth in 1851 noted that its cloth was widely traded through West Africa, but did not suggest that its distribution extended anywhere close to Dahomey (1857, ii: 125–6); the wording here seems to confirm that Hausa cloth was as yet known in Dahomey only by repute.

Mayo-gau speaks, a controversy was entered into about the walls of the Palace, which lasted an hour, but of course finished, with a decision that they were to be repaired immediately it ended at 10 o'clock.

I have seen myself several Breaches in the walls, and Trees have filled the space, so they must have been for some time in that state.

Antonio de Souza makes his appearance

Singers for a few minutes praise the Mayo-gau

Musicians a Gift of 23½ heads of cowries.

An Amazon brought forward and shewn to us having been wounded by a man at the Okeedan war,[524] had received two sword cuts on the head, nevertheless she took the man a Prisoner, her name is Soh-doo-soon-voo.

Amazon Troops sworn in for the next war, their names are called and the number of Prisoners each has taken are mentioned at the Ah-taa-Pam war, according to their statements, 346 Prisoners and 32 heads, 79 not explained prisoners or heads.

Another Amazon brought forward and displayed before us, having received wounds on the head, nose, and hand at the Ah-naa-goo war[525] her name Lah-maa cee-dung-vee.

Nee-dag-baa a bad wound at the back of the neck, I presume it was with an intention to get her head, these three were the whole of the wounded displayed, I presume his Pension list is not extensive, he should have a peep at Greenwich.[526]

4 o'clock rain, King walks from his Tent to us, takes us by the hand, as usual a Glass, shouts, and 6 muskets fired, he showed us three well made country sticks, well made and inlaid with Ivory, coloured wood, he said that he would send a specimen home with us, to get some made by them on It, he asked me, if I would not come again, to see him. I told him it was very likely, he retires

Hum-baa-gee King's officer of his Amazons[527] receives a Gift of 10 heads of cowries and a Keg of rum, she then called all her officers and harangued them on the munificence of the Gift, and said who is there that can act like Gezò our King, give us cowries and rum, an acclamation, and loudly called

---

[524] Okeodan, in Egbado, destroyed by the Dahomians in 1849.

[525] Cf. note 229.

[526] Alluding to the Royal Hospital at Greenwich, London, which paid pensions to retired naval persons.

[527] Later spelled 'Hung-maa-gee', 'Um-baa-gee'; by Forbes 'Hungbahjee' and by Burton 'Humbagi' (1864, i: 252–3), probably representing the Fon name nowadays spelled 'Houngbadji'. She is later described as 'head of the Amazons' (p. 116), by Forbes as 'chief of the King's levees' (Journal, p. 185) and by Burton as the commander of the left wing of King Gezo's female body guards.

out that there is not a nation like the Dahomeians, and perhaps but a very few real ones amongst the people, that were born in the country.[528]

Sing and dance and call Gezo's Praises aloud, receive 1 small & 1 large Bottles of rum and retire.

Caboceers dance a Gift of 1 Bottle of rum

Soldiers men muster and salute the King, a Gift of several calabashes of chop, or provissions.

Poo-voo-soo the privileged [one] advance to us, and receives a glass of spirits, and nips it of.

Soldiers men sing Praises, and finish by stating that if the Dab a Dab Hills were to fall on the King, they would not allow a hair on his head to be injured.

Ag-gaa-hoo [= Ajaho?]	Thiefs [*sic*] Drum plays a short time	2 heads
Ah-coo-huu	Band of music	2 D°
Poo-wah	Drum band 6 fellows	2 D°
Cong-goo	Drum for decapitation	2
a large Band a fellow with a well worn uniform coat		1 head 15 str
Kings Family Brother sons &c		40 D°
3 gallons of rum		
Ah-puni-gan[529]	a Drum—large	2 Do
		54
Band Gao-quu-ah		5 heads
D° Pah-tee		20 D° 10 str
D°		1 D°
D°		2 D°
D°	of Horns	⅓ D°

2 women advanced dressed in white called the Kings Birds[530] salute the King in imitation of Birds, modifying their voices, a Gift of   1 D° 10 str
and a Bottle of rum

Band passing and playing   2 Do
                                                  15 20 str

5.30 got Permission to depart, Mayo-gau and the Caboceer for Whydah, asked if we wished to remain to see the sacrifices, I made no reply only by

---

[528] The words beginning 'and perhaps ...' are clearly a comment by Beecroft, rather than part of what Houngbadji said. Forbes likewise asserted that 'there are few pure Dahomians', only 10 per cent (20,000 of 200,000) being free, the remainder slaves, either purchased or captured in war (1851, i: 14, 19); (cf. also his comment on the composition of the Dahomian army, Journal, p. 157). These statements are probably exaggerated, but it has been estimated that in the late nineteenth century slaves comprised between a quarter and a third of the population of Dahomey (Manning 1982: 192).

[529] Presumably, this is again Kpanlingan (cf. note 396).

[530] Forbes gives this term in Fon (Journal, p. 183).

shaking my head, in disgust, at such awful and horrible atrocities, The Caboceer told Nawhey, to tell us that one of his wives were very ill with Dysent[e]ry, we told him that medicine would be sent for her, by Nawhey, we proceeded home at 6 o'clock when we arrived, weather had become fine, a messenger arrived from Whydah, with a Letter addressed to me, from Mr Hastie enclosed one from the Admiralty, via Ahgway, dated the 4[th] of April,[531] also a Spectator, dated 2nd March,[532] I presume that it is the first that has arrived at Abomey direct from England.

10 o'clock retired to rest.

Programme Monday 17 June

am cool w[r] daylight Ther 75° took an early Breakfast, left at 9 o'clock, at 9.30 entered the Ah-doo-noo Gate,[533] the [King] was dressed in a country cloth, saluted him and took our seats, the court was small, originally called Ah-ga-ja-du-soo,[534] [calab?]ashes of skulls, there are several shady Trees in it introduced by the singing women.

Gift given them		10 heads of cowries[535]		
Mee-gau, Treasurer,[536] Band & Banners		10 heads, 1 demijohn rum		
Mayo-gau—Prime Minister		10 D°		D°
Caboceer [of] Whydah		10 D°		D°
Quahnoo[537]		10 D°	"	D°
Ah-goo-vee		10 D°	D°	D°
King addresses them and states I give you these Gifts for your good offices				
Koo-jaa-ah		10 D°	D°	D°
Nawhey	English servant[538]	10 D°	D°	D°

[531] Not traced.

[532] A London newspaper.

[533] I.e. Adono, the Kpojito of King Agaja. The gates along the north-western side of the palace bore the names of the successive Kpojito, that of Adono being the most northerly (Burton 1864, ii: 169–71).

[534] I.e. Agaja Dosu. Although Beecroft does not specify this, Forbes indicates that the rites of this day, and those on 18, 19, 21 and 22 May, were to 'water the graves' of the successive royal 'mothers'. Forbes places this day's rites in the Adanjloakodé section of the palace (Journal, p. 183), but strictly Adono's gate was in the northern or Agringomè section. The office of Kpojito seems to have been instituted under Agaja—hence the lack of rites for 'mothers' of the earlier kings (Bay 1998: 71–8).

[535] For the following, cf. Forbes' 'Appendix', in TNA, FO84/827, ff. 303–v; Forbes (1851, ii: 246–8).

[536] This description of the Migan's function is aberrant and certainly incorrect.

[537] Again (as on 7 June, p. 77), the first five names following the Yovogan are those of the principal merchants of Ouidah (in a slightly different order): Quénum, Adjovi, Codjia, Gnahoui, Hodonou.

[538] Beecroft later observes that Gnahoui 'styles himself' the 'English servant' (p. 123; cf. also Forbes, Journal, p. 192). Forbes seems to have thought that this meant that he was literally a

Koh-doo-noo	10 D°	D°	D°
Toh-maa-tee [= Tometin] King's Brother	5 D°	2 gallons rum	
Isadore De Souza Cha Cha of Whydah	10	1 Demi John	
Doo-soo-yaa-vuu[539]	<u>9</u>	<u>1 gallon</u>	
	114	49 gall	
Bah-hee-nee[540]	3 heads 1 case B[ottle] rum		
Cam-baa-dee Treasurer	10 D°	3 Gall	
Kings family	10 D°	3 D°	
Ah-maa-gee-pa-see	10 D°	none	
Mee-gau [of the] Amazons	10 D°	3 gall rum	
Poo-vo-soo	6 D° 16 str		
Poo-la-qua	6 D° 20 str		
Da-gaa-ne-gaa	3 D° 10 str		
Goo-noo	3 D°		
Mee-da-huu	1 D°		
Wee-ma-huu	3 D°		
Hoo-goo	3 D°		
Cha-lee-Koo	2 D°		
My-paa-la-lee	2 D°		
Boo-noo-maa	5 D°		
Ah-loo-pa-Ka	1 " 5 str		
Koo-qua-hee[541]	3 " 5		
Loh-faa-lee	1 " 10		
Uh-coo-boo	6 " 10		
Kah-huu-too	1 " 30		
Du-mee-gan	1 " 5		
Bee-tee	20		
Da-ga-na-Koo-que	5 "		
Baa-vee-na-saa	10 " 15		
Bee-mah-suu	3 " 5		
Eh-noo-gaa	25		
Saa-ah	30		
Ah-lok-wee	5		
So-gong [= Sogan?]	40		
Cha-mu-naa	2 " 20		

---

servant of the English fort at Ouidah (1851, ii: 174), but it clearly refers only to his role as interpreter for English visitors (Law 2016: 742).

[539] Dosu-Yovo: i.e. Antonio Dosu-Yovo, de Souza's interpreter between Portuguese and French (Law 2004b: 177–8).

[540] Bahini, the name of a merchant family at Ouidah (ibid., 102–3).

[541] Forbes gives this name as 'Koh-koh-ah-jee' (1851, ii: 247); he also participated in the discussions recorded later on this day.

Ah-qua-dee-see	2
Ah-see	2
Ah-doo-poo-nee	1
Ah-hoo-paa [= Ahokpè]	4
Ah-vaa-gan [= Yovogan][542]	20
Too-bee-suu	13. 30 6 B of rum
	138 10 11 Gall
Kings Brothers to make Custom for Kings sister Maa-vaa-du	36 heads 3 B rum
Woman Mayo-gau	30 D° & ”
Kings Brother	30 D°
Band	10
D°	3
	247 12½

11 o'clock Band & Banners bearing the imitation in miniature the Town of Kan-gaa-roo in Brass which he conquered after Duncan's visit

King retires and changes his Garment[543]

Egboo-zaa head of Kings Family Troop	10 heads
Sing praises Troops salute the King	Total 257 D°

It is as usual bearding[?][544] each other about the Ah-taa-Pam war

Six men advance to the King's presence and lay two skulls before him, apparently fresh ones after going through a formal address, they then communicated that they had to present the two skulls, taken as follows, The Abbeokutians have taken a small Town, in land some distance from Por-to-Novo called Humbo,[545] a foraging party of 20 or 30 men, had straggled away to look for victuals, they had entered a Farm, and taken, I presume, what corn they could conveniently carry, two of the party being some distance in the rear, were fell in with by these men, they endeavoured to escape, but were shot, and their heads the forfeit, the others hearing the report of muskets, made the best of their way, not knowing what number the party consisted of, behind them, those men [i.e. those who took the heads] belonged to a Town called Too-suu, but it was difficult to gain correct information, it appears by the account that I gleaned the Abbeokutians, had been repulsed at the latter place.[546]

---

[542] Forbes confirms this identification (1851, ii: 147, 'Ee-a-voo-gau').

[543] Burton in 1864 witnessed a ceremony (called *avò hùzú gbè*, 'Day of changing cloth') in which the King changed his clothes three times (1864, i: 373–86).

[544] I.e. confronting.

[545] Ihunmbo, in Egbado, 40 km north-east of Porto-Novo: Forbes here says 'a small town in Anagoo', without naming it (Journal, p. 183).

[546] Forbes gives this name as 'Tossoo': not identified, but presumably also in the Egbado area. This town was subsequently attacked and destroyed by Abeokuta, probably later in 1850: see

They received a Gift of half a piece of white Baft each, 2 heads of cowries, 1 small Bottle of rum, and a Keg of rum, 2½ gallons for the Head man of the Town or Village these men came from, Mayo-gau opened his mouth on the matter, bawling that, we have got two heads, we will very soon have the rest.

The 400 heads of cowries we met outside of the court on our arrival in the hands of 200 men, sitting Indian file were brought in and piled up near us, they were to be shared amongst the male soldiers, on all former Customs they had been sent to Ah-loo-pee's house to be distributed, he is an officer of a body of soldiers.[547]

Ah-Koo-too say that the 400 heads of cowries, should not be sent to Ah-loo-pee's House for division, he is one of the King's head war men, and he has disgraced himself, the same way he left Abomey, he returned to it, without discharging his musket, once.

Mayo-gau say it is correct what the last man has stated, they must be taken to his the Mayo's own Porch to be divided,

a man arose and said they should not be sent to the Mayo-gau's, they should be sent to Tin-gaa-vee's.[548]

Too-no-noo the head Eunuch say they must be sent to the Mayo's.

Boo-coo-maa-hoo-nee corroborated the aforesaid.

Hung-maa-gee,[549] head of the Amazons gives her veto[,] that they ought to be sent to Ah-loo-pee's

Ah-loo-pee say that the cowries shall not be sent to his any more for division.[550]

His speech enraged the Old Mayo-gau, and so incensed him, that the man of 70 years, flew at him like a Tiger, and struck him several times, and ordered him to be taken away, he was bundled out sans ceremonie, after a few minutes the King, ordered that he was to be recalled, Mayo say that the said cowries must be sent to the Kings yard, or wherever he the King pleases to order,

---

Mehu (for King of Dahomey) to Queen of England, 7 Sept. 1851 (in Fraser (2012: 217), 'To-soo', where the editorial suggestion (n. 52) that this is a miscopying of 'Itoro', is mistaken.)

[547] Clearly the Fon name nowadays spelled 'Alokpè'. It is noteworthy that another man of this name, described as an 'old warrior' and 'chamberlain' to King Gezo, is recalled to have been killed in a war in the 1820s (Hazoumé 1978 [1938]: 35, 63, 102), and that an earlier officer of the same name is documented in the 1780s (Dalzel (1793: 167–8): 'Allopwee'). This suggests that this name may have been perpetuated by the practice of 'positional succession' (see note 223): when the Alokpè of 1850 was disgraced for cowardice, it was likewise anticipated that his name would be 'given to another' (pp. 122, 124, this volume).

[548] Forbes has 'Tingahlee' (Journal, p. 184)—evidently one or other of these versions is a miscopying.

[549] Forbes gives the name as 'Hwaemazae'.

[550] Forbes says the opposite: 'I have heard all the dispute & still claim my right.'

Ah-loo-pee was powerful sufficient to walk over 50 of the Mayo-gaus calliber.

The King say that the Mayo was wrong for striking Ah-loo-pee.

When he [= Ah-loo-pee] returned and was allowed to speak, he contradicted his former statement, and said that the cowries, had been always sent to his house in former years, and that they ought to be sent this [year].

Mayo-gau enraged said that they should not under any circumstances be sent to Ah-loo-pee's House.

Ah-loo-pee then stated that they hated him.

King directed them at once to state where they were to be sent for division.

An Amazon, say that it always has been the custom to send them to Ah-loo-pee's.

Soo-gan–saa[551] states they may send them to his House.[552]

Koo-Ko-vee-sah, and Ah-Koo-too, decided in [= on] not saying any more on the matter.

King desires them to speak so as he can hear them.

Kao-Ke-see-sah [*sic*], repeats what the King has just repeated.

King again rebukes the Mayo, and states that the cowries must be sent to Kah-mah-dig-bee's House for division.

Ah-loo-Koo-daa states that it is the Mayogaus rights and privileges, to settle all Palavers.

King say that if any man, or woman, do wrong at the war, to report the same and he will punish them himself.

Laa-pee-hoo King's Brother[553] desires to be heard in favor of Ah-loo-pee.

King replies—No! it is finished he is not to have the cowries, he receives a rebuke, and his [= is] desired to reflect on his past conduct,

Mayo threatens him that if he does not look out and amend his ways, he will see after him.

King desires them not to talk any more on the Ah-taa-pam war, as they have destroyed the Town and all its people, a most monstrous exaggeration, more anon about the war, he say that they have too many opinions, when they go to war, disputes arise, and it is now they are to be settled, he again refers to the Mayo, taking him [=Ah-loo-pee] away on account of the cowries, he say that he ought to have removed Ah-loo-pee for cowardice at the war, if it is proved, it would have altered his position wonderfully. I hear all the bickering and

---

[551] I.e. presumably Sogan: although the significance of the terminal '-sar' is obscure, it occurs in connection with another title (see note 566).

[552] Forbes says rather that it was Alokpè who suggested sending them to the Sogan's house (Journal, p. 184).

[553] Spelled 'Lehpehhooh' by Forbes: i.e. Linpehoun (Bay 1998: 172).

disagreements, from my Ah-gow of the woman soldiers, the head general of the male soldiers, ought to have reported if there were any men that had behaved ill at the war.

Lah-pee-hoo Kings Brother, speaks in favor of Ah-loo-pee and states that if any person has anything to bring against him, at once to come forward and speak.

An Amazon speaks and say that the cowries must be sent to Ting-gaa-vee's house after the next war.

King say what is the matter so much clamour.

At the moment all the officers of the Amazon army, came into the King's presence, and threw dust on their heads.

An Amazon rises and say she brings a charge of cowardice against her officers.[554]

King rebuked them and told them to retire on aside [*sic*]

[King says] This Amazon and another were carriers without arms, under protection, took more prisoners than the officers of the whole Troop, took the arms of the vanquished, and fought and distinguished themselves.

King presented them with a Gift of 10 heads of cowries, for their undaunted courage, he told them at their peril to give one of these cowries to their comrades, if he should learn that they did do so he would take of their heads, they salute him and retire to the rear.

Terrible Bickerings between the Amazons, and men Troops, also between the Mayo-gau's men and the Mee-gaus, some jealousy existing, it went so far and in the presence of the King, as to rather astonish me that a Despot would have allowed it, Um-baa-dee one of the Kings Troops, challenged Kak-ah-joo to single combat, the latter belongs to Cam-baa-dee.[555]

An Amazon rises and takes the part of the latter, by stating that should they both meet at the next war, say at Baa-ah, they will be better able to prove to the King, their Prowess of war, to any extent the farther they go the better he will be pleased.

King speaks rather in favor of Kak-ah-joo, he being a young soldier.

An Amazon say that if Um-baa-dee considered Kak-ah-joo a coward, he ought to have brought it forward before.[556]

King desires them to cease their Palavers.

---

[554] Forbes says more specifically that Akpadume (the female Posu) charged Hetungan (the female Gau), with running away.

[555] 'Um-baa-dee' (subsequently 'Um-baa-gee') is clearly a variant spelling of the name Houngbadji (cf. Forbes' Journal, p. 185). The second name is later given in a longer form, 'Koo-koh-ah-gee', spelled by Forbes 'Kookoahgee', and by Burton 'Ko-ko'aje' (1864, i: 230): he is described by Forbes as 'chief of the Camboodee's levies'.

[556] The male pronoun here (and later) is presumably again an error, since Houngbadji is elsewhere identified as female.

A male soldier say they must not talk at each other, in the manner they are doing, for soon they will be going to war, and in a country that they will have to be as one man, not to make enemies of each other before they proceed.

It really appears that every one claims the right of rising and gabbling their own mon[s]trosities, and extolling each other at will.

An Amazon gets on her feet and states, something monstrous, that Kak-ah-joo's party in war, are the best, and superior soldiers excel all others.

Kok-ah-joo requests the King to allow him more soldiers, Koo-Ko-ah-jee say[557] that they are all the Kings slaves,[558] that if they err in war, he will not sell them but cut of their heads.[559]

An Amazon rises and say that she believes the King is not made fully acquainted with what actually transpires at the war, the Head General ought to communicate every offence to His Majesty.

King speaks to Um-baa-gee tells him that when he goes to next war and fails on every [= even?] one point when he returned he will cut of his head, and he would also recommend them to learn, to keep their own secrets, talk less, and perform greater fetes, when they are at war.

An Amazon say that Koo-Ko-ah-gee's adopted mother was extolling him to the skies.

King checked her from going on to an unlimited length.

we got Permission to leave he sent us 10 Heads of cowries, and 3 Gallons of rum, thanked His Majesty, and left, and arrived at our Palace, at 3.30 pm, King sent 3 pieces of the silk that I brought, to take Patterns for much larger pieces, he sent a great quantity of country chop, the day has been remarkably without any rain, we have been under the necessity today to check our Hammockmen, to put a Bit in their mouths,[560] for a day or two, Retired to rest at 9 o'clock.

Tuesday 18 June

Programme

daylight Ther 74° cool and pleasant w[r] I took a walk, down the Canna Road and returned at 7.15. after breakfast wrote for short time, until the messenger made his appearance, at 11.30 we arrived at the Ah-Wha-gee-see Gate.[561]

---

[557] Awkwardly worded, suggesting that 'Kok-ah-joo' and 'Koo-koh-ah-jee' are two different people, but they are in fact the same person.

[558] Cf. also p. 130. This may refer to the employment of slaves as soldiers (see Forbes' Journal, p. 169), but royal authority in Dahomey was conceptualised in terms of ownership, so that all the king's subjects, including 'free' persons, were represented as his 'slaves': for other references and discussion, see Law (1989: 407–8).

[559] Forbes gives this slightly differently, 'we are the king's slaves, but he cannot sell us' (1851, ii: 145).

[560] I.e. restrain them.

[561] Evidently miscopied for 'Ah-wah-gee-lee'. Forbes' Journal gives the name as 'Ahlohwargaelee' (p. 185): i.e. Hwanjile, the Kpojito of the fifth king, Tegbesu. Forbes implies that these rites were

At noon the adopted mother that lived when Abomey was built,[562] entered the inner court, & saluted the King, we also saluted him and took our seats.

Poo-sooh [= Posu] say that the cowries they have received we have fought for, he appeals to his people they answer with a loud shout, he is one of the Kings staunch warriors.

King is dressed in a white robe, a number of armed Amazons on his left as a body Guard.

Too-no-vu-sah[563] say the house of this Court is out of repair, also say that the A-gow or head war-man is sick, and they must be cautious ere they speak, and what sort of reports they make, and what is said before the King, the Agow must take care how he equips, and sends his people to war, this time, for they were indifferently pointed[564] last war.

Ah-hoo-pee Kings Brother states that Ah-haa-see-see has done his duty, he is satisfied there ought not to be any complaint against him.[565]

A-gow of the Amazons, called Ah-tun-gaa[566] say that she heard all that was spoken against her and others of her party yesterday, that she was ready today to answer for her conduct, that whatever orders the King gave her, she had fulfilled to the letter, to the best of her judgement, and that there is not any burthen [= burden] King may put on her, but she will bear, she cannot complain and say it is too much and not to be borne.[567]

Ah-ee-soo-too say that all the Troops are present that fought for the A-gow, they all rose and answered, but not satisfactorily, it was their absenting themselves from their Posts, that left the Amazons unsupported, when the enemy came upon them, they lost seven of their head people, which has much perplexed His Majesty.

Soo-gaa-saa say that whenever he goes to war and acts as a coward, if he returns he cannot beg the King to spare him, his head is forfeited, he further

---

held in the Dahomey palace (and in his book, states this explicitly: Forbes (1851, ii: 146)), but this is presumably a misrecollection, since Hwanjile's gate was in the main palace (Burton 1864, ii: 171).

[562] Forbes here explicitly identifies Hwanjile as the mother of Dakodonu, the first king of Dahomey, but this is an error (cf. note 225). In his book, he amended this to describe Hwanjile as only 'a hereditary title in the harem', but it is not clear whether this reflects awareness of the error (1851, ii: 146).

[563] Forbes, 'Tohkohnoovehseh': i.e. Tokonon-vissau (note 279).

[564] *Sic*: presumably 'appointed', i.e. equipped.

[565] According to Forbes (who gives the name as 'Ahooeesooee'), this man had been accused of misconduct on 17 June (Journal, p. 185).

[566] Spelled by Forbes, 'Haetungsar' (Journal, p. 186; but in the published version, Forbes (1851, ii: 147): 'Hae-tung'); and by Burton, 'Khe-tun-gan', which would be 'Hetungan' in modern spelling (1864, i: 222; ii: 41). Both Forbes and Burton confirm that she was the female Gau.

[567] Forbes has 'but our load ought not to be too heavy'.

states that Mee-gau would have decapitated Ah-loo-pee[568] but His Majesty's clemency saved him, he goes on to state that all the Palaver that was spoken at court yesterday, they must come forwards and prove today.

Ah-loo-pee was called, and four or five others, he was disgraced and with the rest stripped of their accoutrements, the six were divided with the Mayo, Mee-gau and Cambaa-dee, one of the six was manacled at once.

Soo-gaa-saa again state that Ah-loo-pee is a coward [in] plain terms, he cannot express himself beyond that, I really think that he went beyond what he could really prove, still he hoped the King would spare them,

King say that the Agow has the power and privilege of placing the Troops, in their divisions, and giving each officer his station, and duties, but Ah-loo-pee had not the sole charge of that division, that abandoned their Post to Forage, that he could not condemn Ah-loo-pee, for that, nevertheless they were disgraced,

The King requested them to bring back the man that was sent away in Irons, he was immediately produced, and ordered to be unshackled and his arms and accoutrements restored to him, he was pardoned at once, for it appeared to the King to be a malicious act, for he had made a few straightforward statements that gave the King a clue to see directly that this man was not to blame.

King states that there were Guards for the Provissions, and Powder, and that he was still at loss to find out the faulter, now this said man is desired to state if possible, how the enemy could have gained such an advantage, as to attack the right and cut of several of the Amazons.

The five fellows returned with their heads shaved and disgraced to carry a club, to attend as Executioners, they had besmeared themselves with dust for the degradation, and walked of with their clubs on their shoulders.

An Amazon say that [she was?] one of the number that had the share of the 10 heads given yesterday, presented the Basket, and spoke loudly, in her own Praise, and said that the next war she would fill the same with heads of her enemies at the Baa-ah war and present them to Gezo her King and ruler,

Others swear that if they swerve from their King, they hope the small-pox may Kill them.[569]

An Amazon, an officer, stated that the 10 heads that the King gave as a Gift yesterday, she did not receive even a cowrie, they had forgot who [omission] them to be soldiers, and recommended them, she made the King a Present of 5 strings, two or three others did the same, King ordered a fellow to

---

[568] The Migan had, among other functions, that of 'chief executioner' (Forbes 1851, i: 22; Le Herissé 1911: 38).

[569] Evidently, they swore by the *vodun* Sakpata, who was believed to cause smallpox.

take them to the market, to buy chop for the same Amazons, it was given in a scramble like childrens play.

Band. a Gift of	10 heads of cowries
D° D°	3 D° " D°
D° D°	2 Bottles of rum

An Amazon states that the officers are too proud, and haughty, that if the King was not a good and lenient ruler, he would have taken of some of their heads

Band, 1 Union Jack a Gift of 2 heads

Kao-jaa-da, is desired to cover up the hole that Ah-loo-pee has made, so as he cannot rise any more, his name shall be given to another, so as he may be forgotten, and his memory blotted out.

King cathecizes his Troops, and gives them a severe rebuke, and cautions them to behave better for the future.

A strange assertion from a male soldier say suppose ten men, meet five and one of the five fire and kill one of the ten, the other nine would run of, so he pays the men Troops, an awful compliment, as warriors, it may be a malinterpretation

Another goes to an extreme the other side and say that if his small band of Troops, happened to fall in with 1000 men, they would walk through them, his 100 men any quantity of confidence &c &c

Another states that when he goes to the Baa-ah war, if he is not successful he will not be seen he will take of his own head, he will not give the Mee-gau the trouble, receives a Gift of 10 heads for his people.

King say that a man by chance, encounters an enemy, and gets the better of him, and sees two coming to the assistance of his antagonist, he gets afraid and runs of and leaves his Prize.

then absenting themselves from their Posts,

Man-chee-haa a Carrier at the Ahtaa Paam war, not having any arms, but his stick, encountered an enemy and killed him, and in the act of cutting of his head, he saw two of his enemies followers coming upon him behind, having then got arms from his captive he succeeded in keeping them at bay until some of his own party hove in sight, they then made of.

King told him to hold up his stick and display it to the multitude, he did so and saluted him.

An Amazon say that a good watchman will not make a bad report, for he would make himself properly acquainted with every Position.

4 o'clock, we received permission to leave, took a glass with His Majesty saluted him and left, dined at 5.30 after which I took a short walk and called on Count Nawhey, he has a large mansion, a Pond for ducks &c, all sorts of Livestock in his yard, he must have wealth, and a man well of in this country, he asked me to take a Glass of Gin with him, I merely tasted out of

compliment to the English servant as he stiles himself, I left and amused myself under the Tree, until 8 o'clock, and went inside found Capt Forbes better his attack of ague and fever was slight so we have each had a touch of it lightly, 9.30 retired to rest.

Programme Wednesday 19ᵗʰ June

Ther 74° daylight fine dry wʳ I have caught a cold after Breakfast employed writing until 10.30 messenger arrived and we left and arrived at 11 o'clock at the inner Court of the Gate called Cha-hee,[570] saluted the King and took our seats under a large shady Tree.

A-gow sent a messenger to the King with his compliments, stating that as soon as his health was restored he could wait on him, and at the same time begged leave to thank him for the manner he conducted the affairs of yesterday.

The man that received the 10 heads yesterday for the first head at the Ah-taa-Pam war with only his stick, must needs come forward and open his mouth before the multitude and extol his own deeds, with a long harangue, and winding [up] with the Basket that he received yesterday full of cowries, pledges himself to fill [it] with the heads of his enemies at the Baa-ah war.[571]

It is their whole theme for the King to allow them that road, and they all swear by their heads,[572] a fellow held up the same Basket that the man before him had been extolling his own power, strength, and agility on, he taken [= taking] the mania for [= from?] this fellow that the Basket would not hold one third of the heads that he intended to present to the King after the next war.

a man rises and states that they are in reality going to war, not as formerly, skirmishing, he further stated that he had not a sweet, oily mouth, but that he is read[y] and willing to do his best, the King will be better able to judge of his Powers, on his return from the war, should he not fall. They then commence the theme is that the King will not detain them too long, for water is stronger than fire, I presume they do not wish their thirst to be quenched.

An Amazon say that they have gained Power over their enemies by one man's head, only, look at a man without arms, or ammunition, conquers his enemy fully armed, God blessed them with victory.

---

[570] Forbes gives this name as 'Jahhee', described as 'the King's great grandmother' (Journal, p. 187): i.e. Chai, the Kpojito of Gezo's grandfather, the sixth king, Kpengla (Bay 1998: 49).

[571] As Forbes notes, this day's proceedings comprised the taking of an 'oath of fidelity' by the male soldiers, paralleling the oath of the 'Amazons' on 13 June.

[572] Perhaps meaning that their heads would be forfeited if they failed in their duty. However, in Dahomian thought, a person's soul (sé) was thought to reside in his head (Law 1989: 408–9), so the oaths may have been sworn on their souls.

They then sing praises to the King, that he is brazen on their memory, particularly in the war, if any country insult our King by word, or deed, he has only to issue his mandates, and they will soon go and destroy that country.

King say that their former wars they were not so well equipped, and served, as they are now he supplies them with Guns, Powder, flints and shot, no other nation can stand or compete with them, so if any man miss and do wrong his head is forfeited.

A man say that it is not them that open their mouths, and make fine speeches before the King, that does the most execution at the war, 1000 men enters the field, they are not generally all engaged at once.

King say, I merely exhort you to do your duties.

A man rises and rebukes the man that sat down last, and told him that he was not a leading officer, that he ought not to talk such a Palaver before the King.

Another states that the King supplies them with cloth, and everything that is necessary for them, therefore they ought all to be of one mind, to fight right well for their King & Country.

a vast [amount?] of ribaldry is spoken, a fellow states that not any person has a right to interfere with them and sits down.

Another get up and spouts, that the next war is one of boys, the A-gow and head officers, had better stay at home, he was shouted down, and told by one of his comrades that he was speaking against the King, he was too noisy, and clamorous, and had too much confidence in himself.

King interferes and desire them to desist from attacking each other, he has the Power to make and break his officers, as he deems fit.

A Gift of 1 Head of Cowries, and one bottle of rum.

An Amazon a clamorous one she is, say that the King gave her a Knife, and displays it, stating that she has not as yet had an opportunity to use it, but she will give it a trial of her skill, at the next war, and perform some fete to please the King.

2nd gets up and displays a sheet of Blank Paper, given her by Bah-daa-hoo he gave [it] to her and told her to go and look for the King his Father, and show him the Paper, he will put his mark on it, then I shall be satisfied that he is well, for he felt anxious about his Father, after the attack of the enemy on the right wing.[573]

King say that he has not as yet given Ah-loo-pee's name to any other person, nor appointed any person in his place.

---

[573] Forbes also records this flourishing of a piece of paper, but gives the accompanying speech differently: 'This book was given me by Bah-dah-hoong ... to give my "Father" ..., to keep the

Ah-Kaa-Kee-guu an Amazon say the King can use his pleasure, about placing any one in the room of Ah-loo-pee, for he was not the only one, they were all to blame only it has been maliciously placed on his shoulders.

Ah-loo-pee comes into the Kings presence and throws dirt on his head.

King say that the last speaker state that they were all to blame, so they must clear the matter if possible today.

An Amazon states that they must each talk their own Palaver.

King say if you accuse each other in that way of cowardice who will stand in the court

Band a Gift of 13 heads and 1 Bottle of rum.

The Band of soldiers saluted the King and retired.

King say there are several in the midst of you, that deserve their heads taking of, what would you say if I was to do so, would you like it, but he had no desire to do it as it would not be pleasing to himself.

Band, Banners, and soldiers enter, some with halberds,[574] several were dressed in scarlet wrappers, with black striped velvet vests, another carrying a shield, made from a Bullocks Hide, captured from the Eyo's at their wars.[575]

King's sisters salute him a Gift of a few bottles of rum, music cease and singing begin 8 Boys are presented before the King, they were taken at the Ah-taa-pam war,

A Gift of half a head of Cowries was laid across each of their necks.

King then address those in his presence that are in charge of his Father's [= grandfather's?] House, they are called appertaining to that mansion, they prostrate themselves, Mayo say that Phing-gaa-laa[576] went to war with Sahlee-chee but did not take it,[577] it was left to be a laurel on the Brow of <u>Gezò</u>,[578] all places are the same they fall at his appearance, they chaunt Praises to his Grandfather and repeat over all his victories[,] he gained Whydah, and slew the King Ah-baa-muu,[579] he fought against Ah-taa-Paam, but they [i.e. the

---

records of the country on' (1851, ii: 154–5).

[574] A halberd is a combined spear and battleaxe.

[575] Probably referring to the war of 1823, in which Gezo defeated Oyo.

[576] I.e. Kpengla.

[577] Tchereti ('Tchetti' on modern maps), north-west of Dahomey. But later Dahomian tradition says that Kpengla's war against this people, after early defeats, was ultimately successful (Le Herissé 1911: 306–7), and this is supported by contemporary evidence (Dalzel (1793: 163–5, 176–8): 'Sarrachees').

[578] Gezo's campaign against Tchereti was in 1819/20 (Mouléro (1965: 52): 'Séréchi').

[579] Referring not to the town of Ouidah, which had been conquered by Agaja in 1727, but to Hueda-Hendji ('Hueda at [Lake] Hen') to the west, a settlement of refugees displaced by this conquest, whose king, Agbamou, was defeated and killed by Kpengla's forces in 1775 (Le Herissé 1911: 305–6; Law 2004b: 64–5).

Dahomians] were twice repulsed and sent back, defeated,[580] Gezo has conquered them.

King say that the 8 Boys were taken at Ah-taa-Pam he has entrusted them
to be Kept, in his Grandfathers court yard, in commemoration of the event
of that war,[581] and he cautions the old Gentleman that is in charge there to be
particular and look after their welfare, men all sing his Grandfathers Praises,
clapping their mouths with the right hand.

Amazons perform the same acclamations, and him they will serve for ever
the Boys and 2 Girls are taken away.

King sent a Gift of a Basket of oranges
                1 D°   daa-saa fruit
                Several calabashes chop
King address his sister in a tone so low as not to be heard.

Band a Gift of 15 Heads and 2 Bottles of rum

King drinks shouts, and musketry

a Band of his male soldiers advance with their Gifts of cowries, Goats,
Bullocks & fowls

King sends to my Table a country made Liquor case, containing one
round bottle of Gin, and one white china vase containing water, it [i.e. the
bottle?] was made of Hide and ornamented coloured leather, he sent a small
callabash of round country balls, like grape shot and nearly as hard, it is part
of the chop the[y] carry on their war expeditions, I managed to masticate one
it is well salted and peppered.

Ah-pah-doo-mee [*sic*], A-gou for the Amazons,[582] and Eg-boo-sah King's
Brother ornamented with these said Balls in Bag over their shoulder.

King say when they go to war they must stand to eat and drink water, no
taking a seat.

---

[580] Forbes in 1849 heard of a war under Kpengla in which Abomey was 'invested' by 'the
Anagoos', who from the context (including their location 'to the westward') are clearly those of
Atakpamé: HCPP, *Slave Trade*, Class B, incl. 10 in no. 9: Forbes to Fanshawe, 5 Nov. 1849 (cf.
also Forbes (1851, ii: 89), referring explicitly to Atakpamé, but attributing their 'inroads' to the
reign of the following king, Agonglo). This war is not recalled in subsequently recorded traditions
of Kpengla's reign (Le Herissé 1911: 305–9), probably because memory of defeats tended to be
suppressed. A contemporary source alludes to successful fighting against Atakpamé under
Gezo's immediate predecessor Adandozan, but this is also suppressed in later tradition
(Robertson (1819: 268): 'Takpama').

[581] These were probably in lieu of sacrifices: see Endnote 1.

[582] But Forbes (Journal, p. 185) identifies Akpadume as the female Posu. Burton at one point calls
her the female Posu (1864, ii: 76), but at others the female Mewu (i: 224; ii: 41), but both of these
were officers of the left wing, whereas the Gau was commander of the right wing. Beecroft was
clearly confused about the female Gau, since he elsewhere gives the title to two other persons,
Gundeme (p. 105—also wrongly) and Hetungan (p. 120—probably correctly).

Officers of his own Troops salute the King, and sing that if the fowls have not ears they cannot hear their Guns.

Band	2 heads	2 Bottles of rum
"	1 D°	1 D°
"	1 D°	1 D°
"	1 D°	½ a Pint

A Band of soldiers advance with Presents of cowries, Goats, and fowls.

King gave me permission to leave on my arrival found Capt Forbes better had got over his shake [*sic*] of the ague.[583]

I took a slight dinner, 2 Bags of Cowries arrived from Whydah. I took a short walk to the Canna Gate, and returned, a great number of our Blacks sick with influenza & Dysentry, I retired early to rest.

Thursday, 20th June

daylight dull wʳ my cold better 5 Bags of Cowries arrive by men carriers, three more on the road, after Breakfast Peter Brown called and said the King had sent for him, and settled his Palaver,[584] and passed him, so as he may leave for Whydah tomorrow, Noon today fresh westerly Breezes Ther 82°.

The King sent a Gift of three Bullocks to Isadore, Ignatio and Antonio de Souza.

Richards my Interpreter went out for a walk during his stroll he was joined by two young Youribaa men slaves to the <u>Cha-Cha</u>,[585] they were very communicative, for they commenced and told him, that on the death of old De Souza, he left in his will they were to have their freedom, on giving a slave each, but their present master has imposed two each, so they are likely to continue in thraldom all their lives, unless they succeed in the next war.

They then intimated to Richards that the King intends attacking Abbeo-kutta and they would advise him to tell his master that he had better remove the whitemen from there, he asked them from what quarter they had gleaned their information that there were so many white people at Abbeokuttaa, they said they knew that there were a great number of Englishmen in that Town, on my return home I found the same fellows that had accompanied him to our yard. I happened to mention Baa-ah they said immediately the King had Fetish to send to Abbeokutta, that would cause a Revolution amongst them-selves they then would have no trouble to take it and they are certain to pick

---

[583] According Forbes' own Journal (p. 187), he had had to leave the ceremony at noon, because of an attack of fever.

[584] Brown had come on Thomas Hutton's behalf, 'concerning some duties paid for the trade at Badagry' (Forbes 1851, ii: 72).

[585] Forbes says they were from Ijanna, Richards' own hometown (1851, ii: 155).

up stragglers as they proceed in the various Farms, and make use of them as guides &c &c.

It appears that they depend in a great measure on stratagem, and superstition for their success, Bought two pieces of <u>Shea-Butter</u> from the same men about 15 lbs weight for one head of Cowries and thirty five strings, it is an enormous price to what I bought it for five years ago at Swah on the right Bank of the Niger, near <u>Laddie</u>[586] I presume it must come from near that quarter, They have the Tree here, but they dont Know the process of extracting it [i.e. the butter] from the nutt.[587] I told them that it is too obvious that they are under an awful delusion, and their minds were too fully intent thirsting after Blood, rapine, and Plunder even all their movements, in their dances they foster it in their motions, the sawing of a fellow creatures head,[588] all the gesticulations of the children, are shown in that awful similitude, it is really too awful for a mind of congenial feelings with his allwise Maker to dwell upon.

I must leave of here this tale of war and curse on a nation, soon you must be left to yourselves, then awful will be the visitations, you have not any trade their neighbours shun them, as the sheep does the wolf, I do really Pray that the King and his ministers, will become wise and see their own downfall, I think they will listen to good advice from those that are able and willing to give them a lesson, now is the time, he can become a mighty King, exalt himself far above all the Kings in Africa, and link himself in the most durable chain with one of the greatest monarchs on earth in the world thousands and tens of thousands would burst forth in loud hallelujahs to his name. I retired at 9 o'clock.

Midnight fine w^r.

Friday, 21st June

Programme

daylight fine w^r a woman and two men arrived with the cowries, Capt Forbes received a letter from Monsieur Casse, excusing himself from visiting the Fete manificio,[589] The Fort being in such a dilapidated state,[590] he would oblige him by making an apology to the King from him.

---

[586] Referring to Beecroft's expedition up the Niger in 1845, Tshua being the port of Lade.

[587] In fact, Duncan earlier described the method of extracting the butter, by boiling and pressing, but with reference to an area some distance north of Abomey (1847, i: 286–8).

[588] Cf. Forbes (1851, i: 24): 'In every action ... there is some reference to the cutting off of heads. In their dances ... with eyes dilated, the right hand is working in a sawlike manner for some time, as if in the act of cutting round the neck, when both hands are used, and a twist is supposed to finish the bloody deed.'

[589] Portuguese *magnifico*, 'magnificent'.

[590] I.e. the French fort at Ouidah, which Cases occupied as agent of Régis.

10 o'clock messenger arrived we set of and arrived at 10.30 at the Gate called Sah-noo-mee[591] entered and saluted His Majesty, and took our seats opposite the King.

Amazons singing Praises to his Grand-mother and Progenitors, the adopted one[592] was sitting dressed in a scarlet velvet cloak, her head dress silver, round her neck coral, Popoo, and other Beads, also a silver chain round her neck, silver ornaments on her fingers, a great number of skulls, as usual displayed abreast and near the King.

Amazons singing Praises, how he gained his Power &c she sits down, they all chaunt his Praises, they are all armed and well dressed, about 60 officers belonging to the Amazon Troop, on their heads silver ornaments, and wristlets.

At the right of His Majesty men seated unarmed, the court yard is small, two or three small Trees, in this yard.

I saw on one of the skulls, a string of coral to commemorate it, it was from Ear to Ear over the skull.

They all commenced chaunting his Praises, referring to the 8 Boys, the King had sent to his Grandfathers yard, to commemorate for ever the Battle of Ah-taa-Pam.

Too-noo-noo the Eunuch thinks it time, to play upon his silvery Tongue, and say, they sing well, it pleases his master, they must continue their sweet songs, they are grateful to the King's Ear.

Mee-gau for the Amazons, speak and corroborate the Eunuchs [words], but winds up with saying that if they do not sing to please their King, he has Power to cut of their heads, they must well understand that.

Too-noo-noo amends the last and says that the King is wise, that is the reason his people are wise also, from his judicious lessons.

May[o]-gau corroborates the same.

King's Brother Lah-pee-hoo say that the King is wise and has taught his ministers and people wisdom.

singing that the charge of his Grand-mother's House, given to the adopted one she must take special care of it, and not allow it to fall into decay, but apply to right quarter in time.

Mayo finds fault that there is not a sufficient number in the Band, orders them to be increased.

An old Amazon say that the Drum men are asleep they do not please the King.

Mee-gau of the Amazons say, that singing, is not good, it does not please the King.

---

[591] Forbes 'Sehnoomeh', identified as Gezo's grandmother (Journal, p. 187): i.e. Senunme, Kpojito of Gezo's father King Agonglo.

[592] Later called 'the adopted Grandmother', i.e. the person now representing Senunme.

Ah-coo-do-mee[593] corroborates the same.

One of the singing Party spoke and said that if they did not sing to please, they must correct them, that is plain.

The King does not like it they have been too long on the same Theme about his Grandfather.

They then commence a fresh theme, and sing that he had bought them all they were his slaves,[594] he did not allow them to want for anything, God can bless him.

They invite the adopted Grandmother to rise and dance she comes forth, with her Train-bearer, she advances and salutes the King, and drinks, music and shouting she retires.

4 Fetish women in white with beads, armlets, and silver wristlets, one with silver ornaments on the fingers of both hands, they dance and salute the King.

Group sing Praises to the old Lady, it rises her vanity about her dress fitting her so well, & becoming her person, but really it was anything but a neat fit, for she was in the shape of a Cask.

Mee-gau of the Amazons presents her with 5 heads and 1 Bottle of rum.

Old Lady say that she would not have been Known, had the King not paid her a visit[595] and if she had not spoken publickly, she then said that she had maidens, and would bring them to the King.

Ah-hoo-pee King's Brother say that three days after this Custom, Fetish one begins.[596]

Too-noo-noo, the Eunuch say they must sing against the nations on the other side of the river that is Abbeokutta.[597]

Too-no-noo desire the Amazons again to sing Praises for the woman that suckled him [i.e. the King]

A quantity of chop in callabashes brought and presented to a Band of his officers of the war Troop of the men soldiers.[598] they bicker with each other about the war, until they are excited almost to fight on the ground, they talked about their heads, and dying, as a commonplace occurrence, an officer told them to take their chop, and be of without any more clamour or noise.

King speaks so low as not to be heard.

[593] Forbes (who spells the name 'Ahcordemeah') identifies her as 'Amazon head of the band'.
[594] The reference to purchase need not be literal, but may allude to the idea that all Dahomians were 'slaves' to the king (cf. p. 119, note 558). The king symbolically 'purchased' Dahomey, including its inhabitants, at his installation (Law 1989: 407–8).
[595] Forbes has 'who can know he [*sic*] is there?' (Journal, p. 187).
[596] The 'Fetish' Custom began on 26 June and was still ongoing on 3 July.
[597] Forbes attributes this to Ahokpè; he also names the river as 'Agonee [= Agonli, east of Dahomey]': perhaps the Ouèmè, which flows through Agonli territory to the sea and formed the eastern boundary of Dahomey further south, is meant.
[598] Forbes says to 'the Amazon officers and their coadjutors [= male counterparts]'.

Mayo say and repeats His Majesty's speech and state that the language of those officers were unbecoming, they ought to consider their speeches at home, ere they shout them out before the public.

King say that a young man that spoke, and talked so loud must take care that he does not get tired

An old officer said the young man spoke uncautiously, he is a very good young man, and is always ready and willing to obey His Majesty's summons.

An Amazon of the officers say that they must be wary what they say in Public, for it will be repeated in their songs, perhaps to their shame.

Procession of 10 mademoiselles de pavau [= pavé][599]

King say to the officers of both Parties to take their victuals, and depart, and talk not any more nonsense.

They sing praises aloud and say the King is their Power, and as long as he lives they don't care for any person.

Amazon officers present their muskets, and retire.

a Band of men sing that they are the Kings Lions.

Too-noo-noo states any oils the Mayo-gau b[u]y saying he is generous, he gives Gifts of Cloth every year to the Constables, in the Kings Palace yard.

King sent us a Gift of a callabash of oranges, and Daa-see fruit.

An Amazon calls on Ko-Koo-agee, he advances and speaks, that he is not ashamed to state about the war, another interrupts him and say you have not any power but through the King.

She tells him to prove his strength.

He state that he is strong by the Power the King gives him.

a soldier answers him and say his Power is in his having plenty of people, that is his strength, that he must be cautious and take care, else one day he will fall, so says Sum-baa-gee.[600]

Ko-koo-ah-gee say they must wait until they get actually into war, then will be the time to test his Power.

King say he must be cautious, and make proper use of his Power.

another male soldier rises and state, that they fire any quantity of Guns in Town, they must be sure and be as active with them at the war, for it will be proved by and by.

King speaks too low to be heard.

---

[599] 'Girls of the street', i.e. prostitutes (cf. also p. 134 and note 606). A parade of 'ladies of pleasure' was also observed at the Annual Customs of 1772 (Norris 1789: 98–100). For prostitutes in Dahomey, who were licensed by and paid taxes to the king, see Bay (1998: 149, 211–12).

[600] Comparison with Forbes' Journal (p. 188) suggests this may be miscopied for 'Hum-ba-gee', i.e. Houngbadji.

Ko-Kooah-gvee say he has heard the King his master speak, that neither him nor his people can do wrong.

a maid advances very cautiously, with a glass of spirits in her hand, her intended husband came forward, blushed and drank the Balm, a titter of a laugh all round.[601]

Banners, 2 Union Jacks, a Gift of two calabashes of cassavaa, to them, they commence and sing aloud Praises of his wealth, and Power.

De Sous[a] wives enter and prostrate themselves before the King.

Band a Gift of 9 Heads of Cowries.

King drinks and uproar and musketry.

A crier gets up and bawls aloud, oh King of Kings that conquers all other Kings, and sells them to buy rum, for his people to drink, also Powder, and cloth.

Band enters with Banners, and sings God bless the King, he dont make us alike, the head of this band is very aged man, he has a firey [= fiery] eye, and forbidding countenance.

Ah-loo-pee and his Brethren are called to be disgraced, they throw dirt on their heads, The old Mohawk [= Mewu?], asks his name, it is changed he then bellows at them, and all his gang, and say you have fallen, from carrying a Gun, to that of a Club, and named Ga-ga-do[602] they are ordered to retire from the jaws of that old Devils Tirade.

They commence and sing that God made all men with five fingers, on each hand, but the King has extraordinary power in his ten fingers, wherever he places his hand he conquers, he was Born to Conquer, Ah-tah-Pam, God makes every man different, a finish with this old beggar's froth.

Band a Gift of 9 heads.

King comes out and makes a gesticulation or two before the Band and then walks to us, takes a Glass and then enquires after our welfare, he pours a Tumbler of sweet wine down his Brother Ah-hoo-pee's throat and retires.

Band of Whistlers a Gift of 1 Head of cowries.

3.20 a Band makes their appearance and sings aloud Praises to the King, and then to the Cha-Cha their God took care of their Father old Cha-Cha until three of his sons grow up men able to take of [*sic*] care of themselves.

Caboceer of Whydah spoke to Cha-Cha as long as the King lived he would be able to get wood, Cha-Cha said as long as he could get wood and

---

[601] Forbes identifies the husband as the Sogan.
[602] Forbes says that this new name had already been given on 18 June and explains its meaning in Fon (Journal, p. 186).

Keep the Pot a Boiling, Whydah would do but when that failed it would be time to quit, after which Cha-Cha retires.

Sing against the late King that his [omission?] was too strong, and the Town overrun with Bush, and became depopulated,[603] now it is a different Town in good order and plenty of people.

4 o'clock sent for permission to depart, the Mayo, and Caboceer of Why-dah, came and said the King had a great number of Drums to pass, it would take him until dark.

I then said it only wants two hours, you must move yourselves quicker than you have done, the last you have passed, this same fellow has been yelp-ing for the last hour, so we had better leave, it was decided and we left without further Ceremony, Caboceer took leave of us outside, he then told us that he had a few Bottles of Black wine, he would dash us, but it was not every Eng-lishman, he liked so well as us, and could get the same favors.

we took our leave got into our Hammocks and returned home, a partial shower of rain went to dinner,

Evening cool after the rain, went to bed at 9 o'clock, my cold troubled me I was restless all night. midnight dry cool w^r

Saturday 22nd June

Programme

daylight cool pleasant w^r Ther 74° took a short walk before breakfast, after which Peter Brown called to take his leave, sent us a small Goat.

10.30 the messenger came for us we left and at 11 o'clock arrived at the Gate named Sou-tee-mee his [= the King's] mothers yard.[604]

a Band—a Gift of 1 head of cowries, Groups of men squatted in different parts of the yard, Amazon officers of the Troops, on the left of the King armed.

Band a Gift		10 strings of cowries
D° D°	1 head	" D°
Band of Callabashes ornamented with net work, sing a short song		
Gift of	1 Head	
Band one Horn, 3 Callabashes, 2 Gongs,		
Gift of	40 strings	
Band all Callabashes with Pease		½ a head. 2 str
D° 3 Whistles 1 Gong		10 strings
D° 5 Horns		10 D°

---

[603] I.e. Adandozan: the assertion of decay seems conventional, intended to justify his deposition.
[604] Evidently miscopied, probably for 'Gou-tee-mee'; cf. Forbes, 'Ahcontihmeh' (Journal, p. 188): i.e. Agotime, the Kpojito of Gezo.

D°   2 rattles watchmen   10
        Total 6 heads 7 strings

Band of officers Amazons armed singing Praises aloud to their King, he is their only head and Protection, that all nations have their different fashions, and that all the Blacks, and some whitemen, come to look upon one man, and prostrate themselves what overwhelming power he must be possessed of.

Band Plays and sings in corroboration of the same sentiments, all advance and cover themselves with any quantity of dust, both their heads and bodies.

Commence and sing against the Youribaas,[605] and say they tell lies, stating that the Dahomeians cannot conquer them, it will be seen when they meet, if at night, it will appear like day from the firing of their muskets, if it is day the sun will be darkened, with smoke, they appear to consider the Abbeokutians risable [= risible] that is the means they can take to conquer them, with their wealth, they really think them mad or drunk, when they state that they are able to compete with the Dahomeians.

Crier aloud you must sing sweet songs, to please the King.

An Amazon rises, and say you must open your ears, she sung that the Guns his [= the King's] Father had would last 20 years, but what he gets now are spoiled in two or three years, she is desired to sit down.

Deputation of the Ladies of the Town,[606] receives a present and departs after throwing dirt on their heads.

Sing that the King is above all poor and rich, if the song does not please they hope he will forgive them, for they endeavour with all their might to please.

K[ing] fulfils the old Ballad, that the Queen cannot swagger nor get drunk like a beggar nor be half so happy as I.[607]

Sing similies and Phraseology.

A leaf called Guu-boo[608] passes all the leaves, they use it as Fetish before he commences to go to war, he is then sure to conquer.

Crier aloud that he is then all powerful and can do as he pleases.

Ahdoo-muu at the head of the Amazons, singing state that the King must not be afraid, as long as they carry their Guns, Powder, and shot, that when he meets them at the war, he will dance and be merry, when they present their Prisoners.

---

[605] Here referring to Abeokuta.

[606] Forbes says 'public women', i.e. prostitutes (Journal, p. 189).

[607] Referring to 'The Beggar's Song', which includes the line 'A King cannot swagger or drink like a beggar, or be half so merry as I.'

[608] Forbes, 'eeaboo'; but not identified.

An Amazon sings at the King's sons and hope they will be liberal in their donations, of cowries to the Fetish,[609] for to give his Father long life, and the King must pray, for his sons, long lives, all his family and ancestors must pray for his days to be prolonged, also state that Antonio de Souza, must pray for the King, Parable of a Leopard, goes out to forage for its young one, so does the Doe, brings it home to his Kid, by that it appears that Antonio is the Kid, belonging or under the Protection of royalty.

Baa-daa-huu King's son gets up and say, that as long as he has life he will pray for his Father long life, and will always be ready to protect his parent at the risk of his own.

An aged Lady[610] say if you want the Honeycomb you will have danger before you can get it,[611] so you must be cautious, and whatever may await you, keep a good heart.

Kings mother, and five other old Ladies, get up and dance, before the King and people, it is rather awful to see old age embellishing themselves with the skulls, of their enemies, they had each one handed to them, and held it out before them, as they performed their various gesticulations, before the King, and the people, after which they went on their Knees before the King. The Kings mother had on Gold-laced slouched Hat, gold wristlets, checked Print wrappers, she had silk or satin underneath, there were another slouched Hat, silver ornaments the rest with head dresses, and checked wrappers, it was 1.30 when they finished their ceremony, they had two handsome country umbrellas.

The old Lady that spoke of the Honeycomb, called Too-do-stuu received a Gift of ½ a piece of cloth for herself.

3 heads of cowries and 1 Bottle of rum to buy victuals for his mother,[612] they all retire.

Fetish women dressed in white with broad bead ornaments, on their arms, dance and salute the King.

Sweet wine is passed round to the King's Family, singing God bless the King and all his people, Gift of 14 heads of cowries. his mothers Chair was covered with Crimson Cloth, four feet ornaments with skulls.

Enter Band, and Banners, 2 Union Jacks, Bandmaster ornamented with a dirty old shakoo, 10 men and 20 women, with white cloth wrappers, round their heads 2 men with large wooden cleavers richly carved.

all the skulls in copper cans and Brass, and Callabashes &c displayed to the best advantage.

---

[609] Forbes says 'to Seh (God)' (cf. note 519).
[610] Forbes says the 'King's Mother's Sister's Daughter' (Journal, p. 189).
[611] I.e. of being stung, as Forbes makes explicit.
[612] Forbes, 'her mother'.

Any quantity of Callabashes of chop, for the officers of the Kings Troops, about 200 people arrived from Ting-gaa[613] with calabashes of Chop.

A great number of Cruet stands, and small vials full of rum handed to the Kings family, and Caboceers, to refresh themselves in a strange manner, they really looked like so many children playing with toys at a fair.

Ah-lee-paa-hoo [= Linpehoun] Kings Brother is called, and handed a small case containing half Pint Bottles, filled with the various spirits, and Liquors, the King has taken during the Custom, they are all desired to taste and remember him.

Too-no-noo received a case Bottle of rum as a Gift for his people to drink the King's health, he placed it on his head, his gang of eunuchs, at his Tail, went like an Arch [= arc?] past the King, to a corner in the farther end of the court yard, drank the contents amongst them, and then returned in the same procession, with the empty Bottle on his head, passed the King and retired excepting the old Too-noo-noo.

Any quantity of victuals distributed, cooked in various dishes, and ways, a mountain of Palm oil cake, given to all the Drummers, and people it is ground Beans, Palm Oil, Pepper, and salt, it appeared in the distance like a mass of Gingerbread.

Ignatio de Souza	a Gift of	10 heads	3 Gall of rum
Antonio D°	" " "	10 D°	" D° "

a fellow sings wonderful King, white man bring cowries to Blackman, now he gives them away to the white man, Oh King of Kings,

Band   12 heads of cowries

King drinks a shout and a din of muskets,

Band & Banners   3 heads

Mee-gau for Amazons state that the Caboceers &c &c, receive 160 heads of cowries—for the Fetish of all parts of his dominions.[614]

rum [for?] soldiers—60 heads

Ah-hoo-pee King's Brother 2 heads an unknown 2 heads

Victuals distributed in quantities also a quantity of the Daa-saa fruit

Crier announces that they are all ready to eat any thing the King gives them should it Kill them

Crier not anything can hurt the King, as long as they are all of one heart, and mind.

Sing, if the Leopard makes his appearance all other animals run off. 3 o'clock get permission to retire

[some lines of text hidden in binding] write a little dine at 5 " 30 walk until 7 o clock chat until 9 o'clock and retire to rest.

---

[613] I.e. Tindji, which was associated with Agotime (cf. p. 74, note 349).

[614] Forbes says 'to make Fetish with, to clean the town after the custom'.

Sunday, 23rd June

daylight fine dry wʳ Ther 75° my cold continues and affects my spirits, and causes me to be very languid and uncomfortable, it is pleasing to have this day in quiet to ourselves, clear of the noise of Drums, and sycophants, shouting their master's Praise, bickering and quarrelling with each other for the ascendancy, in the Eyes of the King.

I am sure he must be disgusted with the extent of their vainglorious expressions, sometimes it is a continued clamour of self Praise, took an early Breakfast of course very light, for there is not much to be had in the market fit for a stomach deranged, eggs are scarce, indeed all things are very ill to get particularly as it is the Customs all goes to the Palace yard. it is always the fatal consequences, of a country at war with everybody, about them, it has not any neighbours, 10 o'clock Nawhey called to ask if we had a desire to go to the Kings yard, we told him the same as he was told last Evening.[615]

Noon fine dry wʳ we were perfectly quiet not an individual to molest us.

pm a passing shower of rain, accompanied with distant thunder, we told Nawhey to communicate with the Mayogau, to inform His Majesty, as the Custom will be done today, we have a great desire that the King will be kind enough to appoint a day for the conference of our mission from the Queen of England.

Sunset it became fair but a damp air cold and raw. retired at 9 o'clock slept until midnight after which I was uneasy, cought [= cough] troubled me.

Monday 24th

daylight dull cloudy wʳ but fair Captain Forbes went to take his usual walk, 10 o'clock Count Nawhey came in a great hurry, stating that the King wanted us, we could not glean the slightest intimation on what errand we were going to the Kings Palace, at Ah-gue-goo-me [= Agringomè], Arrived there at 10.30 and soon unravelled the mystery, the King himself was not there, we were merely sent for to count a quantity of cowries that is going to be paid away to the people, belonging to the different Tribes, and nations, it was the Kings desire that we should see them & take an account of them, in our Books,[616] 11 o'clock a shower of rain, in the mean time about 200 men entered with 5 gallons Demi Johns of rum from Whydah for His Majesty. continued rain. Noon we went into the large Court yard, where there were a large display of Cowries, Bottles and Kegs of rum, in readiness for payment it still rained. I told Forbes that as he had on a substantial Pair of wooden Clogs, to go and count

---

[615] This was presumably in the section of the text missing at the end of the previous day's entry.
[616] Forbes records this under 23 June and places it in the Adanjloakodé section of the palace (Journal, p. 190).

the cowries, so as to enable us to leave we have now been two hours here, he counted them and made 924 heads and 125 Gallons of rum, they were distributed in rows about the yard, a Bottle of rum attached to each Lot, these people are here only at this first Custom, then return to the different Towns they came from after receiving their pay or Gift for that is all they get for the year, we went through the form of taking a Glass from the Kings Bottle, and took our leave Mayo was anxious for us to stop to amuse him in seeing him issue the cowries and make speeches of the munificence of the Kings Gifts, it was fair & continued so until 4 o'clock, when it commenced with thunder lightning and heavy rain, our dwelling would be inundated if we had a days continued rain, it being on a level with the yard and no shelter from draughts, it rained more or less until midnight, when it cleared away and became fine we retired to rest early. rec^d from Mee-gau a Gift of 1 Duck 1 Guinea Fowl & 2 Pots of Peto or country Beer.

Tuesday 25th June

daylight dull cloudy w^r Ther 75° Capt Forbes took his usual walk. I took a short one to the Canna Gate and returned. after Breakfast Forbes received a letter from Mr Stroove, at Popoo[617] and a small case with 200 dollars for the King to pay the ransom of the two men mentioned in a former part of this Journal[618] a messenger was sent to the Mayo-gau, to come and receive the dollars on account of His Majesty, as early as possible, no eggs to be had in the Abomey market. sent two Hammock[men?] to Canna, to purchase them and oranges, also a messenger to Whydah for Tea and sugar or any small comforts in that way that was to be had.

11 o'clock the old Mayo-gau made his appearance, the Dollars were counted out on the table by myself and Forbes, we then handed them over. The Mayo-gau and Nawhey counted them over and deposited them in the Bag and handed them over to the King's slave, they then started them out and counted them a Clamour arose upon enquiry one of the Mayo's slaves said they were not right, the Kings was perfectly satisfied that was the dispute the Mayo in a great rage snatched the Bag from them, and started them again and went through the same ordeal a fourth time he of course found them all right he then bullied his slave and called him for his confounded stupidity. The

---

[617] Ferdinand Struve, employed by the British Navy to survey the lagoon, at this time at Little Popo (Strickrodt 2015: 21).

[618] There is in fact no earlier allusion to these men in Beecroft's journal, so perhaps this should be 'his [i.e. Forbes'] journal'. The reference is to two Kru men employed on an English merchant vessel which had been wrecked off Little Popo, who were then sold into slavery and who had contacted Duncan and Forbes at Abomey in October 1849, requesting help (Forbes 1851, i: 88).

Dollar Palaver set.[619] We told our Interpreter to ask the Mayo if he could not give us the most distant intimation when we might expect to leave <u>Abomey</u>, so as we might be guided in our orders for necessaries, he replied very innocently that he could not but would ask the King, in the course of the day if he was not prevented by the rain he then said we could get as many Cowries as we required from the King, we told him that we did not require them at a heavy <u>Premium</u>, he then left but soon returned with a silk Hkf in his hand, showing it to me at the same time told me that I had dashed him it.[620] I told him that I was perfectly aware of it, he said I must [put?] it down in my Book for one large pair from England he then left to go and see the King. he said if it was not too late when he returned from the Palace, he would call and let us know the result of his Palaver,[621] we accompanied him clear of our yard and left him, the old gentleman has had fever[?] from cold, so it is not likely that he will wait on the King, during the Evening the Hammock men returned from Canna with 5 dozen eggs, and a quantity of oranges, and a few yams. 8 o'clock we went into our Domicile and chatted until 10 o'clock when we retired to rest. Midnight dry w^r.

Wednesday 26th June[622]

daylight dull cloudy w^r Ther 75° Forbes took his walk as usual, returned at 7 o'clock, took a light Breakfast of Tea and eggs. 10 o'clock the Mayo-gau made his appearance, to report progress it was as I had expected that the King wished us to remain to see the Fetish Custom, and the small Schooner dressed out with Flags and some other fooleries, that would take fifteen days,[623] I told him it would be three weeks for they Procrastinate too much you are never sure of their word, as soon as that was communicated we sent down for 50 dollars more cowries,[624] Noon fresh westerly Breezes Mayo told us the Fetish people were going to amuse themselves with their ribaldry if [we] wished to see them we were at liberty, I told him that I had seen them and got them in my Book. Then at 2 o'clock 78° dined and took a walk to the Gate, where the Fetish women were performing an old Caboceer very polite introduced us to two of the Kings Brothers, and gave us each a Country stool to sit on, sent

---

[619] However, at the final interview with the King, on 4 July, Forbes reports that the Mewu said that the two men had 'not been found' (Journal, p. 194: not mentioned by Beecroft).

[620] On 2 June—as recorded in Forbes' Journal (p. 169), but not by Beecroft.

[621] Forbes (under 24 June) gives the Mewu's message more positively: 'the King not wishing to keep us longer, he would now appoint a day for the palaver' (Journal, p. 190).

[622] Forbes reports this day's events under 25 June.

[623] Forbes says 14 days.

[624] I.e. to the English fort at Ouidah.

small decanters of rum, Gin &c &c and a Pot of water and Peto, or country Beer, we tasted of each with them, they were all women performers, a few of the King's wives, and one of his daughters were present, sent for a Keg of rum and presented to the old Caboceer, it was placed in front. The two Kings sons, and two Caboceers presented it in due form with a long speech, they returned us many thanks Bah-dah-huu Kings Brother[625] was particularly complimentary, and said it pleased him too much to see Englishmen at Abomey, friends with his brother the King. They sung Praises trusting God would take care of us, and Protect us from harm, they said that they would be glad to see us tomorrow as they were going to sacrifice a Bullock, they then retired and we returned home, we received a few necessaries from Whydah from Mr Hastie they arrived at a very convenient season for we were nearly dry, it is truly Kind and thoughtful of him, he states that he has been confined 8 days. retired to rest at 9 o'clock. the Fetish performers were all aged.

Thursday 27th June

daylight fine dry cool w[r] had visit from the saved, recommended them to take exercise so as to better enable them to perform their journey to <u>Whydah</u> as the time was drawing near, gave them a supply of Provissions they returned to their quarters.

Caboceer for Whydah, sent us a message to say he would call to see us during the day.

Noon fresh westerly winds and dry pleasant weather, no appearance of the worthy Caboceer, but he is tinctured the same as the rest, a Procrastinator I have just heard that they are all at the Palace at a conference, Isadore, and Ignatio, Nawhey is denied but I Know from very good authority that he was sent for by His Majesty[626]

4 o'clock took a short walk accompanied by Forbes, and seated ourselves under an old Tree near Mayogaus entrance, under the next Tree near us, amongst it[s]spreading fibers we discovered a skull. I had been near it several times previous without seeing it, upon enquiry found it to be the head womans of the <u>Ah-gow</u> beheaded a number of years ago for adultery, it was left there as an awful example for the future no person dares to remove it, the man was sold we were soon beset by a group of raggamuffins and boys, we soon moved of and prolonged our walk, to a short distance and returned near to our own entrance the Mayo-gau in the mean time was announced, he had been with the King all day, there appeared to be a great mystery about the

---

[625] Evidently a confusion, since Badahun was, rather, the King's son. Forbes names the King's brother here as Linpehoun.

[626] Forbes reports this meeting under 26 June.

whole affair, an anxiety to know what our Account of the Cowries expended or paid away by the King [was], we informed him that if he would call tomorrow we would give him the particulars, he said there were four more Customs, but the King did not wish us to remain for such a length of time, the schooner, watering the ground for his forefathers, and two others which will take six months, ere they are all complete,[627] that we must soon go, but they could not give us a day. Antonio has left under the rose[628] to return, I presume to endeavour to ship his slaves, as report say three vessels have arrived.[629] Domingo, Isadore, Ignatio & Antonio [omission?],[630] Mayo left at 8 o'clock. I have a strong suspicion that they have not any desire that we should see any more of their Customs, retired at 9 o'clock cool day w^r same at midnight.

Friday 28th June

daylight Ther 74° Capt Forbes left at 5.30 and took his usual walk. I left at 6 o'clock and went down the Canna road, as far as the Cannonades.[631] met Forbes, on his way back, he went on, I sauntered home slowly bought a Guinea fowl for 20 strings of cowries on my arrival Nawhey called and said the Caboceer [*sc.* of Whydah] would call if we would let him Know when our Breakfast was over we told him 9 o'clock accordingly he made his appearance at 9.30 he brought us a present of four Bottles of Portugal wine, very little was said so no conclusions could be got at, only the King did not intend to Keep us long, not fifteen days as was mentioned two days go but still it was all a mystery no definite time could be fixed upon, he left at 10 o'clock, the messenger returned from Mr Hastie. Pm Count Nawhey brought 5 Kegs of rum, he said when they were done we could get more, I said we should not require any more as the Cha-Cha was passed and going to leave today, so of course we could not be long we must be of in a day or two, he was asked if he Knew when they were going he very innocently said he did not Know he Knew that he was telling me an untruth, he stared with all his eyes when I told him that he was going to day wondering where we could have gleaned our information, he referred the matter to Ah-taa Mayo-gau's boy, and said to him you hear what the Governor say,[632] you had better tell your master to speak to the

---

[627] Cf. p. 145 (which, however, refers to seven 'customs').

[628] I.e. secretly (translating Latin *sub rosa*).

[629] Cf. Forbes, Journal, p. 191, recording Antonio's return to Abomey on 29 June. One of the reported ships was the *Juliana*, which was captured by the British Navy without embarking any slaves (ibid., note 94).

[630] The listing of these four here is unexplained, but perhaps relates to the attempted shipment of slaves at Ouidah, rather than to any occurrence at Abomey, since Martins as well as Antonio was not currently at Abomey.

[631] Cf. p. 72.

[632] I.e. Beecroft, referring to his position as governor of Fernando Po.

King at once for Maa-di-Ka and myself will have plenty of trouble if they dont get away soon, Pm fresh westerly Breezes Ther 79° 4 o'clock Capt Forbes accompanied me to the Mayo's Gate, just as we reached it a shower of rain prevented us, from going through and returning by another Gate about ten minutes walk NE the Guard an aged Negro advanced and asked for a trifle for looking at the Wicker-Gate ornamented with a skull on each side of the <u>Lintels</u>, it is in an awful dilapidated state, shower was soon over we returned direct by the same path, shortly after our arrival a smart shower. took our dinner, a little while and the Mayo paid us a visit, and apologized for not coming in the morning as the Caboceer was here.

we told him that he did not remain half an hour, he hinted for the account of Cowries for the King; we told him it was dark, that he had better come directly after our Breakfast on the morrow, we enquired of him when the Cha-Cha was going, he did not make a reply, we told him that he had been four or five hours at his place to day, it must be a long Palaver, Nawhey denied being there, we Know from facts that he had been there, Mayo complained for <u>Tooth Ache</u>, and requested leave to go home it was readily granted for Old Nawhey the Knave would rather have been in any place else. 6 o'clock when they left inclined to rain, 9 o'clock retired.

Saturday 29ᵗʰ June

daylight Ther 74° dull cloudy wʳ we took a short walk to the Canna Gate and returned at 7.30 after Breakfast, sent for the Mayo, he made his appearance about 10 o'clock he looked very unwell indeed, we asked him, if the King had requested the account from us, he replied in the affirmative, we then told him, that the whole did not amount to more than 7000 heads of cowries, not any reply was made, after musing for about 10 minutes, he asked about the rum, we then told him that we had allowed 1400 dollars,[633] he then said that he gave more than that, forty Pipe per diem[634] besides what he gave by night, we told him that we were very hard of belief about the night Palaver, we were not to be diverted with such tomfooleries, we were eye witnesses to what was issued in the day time it was upon the most oeconomical plan in Eau de Cologne, and Cruet Bottles, not any more said on that matter, Bullocks were the next discussion, they proposed to be paid 2 heads of cowries, for carrying the two Bullocks to Whydah, we told them as soon as they were ready to start we

[633] Forbes gives the figures as $7,215 cowries, $2,000 cloth, $1,400 rum, $1,500 food, total $12,115 (Journal, pp. 190–1).
[634] Meaning evidently 'during daytime' (over the entire Customs), rather than 'per day': 40 pipes, at the price of $60 per pipe assumed in the Appendix to Forbes' manuscript journal, would represent a cost of $2,400.

would advance the 2 heads. The conference then broke up. Noon strong westerly Breezes Ther 78° 3.45 Capt Forbes accompanied me on a walk, through the western Gate, and took a path to the Nor[th] for 1½ miles, came to another Gate-way, passed through it, and found ourselves still in the country, walked ½ a mile along a Path had a good view of the Dab-a-Dab Hills, and returned home by the same route, arrived at 5 o'clock, this Gate must have been to Protect that Path, when at war with the country in that direction.[635] Cha-Cha left this evening, all the Caboceers have been at the Fetish dance, retired to rest at 9 o'clock a complete din with their drums and singing Praises to the King of Kings.

Sunday 30th June

daylight cloudy cool wʳ Ther 74° shaved washed and took a walk out of the <u>Canna Gate</u>, the other is closed to day on account of all the Kings women going out at that Gate to the Valley, to wash, returned home at 7.30 met Nawhey. he desired me to go with him to look at the Bullocks, tied ready to proceed to <u>Whydah</u>, I saw them one has got an awful bruise on his back, as big as my hand, he said he would come for the two heads after Breakfast, to pay the men for carrying them down, accordingly they made their appearance at 10 o'clock and received their 2 heads, and an order for 4 pieces of romal, and 4 Bottles of rum, if the said cattle were delivered in good order to Mr Hastie, at Whydah. they left at 4 o'clock, took a walk accompanied by Capt Forbes to the western Gate and proceeded along a beautiful road course about NW B[y] N by Compass about 1½ miles until we arrived at a descent, a great number of water carriers on the road,[636] Forbes asked me to accompany him down but I declined being then over heated, he proceeded I remained about a quarter of an hour, to look about me and cool myself, when I returned slowly to the Gate in about twenty minutes, I walked slowly on I had to face about five or six times, on my path for the tinkling of those awful small Bells, slaves to the King's wives, not bona fide his wives, as stated, for some of them are filthy,[637] I reached home at 5 o'clock, met three strangers, on enquiry my steward knew them being Po Poo boys, two of them belongs to old Lawson's

---

[635] Referring to an outer defensive moat with gateways, to the north of Abomey (see Forbes (1851, i: 69); Burton (1864, ii: 235–6); and map in Randsborg & Merkyte (2009, ii: 40)).

[636] Presumably from the water source called by Burton 'Nyassa', north-west of Abomey (1864, ii: 235–6).

[637] In fact, the term *ahosi*, lit. 'king's wife', was applied to all women of the palace, including slaves, not only those who were his sexual partners (Bay 1998, 8).

family,[638] they are up here with Antonio's family,[639] it is too obvious that they are mixed up with the Slave Trade,[640] gave them a Bottle of rum, took dinner after which took a short stroll, weather remarkably fine for the rainy season, returned at 8 o'clock sat until 9.30 and retired to rest.

Midnight fine cool dry w[r].

July 1st Monday

Daylight cool pleasant w[r] Ther 74° Took a Seidlitz,[641] and a cup of Tea, washed and dressed, took a walk in the vicinity, for exercise. Forbes gone to take his morning walk, 8 o'clock, a messenger arrived from some country, that the King must have declared hostilities against,[642] he was ornamented with Palm leaves, as emblems of Peace,[643] he prostrated himself three times, in the presence of the Kings Brother,[644] they then proceeded on, I presume to the King, 9 o'clock our dispatch messenger arrived,[645] successful, two cases of wine, a Loaf of sugar, Bread, Tea, and coffee, I can assure the reader, that it was a great comfort, to get such articles, for the country chop is indifferent for an European, received also Tins of Sardines, the fellow has only been five days absent, so he must have gone over the ground pretty smartly, Nawhey paid us a visit, asked him when he thought we were going, he said he that he did not know, Mayo-gau was sick, we said we had better go to the Palace Gates, and demand admittance to the King, of course he smiled, he went to the Mayo, and returned, and told us that he would call, Noon westerly winds and dry w[r] Ther 78° Mayo made his appearance, now the matter stands thus, that he had not seen the King, so he promised that he would go at once, he is completely knocked up,[646] and of course they require time to collect their senses, I have my own opinion on these matters.

sunset fine w[r] 7.30 the Mayo paid us a visit, he said that he had been to the King, and that our Palaver, would soon be settled, we told him that the great affair had yet to be settled that we came here for, it is of no use preaching

---

[638] I.e. George Lawson, the leading African trader of Little Popo (Strickrodt 2015: 160–1, 171–5).

[639] Antonio de Souza was related by marriage to the Lawsons and had trading interests at Little Popo (ibid., 193, 203).

[640] The Lawsons had certainly been involved in slave trading earlier, but there is no clear evidence that this was still the case by 1850 (Jones 1999: 127–31). Beecroft perhaps merely inferred their involvement in slaving from their connection with Antonio de Souza.

[641] Seidlitz powder, taken as a laxative.

[642] Forbes says 'a chief of the Maha [= Mahi] country' (Journal, p. 191).

[643] Forbes, 'the sign of subjugation', which is correct (cf. Le Herissé 1911: 306, with n.).

[644] Named by Forbes as Linpehoun.

[645] I.e. from Ouidah: he had been sent on 25 June (p. 138).

[646] I.e. exhausted.

about passing, until after this great Palaver, and hear the King's opinion, on it we may then have a faint idea, when it is we shall get away, The old Mayo answered me, he said the Queen of England and the King of Dahomey, are all the same, as these two wine Glasses, they were exactly Pairs, you may change them, from one side to the other, and you cannot see any difference, so much for the old Mayo's wisdom, he has had a lesson from the Cha-Cha for he desired to know how many cargoes, the Queen of England would give him, for to give up the Slave Trade,[647] he then immediately excused himself, and said that he did not wish to talk about that Palaver, he would leave it for the King's mouth, we told him about Lagos, and said that we would route them out and, all those fellows that have no right there, and place the legitimate King on the Throne,[648] I again stated to him that it was my duty, to settle all matters, between the King of Dahomey and British merchants, in his territory, there our debates ended, we sat up rather late discussing the question, with our Interpreters,11 o'clock retired clear w^r.

Tuesday July 2nd

daylight a fresh Breeze and fine cool pleasant w^r shaved and washed, at 6 o'clock left for a walk, went out at the western Gate, I was obliged several times to face about, on the sound of the tinkling of a Bell, resembled a flock of sheep, Ladies of <u>Harem</u>, or rather slaves to them, I walked on to the Valley, and looked at the Dab [a] Dab Hills,[649] and walked home, The Hills were enveloped in clouds to day, with a mist[,] on my way back, I was faced about four times, forbidden to look on the Ladies of the Palace, arrived at our domicile at 7.45[,] after Breakfast it was expected that the Mayo-gau, and the Caboceer of Whydah were coming, to talk some Palaver, shortly after their arrival were announced by the clapping of hands, and snapping of fingers, 9.30 they arrived at our Domicile, accompanied by a few lazy followers, brought with them, two Baskets of cowries, strung, Mayo-gau commenced an harangue, with eight stones from a fruit, I presume the wild Plum, to show the expenditure of the Customs that are to follow,[650] and end in December, there

[647] The wording is ambiguous: 'him' probably means the King, but might be the Mewu himself, since he may have expected to receive a share of the compensation (cf. p. 148).

[648] Cf. pp. 98–9, the 'legitimate king' being Akitoye, currently in exile. It is remarkable that Beecroft should be so categorical about this, since the proposed action had not yet even been submitted to, far less approved by, the Foreign Office in London. This reinforces the argument of Lynn (1992), that Beecroft, as 'the man on the spot', rather than the government in London, was responsible for the action at Lagos.

[649] Cf. p. 88.

[650] On the use of seeds, pebbles, cowries etc. to keep financial (and other quantitative) accounts in Dahomey, see Law (1999: 27–8).

are seven more according to their account, which he named,[651] 1st dancing at daa-gee-coo-doo[652] 2nd dressing the ship,[653] 3rd dinner at Coomassie, with saluting at the same time at Whydah,[654] 4th war Palaver,[655] 5th small customs for his Fathers,[656] 6th Preparation for war,[657] 7th Fetish Customs at Cann[a]-Minna, after his return from the war,[658] Nawhey the mercenary wretch, spake and said perhaps he [= the King] may take 8000 Prisoners all young men, and women, and buy them for 10 heads each,[659] and sell them for 80 heads, that would leave an enormous Profit,[660] but suppose we receive it Nawhey, how will you stand, you are building Castles in the air, but the King does not wish us to remain to see the remaining Customs, that he has sent the account of the last one, in strings of 200 cowries, 10 strings to each bunch, 2000[661] and 16 of them made his account 32,000 heads or dollars,[662] deduct a seventh it will not

---

[651] Forbes' journal also gives a version of this account (pp. 121–2), which is elaborated in his book (1851, i: 17–19): for comparison of the three versions, see Fraser (2012: 266–7). Note that it is in fact only the first five customs listed which 'end in December'—the ceremonial cycle is evidently counted from the Kana Custom to the 'small customs' which preceded the military campaign. Also, the 'Fetish Custom', which began on 26 June, is not included, perhaps because it was not considered part of the cycle of royal Customs.

[652] I.e. Adanjloakodé, here referring to the palace gate of this name, giving onto Singbodji Square. This dancing seems to have been witnessed by Vice-Consul Fraser between 20 August and 4 September 1851 (2012: 75–6, 78, 91–3). He understood that it was 'in memory of the King's father' (ibid., 86): the Adanjloakodé gate is recalled to have been built by Gezo in memory of his father Agonglo (Mercier & Lombard 1959: 12).

[653] That is, 'dressing' in the sense of 'decorating' (cf. p. 139). The exhibition of the ship was witnessed by Blanchely on 18 August 1850 (1891: 575). Forbes transposes the order of the first two customs listed: in this he is probably correct, since Beecroft's own earlier reference to the exhibition of the ship implies that it was the next custom to be performed.

[654] Forbes says 'firing guns along the road to and from Whydah'. This ceremony was witnessed by Fraser, from the Ouidah end, 19–24 November 1851, although he understood that the 'dinner' was then held at Kana, rather than at the Kumasi palace (2012: 126–9).

[655] Forbes adds 'at Cumassee'. Blanchely witnessed these '*palabres guerrières*' on 8 October 1848 (1891: 546).

[656] Earlier, Beecroft called this custom 'watering the ground for his forefathers' (p. 141). Forbes says for 'his father [singular]', and that it took place 'at Ahgongroo', i.e. the suburban palace of King Agonglo, which was in Gbèkon quarter (cf. Forbes 1851, i: 71). These 'small Customs' evidently correspond to those witnessed by Burton in January–December 1863/4, then held for the now deceased Gezo by his son and successor Glele, at Gezo's Kumasi palace (1864, i: 354, 361).

[657] Forbes says 'the war': this was not strictly a 'custom', but presumably included because it also involved expense to the King.

[658] This was the custom which Gezo stated on 28 May that he had lately 'finished' (see p. 28).

[659] I.e. from the soldiers who had captured them (cf. p. 104, and note 503).

[660] This calculation omits the commission taken by the merchant who sold the slaves at Ouidah, given as $16 per slave in other sources (Law 2004b: 145). The King's net return (even without allowing for expenditure on war supplies) would therefore be only $54 per slave.

[661] Beecroft seems to have his cowry terminology muddled: a 'string' is 40 shells and 2,000 is a 'head', while the 'bunch' is given elsewhere as 5 strings/200 shells (e.g. Burton 1864, i: 162 n.).

[662] I.e. each cowry represented one head of cowries (2,000) expended.

be more than 27,000 heads,[663] he makes his ⅔ more than our account,[664] and I'm certain that we allowed more than was actually expended, it is a different account, to what Nawhey rendered in the first day, 26,000[665] he blushed to day if it was possible for such a miracle to happen, Mayo was anxious that we should relate to the Caboceer, what passed last evening, so we gave it him, in detail as near as possible, what we were discussing about Brown they were very anxious to know, what he had been saying, we told them that he did not say a word, that was derogatory to the King, but embellished his wealth, &c[666] 10.30 the conference broke up, after taking a Glass of wine, they left to visit the King, the Caboceer was very silent, in the matter, I really expected the account would have been a good deal more, noon fresh Breezes, the King passed the Brazillians today, gave them 10 heads and a Keg of rum, amongst 15 of them, the two head men, a head each, so it would only be 2s/6d each,[667] not anything particular transpired during the remainder of this day, retired to rest at 9.30, Drums, and singing the whole night through, Fetish people keeps it up, Midnight dry cool w^r.

Wednesday 3rd July

daylight fine dry cool w^r Ther 74° shaved, and washed, 6 o'clock started for a walk, went through the Ah-gaa-hee market Place, and proceeded through a Gate westward, then turned N.E. for ten minutes, entered another Gate, and returned by the market place, and walked home by the Bee-Kon Gate, 10 o'clock the Mayo-gau, and Caboceer of Whydah, and Nawhey came and reported progress, and said that the King would see us tomorrow, and talk our Palaver, they then counted a parcel of stones, as before, and said the remainder of the Customs would cost the King 11,800 dollars of heads of Cowries, they then further stated, that if three vessels arrived for slaves, that

---

[663] Forbes in his book gives $28,000: actually a $^1/_7$ deduction would yield 27,555: the difference was based on the fact that the palace issued cowries in strings which contained fewer than the nominal 40 (Forbes 1851, ii: 183–4). However, this reduction was not applicable to goods other than cowries, and indeed not all of the cowries distributed were strung: an alternative calculation by Forbes assumes that strung cowries accounted for less than a third of the total (see Appendix 2). Forbes' original journal here proposes a reduction of one-fourth: see p. 192 and n.96. These adjustments served, of course, to reduce the gap between the King's claimed expenditure and the compensation the British were offering ($15,000).

[664] Awkwardly worded, as the King's claim ($32,000) was nearly three times the English party's estimate ($12,115).

[665] Cf. pp. 32–3.

[666] But Beecroft's account of his conversation with the Mewu 'last evening' does not mention Brown (pp. 144–5).

[667] Based on the official valuation of the dollar at 4s. 2d. (50 d.): if 13 persons (i.e. other than the 2 'head men') received 8 heads among them, this would make $^8/_{13}$ of a head each, which approximates to 30d., or 2s. 6d.

the King took two, and gave one to all the other Traders, or Slave dealers,[668] so it is inferred that he must pay on[e] third of the subsidy to the people, I certainly did expect to hear today of an awful advance, it only amounts according to his own statement to 42,000 heads, its intrinsic worth 36,000[669] so it goes to prove the exaggerated reports, of this great mans riches, himself and all his ministers, and Caboceers, depend totally on their rapine, and plunder, all the liberated Brazillians left this morning, Ignatio, and Antonio, are to leave tomorrow; so we shall be the last of the strangers, great doings at the Bee-Kon today; Fetish play, pm Ther 78° 4 o'clock it commenced to rain, and continued heavy until 10 o'clock, retired to rest. Midnight rain.

Thursday 4th July

daylight continued rain, Ther 74 8 o'clock it rained heavy, it is rather unpleasant on this eventful day, after so many days of fine w[r] since the full moon, it rained until noon when it partially cleared away, 30 minutes pm Nawhey made his appearance, and in his customary rude manner said come let us go, so we started of and walked to the Palace Square, we were seated under a half shed until the messenger returned, from the King, which was full half an hour, we entered the Palace at 1 o'clock and of course were courteously received, after our usual ceremony we took our seats, opposite the King, at the door entrance of his bed-room he was as at our other interviews, on his bed, with about 12 elderly women about him, and Cam-baa-dee his Treasurer at the foot of his bed, outside in the rear of us, the Mayo-gau, Caboceer of Whydah, his second Nawhey, Cou-pah Store-Keeper to the King[670] two Interpreters one on each side,[671] after a few minutes he said that he expected we would have remained to have seen some part of the other Customs, we told him that we had seen the first, that was all he desired, it is full six weeks[672] and it will be two or three before we get away, he then said the whole of his Annual Customs will not be over before December, it would be too long for us to wait, also too much rain will fall, after a pause he then told us to commence

---

[668] Forbes gives a fuller version: 'if one ship comes to Whydah the King monopolizes half the trade; that of three he takes two' (Journal, p. 192). The estimate of the king's revenue from the slave trade given to Cruickshank in 1848 assumed a somewhat lower royal share—3,000 of 8,000 slaves (Cruickshank's Report, 15–16). This evidence refutes the common assumption that the king exercised a 'monopoly' of the slave trade—at least with regard to the mid-nineteenth century: see further Law (1977b).

[669] I.e. deducting one-seventh (cf. note 663): Forbes says, more precisely, 43,800 heads, equivalent to $37,543 (Journal, p. 192).

[670] Forbes, who gives this title as 'Caoupeh' or 'Caoopeh', describes him as the 'sub-treasurer', i.e. deputy/assistant to the Kanbode (1851, ii: 18); spelled 'Kakopwe' by Burton (1864, i: 230).

[671] I.e. Gnahoui, the King's interpreter, and Madiki Lemon, for the British party.

[672] Beecroft had actually been at Abomey rather less than six weeks (since 27 May).

our Palaver, we asked him if it was necessary for him to have Her Majestys letter to him on the important question read again, he said no that he was fully acquainted with its contents. We then produced a List of goods amounting to 15,000 Dollars,[673] worth at Whydah, or Abomey 25,000[674] viz.

muskets	500	250 £
Kegs of powder	1000	200
Pun[cheons?] of rum[675]	100	800
Dollars	2000	500
Cowries	2000 heads	500
Pieces of silk	200	300
Cotton Prints	250	100
romals	1000	100
sloutched hats	50	75
1 Pipe of Lisbon[676]		25
250 rolls of tobacco		150
		3000[677]

This amount was carefully communicated to His Majesty, two or three times, and under consideration Capt Forbes and myself deemed it Politic to mention five instead of three years, subject to ratification,[678] he mused for some minutes he did not make any remark that it was a generous offer from his friend the Queen of England, or otherwise, but commenced in detail to relate the state of Abomey a century back, that it is just the same at this day;[679] The French was the first nation at one time,[680] but after they [= the

---

[673] I.e. the annual compensation offered for renouncing the slave trade.

[674] This mark-up of ⅔ in value is not implausible: Vice-Consul Fraser in 1851/2 (2012: 198) found that linen cloth was bought at 4 heads (8,000 cowries) per piece of 15 fathoms and retailed at ½ a head (1,000) per fathom (a mark-up of 47 per cent), while tobacco was purchased at 6 silver dollars (now equivalent to 10 heads of cowries) per roll, resold at 30 heads (+200 per cent). However, the British evidently had an interest in inflating the value of the compensation offered.

[675] But Forbes has 'pipes': a puncheon was 84, a pipe 126 gallons. The price assumed (£8 = $40) suggests that the puncheon is intended: Forbes' calculations, in the Appendix to his manuscript journal, although not entirely consistent, generally assume a value of $45 (£9) per puncheon and $60 (£12) per pipe of rum.

[676] I.e. Portuguese wine.

[677] The conversion between pounds and dollars here assumes a rate of $5 to £1 ($1 = 4s.), as opposed to the official valuation of the dollar at 4s. 2d.—although, oddly, the valuation of the actual dollars (and heads of cowries) in the list is based on a rate of $4 to £1 ($1= 5s.), which has the bizarre consequence that the 2,000 dollars are valued at $2,500! These adjustments serve to inflate the value of the compensation offered.

[678] I.e. the offered compensation, which in the draft treaty was to run for three years, was now extended to five.

[679] Forbes is more explicit: 'throughout, the Dahomans had sold slaves' (Journal, p. 193).

[680] Forbes understood this to refer to priority of settlement: 'First, … the French came to Whydah' (1851, ii: 187): the French were indeed the first European nation to establish a permanent post in Ouidah, in 1671 (followed by the English in 1683).

Dahomians] conquered Whydah,[681] the English became the first[682] and most confidential friend, of the King of Dahomey, not any other nation, knew the extent of their Friendship it continued so, and two of his Grandfathers children were sent to England to be educated,[683] after which he very soon expressed himself, that he could not leave of the Awful Traffic in slaves, it very soon came to that, he then commenced to state, that we ought to commence with those inferior places, Popoo, Aghway, Porto Novo, Badagry and Lagos, then to come to him and talk the Palaver he would then try, but I am quite satisfied that it is too obvious he has not the most distant Idea, of leaving of the abominable Traffic, he expressed a strong desire that Her Majestys Government should Blockade all these above mentioned places, for they were not like him, liberal and munificent, they kept it all from their people,[684] His Majestys desire was that Whydah was to be a Free Port, for he acknowledged that he had five men to attend to his merchants in Whydah &c mentioning at the same time their names, Isadore, the Cha-Cha of Whydah, Ignatio Caboceer, and Antonio King's Friend[685] three Bastards to the late De Souza's, Domingo Martins, and Joachim Antonio,[686] he wanted Papers, and Colours for five ships to pass without Hinderance, or molestation, from Her Majesty's cruisers, we told him at once No, he then ardently requested that we would mention in the Letter to the Queen to allow himself one Ship to pass without molestation, The Queen of England his friend surely could not object to that, allow him Papers and Flag for one solitary ship, we then told him that it was impossible we could not write that to the Queen of England for she had Treaties with all nations, about the same accursed Traffic, he must take his chance, like the rest of the Slave dealers, as he had declined to enter into a Treaty with Great Britain, he said he certainly thought it very hard that his friend could not allow one vessel to pass, to bring articles for himself and his people. We mentioned Cotton he said that his people were a warlike people,

---

[681] I.e. in 1727.

[682] Forbes again understood this to mean priority of settlement (following the abandonment of the European forts during the reign of Adandozan, 1797–1818): 'the English traders were the first who landed there, and bought slaves' (1851, ii: 187). This presumably alludes to the reoccupation of the English fort by Thomas Hutton in 1838, although he was buying palm oil, rather than slaves.

[683] Presumably referring to two boys sent for education in England by Gezo's predecessor Adandozan, who were initially by mistake sold into slavery in the West Indies, but subsequently liberated and repatriated to Dahomey in 1803: however, these are described as 'younger brothers' of Adandozan, so were sons of Gezo's father Agonglo, rather than of his grandfather (M'Leod 1820: 102–7).

[684] Alluding to the King's expenditure at the Annual Customs.

[685] Antonio de Souza had been granted the honorific title of 'amigo del rey', 'King's friend' (Forbes' Journal, pp. 155–6).

[686] Joaquim Antonio was a Spanish merchant, based at Great Popo, on the coast between Little Popo and Agoué (Strickrodt 2015: 202).

unaccustomed to the agricultural pursuits, he could not attempt to send his people to Plant and cultivate cotton, and make Farms, that they were warriors, and he did not wish to be laughed at by other nations, all the nations that had planted and sold cotton he had conquered, so there is very little cotton for sale, he asked us from the swamp[687] to Abomey did you see any Farms,[688] I cannot take my women to Plant Farms, so he felt somewhat excited and annoyed evidently that his friend the Queen of England would not allow him a vessel to pass, he Harped upon it for some time, until he found we could not be induced to write the same in the Queen's Dispatch,[689] he left it and gave it up as a bad case, we asked him if he had come to his final decision, or if he had any more to say on that point, His Majesty then commenced about Freemans visit from Cape Coast, and said that he promised to send a white man to Abomey, but he had not Kept his word,[690] he gave him two Boys, and two Girls to be taught English,[691] he has had them Five years,[692] and will not send them back[,] one is dead, Capt Forbes mentioned the affair to Freeman when at Cape Coast,[693] he said he wanted payment before he sent them to Abomey we told the King that it had better be mentioned in his dispatch to the Queen of England, the matter would soon be adjusted, and no doubt orders sent to Governor Winniett to arrange the affair,[694] next matter was relative to Abbeokutta, with the King's permission, I read the Earl of Chichester's letter from the Queen of England to Sagbua Chief of that place,[695] he appeared to be excited when it was mentioned, I told him that, I was going to visit it after the rainy season,[696] he then said he was going to attack it, that I must remove all the white people, he appeared to be very jealous about white men being sent there, The Mayogau remarked and said that the white man had not any right to go and teach those fellows Book,[697] I must go and take them away. So the case ended.

[687] I.e. the Lama.

[688] Forbes adds 'except in the neighbourhood of towns' (Journal, p. 193).

[689] I.e. the letter to be written on the King's behalf to the Queen.

[690] In 1843: by his own account, Freeman had told Gezo only that he would 'try' to arrange for a missionary to be sent to Dahomey (1844: 261–4).

[691] Ibid., 273.

[692] Actually seven years (1843–50).

[693] Presumably, Forbes had visited Cape Coast after his earlier mission to the King in October–November 1849.

[694] William Winniett, still Lieutenant-Governor of the Gold Coast.

[695] Earl of Chichester (President of the CMS) to Sagbua, n.d., in HCPP, *Slave Trade*, 1850–1, Class B, incl. 2 in no. 15, conveying best wishes and thanks for protection of the missionaries. This was among papers which Beecroft had been given by Lord Palmerston, in his briefing for the mission. The point of introducing this letter was to emphasise that Britain considered Abeokuta a friend.

[696] Beecroft did visit Abeokuta, in January 1851.

[697] I.e. reading and writing.

Next was a case about Mrs McCarthy from Sieirleon,[698] I stated to His Majesty that she had complained to me that her Husband John McCarthy was a Prisoner in the Kings yard, not any person appeared to know any thing about him, King ordered the old Mayo-gau was to see about the matter.

His Majesty was very anxious to have some person from England to reside at the Fort,[699] he said you live close to me at Fernando Po, he wished C[aptain] Forbes as he knew him, and desired us to mention it in the Queens dispatch, which has been done,[700] he then said he hoped that I would come and see his next years Customs he would send me a Book to Fernando Po, if he wanted me at any time, I told him if my health permitted I would attend to His Majesty's request, I then informed him that any disputes between British merchants and natives &c that it was my duty to enquire and endeavour to settle them so the whole of our conference ended. It rained we waited a short time and then asked permission to depart, we went through the form as usual of taking a quick Glass, without any shouts or musketry, he then conducted us outside of the Porch, shook hands, and wished us a good and safe arrival at our destination, we got into our Hammocks, and arrived at our Domicile at 4 o'clock, sent for the Sieirleon woman, she came but Nawhey and <u>Maa-daa-Kee</u> did not know any thing about her, the Mayo was present and we told him all the particulars, after we had talked the matter over he left, I told him [as] last words that he must let us know in the morning about McCarthy, he asked me if I wanted to buy him, I said no he was a British subject, he said he would see the King on the matter, and left, we dined shortly after[,] about 6 o'clock, I was astonished to see the Mayo-gau, Nawhey, and Cow-paa, make their appearance, wishing to have the account we had laid before the King, we were rather annoyed or rather appeared so, that they should come to annoy us at dinner for no earthly use whatever, at last we gave them the account we were sanguine that we might have another conference on the matter, but it was merely to show to his agents at Whydah, or rather his five agents, or Partners.

During our conference the King expressed a desire that a white man might be sent to Teach.[701] I asked him if he would ensure him his Protection, and a grant of land, and assist them to build a House. he said certainly the Interpreter the fool said it was too cold for Whitemen at Abomey, he must remain

---

[698] Cf. p. 100.

[699] I.e. as Vice-Consul, in succession to the late John Duncan.

[700] Beecroft's dispatch to Palmerston (in Appendix 3, doc. 8, see p. 210), indicates that it was at this point that the King's letter to Queen Victoria was dictated and signed. Forbes, however, places this earlier, before the discussion of Abeokuta (Journal, p. 194): the latter version seems more plausible, since the letter makes no mention of Abeokuta.

[701] I.e. a missionary: the request was included in the postscript to the King's letter to Queen Victoria.

at Whydah. I told him to ask the King, and he said he must remain at Whydah, so I don't think that he is anxious to have Gods word Preached at Abomey. I retired at 9 o'clock.

Friday July 5th

Daylight drizzling rain 8 o'clock Mayo-gau Caboceer of Whydah and Nawhey made their appearance with Presents from the King, & to pass us on the road, viz.

> 1 Handsome country cloth for Queen
> 1 Plain [cloth] for each of us
> 1 country stool, D° Large and a Foot stool
> 1 Keg of rum 2½ Gallons
> 10 Heads of cowries
> 1 little girl each

Interpreter deputy Governor of the Fort at Whydah,[702] 1 Piece of cloth, 4 heads, and 1 Bottle of rum

Richards my Interpreter from Fernando Po	1 Head of cowries and 1 Bottle of rum		
Nawhey	2 Heads	1 D°	of D°
Hammock Bearers	2 Heads	1 Bottle of rum	

after the distribution outside, we went inside and held a short conference. They commenced that before the King went to Ah-taa-Pam war he gave 4000 muskets, to the Ah-goo-nee people indeed they made out 8000 more muskets to new Troops.[703] Mrs McCarthy was here; I told Mayo-gau that she had seen him [i.e. her husband] at Cambaa-dee's house in the morning, he sent her of with a messenger, and said they would both be here again some part of the day. She left taking her child with her, we then told them that we should leave in the morning, they said they would be here early—fire a salute of 21 guns for the Queen of England, and 13 for each of us, Mayo-gau then said to me that I was not far from the King, he could always send me a Book or send a man to tell me his Palaver, that if I cannot attend I must send my Interpreter Thomas Richards it would do all the same. So ended the conference, they took a Glass of wine and left, Kings demand is not large, but he did not mention a word at his last conference. these articles were mentioned before, viz

---

[702] I.e. Madiki Lemon.

[703] Forbes (Journal, p. 195) gives the details differently: 4,000 to 'the soldiers' and 4,000 to the Agonli people for the 'last war', and 4,000 to 'the new War men'; in his book, he explains that the 'new' soldiers were those raised for 'the next war' (1851, ii: 193). The point was evidently to emphasise that the King incurred expenditure for military supplies, as well as for the Customs.

1 Tent, 1 Large sofa, several pieces of cloth, a few good Dogs—
A quantity of Blunderbusses—and musketoons.
showers of rain at noon Ther 76°
Paid the different people about the house, as under

Sogong	2 pieces of romal			
Ma-chee	2	D°	"	D°
Ah-taa[704]	2	D°	"	D°
Le vee see	1	D°	"	D°
Carriers of firewood	2			
" of water	1			
	10			

Pm rain employed getting packed up for a start in the morning. Sunset no appearance of the McCarthy's—sent my Interpreter Richards with a Hammockman that knows where she formerly lodged, to enquire about her, he returned at 9 o'clock and stated after a long search they found it and they told him that she [had] been taken with her Cloathes in the morning by some of the Dahomeians but they did not know where they had taken them. sent the other interpreter Maa-daa-Kee to the Mayo to inform what we had heard, and that we could not leave until we had a finall answer from the King what was his intentions towards those people as British subjects. he returned later and said that the Mayo would see the King about the matter retired to rest at 10 o'clock a fine night hopes of fair wʳ tomorrow.[705]

I should certainly recommend that not any more Presents should be sent to the King of Dahomey under the Present circumstances of the case. I have finished the greater part of this Journal in a very hurried manner. I must amend the Duplicate at Fernando Po and send it by the 1ˢᵗ opportunity.[706]

---

[704] Identified earlier as the Migan's 'boy' (p. 141).

[705] For the return journey to Ouidah, see Beecroft's dispatch to Palmerston, 22 July 1850, in Appendix 3, doc. 8 (see p. 211), and Forbes' Journal (pp. 196). The English party left Abomey on 6 July and arrived at Ouidah on 9 July. En route, they were overtaken by Gnahoui, who belatedly delivered the McCarthys into their custody.

[706] The promised revision does not seem to have been done: cf. Introduction, p. xlvii.

APPENDIX 1

LIEUTENANT FORBES' JOURNAL

The original of Forbes' journal does not appear to have survived. It exists in two versions, a manuscript text preserved in the National Archives and a printed text included in the Parliamentary Papers.[1] The manuscript version is not in Forbes' handwriting, so is evidently a copy of the original text, and it does not seem to be the source of the printed version. It therefore has no greater authority than the printed text, and indeed in certain details seems to be a less accurate copy of the original,[2] although the printed text perpetrates inaccuracies of its own. The manuscript version, however, includes some material omitted in the latter.[3] The text as presented here represents a conflation of the two versions, with significant textual discrepancies noted; account is also taken of variant readings in the reworked version of the journal included in Forbes' book. The text is offered with limited annotation, in order not to duplicate annotations to Beecroft's journal.

May 13—Arrived off Whydah, and embarked on board Her Majesty's ship 'Phoenix', where I had the honour of being introduced to Mr. Beecroft.

May 14—Landed, surf rather high, one chest of muskets; twenty lost. Her Majesty's ship 'Kingfisher' saluted, twenty guns. British fort saluted as we entered the town of Whydah.

May 15—6 A.M. Visited Viceroy, and introduced Mr. Beecroft as Her Majesty's Consul, and explained to him our position as Her Majesty's Plenipotentiaries. Took private apartments in the British fort.

May 16—Viceroy sent to apologize, as a King's Messenger had arrived, that he could not call.

May 17—Viceroy called. He starts [i.e. for Abomey] on 20th, we are to start 21st. Isidore da Souza is Charchar, Ignatio da Souza, Cabooceer, Antonio da Souza, Amigo

---

[1] TNA, FO84/827, ff. 234–81; HCPP, *Slave Trade*, 1850/1, Class A, incl. 2 in no. 220; also reproduced (with minor spelling variations) in *Papers Relative to the Reduction of Lagos* (1852), incl. 3 in no. 13.

[2] Note e.g. pp. 162, 190, where the MS version has 'names' and 'palaver' but the printed version 'manes' and 'palace', the latter being clearly correct.

[3] See pp. 156, 193.

del Rey;[4] three appointments out of one that their father enjoyed—the reason obvious: His Majesty receives three presents.[5]

May 18—Called on the Charchar to thank him for the use of his canoes to land Her Majesty's presents. All appeared poverty and decay.

May 19—Sunday.

May 20—Received 2 casks 80 dollars of cowries.[6]

May 21—Sent on baggage. Mr Hutton having conferred with me, gave him the following Letter.—

Mr Hutton having explained to me his intention of sending Mr Hastie to England unless he could clear himself of the charge of aiding and abetting the Slave Trade in lending his Canoes to Antonio Da Souza, Mr Hastie called upon me to state whether I was aware that such was the case or not.

Mr Hastie has apologized to me for his conduct to me on the occasion of my former visit.[7] In my second I had occasion to remark on Mr Huttons kindness, and that he had offered me Apartments in the Fort. Mr Hastie is in the habit of talking indiscreetly with regard to the charge made by the late Mr Duncan I can only say I heard it from Mr Hastie, and from no one else; I therefore hope he might have stated it in Bravado.
Signed F.E. Forbes.[8]

At 5 started, and at 9 arrived at Torree.

May 22—Arrived at Allahdah. In the evening, Charchar and Ignatio da Souza arrived with the ostentation, dirt, and display of African officials

May 23—Arrived at Wybagou [= Houègbo].

May 24—Crossed the swamp, rather bad; arrived at Zobardoh [= Zogbodomè], and put up in a neat farm-house in a fine cultivated country.

May 25—Arrived at Canamina.[9] This being the same route I took in my last mission, I do not describe it. Cana deserves a line in praise. The level park lands, the high state of cultivation, neatness and cleanliness of habitation, aged of both sexes, sereneness of atmosphere, all combined, lead the ideas far from Africa, slavery

---

[4] Portuguese, 'friend of the King'.
[5] Referring to the annual tax on income/wealth, elsewhere called 'tribute'.
[6] If these were the same-sized casks as those purchased from the French factory earlier (cf. Beecroft's Journal, p. 7, n. 40), they were obtained at less than half the price then paid.
[7] At Forbes' initial interview with the Yovogan, Hastie had disrupted proceedings by threatening coercive action by the British Navy: HCPP, *Slave Trade*, 1849/50, incl. 9 in no. 9, Lt Forbes to Commodore Fanshawe, 1 Nov. 1849, journal entry for 5 Oct. 1849.
[8] This letter is omitted in the printed version.
[9] MS version has 'Cannah Ninah'.

and sacrifices. Dahomey, carrying war and devastation into all the neighbouring countries, has herself enjoyed the sweets of peace, It is not the Dahomans
who war, but forced mercenaries;[10] nor are the Dahomans much the gainers by
these harassing slave-hunts—old age is decapitated to ornament the Palace,[11]
strength and youth sold to enrich the Brazils, their proceeds wasted at the horrible and ridiculous customs of Hwae noo ee wha, occurring once a-year.[12]
Charchar arrived. Sent to Abomey to report our arrival; received an answer that
we rise at cock-crow and proceed.

May 26—At 7 arrived at Abomey. Immediately inside the gate, on wheels (a present
from the late Charchar) was a brigantine about twenty-eight feet long, well
rigged, under all plain sail, union-jack at the fore, French tricolor at the peak [*in
margin*: French flag last visit was white].[13] Dressed in full uniform, Charchar
and Brazilians arrived and took ground a-head of us, attended by 140 armed
slaves in Dahoman uniforms. At 9 we were met by the Cabooceers. I have
described a meeting before. The Charchar was bent on giving us his left, in
which he failed, and to show his bad taste muttered audibly, 'politico, politico'.[14] A messenger arriving from the King addressed him, in hopes that he and
all his 'whites'[15] were quite well, he was constrained to pass on to us and thus
showed we were two parties. [*In margin*: Antonio did not accompany the other
Da Souzas, he remained to ship slaves for the family, but fortunately the 'Gladiator' took the slaver. She was consigned to the Charchar.[16]] It is somewhat odd
that the late Da Souza was the patron of nearly all English visitors to Abomey,
Mr. Duncan, Dr. Dickson,[17] and nearly so to Mr. Cruickshanks. Forming procession, the Cabooceers preceded them,[18] Mr. Beecroft and myself followed by
the Charchar, the guns of the saluting battery firing twenty-one guns in honour
of Her Majesty Queen Victoria, and thirteen each for Her Majesty's Plenipotentiaries. The King's reception was much the same as described in my former
mission, we were received first, and the Charchar 'passed' first; honours were
divided. The court-yard was decorated with flags of all colours, among them
many union-jacks, intended doubtless as a compliment, although the only other
great display was of human skulls. I remarked last journal, that the skull-orna-
ments of the wall were in many parts blown down; now there are few left, and
the King has no intention of renewing them: yet how inconsistent! the Palaver-House in the centre of the square was ornamented with 148 newly cleaned
from the Okeadon war (one of the most cowardly acts that ever disgraced a
tyrant), the only other ornament was a gaudy tent in front of the Palace, under
which was a state chair. At noon we were permitted to retire to our new home
in the Mayo's palace, having taken a mixture, in the United States called 'stone

---

[10] Subsequently, he says slaves (p. 169).
[11] Referring to the exhibition of severed heads on the walls of the palace.
[12] I.e. the 'Annual Customs'. For interpretation of Forbes' names for ceremonies, see Endnote 1.
[13] I.e. the French royalist flag: the monarchy had been overthrown in the revolution of 1848.
[14] Portuguese 'political', i.e. devious.
[15] Printed version omits 'all'.
[16] The *Bom Fin*, taken on 25 May 1851: cf. Beecroft's journal, p. 86, n. 407.
[17] Thomas Dickson, an explorer who travelled through Abomey into the interior in 1825/6.
[18] *Sic* in both versions: but it seems likely that this should be 'preceded, then ...'.

wall', of rum, gin, brandy, beer, hock, limonade gazeuse, besides liqueurs. In the Evening the Mayo visited.

May 27—The Mayo visited and invited us to be present at his levee.

    The Palace of Dangelahcordeh has many gates; to-day at each gate a Minister held his levee. At 2 P.M. we arrived at the Mayo's, whose canopy of umbrellas formed the apex from which a ring was extended here and there studded with umbrellas and banners: on a high stool of state sat the Minister, surrounded by his officers, who left a lane in front for new-comers to advance through and salute the chief. On our arrival we were seated on his right, and exchanged compliments in a glass of Frontignac.[19] In this ring were two bands, and in gaudy attire two troubadours (the only appropriate names for them; they were not minstrels and certainly not ballad-singers, but between the two); each carried a staff of office,—a blue crutch stick[20] with a device carved in the staff, and to each stick was a yellow handkerchief. They sang about the wars of the Dahomans and histories of the Kings of Dahomey; in this way only are the records kept. The troubadours were father and son, and the office is hereditary and lucrative; if failing [a] male heir, by adoption. First, the elder sang how the King had conquered Attahpam;[21] but the greatest achievement appeared to be in the capturing of a lady, on which he had bestowed a largesse on the troubadours; then how the King had killed Ahchardee, King of Jena;[22] and, pointing to a handsome tunic and Damask-silk crimson Turkish trousers, gave me his clothes. He then sang at length in praise of Queen Victoria, the friend of Gézo, for which we gave him a breaker[23] of rum. A court fool with white-washed face, surmounted by a slouched hat, exercised his ingenuity; but not being initiate in the Idiom of the language his witticisms were lost to us.

    About an hour after our arrival, headed by guards, banners and official emblems, arrived His Majesty's sisters and daughters, followed by bands of discordant music and attendants carrying changes of raiment, gaudily dressed in cotton cloths and coral and Popoe beads. The Princesses, about thirty in number, took position on our right in front, and made it very warm. The elder troubadour was soon dismissed, the younger pleased better. After remaining about an hour, the royal ladies rose *en masse*, and each producing a small decanter, which it appeared her prerogative to have filled with rum, assailed the aged Minister. A scene followed, highly derogatory to the dignity of royalty. As soon as all were satisfied, they took leave, and forming procession, marched off to the next gate, where a similar scene followed. During this time the Mayo received his friends, and entertained each with a glass before he dismissed him; all knelt when approaching him, and threw dirt on their heads. Taking leave, we called in at the Viceroy's levee, who regaled us with beer and effervescing lemonade. These levees are called *Zandro*.[24]

---

[19] A variety of white wine.
[20] I.e. one topped by a cross-piece.
[21] MS version has 'Attassam'.
[22] See further p. 160.
[23] I.e. a small cask.
[24] Fon *zàndló*, '[over]night wake'.

May 28—At 8 A.M., in full uniform, we were commanded to the Palace, and according to the court etiquette were gazed at by the many-headed[25] for an hour. During the customs each Minister, Cabooceer, or military officer, has to assemble his men at 6, and when dressed and ready (every morning), to make the circuit of the Palace Square in procession three times. At the arrival at the gate in each round, he has to prostrate, while his retainers fire, dance and sing; this finished, if on duty, he places his insignia of office under a long tent, and stretches himself on a mat until required; if not, he plants his umbrella, and, seated on a stool holds a short levee, and then retires. At 9 we entered the Palace, and were shown to the entrée of the audience-chamber; His Majesty lounged on a bed. There were present the Mayo, Eeavoogau, Camboodee, Toonoonoo, and Maehaepah, Minister of Foreign Affairs,[26] Viceroy of Whydah, Treasurer, Head Eunuch, and the Amazon Grand Vizier. The seal of Her Majesty's letter having been broken by the King, Mr. Beecroft read it in short sentences to the Interpreters (three, and unfortunately none of the best).[27]

As far as could be judged, His Majesty received its contents with pleasure; promised to consider the question. Directed us to view his customs well.

From certain remarks elucidated concerning the emoluments of the Slave Trade, we considered it prudent to acquaint His Majesty that we were authorized to offer a subsidy and we were in power to put it in force immediately His Majesty should enter into treaty; but that it was impossible to pronounce the sum until we had witnessed his disbursements.

The interview was flattering. On our return sent the Queens gracious presents. (List annexed.)

The Ministers and Caboceers paraded the town at the head of their bands and retainers, firing constantly.

May 29—At 7.30 we were again ushered into the audience entré[e], now occupied by Maehaepah, very busy winding up, one after another, eight Sam Slick's clocks,[28] some upside down, others on their sides, and one, by mistake, in its proper position; from this state we rescued them, but not before I had horrified the stately dame by placing one foot within the sacred precincts of the Harem, To prevent so unprecedented an occurrence, the Maehaepah and Toonoonoo knelt one on each side the threshold, and thus exhibited clocks, musical-boxes, watches, &c, on the particular efficacies of each of which we were called upon to dilate.

At 10 we passed through another gate, entering a large court-yard; on the opposite side, under a canopy of umbrellas of every colour, and ornamented with strange devices, sat the King on a sofa, and over him a small European parasol of crimson velvet and gold. His Majesty wore a blue flowered satin robe, a gold laced hat, and sandals ornamented with silver, round his neck a neat gold chain.

[25] The 'many-headed beast', i.e. the common people.
[26] The Mewu's responsibilities included relations with Europeans (Le Herissé 1911: 41): however, in his book Forbes calls him the 'Grand Vizier'.
[27] Referring presumably to the mission's interpreters Madiki Lemon and Thomas Richards, and the King's interpreter Gnahoui.
[28] Cf. Beecroft's journal, p. 20, n. 124.

On the side of the court occupied by the throne sat the royal wives and female officers, all well dressed in a variegation of silks, cloths, &c, and the Amazons in full uniform, all seated on their hams, rested the stocks of their long Danish muskets on the ground, while the polished barrels stood up like a forest. In one part of the female group sat twenty-eight with blue crutch sticks, each ornamented with a yellow handkerchief: these were the sticks of office of the female troubadours, and each was to relate in her own way the romance of the history of Dahomey.

Standing facing the throne (the Mayo, Eeavoogau and Caboceer of the British fort, Heechelee lay prostrated, throwing dirt on their heads), we bowed three times to the King. This was a neutral ground, and was occupied during the day by the Maehaepah and Toonoonoo, or the female grand vizier and head eunuch, who, on their knees, communicated the royal pleasure, or any message; the King being guarded by his Amazons, could not be approached by one of the opposite sex. On this neutral ground were the skulls of kings in calabashes, surrounding a newly-formed heap, which contained the head of a victim sacrificed last night, his body is to be buried under the tent (pole) to be used by His Majesty to-morrow. Some of these skulls were ornamented with brass, copper, coral, &c.; one in a copper pan illustrated a fearful tale of treachery and murder, the skull of Ahchardee, Chief of Jena. The history may not be out of place in this Journal.

Onsih, King of Jena, died; and Dekkon, heir-apparent, hated, was rejected. He escaped to Dahomey, then reigned over by Adonooza [= Adandozan], and implored him to march upon Jena; Adonooza refused, his mother being a Jena Woman. Ahchardee (until they should choose a king) was nominated President; Adonooza deposed. Gézo marched an Army three successive years against Ahchardee, and was each time defeated. Resolved to effect by stratagem what he had failed to do by open war, Gézo invited Ahchardee to Dahomey to witness his customs. Receiving hostages and presents he came, and was returned, loaded with presents. A second year he was allowed to go back unmolested. The third, he came with near a thousand traders, at the Custom called 'Eh que noo ah toh-meh'.[29] He was thrown with the victims, sacrificed, his people taken into slavery.[30]

After saluting the Monarch we turned round, and on the opposite side were from 300 to 400 males, Ministers, Caboceers, officers and soldiers. As with the Amazons, in one part were twenty-eight sticks belonging to troubadours; all were shaded by large umbrellas. Immediately opposite the throne were chairs and a table set with decanters and glasses for ourselves, under a canopy of handsome umbrellas; on the right sat the Charchar and the Brazilians, similarly accommodated.

Taking our seats, the *coup-d'-oeil*[31] was very pleasing; all were well dressed; the Ministers and Caboceers in flowing robes. Besides the diversity of colour

---

[29] Both versions here have the second syllable as 'anee', but Forbes (1851, ii: 26), has 'quee', which is correct, i.e. Fon *hwè*, 'year'.

[30] This story is muddled. 'Jena' is Ijanna, in Egbado, but the town destroyed by the Dahomians (*c*.1837) was not Ijanna, but Refurefu (cf. Beecroft's Journal, p. 72): Ijanna itself was also destroyed (*c*.1833), but by Abeokuta, rather than Dahomey. 'Onsih' represents Onisare, the title of the governor (not in status a 'king') of Ijanna; Dekun and Asade were chiefs of Ijanna who left to found Refurefu (Law 1977a: 276–7). The deposition of Adandozan had occurred several years earlier (1818), so cannot have been directly linked to the war against Refurefu.

[31] I.e. 'view' (French).

in dress and umbrellas, there were also numbers of banners and fetish ornaments. The days jubilee is named, 'Eh nah ek begh' (the day of giving).

Business commenced by two male troubadours introducing themselves;
then one at a time recited the exaggerated accounts of the wild warlike adven-
tures of Gézo and his ancestors; interlucent praises[32] and visionary accounts of
the future. As though gratifying to the Monarch who had deposed him, they
desecrated the memory of his brother Adonooza, as totally unfit to reign over a
powerful and brave nation such as the Dahoman. At the mention of the name
of any member of the Royal Family deceased, all the Ministers, Cabooceers,
and officers, male and female, had to prostrate and kiss the dust, &c. The troubadours by no means spared them: they hailed Gézo as the greatest of African
Monarchs; he had only to command and it was done; enumerated all the conquered states. That any country that insulted Dahomey must fall; and there still
remained three to conquer, Tappah, Yaruba, and Abbeokuta.[33] (In the Jena war,
the Yarubas—a part of whom the Dahomans consider a separate nation from
the Abbeokutians—assisted against Dahomey.[34] In the Okeadon War in 1848,
the Abbeokutians took an Amazon general, (umbrella) and standard and regiment, and as the Dahomans term it, 'made children for them'.[35]) The Amazons
next spouted their visionary lore, amusing themselves at times calling on the
multitude to laugh for joy at the recital of the King's exploits; when first the
females would exercise their risible faculties, then the males give a sort of Irish
howl; now and again the singers called on the multitude to join chorus, which
was readily complied with. As each two were attended by a discordant band,
there was no lack of music.

The only innovations were: 1st Ahhopeh, the King's brother, spoke of the
impropriety of removing cowries, to be distributed from the market[,] at night,[36]
stating that as there were so many strangers in the town, it would be dangerous
to tempt them, particularly as the penalty, even to a Prince, would be death. The
King concurred, and agreed that the cowries should be distributed on the 31st,
and removed at 4 A.M. of that day. 2nd. At noon His Majesty crossed over, and

[32] 'Interlucent' means shining in the midst of other things.
[33] 'Takpa' (or 'Atakpa') in Fon usually means Nupe (in the interior, north-east of Oyo), but this
was beyond the range of Dahomian military operations: probably here it refers to Atakpamé (the
last syllable of which name represents a locative suffix, 'in'), which was regarded as 'defeated
[earlier in 1850] although not annexed' (Forbes 1851, i: 8). 'Yoruba' usually means Oyo, but this
had been defeated in 1823, and was now claimed (with some exaggeration) to be 'under the
Dahoman yoke' (ibid., i: 20), so perhaps the reference here is to one of the states which were
vying for the succession to Oyo power, Ijaye or Ibadan (both north-east of Abeokuta). Ijaye was
certainly encroaching into Dahomey's sphere of influence at this period, with raids into the
territory of Savè (recently conquered by Dahomey), which culminated in the destruction of the
Savè capital in 1851 (Palau Marti 1992: 209–10). However, in 1852 there was a rumour of a battle
between Dahomey and Ibadan, which although false is evidence that the latter also was
considered a potential enemy (HCPP, *Slave Trade*, 1852/3, Class A, incl. 1 in no. 89, Commander
Strange to Commodore Bruce, 7 March 1852).
[34] Egbado had earlier been a province of Oyo (so itself part of 'Yoruba'), but Oyo authority here
had collapsed in the 1830s (Law 1977a: 276–7): presumably the reference is to Ijaye or Ibadan.
[35] This seems to be a confusion: the campaign in which the Abeokutans captured a royal umbrella
and other trophies was not that against Okeodan, but the earlier battle of Imoloju, in 1845
(Folayan 1972: 20).
[36] I.e. of moving them to the market, ahead of their distribution, as Forbes in his book says more
clearly (1851, ii: 28).

took a glass of liqueur with us (being covered by cloths while he did so). Guns fired, Ministers and Caboocers danced, and all huzzaed.

As each two, male or female, of the troubadours finished their lays, they received a present for themselves and bands in all about thirty, thus:–

        Cowries, 28 heads or dollars.

        Cloth, 28½ pieces, or 28 dollars.

        Handkerchiefs, 4 pieces.

        Rum, 2 gallons.

The total expense of the day by my calculation was cowries, 784 dollars; cloth, 784 dollars; handkerchiefs, 102 dollars; rum, 28 dollars: in all 1698 dollars.

At 3 P.M., raining hard, we were commanded to retire.

Seated five hours over damp ground. Had it not been for the novelty, would, doubtless, have been irksome.

In the evening, the Mayo, Eeavoogau, and Nearwhey, attended by the royal command to explain to us the expenses of the day, and brought strings of cowries, which we had to count, to satisfy ourselves of the correctness of their statement, which ran as follows: cowries 7,540 dollars: cloth, 644 pieces; iron armlets, 92 in number; rum, 140 bottles. Further, that His Majesty had that morning thrown away 400 dollar heads of cowries, and 40 pieces of cloth, and intended that night to throw away 800 dollars heads of cowries; that the sum total of the days expenses was 26,000 dollars in value.

At 3 P.M., when we left, only four males and four females had been paid; we allowed all to be paid, and that would have taken till at least 8 P.M., and these officers were with us at 6 P.M. His Majesty, we had expected would take every advantage of us; but this was rather too much; it reminded me of the stories handed down by the late Da Souza, with which he fed English visitors. And well may the Royal Exchange be laid at 300,000 dollars per annum,[37] when (at the most liberal allowance) the expenses, actually 1698 dollars, are given as 26,000 dollars. The description of the 'Eh quee noo ah toh meh'[38] will, I trust, prove together with Ahhohpeh's speech, that neither the 800 nor 400 dollars were distributed; whilst the custom called 'Ak bah tong ek beh'[39] will pretty well illustrate the impossibility of the gross sum, 26,000 dollars in cowries and cloth, being distributed in one day by the Dahoman Monarch.

Before leaving, the Mayo solemnly charged us, that neither ourselves nor our servants be found in the streets to-night; His Majesty was going to sacrifice to the manes[40] of his ancestors.

May 30—At 7.30 we started for the Palace. At a little distance from our house, the road was fenced off; the King's wives were going to carry goods to market, and no one might meet them.

At the foot of the ladder ascending to the Palaver-House, in the square of the Palace of Dangelahcordeh, lay six newly cut off human heads, the blood still oozing; at the threshold of the entrance gate was a pool of human blood.

---

[37] Referring to Cruickshank's Report, 16.

[38] On 31 May (below, pp. 164–5). Both versions have the second syllable incorrectly as 'gnee'.

[39] On 30 May (below, pp. 163–4).

[40] I.e. spirits of the dead (Latin). The MS version has 'names'.

Within, the scene was entirely different from yesterday; in the centre of the Palace court stood a huge crimson cloth tent, forty feet high and of forty feet diameter, ornamented with devices of men cutting off other's heads, calabashes full of human heads, and other emblems of brutality and barbarity; on the top stood the figure of a Dahoman, with half his head shaved,[41] supporting a staff from which flew a white standard; on it was emblazoned a jar having one skull for a stopper, standing in a large dish on three other skulls (blue). Although the King had not arrived, we had to pay the same compliment as yesterday (similarly attended) to the throne, which was inside the tent, around which were the Amazons, wives, &c. On the neutral ground were the same skulls. Turning round our position faced His Majesty's, and about were the Ministers, &c., all dressed as nearly as possible alike, in red striped flowing robes, and laden with necklaces. In a short time His Majesty arrived dressed in a coloured silk robe and laced hat. Having taken his seat on the throne under the tent, the business of the day commenced by a procession of fifty-eight Ministers and Cabooceers, each carrying a sword, a scimitar, and a club; after passing the throne three times, all prostrated and threw dirt on their heads.

To give the whole account would be to make this Journal prolix; I shall therefore annex a programme of the processions which lasted till 3 P.M., and comprised between 6000 and 7000 people, and here merely make a few comments.

The days custom is called 'Ak bah tong ek beh' (carrying goods to market), and is really a display of as much of the whole wealth of the Monarch as can be, without material damage, drawn or carried to the market of Ahjahhee and back, a distance, both ways, of about a mile. The day was cloudy, and the dresses by no means good. From the programme a very fair calculation of the actual wealth of the King may be made: 1793 women, carried cowries, each three heads, on an average, some not more than half a head: being in total 5,379 heads of cowries or dollars. Among the display of wealth were many articles of little value—some 50 pots-de-chambre, to wit—His Majesty could not be aware of the use of; 90 women carried common jugs; 170 carried each one piece of cloth cut in two and rolled; 46 ditto white baft ditto; 47 carried each six Dutch pipes; 70 ditto empty blue bottles; 50 carried a washing-jug each. It has been frequently related to me that His Majesty possesses whole services of plate. How ridiculous! All his silver ornaments were displayed to-day, and his artisan brother, Sohsar, and Hatongee,[42] the silversmith, were by command seated near us to explain their value. In all they were 90 in number, carried by as many women; among them coffee-pots, tea-pots, cream-jugs, and baskets of European manufacture, 33 were silver-headed canes, and the remainder large hollow ornaments of native make [*in margin*: At least so we were told, but they were wrapt in cloths]. Of the fashion of His Majesty's knives and forks we had a daily sample, and certes,[43] they would be of equal curiosity in England as in Dahomey, of iron.

---

[41] Royal messengers had one side of their heads shaved and were consequently called 'halfheads' by Europeans (Bay 1998: 114).
[42] 'Hootoojee' in Forbes' book (1851, ii: 38), which is more accurate, i.e. Hountondji.
[43] I.e. 'certainly' (French).

The collection of a country fair, carried in a similar manner would have far exceeded the wealth displayed in value and appearance. The dresses of a minor theatre would have excelled.

In a country like Dahomey, it is an immense collection, but when the exactions of the Monarch are considered, scarcely to be wondered at; if a Dahoman receives a present he must lay it before the King, and if admired, even the Prime Minister[44] would find it more to his interest to forego it.

Besides goods carried, there were several bands of troops, male and female, and several tasteful groups at different periods took position, danced and sang before the King. Bands were playing in all directions: dwarfs, hunchbacks, court fools, albinos, besides an ostrich and an emu,[45] and several dogs of strange breed strolled about the neutral ground; lastly came the ancient ladies and those holding offices of regal rank, with the insignia of their separate offices; among them numbers of human skulls in drums, banners, knives, &c. These were disgusting enough, but to behold twelve unfortunate victims for to-morrow's sacrifice—carried round, eight on men's, four on women's heads, bound hand and foot and tied in small canoes, dressed in white with high glazed red caps, followed by an alligator and a cat, also for sacrifices,—was fearfully so. As the victims passed the throne of their superstitious tyrant they were halted, and addressed by the Mayo on the munificence of the Monarch, who sent them each a head of cowries, wherewith to purchase a last meal.

Once during the day the King left his tent, to pay us a visit and drink a glass of liqueur.

As yesterday, the Maehaepah and Toonoonoo were continually engaged, and each point of the proceedings was explained to us through this channel from His Majesty.

At 3 It rained hard, and we were allowed to leave, with much to reflect upon.

Rum was distributed in bottles to the different companies, and about 800 dollars in cowries.

May 31—At 7 A.M. we were summoned to witness the custom called 'Ek que noo ah toh' (throwing away cowries from Ahtoh).[46]

As we left our house His Majesty was passing, and sent us a bottle of rum. Joining in procession we were followed by the Amazon host. Passing round the walls of the Palace of Dangehlahcordeh we arrived on an open ground called Ahjahhee, at once the market-place and parade-ground, and now occupied by a huge raised platform, hung with cloths and ornamented with banners of every hue, among them two union-jacks, and surmounted by huge umbrellas and small tents. On the west side of this platform of Ahtoh was a fence-work of prickly acacia, outside of which was a band of soldiers, inside fourteen human beings for sacrifice. As soon as the King arrived he ascended the Ahtoh, and immediately several bands of naked men (unless a grass cloth bag round the waist be termed clothing) marched past; in each band several rode on the

---

[44] I.e. the Migan.

[45] Forbes also recorded seeing an ostrich and an emu on 3 June (1851, ii: 233), when Beecroft refers only to ostriches (Journal, p. 59). The identification as an emu (a specifically Australian bird) is evidently an error.

[46] Fon *atò*, 'platform'.

shoulders of others; headmen; these were the soldiers of the King, his sons, the Ministers and Cabooceers.

I believe it has hitherto been supposed that on this particular day of the Customs His Majesty enjoys a species of liberality unknown in the annals of the histories of any other known nations, in the scrambling to his people, goods of all descriptions—cowries, silk, tobacco, rum, &c., and also live sacrifices. I say I believe so, for such has been my own opinion, deduced from Dalyell[47] and from report. Such is by no means the case.

The public are not admitted to the scramble, and the whole performance is a cheat. The scramblers, as has been stated, are the soldiers (about 300), and the goods are their pay, and this day did not amount to more than 1000 dollars in cowries and 300 dollars in cloth. The throwing away occupied between seven and eight hours.

Taking seats on the left, the King (all being hustled together) addressed the scramblers, directing them not to fight or quarrel, and having thrown a few by way of trial commanded us into his presence. Ascending the Ahtoh, the scene was extraordinary; the floor was laid with rushes, and on it about 3000 heads of cowries, and 500 pieces of cloth, besides rum and tobacco: at one end, under a gorgeous umbrella, dressed in a black waistcoat, a cotton cloth around his loins, and a white nightcap, stood the King, labouring hard 'throwing goods'. Under a range of umbrellas, facing the multitude, stood the Ministers and Cabooceers, one of which remained vacant for our use; the back part of the Ahtoh was occupied by small tents for the ladies of the Harem; while, as we entered, under separate canopies, were two tables set with decanters, &c., for ourselves and the Charchar to retire to.

Taking our stand under the umbrella, the crowd appeared to be one living mass of humanity. Cowries became the property of the lucky ones who caught them; but not so the cloths,—no sooner caught, than if not handed to the headmen riders, a fight ensured terrible to behold, the riders running over the mob as if on dry land, and it was sure to be found.

As the mass oscillated, it emitted an effluvium only to be compared to the fetid vapour that rises from the over-crowded decks of a slave-ship, and a steam arose as dense as the miasm from a swamp. A guard of soldiers paraded the area during the day.

Soon after our arrival His Majesty sent us a present of ten heads of cowries and two pieces of cloth.

During the day, as will be seen by the programme, several presents were given, altogether to the amount of 1000 heads of cowries, and about 200 pieces of cloth, a little rum and tobacco. Among the recipients were two Kings, an Ashantee ambassador, a head mallam, &c.

About noon the brigantine before alluded to was drawn up, and a lane made through the mob; a boat on wheels put off to land her cargo of rum, cloth, and cowries, &c. At 10 we breakfasted, supplied by His Majesty, and after breakfast joined the King in 'throwing away'. It was easy to observe that one party was the grand receiver, and that party the King's. Acting on this, a man named Pohvehsoo, captain of musketoons and court fool, and as we have since

---

[47] I.e. Dalzel (1793).

heard, headsman,[48] had ingratiated himself; knowing him to be the King's friend, we aimed three cloths filled with cowries at him; having received the third, His Majesty ordered him off, as having had enough.

If I were to conclude the history of this day's customs here, I should merely remark that there might be a policy in making appear munificence, the distribution of a sum of money, that if doled out to each individually would prove a miserable pittance, although it tended much to debase the minds of his people, if that were possible. But what followed is almost too revolting to be recorded.

As if by general consent, and evincing a slight dawning of decency, hardly to be expected from these truly barbarians, silence reigned, and when broken, the eunuchs would strike a metal instrument each was supplied with, to enforce it, sounding the knell of eleven unfortunate human beings, whose only crime, known to their persecutors, was that they belonged to a nation Dahomey had warred against, Attahpam. Out of the fourteen now brought upon the platform, we, the unworthy instruments of Providence, succeeding in saving the lives of three. Lashed as described in yesterday's journal, except that only four were in boats, the remainder in baskets, these unfortunates, gagged, met the gaze of their enemies with a firmness perfectly astonishing, not a sigh was breathed. One cowardly villain put his hand to the eyes of a victim, who sat with his head down to feel for moisture; finding none, he drew upon himself the ridicule of his hellish coadjutors.

Ten of these Human offerings to the vitiated appetite of his soldiers, and the alligator and cat, were guarded by the male soldiers, and to the right of the King; four to the left were guarded by women.

Being commanded into the presence, the King asked if we wished to be present at the sacrifice; with horror we declined, and begged to be allowed to save a few by purchasing. After a little hesitation, we were asked which we would have; I exclaimed [*sic*: = claimed] the first and last of the ten, while Mr. Beecroft claimed the nearest of the four, and 100 dollars being stated as the price, was gladly accepted. In all my life I never saw such coolness so near death; the most attentive ear could not have caught the breath of a sigh—it did not look reality, yet it soon proved fearfully so.

Retiring to our tents, the King insisted on our viewing the place of sacrifice. Immediately under the Royal canopy were six or eight executioners, armed with large knives, grinning horribly; the mob now armed with clubs and branches, yelled furiously, calling upon the King to 'feed them—they were hungry'.

Scarcely had we reached our seats, when a demoniac yelling caused us to look back. The King was showing the immolations to his people, and now they were raised high over the heads of their carriers, while the Monarch made a speech to the soldiers, telling them that these were of the prisoners from Attahpam; he called their names. The Charchar left at the same time with ourselves; but Ignatio and Antonio da Souza remained spectators.

The unfortunate being nearest the King, stripped of his clothes, was now placed on end on the parapet, the King giving the upper part of the boat an impetus, a descent of twelve feet stunned the victim, and before animation could return, the head was off; the body, beaten by the mob, was dragged by the heels to a pit at a little distance, and there left a prey to wolves[49] and vultures.

[48] I.e. executioner.
[49] I.e. hyenas.

After the third the King retired; not so the slave-merchants. When all was over, at 3 P.M., we were permitted to retire; at the foot of the ladder in the boats and baskets lay the bleeding heads. It is my duty to describe; I leave exposition to the reader.

The expenses in money, &c., expended this day was 2,700 dollars; out of the 3000 heads on the platform, 1000 remained when all was over.

June 1—At noon we sallied forth to witness a novel sight; a review, half males, half Amazons. The custom is called 'Eh dah soh ek begh' (firing guns).[50] The parade-ground in the Ahjahhee market-place was now clear, the Ahtoh had disappeared, and all that remained to mark the fearful tragedy of yesterday, were the stains of blood, emitting a pestilential stench.

Having taken our seats under some shady trees, the troops marched past in the following order. First came the Cabooceers and their retainers, some 300; lastly, the King's levees and those of the Royal Family, in all 4,400 Men; then came the Amazons in the same order, 2,400. In each regiment or company, first came the armed, then the banners, stool of office, followed by the officers under umbrellas; lastly the band. In the rear of each of the King's levees, male and female, was an equal number of stools, banners, drums, and umbrellas, all ornamented with skulls and jaw-bones.

At 12.30 His Majesty arrived, and took his seat on a high stool under a canopy of umbrellas. On his left the Charchar; on his right Mr. Beecroft and myself. Under the Canopy were none but males. Toonoonoo remained outside and Maehaepah hovered in the neighbourhood, ready to communicate if required.

The King must be aware of the consequences of too often raising the evil passions of men, and too long indulging his people with murder. As if by the power of Aladdin's lamp, to-day they were a changed nation, totally military; the King was a soldier, in French grey tunic, short trousers, and fur skull-cap, no sandals and no ornaments except a neat cartouche box and other military apparel. The hunchback and dwarf vied with the court fool in military address; in all this, there was nothing very extraordinary; but when, in the midst of the Amazons stood the royal mother, wives, female ministers, all in uniform, and armed each with a musket, sword, and club, and which each by her actions showed she knew well to use, the Monarch looked to us, as if to say, 'Did you ever witness the like of this?' All were well, and many handsomely, uniformly, dressed.

The whole marched past, a second or third time. 77 banners and 160 huge umbrellas flirted by the bearers, muskets ornamented with ribbons, flying aloft to be caught again, together enlivening the scene; while 55 discordant bands, and the shouts of the soldiery as they hailed the Monarch, almost deafened the observer.

The retainers of the Ministers and Cabooceers now occupied the ground at the farther end of the field, when first the royal male levees (headed by an emblem of a leopard killing a snake, on a staff) advanced, skirmishing to the foot of the throne, keeping up a constant fire. In front was a regiment of blunderbuss-men, bush-rangers in green grass surtouts.[51] Halting in front, they gave

---

[50] Both versions give the third syllable as 'sol', but Forbes' book has 'soh' (1851, ii: 55), which is clearly correct, i.e. Fon *sò*, 'thunder', and hence 'gunfire'.

[51] I.e. overcoats.

the salute, holding up their muskets with their right hands, their left rattling a small metal rattle, each soldier wears round the neck; while some having light pieces, flung them aloft to catch them again; all the officers prostrating, and throwing dirt on their heads.

The King rose and left the canopy said one or two words to them, and receiving a light musket from an aide-de-camp, fired it and received one of many now offered. He then danced a war-dance. It commenced with a quick-step march; presently he halted, and putting his hand over his eyes, scanned the distance, sent out scouts; danced again, again halted; now certain the enemy was in sight fired his piece, [*in margin*: Bringing his piece to the shoulder]. The soldiers shouted, fired, advanced, and retired, and the King returned to his seat, shaking hands with us, telling us he had been to war.

Domingo José Martins arrived (sixteen hours from Whydah) [*in margin*: He had hammock-men all along the road]. The soldiers sang, and in their song thanked Martins for some powder and muskets he had given last war. As these marched off, the Amazons advanced in the same order, keeping up a constant fire from muskets, blunderbusses, musketoons and wall-pieces;[52] forming a half-circle in from of the canopy, they saluted the King, who, after a parley between those two grave reasoners, the Mahaepah and Toonoonoo, again quit-ted the stool, and performed a war-dance. The Amazons now sang, and intro-duced Domingo, for the same reason, in the following verse which they repeated several times:

> June, Juna long[53] Jose
> Dae mee goo o
> Sooto ah noo o
> Ah dae mee Gézo
> (Domingo gave us Muskets to fight for Gézo).[54]

After much dancing and singing, they marched off and took ground to the left, forming a canopy of umbrellas in their centre for the officers, all seated on their hams, their Danish muskets on end, became Spectators of the remaining part of the review.

The remainder was a sort of presentation of chiefs and officers to the King, while the retainers marched past, firing constantly. The order was as follows:– First, the retainers enfilading between two Fetish-houses, about 200 yards from the throne, would commence firing, and march, edging to the right; the Caboo-ceers and officers would leave the body, and, arrived at the foot of the throne, prostrate, and throw dirt on their heads, while the Toonoonoo called their names and rank. The Cabooceer then knelt, and receiving a bottle of rum, fol-lowed his retainers. All the Cabooceers having passed, among them Ignatio da Souza (who stood),[55] to whom the King went out, and he having declined to dance, His Majesty shamed him into doing so by setting him the example. The Ministers went through the same ceremony. The only other time the King left the tent was to throw some rum on a black pudding of human blood, carried by

---

[52] I.e. large muskets, designed for firing from walls.

[53] Printed version has 'Jim along'.

[54] Not deciphered, but 'Dae mee goo' is presumably 'Domingo', 'sooto' perhaps includes Fon *tù*, 'gun', and the second 'mee' is presumably *mĭ*, 'we, us'.

[55] I.e. he did not prostrate himself.

Fetish-men. At 6.30 the review ended, and we were permitted to retire, much pleased with the days amusement.

During the whole proceedings, order and discipline were observable; the uniformity of dress exceedingly striking. The show of colours, variety of the flat-topped umbrellas, various devices and emblems like the eagles of the Romans, the highly-polished muskets, all combined,—the effect was as pleasing as it was novel.

I am now accustomed to skulls, but a sense of disgust arose when the King sent the Meigau's drinking (war) cup for our inspection—it was a polished human skull. The Meigau, the highest officer in the realm, holds, among other offices, that of hereditary headsman,—under a Dahoman Monarch, no sinecure, although he has a band of subordinates.

The 6,800 soldiers reviewed, with perhaps an equal number on the frontiers, form the standing army of Dahomey; certainly not more than 14,000 male and female, and nearly all foreigners, bought, or prisoners of war.[56] When the King makes war he levies, according to its capabilities, from each town and district; but I should say never marched more than 20,000 to war, leaving about 8000 armed men under the Mayo to protect his capital and frontiers. [*In margin*: To leave the frontiers open, said the King, would be to invite an attack.]

I do not think his Majesty gave us credit for being able to count his troops, but we had done so before he arrived on the ground; and luckily we had, for afterwards several of the largest regiments would march past twice, and one of them three times, thus swelling out the apparent numbers.

During the day he appeared anxious we should have every information, and frequently sent the names of the chiefs as they passed.

June 2—Sunday, and luckily a quiet day. The Mayo called, conversed on trade, but I am not of opinion we made much impression on the Minister, who, besides being himself a slave-dealer, is too old. He did pretty well by his visit in obtaining two gold rings and a new silk handkerchief as a present. His call was to ask us to obtain for His Majesty some silk of a certain pattern the King had had twenty years.

June 3—Again the custom called 'Ek bah tong ek begh', and preceded as before by six human sacrifices, which lay in two heaps under the steps of the Palaver-House as we passed into the court of the Palace of Dangelahcordeh at 7.30 A.M.

The day was fine, and the dresses beautiful in appearance; the tent and positions the same. The opening scene, the procession of Ministers and Cabooceers, was as splendid as it could have been; all wore crimson and yellow slashed silk robes, and over these the Ministers wore crimson silk velvet cloaks trimmed with gold. Bands of singers, males and females, dressed in scarlet tunics and many silver ornaments, were grouped in different parts. The procession was mainly the same, the dresses of the carriers finer or rather more gaudy. Several carriages and wheeled chairs were drawn past, and cloth. velvet, silk, coral, &c., took the place of cowries. As the procession passed, ladies (attended by guards of Amazons) magnificently dressed in the most showy silks, satins, and velvets

---

[56] Cf. Forbes (1851, i: 19), 'the officers are natives, the soldiery foreigners, prisoners of war or purchased slaves'. See also further reference to slaves employed as soldiers, below p. 186.

with hats and plumes of the time of Charles II, would take position opposite the throne, and dance before the King, who was habited in a black slouched hat almost covered with gold embroidery, a blue and white robe and sandals. His Majesty seldom left the tent. A great part of the Amazons were in scarlet or crimson tunics.

The aged ladies, dressed out in scarlet, crimson, or light blue, as they passed in procession, attended by a paraphernalia of skull ornaments, as banners, drums, &c., had their trains borne by maidens in gaudy attire, and were each followed by a guard of Amazons.

Among the groups the most showy were the Paussee six ladies;[57] one wore a Charles II hat and milk-white plume; the other five wore gilt helmits [= helmets] with red and green plumes, tunics of scarlet and gold, with bands of green satin, and waist-belts of blue and green silk; coral bead necklaces, silver gauntlets and armlets, attended by 200 Amazons under Arms in scarlet tunics; also a group of six ex-ladies of the royal chamber, all mothers by the King, and his present favourite wife, in tunics of country cloth, and similarly ornamented as the above, except that each wore at her girdle a polished human skull-cap, and each wore a white slouched hat trimmed with gold lace. The scene was much more brilliant than on the last day [*in margin*: May 30th].

Let it be remembered that these customs occur only once a year and have been annually for 100 years, and that many of the dresses (which are worn on no other occasion) are much older. I had almost forgotten to mention that these dresses did not save the eternal prostration.

One article deserves mention: the programme must be referred to for the rest. A model of a hill in Kangaroo, taken by storm by the Dahomans; by command it was placed near our position, and those two important functionaries, the Maehaepah and the Toonoonoo, knelt with their heads locked for about half an hour, when the mystery was explained to us. The late Mr. Duncan, in his travels to the mountains of Kong, being in the vicinity, asked permission to ascend the hill, which was refused; this, as Mr. Duncan was travelling under Dahoman protection, was construed into an insult. Kangaroo Hill was surmounted by a large town, supplied for a siege and with large tanks of water; the rear was a perpendicular, the front was a slope, round which was a high wall and gate. This wall was escaladed by Eeawae (the English Mother),[58] at the head of a party of Amazons, and her stick of office was placed in honour on the model, where it looked very much out of proportion.

Several musketoons, wall-pieces, and a five-barrelled blunderbuss, all English, were shown us; and His Majesty sent to say, as these were getting old, he

---

[57] Cf. Beecroft's Journal, p. 62, n. 317.

[58] I.e. the person appointed to look after English visitors to Abomey (see Beecroft's Journal, p. 63). She is also mentioned by Freeman in 1843, who spells the name as 'Yaway' (Bay (1998: 208); but 'Yawa' in his published account, Freeman (1844: 257)), Duncan in 1845, who gives it as 'Knawie' (1847, i: 231) and Fraser in 1851, who has 'Yarwhay' (2012: 66); Burton later spelled it 'Yewe' (1864, ii: 75), but in view of the consistent evidence of earlier sources, this should probably be 'Yawe'. Duncan describes her as the 'commander' of a female regiment called 'Apadomey', which presumably means that she was a subordinate of Akpadume, the female Posu, but Fraser and Burton later state that she was the female Mewu, the civil counterpart (and superior) of the Posu: presumably this represents a promotion subsequent to the 1850 mission. Forbes understood that the previous female Mewu had been killed in the recent Atakpamé war (below, p. 185), which might have been the occasion of this promotion.

would be obliged if the Queen, his friend, would send him more, particularizing that flints were preferred. We made a note of it.

Before going away, His Majesty invited us into his tent, to the too well expressed astonishment of 200 ladies, who must have thought the King had parted with his senses when he admitted men and strangers into their sanctuaries. His Majesty proved himself to be sane, by telling us, that to-morrow he wished us to measure the tent, and put down in our note-books that he wanted two, and two sofas.

Inside, the tent was supported like an umbrella, and apparently very old; in the centre was the sofa, and over it a white umbrella; on the sofa were child's toys.

At 5.30 we left, having sat for too long over damp ground, at 7 we were again commanded to attend the King to an Evening Custom 'Ee doo beh pah meh',[59] 'Go to Pah meh (to eat).'[60] His Majesty went in procession, attended by all the Ministers, wives, Cabooceers, and both armies.

Arrived at the market, some edibles were brought to us; but as it was very dark, we did not eat of them. The King was said to be throwing away eatables to the people; we did not see or hear it. His Majesty sent us four heads of cowries each, and permitting us to depart, we reached home at 10.

June 4—Measured the tent and sofa. In the yard lay 800 heads of cowries, said to be to pay parties employed yesterday, but I much doubt that more than 200 were paid away, we witnessing that payment, and the rest remaining when we left. In the evening the Mayo brought the three (saved) victims, one ill. Gave him some medicine, and clothed the whole.

June 5—One of the King's brothers called,[61] and seeing we were employed, said, 'I am a working man, and when employed do not like visitors; I therefore take my leave.'

June 6—Most of the town was closed to-day, as the ladies of the Royal Harem went forth to bathe. Mr. Brown arrived.

June 7—At 9.30 we entered the Palace of Dangelahcordeh to witness the first day of the customs called 'Se que ah hee' (throwing water).

Passing through the first court we entered an interior court-yard by a gate ornamented with two human skulls, in shape a parallelogram; at the further end were three small tents, the centre surmounted by a large silver ornament,[62] each of the other two covering a large glass chandelier. The right was formed by a long low shed-like building, in which were two canopies; under the central one, on a couch of crimson and gold, lay the King, while in front was a crimson damask cloth for the recipients of the royal bounty to kneel upon; under the second were the females of the Royal Family, [*in margin*: Dresses by no means good, as nearly all had to prostrate]; while under the shed and immediately in

---

[59] The first syllable is given as 'El', but Forbes' Fon vocabulary gives 'ee' for 'go', i.e. *yì* (1851, i: 240).

[60] Fon *kpámè*, 'enclosure'.

[61] In Forbes' book identified as 'the king's artisan brother' (1851, ii: 70), i.e. 'Sohsar' (above, p. 163).

[62] Forbes' book specifies that this was in the form of an ostrich (1851, ii: 74).

front, were Amazons under arms, and other ladies of the Harem. Again, in front, were the skulls; a space of twenty yards (a neutral ground) was unoccupied. Facing the throne, beyond this, was a band of minstrels, and in their rear, Ministers, Cabooceers, military officers, and visitors. Scarcely seated when the business of the day commenced.

A crier stepped to the neutral ground and called by direction of the Maehaepah, the Toonoonoo and Camboodee [*in margin*: eunuch[,] treasurer];[63] the three then seated themselves on the edge of the crimson cloth, and the Meigau was called; he being sick, ten heads of cowries were sent to him. The Mayo being called, went through the following ceremony, which was followed by all, and a reference to the programme will give the names of the recipients and sum received by each. Prostrating at a little distance from the throne, he crawled on to the crimson cloth, and there received in his robe, poured from a basket by the Royal hand, eight heads of cowries (eight dollars), which he carried away, staggering round the yard as if under the enormous weight. After having counted them he returned, again prostrated and covered himself with dirt.

I have before mentioned a man, Pohvehsoo; it may be necessary here to describe him. His origin is humble; he was a carrier of Whydah; he is now a captain of musketeers, a headsman, and a privileged court fool; he has a coadjutor in the Amazon ranks; they dress meanly generally, and have their faces covered with whitewash, like a skull; take great liberties with the Monarch and the nobles; and for a headsman, or even otherwise, I never saw so benevolent a black countenance; in age he is about sixty. To-day they executed every ingenuity to obtain largesse. At one time Pohvehsoo was rolling about in a bag, imitating the call of the guinea fowl, the King feeding him with cowries, causing the court fools and sycophants to exclaim, 'Was there ever so generous a Monarch? See, he throws away cowries like corn.' At another, with a mask of a monkey, he would be dipping his paws into baskets of oranges, corn, &c., and removing their contents. But the main cast was Pohvehsoo and his coadjutor, each made a present to the King. From each end of the yard a party heavily laden arrived (apparently), and it required all the care and attention of each to get his or her party before the King, the weight appeared so excessive, that the carriers had to be wiped down and fed with corn; at last they reached the foot of the throne, and the King made a present of cowries in return, when on examination, two huge baskets of shavings and two huge stacks of the Pith of Bamboo, assimilated a like quantity of corn and firewood.

In the middle of the disbursements, the Charchar, his two brothers and ourselves were called, and received six heads of cowries each, and drank with His Majesty, amid firing, &c. Altogether he disbursed 600 heads.

Two crown birds and a beautiful gazelle played about the Yard. In the intervals the minstrels took advantage and praised the King in a most disgusting manner; when one band had sung their praises they were paid, and another took their places, and either sang or danced, and some both. At 2 we took leave, and going home I asked my interpreter, how many heads had been given away, during the day; at first he would not answer, but being pressed, gave it as his opinion 10,000 dollars. Such is the idea the Dahomans have of the liberality of

---

[63] Both versions have 'treasurers' (plural), which is clearly wrong.

their Sovereign.[64] Visited the Ahjahhee market, a four-day market, well supplied as far as variety of articles was concerned, but with little of each.

June 8—Visited the Behkon market [*in margin*: Hungooloo],[65] a four-day market also, just outside the Cumassie gate, similar to the Ahjahhee. Called on the Mayo, who reclined on a mat in the shed before described for the Ministers and others on duty at the Palace.

June 9—Sunday—The Charchar, his brothers, and Domingo, have been closeted all day with the King. The late Da Souzas debts is said to be the Palaver.

June 10—At five miles north-west of Abomey is a beautiful view, which we visited this morning. Leaving the town, the ground gradually rises and suddenly the road opens on a deep extensive valley of undulating ground. Far as the eye can see are the Dabadab mountains, looking blue in the distance; our eye having been so constantly accustomed to level views, looked upon this as magnificent, and the keen air blowing clear from such a distance, gave us an excellent appetite for a picnic breakfast; on the upper ground was clay with ironstone, sandstone, conglomerate, and chalk. Descending into this valley, a walk of a mile and a half brought us to a swamp of discoloured water, the only watering-place of Abomey,[66] and from here the water is carried on the heads of women. In the valley the soil is oozy and fertile, but unfortunately except here and there, miles apart, there are no habitations.

Passing the Palace of Dangehlahcordeh, on our return, His Majesty was taking formal leave of Domingo José Martins, honouring him with a review of two regiments of Amazons. According to etiquette we had to descend from our hammocks and make our bow. Having drank with His Majesty, he asked us if we had brought him any specimens from the bush; we told him our canteen was gone on, but we would bring him some after we had dressed. Taking leave, we returned with five breakers of rum, two large case-bottles of gin, and two of liqueur. Domingo had left, and the King entertained us with some very good dancing, first by men, then by Amazons. The dance offered great variety of positions, and was very spiritedly performed. The band was not so good as it might have been, and one of the dancers would now and again sound them the tune. At 5 H.M. sent us two bullocks, some flour, peppers, and salt. In the evening His Majesty passed our gate in procession to the Palace of Dahomey. First came the Cabooceers and all their pomp and array of war; then the Ministers, the King's levees, the King in a hammock (who halted and sent us a bottle of rum), followed by skull ornaments, as instruments, banners, &c., (a space), then the Amazons, Cabooceers, Ministers, main body, and a similar hammock, skull ornaments, &c.; lastly, the Camboodee and his retainers.

---

[64] However, it is likely that the figure 10,000 was not intended literally, but signified only 'a large amount'.

[65] I.e. Houndjro.

[66] In fact, there were other water sources to the north-east and north-west of the town (Burton 1864, ii: 234–6).

In the Evening Domingo José Martins, the greatest slave-dealer in all Africa, called to take leave, He remained upwards of an hour, and, in conversation, told us that last year, by palm-oil alone, he cleared 70,000 dollars, and shipped in one month from Porto Novo, 300 tons of oil, or 10 tons a-day. In conversing about the Slave Trade, he said the only thing that supported it was its being contraband. In speaking of his individual position, the monopoly of Porto Novo, that one trade helped the other.

June 11—As an introduction to the day's proceedings (the commencement of the War Palaver), it is necessary to give some account of the present state of the Dahoman army, which is at once divided into two divisions, the right and the left, the advanced and the rear, or the Meigau's and the Mayo's, or the generals' titles, the Agaous and the Passoos. In each of these two divisions is a battalion of males and one of Amazons.

The army has another extraordinary division—the male and the Amazon. In each army is a Meigau, a Mayo, an Agaou, a Passoo; and each male officer or soldier has an equivalent in rank in the Amazon lines, termed 'mother'. The Meigau's levees are 140, the Mayo's 300, &c.; those of their coadjutors are equal numbered, or nearly so. The Charchar and all visitors have 'mothers' also. Our 'mother' the Eeawae, is a most distinguished soldier.

Their pay is precarious; clothed and fed, armed and supplied with powder; as will be seen, they swear to conquer or die. Prisoners and heads are purchased from the captors,[67] and the reward at the customs depends on the success in the War.

In or about 1625 Tahcohdohnoh [= Dakodonu] King of Fahhee,[68] marched upon a small Town (now called Abomey), and accomplished a vow to the Fetish by ripping open the belly of the captured Prince and placing his body under the foundation of a new palace, which he appropriately called Dahomey or Dah's belly, hence the name also of the Kingdom of Dahomey.

At 10 A.M. we entered the Palace of Dahomey at a gate called Ah goh doh meh.[69] The King reclined under a canopy in a low shed-like building; the positions were similar to those described on previous days. In our rear were the mausoleums of Kings—small thatched round houses, each surmounted by a silver ornament of large size; in front of each was a heap of human skulls and bones and at the door of each a pillar of cloth, shaded by an umbrella, On the neutral ground was strewed cooked meat, &c., and hundreds of Turkey buzzards flew about with sickening familiarity.

The custom, called 'Seh-que-ah-ee' (watering the graves) is in honour of Tahcohdohnoh and his successors.

Singing had commenced and shortly after, from the tenor of the song, a dispute arose which became a war palaver.

Ahpahdoonoomeh, an Amazon general, addressing the singers; she said Attahpam was conquered, the town taken and destroyed. But it was the Amazons who saved the war!

---

[67] I.e. by the King.

[68] Both versions have 'Tahhee', but this should clearly be 'Fahhee' (cf. 'Fahie' in Forbes (1851, ii: 87), i.e. Fon, an alternative (in fact the original) name for Dahomey.

[69] *Agodomen*, the inner courtyard, containing the royal funerary shrines (Monroe 2014: 184).

Ahhohpeh, the King's brother, said that her speech was true.

Ahpahdoonoomeh. The Attahpams have sought refuge in Ahjah; let the King make war upon Ahjah.

Ahhohpee. True, the Amazons saved the war: some of the King'ssons [*in margin*: idiom, Male soldiers] gave way.

King. My opinion is that their Chief knows more about counting cowries than the art of war. If men run away like goats, unless followed, it is not likely they will be caught. [*In margin*: Alluding to the few Prisoners]

Ahpahdoonoomeh. I cautioned them to be wary.

An Amazon. If the King eats out of a plate, it must be cleaned before it is used again. After use, my musket requires cleaning.

The party of soldiers charged with neglect advance to the neutral ground, and their remuneration, some pieces of cloth in six bags, is placed before them; they kneel and throw dirt, while a sort of trial takes place to discover if they are worthy of the royal bounty, in which great liberty of speech is used by all classes and any one may give his opinion.

An Amazon. Let the King give us Bah [*in margin*: Abbeokuta] to conquer.

Another. Let Ahjah be the seat of war; let the Mayo lay this request before the King, who will cause him to send messengers into Attahpam, calling upon the people to return and fight again on pain of being attacked in Ahjah. Did they not invite Gézo to war and then ran away?

Mayo. I have already sent messengers, telling that if the Ahjahs protect the Attahpams, the King will annihilate them.

An Amazon (addressing the King). For my part I am in debt for provisions for last war and must go again to get money, whether you give Bah or Ahjah. [*In margin*: alluding to the small booty at Attahpam] If a bone is thrown to a dog, he will break it and eat it, so will we either.

A procession of fourteen *demoiselles du pavé*.

Mayo (to the Amazons). Don't beat about bush, but come to the point. Your charge? Explain at once your wishes. If this is to be a war palaver the Agaou should be present.

A stormy debate ensures. The Amazons supporting their charge that the males behaved cowardly, and left the brunt of the action to them, saying, to be overloaded is to be made a laughing stock. The men try to cry them down, when they resort to singing, 'If the King's soldiers go to war they should conquer or die.'

Male Officer. The Amazons are 'sweet mouthed'. If the King commands, the Agaou will see the work done.

Passo. If the King sends me I shall do my best: there has been too much palaver about nothing.

An Officer. The King made sacrifices to the River Mono. We are ready to return, re-conquer the Attahpams, or die.

Ekbohsah, captain. if we are not able to go to Bah, we should say so, and let some other party go.

Tookonoovehseh, another officer. Goat's blood is goat's blood. [*In margin*: Truth]. *Ahpahdoonoomeh*, you had better have held your tongue.

Ekbohsah. To interfere in a palaver is not right; I do not make war; the King makes war. The King knows how the Attahpams escaped and who is in fault. If the King hears for certain where the Attahpams have sought refuge, that place will be destroyed. As for myself, I think more about the matter than I am able to express, therefore finish my palaver. I did not come to quarrel; where the King sends me there will I fight. Is this a day on which to find fault? If I am not fit for my situation let me be degraded. If my actions are not right, let my accusers look me in the face and make their statements. I will not allow my name to be bandied about because a part of the soldiers did not do their duty. I call upon my 'mother' to say what she knows.

Ahpahdoonoomeh. I will explain myself and my reasons for requesting the King to give us Bah. (Interrupted by Bohnohmahseh (male officer), who says where the King's sons (male army) are, there the fighting will be)—What I speak in the house I will enact in the field. There is a fish in the River called Pah tah seh heh[70] (this fish has a natural protection). (Loud cries, you talk too much.)

An Amazon. What right had you to interrupt? What are your reasons? Does one do wrong, if in seeking a livelihood one gives a part to the King?

Mayo. The King has said, If a man eats too much for supper, he is heavy-headed in the morning; that man's a fool.

King. If a man be too lazy to labour for his livelihood, he is of no service to the King. If one leave a country (partly destroyed) [*in margin*: alluding to Attahpam] he is not likely to return in open day. He will return in the dark.

Hoomahhee, drum-maker. If the Kings daughters go to war, the King's sons will go also. [*In margin*: Males and females] I and my 'mother' will go together; where war is, there the drum will be, and I am the drum-maker. The army was six days in Attahpam without seeing anybody, yet there is one who calls himself King there.

Sings—all join, males and females

    So wae ee jar

    jor gee

    Ah Jor gee sar.

If a man cries his goods in the Market, he will meet a sale.[71] [*In margin*: alluding to the Attahpams having challenged]

Bahsolsar, one of the singers. When the King gives us Bah I will speak; we can go to war with our clothes on (no preparation). Ahpahdoonoomeh has raised this Palaver.

Ahpahdoonoomeh. If I am the cause I will have my say; If the King decides against the Attahpams we can have Bah also. [*In margin*: meaning the men can take one, the Amazons the other.]

Hoomahhee. Where the women go, the men must go also.

Ahpahdoonoomeh. Who are you to speak thus confidently? Are you the Agaou?

Another singer. In time of peace my eyes are everywhere, in war concentrated into one focus. I wish to speak to the Meigau and Agaou. Why are they not here? It was not yesterday we returned from Attahpam; why bring that palaver in question now?

An Amazon. If men give cause for a palaver, do they think a woman can hold her tongue?

---

[70] Both versions have the last syllable as 'hed', but this is linguistically impossible, since Fon does not have closed syllables: Forbes' book gives 'heh' (1851, ii: 98).

[71] Not fully deciphered, but 'jar' = Fon *jlă*, 'cry'/'hawk'; 'sar' = *sà*, 'sell'; 'ah jor' = *ajò*, 'trade' (but 'goods' is *ajonŭ*).

Hoomahhee. If Attahpam sent parties to treat, their feet would blister on the road; let the King follow and take all.

Another drummer. The reason we talk about Bah, is, that the Bahs have insulted the King and killed Dahomans. (A general murmur.)

Toonoonoo. Why is this man not allowed to speak?

Ahpahdoonoomeh. After a great deal of flattery says, the Amazons are the King's sandals.

King. (Not loud enough to be heard.)

All held up their muskets and saluted the King.

Two of the King's brothers held a palaver on the agricultural state of the country, that but little grain is grown in the neighbourhood of Abomey; formerly they brought from Ahjah, now they cannot. Hungbahjee, one of the King's officers, says, formerly goats were plentiful, now there are but few in the market. Fowls are dear. The roads are uncleaned.

Singers sing. Tehpehseh and the party of soldiers in disgrace have a parley with Hungbahgee, who says they do not deserve their pay; they appeal to their 'mothers' in the Amazon army, who say they deserve it as, their party killed the King of Lefflefoo (another war). One Amazon questions Hungbahgee's right, and another represents the present being given to Tohkohnohvehseh. The King confers the present on Tehpehseh and his party. A long parley ensues and they take it. Some cowries are now distributed, among them, two heads (dollars) to the Royal Family. Much rain. At 3 we left. Before breaking up, four human beings were sacrificed (decapitated). The cowries distributed did not exceed 30 dollars (heads).

June 12—A respectable liberated African woman called to say that her husband, also from Sierra Leone, was a prisoner of war. Her story is as follows: Ten years since they came to Whydah. Her husband has been much subject to the hooping-cough, and hearing of a doctor (native) in Attahpam, went there. War came, and both he and the doctor were taken prisoners. We promised to intercede. His name is John McCarthy.

June 13—At noon I arrived at the parade ground; Mr. Beecroft unwell. His Majesty occupied a similar position to that of June 1, and I joined him under his canopy: on his right, under canopies of umbrellas, were the principal ladies and Amazon generals, &c.; scattered over the field were the different regiments of Amazons, one had passed and another was advancing to the foot of the throne. The custom was the Amazons swearing to be faithful next war. In these swearings it is customary to ask for a particular place for attack, and if asked for three times it is generally granted. Bah or Abbeokuta has been asked for twice; first the King went to Kangaroo, then made a feint and fell upon Okeadon; now they act confidently. The language was constantly in parables and metaphors, continually a crier hailed the King as

'Ah hau soo lae hee Haussoo'.

Oh! King of Kings.[72]

The regiment now before the King was of bushrangers, with three stripes of white-wash round each leg; they first saluted their officers, then the King, when

---

[72] Fon *ahósù lé áhósù*.

one after another, three stepped forward and swore in the name of the regiment to conquer or die.

The first spoke of the Mohee [= Mahee][73] wars, how Dahomey conquered. If we don't let us die.

2nd. Of the Attahpam war. The Attahpams fled; if we flee, let us die; whatever the town be we will conquer or bury ourselves in the ruins.

3rd. We are eighty, and of the advanced guard; never turned our backs; if any one can find fault with us let him do so.

A male officer about to speak is interrupted by a Fetish-man, who says, 'You cannot speak; that woman is Fetish, you are not; we marched against Attahpam, thinking them men; we found them worse than women.' Sing, in derision, salute, and march off.

Parts of two regiments now advanced, one called Ahbohgoh (firehorn),[74] the other Ahkoongahdoh[75] (turkey buzzard);[76] appropriate names as they are, as they are also, bushrangers.

One says, I have nothing to say, I will be proved by action.

2nd. By the King's children I swear never to retreat; if I do, let me die.

3rd. Without war there are no clothes or armlets; let us conquer or die.

4th. I am a wolf, the enemy of all I meet who are not the Kings friends.

5th. Calls the names of all the conquered countries to Eeawae, who repeats them to two criers, who cry them. She then says, 'Let us catch elephants if we can; if we cannot, flies; we cannot come home empty-handed, if we do we deserve to die.'

The colonels now step forward.

1st. Clothes are made by fingers, we are the King's fingers.

2nd. Carriages cannot be drawn without wheels; we are the wheels[.] both; we have destroyed Attahpam, let us go to Bah, if we don't conquer let us die.

The King tells them to finish their speeches and reserve themselves for War. They dance, sing, and salute the King, then crawl off on their hands and knees; at a signal give a yell and then scamper off.

The Kings own regiment now advanced and deposited their Fetish in front (about 300). They are joined by about 200 women belonging to the late Charchar, who state they are young soldiers and are come to witness the review. All sing (to the King), 'you alone on Earth we will serve'.

The colonel advances and prostrates, then says, The Attahpams wanted strength to fight against Gézo. Let us go to Bah, and if we do not conquer, our heads are at your disposal; they will run; if into water we can follow; if into fire or up trees we can catch them.

Another. There is a town standing that must fall, it is Bah. (All dance and sing.)

---

[73] MS version has 'Mother'.

[74] The term 'firehorn' is not recognisable, but apparently the hornbill (or toucan) is meant: *agbògbò* is a Fon term for the latter, which is frequently depicted in Dahomian art, from having been adopted as a symbol by Gezo's father Agonglo and later also by his successor Glele (Waterlot 1926: plate XVIIA; Adandé 1962: 40; Djivo 2013, i: 90).

[75] Both versions have the last syllable as 'dol', but Forbes' book has 'dah' (1851, ii: 108).

[76] Fon term not identified: the usual word for 'vulture' is *aklasú* (cf. Forbes (1851), i: 229, 'ah klah soo').

Another. Attahpam is destroyed, let Bah be also; a man entered a room where lay a corpse, he lifted up the clothes and was asked why; he said he wished to be where that man was; we must go there or take Bah.

Another. Talk of Attahpam, it was unworthy of our arms; as grass is cut to clear the roads, so will we destroy the Bahs.

The Standard-bearers. If we lose the flags let us die. (All salute and retire at the double.)

Kings daughters regiments. *One*. The King is like a hen; when the rain comes she takes her young under her wings; we are under his protection; if we don't fight, let us die.

The King now rose and drank with me, and gave the Passoo of the male army a tumbler of liqueur. An Amazon steps out and says, If the Passoo heads us in war, let us die. Send us to Bah, and we will conquer or die (a male officer tells them, 'if you don't you will lose your name'). The King has borne us again; we are his wives, his daughters, his soldiers, we are men, not women.

Another. I am the King's 'Daughter' [*in margin*: 'Title']; the King gave me [to] the Charchar; he died. I now belong to Antonio; let me go to Bah; if we don't conquer we'll die.

The Colonel. These soldiers have done nothing yet, send us against the strongest; war cannot suffice us; wherever they go I will be at their head. Although a snake casts away beads, [*in margin*: There is a tradition that the Popoe bead is cast away by a large snake] it never changes its colour; I cannot change my tongue; what I say here I will do in war.

Another. Attahpam is no more, let Bah be likewise. Salute and scamper off.

Another regiment attended by the present Charchar's head wife, orna-mented with much Gold. They salute me and beg me to convey their thanks to Her Majesty, for 2000 caps sent them by Cruickshanks; wherever they wear them there they will be victorious. One in the crowd of courtiers made a remark that hit the Toonoonoo, who said sharply 'if you have anything to say, here is the King say it to him'.

An Amazon. The horse has broken its halter, and the robber knows he is loose. Open Bah to us and we will take it; if any one return, and not a con-queror, let that one die.

All 2000 Amazons assemble in front of the throne. 'If beans be dried in the fire, cannot one put her fingers in to take out to eat.' All sing. When we went to Attahpam we found nobody; all ran away; if they reached the water (sea) they will be turned into salt. At Bah let the rear be the advance.

It rained hard and a mat was sloped over the King and myself; still the Amazons kept their ground, and as they were not likely otherwise to be heard several danced while all sang, after which they all swear again.

One. We will pass thro' fire to Bah.

Another. Fetish-men never initiate the poor; there is no use fighting without booty; Attahpam is totally destroyed; let us have Bah.

Souza's Women sing. See the Amazons are ready to die in war; now is the time to send them.

Toonoonoo tells them, When you go, make good use of your arms.

All. They are the King's, and with them we must conquer. All sing and dance. The generals and ladies leave their stools and join; all salute the King. A girl six years old came forward and said, The King opened his mouth three times when he spoke of war, once now will be sufficient; let that once be on Bah.

All call on Souza to act like his father, and get plenty of ships for the King, 'when the porcupine sheds a quil[l] another takes it place'. [*In margin*: 2,600.] All prostrate, and throw dirt, while criers call the King's names. He receives a new one for the Attahpam War, of 'Haussoo Ghah Glah',[77] King of Chimpanzees, that drives men from their farms.[78]

An Amazon. As the blacksmith takes an iron bar and fashions it, so have we changed our nature, we are men. We have powder, and the King has promised to tell the Agaou the intended seat of war; we have been waiting long; let us lead at once to Bah. The King gives us cloth, but, thread is required to make the garments; we are the thread. Corn put out to dry should be looked to or, the goats will eat. Look to Bah, lest like the Attahpams they remove all their treasure. A cask of rum cannot roll itself. A table in a house becomes useful when anything is placed on it. The Dahoman Army without the Amazons are as both.

Another. If one does not spit, the belly is uneasy; if the hand be not outstretched it receives nothing.

All the Officers stand in front. all the Amazons raise their muskets and shout—
'Soh jae mee'

(May thunder kill us if we break our oaths)[79] They hail the King as 'Kokparsalmee' (the eagle).[80] As he leaves the canopy, all prostrate, and rise as His Majesty receives an ebony club. He then addresses them: 'if a hunter buys a dog and trains it, he takes him into the forest without telling him his errand; if he sees a beast he sends the dog after it; should the dog return without the game, the hunter kills him, and leaves his carcass to the turkey buzzards. If I tell my daughters to put their fingers in the fire, they must obey; if I order you to clear the bush and you do not do it, what will I do to you? If you are taken prisoners you know my [= your?] fate? your heads become ornaments and your bodies feed the wolves and vultures. Where you are sent there you must fight.' King dances and drinks; then hands round rum in a tin dish, Amazons drink, he returns to the tent and all march off.

June 14—The sham fight. At 10 the Ministers and Cabooceers, attended by their retainers, &c., arrived by the left, and had scarcely all reached the ground, when the King, attended by about 600 armed soldiers appeared on the right, the Amazon army marching by another road in front. The ground was the same before described, the Ahjahhee market, and His Majesty took up a similar position; on his right were his own male troops; on his left, in front, a court of ladies and Amazon generals, &c.; on the left, Cabooceers and retainers; in front the Amazons; in the rear, a stockade made of palm-branches; and in the rear of

---

[77] Forbes' book has 'Glah-glah' (1851, ii: 119).

[78] Fon *ahosu*, 'king'; and cf. 'gha', reported by Burton as the name of 'a huge anthropoid ape' (1864, ii: 246): this is clearly *hă*, which nowadays refers to baboons, but may earlier have been applied also to chimpanzees, which are now extinct in this area. The final syllable may be *glă*, '(be) brave/strong'.

[79] Fon *sò jè mi*, 'thunder strike us'.

[80] Forbes' book has 'kok-pah-sah-kree' (1851, ii: 120). This is not readily identifiable (the Fon term for 'eagle' being *hŏn*), but is possibly a corruption of *kpákpású*, '(male) duck', which is attested as part of a praise-name of Gezo, alluding to the belief that duck's blood is poisonous to drink (Mercier 1952: 66).

that again, three towns full of slaves. Around the King, besides the Charchar and ourselves, were courtiers, eunuchs, fools, and hunchbacks, all *en militaire*.[81]

The King's male soldiers advanced and saluted, flirting umbrellas and banners, and throwing aloft the light ornamented muskets, then retired. Next all the Ministers and Cabooceers prostrated, and threw dirt on their heads. One of the King's brothers produced some tools, which he explained wanted repair. The King having given the order, Toonoonoo was directed to command the Amazons to advance, who alone took part in the day's performance.

First came an advanced guard in single file followed by two battalions, in open order, their muskets over their shoulders, muzzles in front. As the first passed they planted sentinels, which were relieved by the second, and sent on to report; next came the Fetish gear, the King's stools, horse, and body guard; last a reserve and the Commissariat.

Criers crying: 'Oh! King of Kings, war is coming, let all come and see it.'

A servant of the Mayo's enters the tent with dirty clothes on. Toonoonoo tells the Mayo he ought to know better.

The Amazons marched past a second and third time, having reversed their muskets. The Eeavoogau's mother leaves her ranks and says, 'I am ready to serve the King. You (to the Eeavoogau) cannot hear badly of me.' Heechechee's [= Heechelee's?] mother says the same.[82] The pioneers now advance with a spy, sit down and hold a palaver; scouts are sent out, who soon return with six prisoners, who are examined before the Council.

His Majesty was joking to his courtiers all the day who laughed immoderately at the royal wit. On one of these occasions His Majesty coughed. It is not to be supposed that the Kings of Dahomey cough: all hummed and sang and danced to drown the noise.

The prisoners are marched off to the main body; a council of war attend at the foot of the throne; the position of the stockade, &c., is explained, and the King orders the latest levees to attack first. We now change position to in line of the stockade and the King goes close to superintend the manoeuvres. The remainder was very tame and more like a school of war than a sham fight. As the troops advance the slaves cry 'war is coming'. A gun fired at 12, and opening the palm-branches a party entered and presently returned with slaves and tufts of grass to imitate heads. Again a gun fired, and several regiments entered; the slaves break out from the towns, and a regular slave-hunt ensues; all being caught they retire. Again a musket is fired, and rushing at the stockade by force of weight, down it all comes. At 2.30 the King returned to the canopy, the whole Amazon army formed in front. A man asks leave to kill a snake, which he says has crawled into the tree; he fires and down falls a large yellow snake, which has been killed for the occasion. Amazons take a circular position, surrounding the country; the slaves are loosed again, and at the firing of a musket, there is another slave-hunt. A tornado coming on, the King presents us with some food used in war, dry cakes of beans, palm-oil, salt and pepper, &c., and we take

---

[81] I.e. in military dress.

[82] This reference to the 'mothers' (i.e. female counterparts) of the Yovogan and Hechili refutes the assumption of Law (2004b: 250), that the system of appointing such 'mothers' was not extended to the administration of Ouidah until the reign of Gezo's successor Glele.

leave. [*In footnote*: There was a method said to be for measuring time by threads and two sticks at twenty paces distant, but I could not make it out, nor could the Interpreters explain, nor again did the King refer to it. I therefore think it must have been a blind.]

June 15—The Se que ah ee, to the memory of Agahgah Dasso, great grandfather to Gézo, took place today in the palace of Ahgrimgohmeh [= Agringomè], adjoining Dangelahcordeh. The description of the position on June 11 will save a repetition; there were similar mausoleums, &c.

As we made our bow to the King the singers hail the advantages to trade (all trade), that brought white men to their customs, for which the Mayo, the Eeavoogau, Heechelee, and all the traders from Whydah, had to prostrate and throw dirt; they then sang in praise, and asked the King to come forward and dance. Maehaepah tells them the king hears; they call for Ahpohdohnohmeh, an Amazon general, and sing the praises of the Amazons.

The Mahhaepah with a sly look, leads forth two coy maidens, each bearing a glass of rum; she then calls Heechelee and Ahkootoo [*in margin*: Two Cabooceers], who very sheepishly prostrate and receive each a glass. Henceforward these are their wives.

A slight divertissement takes place. The Cabooceers advance to receive some cowries for the singers, when one of the royal nephews is found among them. On suspicion that he intended to defraud the King, he is seized, and ordered to immediate execution. Ahhohpeh, the King's brother, takes him in charge, and with assistance is marching him off, struggling and begging for mercy. Pohvehsoo, the headsman-fool, is exercising his wit on the opposite side of the yard, sees the prisoner, and with eyes dilated and horrible countenance rushes at him; a party attempt a rescue, when the King grants a parley; the headsman resists, until one of the party wrestles with him; the headsman is nearly down when the King, having forgiven the prisoner, he rushes to his assistance and throws his antagonist. All laugh, singer sing, praises.

The King came forth to dance, Toonoonoo carrying his distaff, surmounted by the skull of Kohcharnee, King of Anagoo. Criers, crying 'Oh King of Kings'. Expenses to the singers about 30 dollars. During the day much food given away. Nothing but singing praises; no palaver.

June 16—At 10 we again entered the Palace of Agrimgohmeh. Positions, &c., the same as yesterday. Singers singing in praise, hail the King as 'Paugh' (a leopard), the Dahomey Fetish. There was not a well-dressed person in the yard. Singers address the Mayo on some rum having reached Abomey watered, and caution him and the Eeavoogau to be more careful; both have to prostrate and throw dirt. In another part they attacked the Ministers for not repairing the Palace walls, in which they are joined by an old soldier who comments on the absence of the Meigau and Agaou: 'If they are sick, why do they not daily report the state of their health? If a house catches fire, one does not run away, but endeavours to put it out, and re-thatch it, in case rain comes.'

Mayo acknowledges the speech.

Toonoonoo. The King is already aware of the state of the walls, and has told the Mayo how to act.

Ahhohpeh, King's brother. I spoke to the Saugau, and he said he had not time.

Saugau. I have other work in hand; when that is finished I will take the walls to repair.

Mayo. All my men are at the King's command.

Hungbahgee, a military officer. I will undertake to repair them myself.

Mayo, in a rage, defies him, says he talks too much. Singers sing of Attahpam and Bah.

An Amazon Chief. Tells them that Gézo alone of all the Kings of the earth, has an army of women; there is no King like him.

A muster of all the Amazons who had taken prisoners last war. They advanced in parties of fifteen; two officers attend, while one of the generals kneels before the King, repeats the name of the soldier and of the prisoner, adding 'Given to the King to sweep the yard Bologee';[83] these are 425 in Number. Then come thirty-two who have brought heads of enemies, 'Lau see dee'.[84] During the muster, three women were introduced to us as having received very severe wounds in war; one, named 'Seh dong hung boh' (God speak true),[85] had a fearful scar on her head.

The King left his throne and danced, then came over and drank with us, pointing out that a stick he held belonged to the Chief of Attahpam

Maehaepah makes a long speech to a party of soldiers, and gives them food for themselves and families; after which several Bands advance, play, and are replaced, one called 'Hausso Hwae' (the King's birds).[86] At 5 the King gave us leave to go. after asking if we wished to witness the human sacrifices. I regret to state that Ignatio and Antonio da Souza remained. It is the duty at this day's custom of the Mayo and the Eeavoogau to decapitate each one victim; they receive each one head of cowries. The Mayo performed his; the Eeavoogau paid 15 pence to the public executioner.

June 17—Again the Se que ah ee, held in a ruinous court in the Palace of Dangelah-cordeh called Ahdohnoh. Ahdohnoh was the mother of Ahgarjah Doossoo[87] (1730), and her name is now a title in the Royal Family. The positions were similar, except that the King sat in a high-backed chair, and in his rear stood a guard of Amazons; on the neutral ground was a heap of 400 heads of cowries, and besides, lay strewed 430 more. Facing the King was a band of singers, and each recipient of the royal bounty had to dance, kneel, and receive the cowries first on his head, and then the rum, which he carried off. A reference to the programme will show the numbers, &c. After the disbursement, a palaver ensued; during which there were two interruptions; first, a procession of public strumpets; 2nd, two countrymen arrived, each with a boiled man's head, and, prostrating, told their story [*in margin*: I do not at all feel certain that this was not a scene to cause us to believe that the Abbeokutians were the aggressors]. A party of horsemen from Abbeokuta had attacked a small town in Anagoo, which they had taken and destroyed; a few stragglers detached and foraged in a

---

[83] Not identified—unless a miscopying of 'podogee' (cf. 'podoji', in Burton (1864, ii: 31, 109)), i.e. *kpodojí*, the outer courtyard, in which visitors were received (Monroe 2014: 183–4).

[84] Not identified.

[85] Fon *sé dò nù gbó*, 'god speak truth [lit. big thing]'.

[86] Fon *ahósú hé*.

[87] Both versions have 'Wossoo', but Forbes' book gives 'Dooso', i.e. Dosu (1851, ii: 135).

country called Tossoo; the two whose heads they now held up, they had shot. His Majesty gave them half a piece of white baft and two heads of cowries each, and a keg of rum for the headman of their town.

Mayo. Go to my house and receive powder, as you have killed these two so well; the King kills all. A party of Cabooceers and officers prostrated and kissed the ground, and then opened the palaver. The 400 heads by custom have for years been carried to the house of Ahlohpeh (who distributed them to parties not attending the Customs), who, it appears ran away last war.

Ahkohtoo, military chief. Ahlohpeh proved himself a coward in Attahpam, and does not deserve to have the distribution of these cowries.

Mayo concurs; and as Ahlohpeh belongs to my party (the left), they should go to my house.

A Military Officer. If Ahlohpeh is unworthy, it is Tingahlee's right.

Toonoonoo. They shall not go to Tingahlee's; the Mayo is the head man.

Bookohmaesonoo, military chief. Ahtingalee is one of the Mayo's servants. Why should they be sent to the servant, and not to the master?

Hwaemazae, an Amazon chief. As in former customs, so let it be now. Ahlohpeh has the hereditary right.

Ahlohpeh. I have heard all the dispute, and still claim my right; it belonged to my father, and descended to me. If I did wrong in war, why was I not accused—, I and all my people? It was not yesterday we came from war, nor is this a time to rip up old grievances. I will not yield my right to the Mayo.

The Mayo rushed at him, and dealt him several blows; then arrested him, and in a moment he was forcibly removed. The whole yard was instantly in an uproar; several armed Amazons ran across; all clamoured, yelled and shouted, when the King ordered Ahlohpeh to be brought back. The Mayo then impeached Ahlohpeh as a coward, and said he nearly lost the Attahpam war, and that his head was forfeited.

King. You had no right to strike him.

Mayo. I was irritated at the man's presumption.

King. If you had reason to find fault with him about the war, you should have done so before, and not now.

Ahlohpeh. I was only protecting my hereditary right; the cowries ought not to go to the Mayo.

The Mayo again flies into a passion, and tries to speak, but is cried down.

Ahlohpeh. As I behaved, so did my people; I am not one in the war.

King. Come to some determination, and be less personal.

Ahlohpeh. The people call me a coward, and will not let me speak out. If they cannot be taken to my house, let them go to Sohgausar's.

Bohkohmaesonoo. They cannot go to Sohgausar's; he is as much to blame as Ahlohpeh; let them go to Ahtingahlee's.

Ahkootoo. After a long speech, says the Mayo, as head of Ahlohpeh's party, is the proper person.

After many opinions, some for the Mayo, others for Ahtingahlee.

King. You will not decide, I will; let them be carried to Karmardigbee's house and there distributed. The Mayo did wrong in striking Ahlohpeh. If any one interferes I can punish him; for the future if a man acts badly in war, let him be charged at once and not afterwards, to serve other purposes.

Lehpehhoo, King's brother, intercedes for Ahlohpeh.

King. It is no use talking now; Ahlohpeh must reflect on his past conduct, and endeavour to do better in future.

Mayo warns Ahlohpeh to beware for the future.

King. We have heard enough of Attahpam, that is finished; the country overrun, the town destroyed, and the King killed. Attahpam is no more. [*In margin*: As will be seen by the Palavers there is great doubt upon the matter.]

Bohkohnoovehseh. Ahooeesooee behaved ill last war, I charge him.

King. There is, I say, too much palaver about it. I asked the Mayo why he attacked Ahlohpeh; if you wanted to quarrel about the last war, there was a time for it. I have heard all the war palaver.

Several Amazons. Ahooeesooee is a brave man.

King. The palaver is that Ahlohpeh had 80 men; Ahooeesooee 80 men; the latter charges the former with not coming into action, therefore he could not act.

Ahpohdoonomeh, Amazon Passo, charges Haetungsar, the Amazon Agaou, and her party with cowardice and running away. [*In margin*: The Amazon Mayo was killed—the Amazon Agaou ran away, at meeting the King she was sent back again.]

King. I am aware of it. (Calls three Amazons). These without arms took prisoners, thus I can reward them. Gives 10 heads of cowries. (A great deal of self-praise and much recrimination takes place for some time.)

Kohkohahgee, chief of the Camboodee's levees, makes a long speech in his own praise; hints he is better than his neighbours.

Hungbahgee, chief of the Kings levees, challenges him to single combat on the spot.

Kohkohahgee. I will take my gun to Bah, and there take more prisoners than you.

From the conversation that ensued it appeared that this was an old sore.

Ahhohpeh, the king's brother, tells the king that they hate each other, who dismisses them. [*In margin*: As the names are so nearly alike I make a note 'Ahlohpeh' is the coward 'Ahhohpeh' the kings brother.]

An Anagoo[88] addresses the meeting and recommends less quarrelling and more reasoning as they are going to war against a people who can fight. Bah.

This speech being distasteful all yell and shout, then sing: 'The Wolf will be abroad, let the sheep fly.' A lengthened palaver ensues, each party praising his coadjutors in the Harem; and *au contraire*, when the King says, 'you had better reserve your strength for war, and not exhaust it in palavers. If any one distinguishes himself, I can hear of it and reward it; if any one disgraces himself let me know at once that I may punish him.'

At 4 we left, the King making us a present of 10 heads and 3 gallons of rum.

June 18—Again the Se que ah ee, to-day in the court called Ahlohwargaelee, after the mother of Toocoodoonoo (1625), the founder of this palace of 'Dahomey'. Position similar to yesterday. As we entered a strong and stormy debate on the late war occupied all parties.

[88] Printed version has 'an Agauo'.

Tohkohnoovehseh and Tohvohveesar, two officers, say the Agaou is sick;
'we can hear for him and explain what passes; [*in margin*: The belief is that the
Agaou is killed The fashion is that if a high officer is killed, to report him sick,
and some time afterwards to say he has died.] Last war the troops were badly
generalled, the Agaou must do better next war.

Ahhohpeh, Kings brother. With regard to yesterday's palaver, Ahooeesooee
is not guilty; there is no necessity to try him.

Haetungsar, the Amazon Agaou. What the King said yesterday we heard.
We are the King's wives, daughters, and soldiers, and must endeavour to do our
duty, but our load ought not to be more than we can carry.

Aheesartong. If the Agaou's people did not do their utmost, the Agaou is
not to be blamed.

Saugansar, M[ilitary] Chief. If I behaved like a coward, I must die; I could
not ask for mercy. Ahlohpeh would have lost his head, had not the king inter-
ceded. Although Ahlohpeh was not arrested yesterday, the matter is not settled;
it is our duty to find if he is guilty or not. I call upon Ahlohpeh and the five men
charged to appear and answer for their conduct. (They come forward, and prostrated, throw dirt.) After a stormy debate, in which the prisoners join, far too
quickly spoken to be understood he continues) They are guilty, and should be
disgraced, let the King take two as headsman, and give two to each the Meigau
and the Mayo.

Another soldier is brought forward, stripped of his arms and accoutrements, tied. Again a long palaver, in which Saugansar tells the King he buys
slaves and makes them soldiers. He must expect good and bad.

King. Ahlohpeh is not so much responsible as may be supposed; he was
headman of eighty, his people left him to forage, against his orders. Ahooeesooee swore by the Fetish to conquer or die; Ahsohnee swore also, she saved the
war. Let Ahlohpeh and the five be disgraced; let them be taken away and their
heads shaved.

Ah hoh-peh. Saugansar has spoken well; who but him could have spoken so
firmly?

King. The man before me I tried on the field; I cannot try him again. His
story is this. He was second of eighty; the Chief fell, and this man fighting, was
separated from the party. Let him be released.

Ahlohpeh and his party return with their heads shaved, and armed with
clubs as headsman; all prostrate, and kiss the dust, throw dirt on their heads.

One of the three Amazons, who received ten heads of Cowries yesterday. I
cannot return this basket; I will take it to Bah and fill it with heads of the enemy.
If I do not, may I die of small-pox!

Ahlohpeh again comes forward and receives the name of 'Garjardoh' (fallen
house).[89]

Ahhohpeh, apostrophizing says, 'No sooner is one man fallen than another
is ready to take his place.'

Ahlohlohpohnokou, next to the Possoo (in the left or Mayo's army), is now
called, and his people swear in a similar manner to that described of the Amazons, to conquer or die, ending by all saluting and singing, 'if we don't conquer,
may we lose our lives'.

---

[89] Not deciphered, except *jà*, 'fall'.

June 19—This day Se que ah ee took place in the court, named after the King's great grandmother, of the Palace of Dangelahcordeh. The Jahhee is a title, and the lady enjoying it sat to the right of the throne, in crimson velvet; the only showily dressed person present, otherwise the positions were the same as yesterday. The days proceedings commenced with more swearing fidelity on the part of the male troops, and much braggadocio. Having an attack of ague, I had to leave at noon; after which the swearing continued, and the King presented eight boys to the yard; stating that his grandfather was beaten by the Attahpams, now that he had conquered them he gave these boys to keep his Grandfathers yard in order. Several presents of goats, &c., were given to the King.

June 20—Mr. Brown had an interview with the King. Charchar, Ignatio and Antonio da Souza received a present of three bullocks. The captains of the Charchar's troops told one of our Interpreters to tell us if there were any whites in Abbeo-kuta we had better warn them, as the King intended to make war upon Abbeokuta.

June 21—The Se que ah ee was performed in a court called Sehnoomeh, named after the King's grandmother.

Outside the Gate was an oven of earthenware, inside which was a duck alive; on the top in a dish three human skulls covered with palm-oil. The yard and positions much the same as yesterday. The Sehnoomeh (represented) was dressed out in crimson velvet, attended by the lady enjoying the title of King's mother, and many other ladies of rank. Among the skulls displayed was one ornamented by a string of coral beads. Besides the band of singers and players, all the Amazon officers and a band knelt before the King, sometimes speaking and singing in praise of the King, his ancestors, and his family.

Toonoonoo. The songs you sing about the King are sweet to hear; sing again.

Amazon Meigau. Sing again sing well; you know if you do not it is in the King's power to decapitate you.

Mayo. The songs you sing are sweet; sing again.

Toonoonoo. The King is wise; hence wisdom is diffused through the nation.

Crier cries. The King is wise; hence so is the nation.

Lehpehhoo, King's brother. Toonoonoo spoke truth when he said Gézo is wise.

Amazons sing. This house is in charge of Sehnoomeh, and she must take care of it.

Mayo. There are not enough in your band.

Toonoonoo. Mayo says true; it should not be.

Amazon Meigau. The band is the same, but they don't sing properly; hence the band does not sound well.

An Amazon Officer. If we don't sing properly you can correct us.

Ahcordemeah, Amazon, head of the band. The Meigau spoke truth; they don't sing properly. It is the singers, not the band.

Amazon Officers sing, and call upon Sehnoomeh to dance. Her train borne by a maiden, she dances. They receive five heads of Cowries.

Sehnoomeh. If the King comes to the house and does not speak, who can know he is there. To-morrow let him go to the house of her that gave him milk.

Ahhohpeh. To-morrow you must sing in favor of her that gave birth to Gézo. If you have any song about the people beyond the Agonee river [*in margin*: Abbeokuta] sing, it for in three days comes the Fetish custom.

Maehaepah gives the Amazon officers and their coadjutors food, over which there is much palaver about what they will do next war. Interrupted by a procession of public strumpets. King tells the soldiers to retire and eat. All sing, 'Gézo is the King of Kings; what King so liberal? we are his soldiers; under him we are not men, but lions.' More praise in which Kohkohagee and Hungbahgee again come to a war of words.

The Saugau receives a glass of rum from a delicate maiden, led by the Maehaepah; as he sips it the Maehaepah tells him he cannot divide it, nor even let one of the Cabooceers taste it.

Sehnoomeh received seven heads of cowries, and marches off, attended by her paraphernalia of skulls, &c. Band advances and sing in praise of Gézo, who comes out and dances; drinks, guns fire, Cabooceers dance, &c. Crier cries, 'Oh! King of Kings that can take all other Kings and sell them for rum.' The band is replaced. After singing about the King, the leader calls for Ahlohpeh and the others in disgrace, and asks his name; then sings—.

> Oh fallen house! 'Gar jar doh'
> That was once considered worthy to carry arms,
> Be thou now disgraced to carry a club.

Garjahdoh kisses the dust and throws dirt, &c. King comes out again and dances then drinks with us; after which we retire.

June 22—At 10:30 entered the Palace of Dangelahcordeh at the Kings mothers gate, called Ahcontimeh:[90] the position much the same as before. At the gate was a similar oven similarly ornamented. Under two umbrellas, to the left of the King, sat the Ahcontimeh, and one lady handsomely dressed. [*In margin*: Mr Brown left I have no reason to alter my opinion expressed in last Journal, indeed it is much strengthened.][91] First passed a number of Amazons, band of music playing, and receiving a few heads of cowries; then the Amazon officers advanced and saluted the King. Sung—Called upon all eyes to behold the Glory of Gézo, there are not two but one, one only in the world—Gézo. Every nation has its customs, but none so brilliant or enlightened as Dahomey. See, all nations send their ambassadors, black and white.

> Chorus.
> Look round and behold
> Ambassadors of all nations.

All officers, male and female, prostrate and throw dirt.

All Amazon officers sing, Yarubas lied when they said we could not conquer them. When we meet we will make their day as night. Let the rain fall quickly, that the river may be dried soon. Yaruba and Dahomey cannot drink out of the glass; two rams cannot drink out of the same calabash. The Yarubas must have been drunk when they said they would conquer Dahomey.

---

[90] Both versions have 'Ahcontihneh' here and subsequently, but Forbes' book gives the name as 'Ahcontimeh' (1851, ii: 166), which is clearly correct, i.e. Agotime.
[91] Forbes in 1849 regarded Brown as a 'spy' for the slave-trader Domingos Martins (1851, i: 53).

An Amazon. In days gone by, the white traders brought good articles; they do not do so now. Then a Musket lasted twenty years, it now lasts three.

Deputation of public women.

Toonoonoo. You have sung sweetly; sing more

All sing (Amazons). There's a difference between the King and a poor man. There's a difference between the King and a rich man. Let a man be ever so rich and Gézo is still King over him. All guns are not cast alike; some are long, some are short. If men are drunk they are not fit to live. There is a nation that must fall: Abbeokuta. Then we will dance before all (Dance). [*In margin*: Alluding to the saying that the Yarubas must have been drunk to say they could conquer the Dahomans.] Criers cry the King's names, and say there is a leaf called Eeaboo [*in margin*: Poison perhaps]: let the King cause a Fetish to be made with it, and Bah must fall. Everything Gézo does is well done. His power is supreme over the male and females of all kinds.

Mehtohseh, Fetish Chief, addressing the Amazon officers. Your songs have been pleasing, you cannot do better than sing again.

All Amazons sing. With these guns in our hands and powder in our cartouche-boxes, what has the King to fear? When he go to war let the King dance, while we bring him prisoners.

One Amazon officer calls the King's sons and sings to them. Pray to Seh (God) that your father's days may be long in the land. Let all the King's family pray to their ancestors for long life to Gézo. If a leopard kills her prey, does she not feed her young first? If a deer bears young, does she not chop the grass for it?—

Bahdohhoo, the King's eldest son. All the days of my life I shall pray for longer life for my father.

All officers of both sexes salute the King.

Tohdarsar, King's mother's sister's daughter, to the Amazon officers. If you try to take the honeycomb, you must be wary; go to work carefully, or you will be stung.

The Ahcontimeh and her companion, attended by four other ladies, come forward and dance, each bearing a skull. Tohdarsar receives three heads of cowries, half piece of cloth, and a bottle of rum, and is told by the Amazon Meigau that the cowries are to buy some food for her mother.

Amazon officers sing. We have sung our lays, now we are going let Seh (God) bless the King and the people.

The Ahcontihmeh marches off with fourteen heads of cowries, attended by her paraphernalia of human skulls and bones, &c.

A Toby Philpot's jug and a dog musical toy being sent for the Ministers and Cabooceers to admire, all prostrate, and throw dirt, prior to the inspection— Food is distributed to all present, a band of singers singing in praise of the royal liberality.

A long inaudible conversation takes place between the Maehaepah and the Toonoonoo, relative to the distribution of some liqueur in the bottles of two cruet-stands, and some more equally curious decanters, which ultimately go to the Ministers and Cabooceers. The Maehaepah makes a speech to Lehpehhoo, the King's eldest brother, and presents him with a sample of every kind of liqueur the King has drunk during the customs, in a small box of phials. All the men and women belonging to all the bands that have played during the customs assemble, and are fed (300). Ignatio and Antonio da Souza receive ten heads of cowries each. Singers sing: 'Oh, wonderful King, to purchase cowries from the

white man, and give them back again.' Gives 160 heads to the Ministers to make
Fetish with, to clean the town after the custom. Gives 60 heads to the soldiers.
[*In footnote*: A word of two about the customs will not be out of place. All night
a crier paraded the Palace walls, calling 'Hausava Haussoo', King, [of] Kings:
the names of the conquered nations and the King's names. The rum distributed
was very small quantities (about half a tumbler to each). The food was always
craved after, and devoured rather than eaten. There was a rule in all, and except
Ministers, Cabooceers, and Merchants, no one received more than 1s at a time,
4s in all.]

Another palaver commenced, but the yard was too much crowded for us to
hear much of its meaning; it was a war palaver. Hungbahgee and Kohkohahgee
became personal, and the King cautioned them not to promise too much. The
Amazons, like turkey buzzards, preyed upon the fallen; in short there was the
usual quantity of squabbling, yet it had to us one glorious lustre, rendering it
more valuable than the diamond to the miner. From the conversation, it
appeared that this was the last of the Se que a hee; nor do I envy any future
visitor that may have again to set [= sit?] out the Hwae noo ee wha.

The expenses of the above custom, by my calculation, were as follows:–

Cowries	5,889
Cloth	1,551
Rum	0,765
	8,205
Food	1,500
	9,705 dollars

actually given away under our eyes.

The account we gave the King, admitting in some measure his exaggeration
was:–

Cowries	7,215
Cloth	2,000
Rum	1,400
Food	1,500
	12,115 dollars

June 23—Three hours were spent in the Palace[92] of Dangelahcordeh, while the Amazons arranged 924 heads of cowries and one pipe of rum, in portions, for about
1,000 different people from distant towns. As it rained much, we counted them
and left.

June 24—Mayo called and told us that the watering of the graves being finished, the
King not wishing to keep us longer, he would now appoint a day for a palaver.

June 25—Mayo called, and reported that the King was about to make a Fetish, and
that it would be perhaps fourteen days before we could hold palaver. Visited the
Fetish custom. About 100 women in a variegation of cotton clothes, and decked
out with strings of cowries, dancing. Present, Lehpehhoong, the King's brother,
and three other Cabooceers. Among the dancers was one of the King's daughters. Gave them a keg of rum in return for some gin and liqueur set before us.

---

[92] MS has 'Palaver'.

June 26—Mayo, Eeavoogau, Charchar, and Ignatio da Souza, were closeted all day with the King.

Grand Fetish-dance, and sacrifices of a bullock, some goats, &c.

June 27—Visited the Palace of Bahdahhoong, the heir-apparent.[93]

June 28—Eeavoogau called in the morning; Mayo in the evening. Conversation on the Slave Trade; both slave-dealers on a large scale. The Charchar, Ignatio, and Antonio, have been closeted all day with the Mayo.

June 29—Mayo called in His Majesty's name to receive our account of the expenses of the customs, which we gave as follows:–

Cowries	7,215
Cloth	2,000
Rum	1,400
Food	1,500
	12,115 dollars

Having been closeted all day with the Mayo, the Charchar left for Whydah. [*In margin*: Antonio da Souza had been absent some days; he returned to-day. It appears that he went to Whydah to meet a schooner and arrived on the 22ⁿᵈ, in time to see her taken by the 'Gladiator' on the 23ʳᵈ, in Whydah roads.][94]

June 30—Sunday.

July 1—Mayo called to inform us that he was going to the King to ask him to appoint a day for a palaver. In the evening he returned, and informed us the King would appoint an early day. We had long conversation with him about the Treaty.

This Morning a Chief of the Maha [= Mahee] country, who had not before sworn allegiance to the King, arrived with the sign of subjugation, a wreath of palm leaves round his neck. Lehpehhoong, at the head of the Cabooceers, received him at the gate of the Palace of Agrimgomeh. Having marched three times round the square, he prostrated and kissed the dust, together with his three attendants. In front of the Cabooceers was a party of soldiers, headed by Pohvehsoo, armed besides their muskets with clubs; having prostrated and thrown dirt three times, the soldiers beat the ground with their clubs to signify they must go through the ceremony again. This they did several times.

July 2—Mayo and Eeavoogau called to give us the King's account of his expenditure during these customs, first explaining that there were seven more to go through: the cleaning of the ship—dancing and singing at the Dangehlahcordeh gate— dinner and firing guns along the road to and from Whydah—war palaver at Cumassee—custom to his father at Ahgongroo—the war—Fetish custom,

[93] Badahun's palace was at Jegbe, south-east of Gbèkon quarter (Burton 1864, ii: 253, 255).
[94] The date of Antonio's arrival at Ouidah cannot be right, as he was still at Abomey attending the Customs on 22 June (p. 189). The ship captured was the *Juliana*, reported taken on 24 (*sic*) June 1850: HCPP, *Slave Trade*, 1851/2, Class B, incl. in no. 147: List of Vessels Captured or Detained, 1 March 1850–28 Feb. 1851 (not included in TASTD).

which last up to the time of the next watering the graves. They brought 16 strings, each containing 2,000 cowries[95] and 26 odd cowries, or the whole expense for everything 32,000 heads of cowries, or, deducting one-fourth the difference, 26,000 dollars.[96]

This was an exaggeration, but only proves that His Majesty has some idea of the use of note-books, since the reader may remember that the first day we were told 26,000 heads or 22,000 dollars[97] had been that day and night distributed which we positively explained was not the case. Again a long palaver about the Slave Trade. On leaving they told us they were going to the King to explain to him our conversation.

July 3—Mayo and Eeavoogau called to tell us the King would see us to-morrow, and brought accounts that the remaining customs would cost 11,800 heads of cowries, making in all, by his own account—

> 32,000
> <u>11,800</u>
> 43,800 heads of cowries
> <u>6,257</u> difference one-seventh
> 37,543 dollars[98]

They added that the King desired them to explain that if one ship comes to Whydah, the King monopolizes one-half the trade; that of three he takes two. Much rain.

July 4—At noon (it had rained hard all the morning) we arrived at the Palace, and at 1 P.M. were ushered into the audience *entrée* before described. There were present the Mayo, Camboodee , Eeavoogau, Toonoonoo, and Caoupeh, and their coadjutors in the Harem, and also Maehaepah, all slave-dealers of a large scale. Besides there were Mudiki [= Madiki], Narwhey, Magelika,[99] and John Richards,[100] interpreters. Narwhey, one of the greatest slave-merchants, *soi disant* servant of the English Fort, told Mudiki in conversation, that he was working against his own interest in explaining matters to us, saying that the Slave Trade was sweet to him: however, a true translation was given both ways by John Richards. After the usual compliments, the King asked us to make our statement, which was as follows:–

> 'We have seen your customs and know your account of expenses. Her Majesty the Queen of Great Britain, for the welfare of the human race, is anxious to stop the trade in slaves, and knowing you cannot relinquish it without an equivalent, has sent us her Plenipotentiaries ("Ah Hausso

---

[95] 2,000 cowries is actually a 'head', the 'string' being 40.

[96] The calculation is inexact: the result of a ¼ deduction would actually be $24,000. This conversion is presumably based on the fact that cowries had recently depreciated against the silver dollar, which was now exchanged at between 2,400 and 2,500 rather than 2,000 cowries (Forbes 1851, i: 36).

[97] This conversion is not explained, but is presumably an approximation for a $1/_7$ reduction, as applied on the following day: from 26,000 this would in fact yield 22,286.

[98] For the rationale of the $1/_7$ difference, see Beecroft's Journal, p. 147, n. 663.

[99] I.e. Midjrokan: see Introduction, p. xlii, note 176.

[100] Actually, Thomas Richards.

Nou beh", the Queen's mouth),[101] to endeavour to arrange a Treaty. In the first place we recommend you to cultivate the soil; all the palm-oil and cotton you can produce cannot supply the British trade, and the present duties on vessels employed in legal trade, being (if you stop the other) insufficient, we recommend you to raise it one-half. If you have enemies and are induced to war, make a treaty of trade with the chiefs of these countries, and instead of destroying, cause them to be tributary, and make your prisoners of war the means of enriching your country by the cultivation of the soil. Beyond these means of making your country rich and your name everlasting, Her Majesty, for the term of five years will yearly send you a present.['] (To attempt to treat with subsidy for three years we deemed imprudent, and in order to swell out the value of the £3,000 divided it as follows).

		£
Muskets	500	250
Powder Kegs	1000	200
Rum Pipes	100	800
Dollars	2,000	500
Cowries	2,000 h[ea]ds	500
Pieces of silk	200	300
Cotton Prints	250	100
Romauls	1,000	100
Hats	50	75
Tobacco Rolls	250	150
Lisbon Pipes	1	25
		£3,000[102]

The Treaty if entered into to be subject to ratification, and not to commence until the first instalment was received.

In answer, His Majesty gave us a history of the foreign trade of Dahomey, from its earliest dates, and the continued good feeling that had always existed between his ancestors and the former Kings of Great Britain; that throughout the Dahomans had sold slaves. He continued, 'my people are a military people, male and female; my revenue is the proceeds of the sale of prisoners of war. Did you, after you passed the swamp, except in the neighbourhood of towns, meet any farms? Other nations deal in slaves, but not like me; they keep all the proceeds to themselves; I give mine to my people. I would wish the ports of Little Popoe, Ahgweh, Great Popoe, Porto Novo, and Lagos, to be forced to stop the Slave Trade, before I could treat. In the meantime let the port of Whydah be thrown open to my Slave Trade; not to all the merchants there, but to my agents, Charchar, Domingo José Martins, Joaquim Antonio, Ignatio and Antonio da Souza; let the ships belonging to these five pass free.' We explained to him that what he asked was impossible; and the interpreters wishing it to be put down in a letter to the Queen, we gave them the short negative which the King understood, and said—

'Charchar has given me one ship, Domingo and Joaquim also one each, make a letter to the Queen to grant me a flag and protection for these three.' We explained that such was impossible, and again had to be expressive and say. No.

---

[101] Fon *ahósù nu gbè*, 'king's mouth voice'.
[102] This list of goods was omitted in the printed version.

At this time the King's countenance was almost blanched, his head down, his right hand rubbed his forehead, while his veins swelled, and in a tremulous voice he added, [']write to the Queen and ask her to direct her men-of-war to allow "one" ship to pass in my name to the Brazils, to carry a cargo of slaves, and bring back goods for me'. Again we answered, No; the removing of one slave would not be allowed if it could be helped.

'If I stop the Slave Trade how can the Meigau, the Mayo, &c., each of whom, and the merchants, Narwhey, Ahjohbee, Quenung,[103] &c., who pay me 5000 dollars annually (considerably exaggerated) duties and presents, afford to pay their customs.[104] I cannot send my women to cultivate the soil, it would kill them. My people cannot, in a short space of time, become an agricultural people. War has destroyed all the neighbouring countries, and my people have to go far for food. All my nation—all are soldiers, and the Slave Trade feeds them.'

We now explained to him that if he made his prisoners of war cultivate the soil at home instead of selling them to enrich a foreign land, they would soon be rich; and read to him a second time the Articles offered. Finding we could make no impression, we asked him to dictate a letter in answer to Her Majesty's oft-repeated request, telling him that his wishes regarding the flag and free egress from the port of Whydah were impossible to grant. The Mayo explained that if the Slave Trade was stopped, the King must send to the beach for sand to feed the people. After some dispute he dictated as follows:–

[For text, see Appendix 3, doc. 7]

This letter having been read to the King, Mr. Beecroft produced a copy of a letter from the Earl of Chichester to Sagbua, Chief of Abbeokuta; we explained to His Majesty it was too evident he was going to war with that people, and that they were friends of the English people, and that English missionaries resided there. The King answered that he intended making war upon Abbeokuta, and Mr. Beecroft had better warn the white men to leave. (I am convinced he intends to attack Abbeokuta after these customs.) The Mayo declared that the two Kroomen I had seen last visit had not been found.[105] The next question was concerning the imprisonment of John McCarthy; the King, evidently annoyed at these questions, ordered the Mayo to enquire about him.

Thus ended the palaver; and I am of the opinion that future attempts, unless by force, will fail in causing Gézo to give up the Slave Trade, or his pride admitting him to accept a subsidy. What he recommends to be done to other ports, stopping all trade, if enforced at Whydah, and Lagos be destroyed, the Slave trade in the Bights will be at an end. The King's selfishness does not save his agents. Little Popoe is almost a monopoly of the Charchar's;[106] Great Popoe is of Joaquim Antonio; Porto Novo an enormous monopoly of Domingo José Martins.

---

[103] The printed version has 'Queming', i.e. Quénum, the others mentioned being Gnahoui and Adjovi.

[104] Other sources give lower figures for the annual tax paid by the Migan and Quénum (see Beecroft's Journal, p. 99, note 481), but the higher figure here includes duties paid on the sale of slaves (and other commercial transactions). For argument that, at least for the leading merchants, the total of $5,000 may not be exaggerated, see Law (2004b: 146).

[105] Cf. Beecroft's Journal, p. 138, n. 618.

[106] Isidoro de Souza had been based at Little Popo before 1849, but removed to Ouidah after his father's death (Strickrodt 2015: 199, 202–3).

In everything he said he illustrated simply a desire to enrich himself at the expense of his neighbours.

If his trade be stopped his power is done. At the head of a military nation surrounded by enemies, he must have money, and would then treat for any trade.

In a word, nothing but coercive measures will cause Gézo and his Ministers to give up the Slave Trade.

July 5—Mayo, Eeavoogau and Caoupeh came to deliver His Majesty's present, which was as follows:

—For Her Majesty's, two pieces of cloth; Mr. Beecroft and myself, each one girl to wash our clothes,[107] one Cabooceer's Stool and foot-stool, one piece of cloth, ten heads of cowries, one keg of rum; Mudiki, four heads of cowries, one piece of cloth, one bottle of rum; Richards, two heads, one bottle; hammock-men, two heads, one bottle. After the present, they explained that His Majesty had given last year 4000 muskets to his soldiers, 4000 to the Agonee people, and 4000 he had to give to the new war men, and that he had equipped these 12,000 soldiers (humbug); asked when we would start, as he wished to salute Her Majesty and ourselves. The wife of John McCarthy being present, the Mayo took her to recognize her husband, promising to produce him.

July 6—At 7 A.M., the Mayo, Eeavoogau, called, and at the same time the battery fired a salute of twenty-one guns in honour of Her Majesty Queen Victoria, and thirteen each to Mr. Beecroft and myself. Drank the health of their Majesties of England and Dahomey.

The Mayo told us that John McCarthy would be sent to Whydah as soon as the King gave orders for his release.

I now asked the Eeavoogau whether, in case Mr. Beecroft and myself coming to Whydah, he would be ready to produce the said John McCarthy; he evaded the question, telling me it was a small palaver, and that the man would be sent.

I then addressed both thus: 'I am going to England, and shall acquaint Her Majesty that the King of Dahomey holds a British subject prisoner; you know the consequences to your trade.'[108] The shock was electrical; and they begged of me not to be angry. I then threw myself into a passion; dashed a book on the table; and told them that I should act as I had told them. They looked much disconcerted.

---

[107] In his book, Forbes notes that the girl he received had been taken captive in the war against Okeodan (1849): she was taken by him to England, where she was received into the care of Queen Victoria and baptised as Sarah Forbes Bonetta (1851, ii: 206–9). For her later life, see Myers (1999), but note that his account that she was one of those redeemed from being sacrificed on 31 May 1850 is fictional: the two persons then saved by Forbes were both adult males (from Atakpamé) and were resettled on Fernando Po.

[108] In his book, Forbes claims more explicitly that 'I threatened to stop his [i.e. the King's] trade' (1851, i: 144). Beecroft's account of this episode (in his dispatch to Palmerston, in Appendix 3, doc. 8, see pp. 210–11) mentions no such threat, which perhaps suggests that Forbes has embroidered, if not invented, it; alternatively, however, Beecroft might have omitted it because it was unauthorised by the mission's instructions.

At 10 started en route to Whydah. Arrived at Cana. One of the purchased men[109] was so ill he could not walk, and it occupied me two hours to obtain two men to carry him; and then only because I had declared he should be carried in my hammock if I did not succeed. After leaving Cana, at 4 P.M., a messenger overtook me, and desired me to stop, explaining that Narwhey and a King's messenger were on the road and wished to speak to me. In a short time they joined, with McCarthy and his wife, and a message from the King, saying that he could not keep a British subject in prison. The wife had been stripped and ironed in the condemned cell.

Narwhey hinted that a present would be acceptable to the King, which was sent from Whydah. (See list.) Arrived at Zooboodoo.[110]

July 7—Crossed the swamp; twelve hours on the road. Arrived at Whybagon.

July 8—This morning, outside our door, was a party of soldiers guarding two dead bodies of Cabooceers. All headmen are buried in Abomey. Besides that the generality of them have their ancestral houses there, it is a more sure report to the King. Arrived at Allahdah.

July 9—Arrived at Whydah, and found Her Majesty' ship 'Bonetta' had anchored the day before.

July 10—Paid all the debts of the expedition. (See list.)

July 11—Embarked in one of Mr Hutton's canoes, with our hammock-men, all others being directly refused by all parties.[111]

Leaving the fort, a Fetish snake[112] had, during the night, killed a cat in the kitchen, and had swallowed all but the two hind legs and tail, which remained ungorged; a Fetish woman was sent for to remove it.

---

[109] I.e. those redeemed from sacrifice on 31 May.

[110] 'Tooboodoo' in printed version.

[111] Although this implies that they embarked on 11 July, Forbes' book (1851, ii: 202) gives the date as 12 July, which is confirmed by Beecroft's dispatch (Appendix 3, doc. 8, p. 211).

[112] I.e. a royal python, sacred to the *vodun* Dangbe.

APPENDIX 2

FORBES' CALCULATION OF THE COST OF THE CUSTOMS

The manuscript version of Forbes' journal has an 'Appendix', listing persons involved in the various ceremonies of the Annual Customs and detailing the gifts they received from the King.[1] This material was not included with the version of the journal printed in the Parliamentary Papers, but most of it was included in Forbes' book.[2] This published version, however, omits some of the financial details. In particular, it does not include a concluding calculation of the royal expenditure on the Annual Customs, which is of sufficient interest to warrant its inclusion in this edition.[3] This elaborates (but also differs from) the information included in the journal proper. In the latter, Forbes in fact offers two different sets of figures for the cost of the King's largesse at the Customs, giving the value of the cowries, cloth, rum and food 'actually given under our eyes' as $9,705, whereas the estimate submitted to the King was $12,115.[4] He explains the higher figure as 'admitting in some measure [the King's] exaggeration', but it seems possible that it also reflected the views of his co-envoy Beecroft, while Forbes thought it should be lower. The calculation at the end of Appendix gives a figure slightly higher than the one in Forbes' journal (though still significantly lower than that submitted to the King), but also adds estimates of expenditure at other ceremonies in the annual cycle, to yield a total figure of expenditure for the entire year, as follows:

Making a total to all the Officers of the Kingdom distant Governors visitors &c.

Of cowries		6,144 Kings measure
	[minus]	250 for those strung $^1/_7$[5]
Cowries		5,894
Cloth		1,551
Rum		1,300 much more than we saw
Food		1,500
Sundries		500
		10,745$

[1] TNA, FO84/827, ff. 285–304.
[2] Forbes (1851, ii: 213–48).
[3] TNA/FO84/827, f. 304.
[4] See Forbes' Journal, pp. 190–1.
[5] As explained earlier (see p. 147, n. 663) the $^1/_7$ deduction was due to the fact that cowries were issued from the palace in strings containing less than the nominal 40. Forbes evidently assumes that less than a third (1,750/6,144 heads) of the cowries distributed by the King were strung.

Besides these customs there are three others[6] which I allow from what I can hear
to cost the King

Fetish[7]	2000
The above	10,745
Ships & firing to Whydah	1,000
Prior to going to war custom[8]	<u>3,000</u>
	<u>16,745</u>

The only other expense that I am aware of is the purchasing the slaves and the
heads from his soldiers the remainder of the slave trade is clear again [= gain?].

No explanation is offered for the deviation from the figure for the cost of the main
Customs given in Forbes' journal, but most of the difference is accounted for by a
larger allowance for rum (increased from $765 to $1,300, thus moving closer to the
figure submitted to the King, which was $1,400) and the addition of $500 for 'sun-
dries'. It will be seen that while Forbes' estimate of the cost of the main Customs is
only around one-third of the Dahomians' own estimate of $32,000, his figure for the
other Customs in the year, $6,000, is around half of the Dahomian estimate, which
was $11,800. Forbes' grand total of £16,745 represents around 38 per cent of the
Dahomian claim of $43,800.

It is not clear how this conflict of testimony might be resolved. Evidently, Forbes
and Beecroft had an interest in minimising the royal expenditure, in order to limit the
value of the compensation they would need to offer the King for giving up the slave
trade—just as, conversely, the Dahomians had interest in inflating it. It therefore
seems reasonable to suppose that the true figure lay somewhere between the two. It
should be noted, however, that Forbes' figure of $16,745, even if thought accurate,
relates solely to expenditure for the Customs. He acknowledges, in a final note, that
the King also incurred expense in purchasing captives and heads from his army at the
conclusion of the annual campaign, and this would probably have represented some
thousands of dollars.[9] Forbes claims to be aware of no 'other expense', but this seems
disingenuous, since the King also incurred costs for military supplies (guns, gunpow-
der, flints and shot) expended in the military campaigns: the Mewu and Yovogan on 5
July claimed that the King had supplied no less than 12,000 guns to his soldiers over
the last two years, which at the price assumed in the calculation of the compensation
offered (10*s.* = $2.50 per gun), would have represented an average annual cost of

---

[6] The account given by the Mewu and Yovogan on 2 July, as recorded in Forbes' and Beecroft's
Journals (pp. 145–6, 191–2), actually listed six additional customs (or seven, including the annual
military campaign), but Forbes here conflates two of these into one (the ship custom and firing
to Ouidah), and omits two others, perhaps because he assumed they involved no significant
expenditure.
[7] I.e. the Custom at Kana, following the annual military campaign and immediately preceding the
main Customs.
[8] I.e. the 'small customs' or 'custom to [the King's] father', immediately prior to the military
campaign.
[9] Beecroft was told that captives were purchased at $10 per head, though other sources give lower
figures (see his Journal, p. 146, but cf. also p. 104 and note 503). A lower price was paid for heads:
Burton in 1864 reported one head of cowries for heads and between one to two and half heads
and cloth for live captives (1864, ii: 223).

$10,000.[10] Moreover, imported goods would also have been consumed (and presumably cowries paid out for goods and services) by the King and other occupants of the palace throughout the year.

There is little evidence on which to base an estimate of total royal expenditure or of revenue received. The figure of $300,000 annually given in 1848 for the King's income from the slave trade alone may reasonably be dismissed as exaggerated, as noted.[11] On the same occasion, Gezo declared that the sum which the British were then offering as compensation, $2,000 annually, 'would not pay his expenses his expenses for a week'.[12] If intended literally, this would indicate expenditure in excess of $100,000 per year, or indeed (if Gezo was thinking in Dahomian 'weeks' of only four days) over $180,000.[13] It can be said, at least, that such figures do not seem inherently implausible. The French colonial administrator Auguste Le Herissé estimated that the royal revenue under the last independent king Behanzin (r. 1889–94) was no less than 2,500,000 francs annually, equivalent to $500,000,[14] of which income from the sale of slaves and the produce of slaves' labour (i.e. palm oil and kernels) accounted for 1,000,000 francs, or $200,000.[15] It is questionable whether this figure can be extrapolated back to 1850, since the value of exports of palm produce in the 1880s was substantially greater than that of slaves had ever been, although it is likely that the King's relative share of export earnings was smaller in the palm produce trade than in the slave trade. A modern scholar has judged Le Herissé's estimate to be implausibly high, since it exceeded the level of taxation taken by the French authorities from the whole of the colonial territory of 'Dahomey' (which was more extensive than the African kingdom) in the 1890s.[16] However, the possibility that the Dahomian state in fact imposed higher taxes than the early colonial regime should not be lightly discounted.[17]

[10] See Beecroft's Journal, p. 153; Forbes' Journal, p. 95. Forbes dismissed this figure as 'humbug'; it might seem disproportionate to the size of the standing army, which he estimated at only 14,000 (p. 169); but note the reported statement that a gun lasted only two to three years (Beecroft's Journal, p. 134; Forbes says three years, p. 189).

[11] See Introduction, p. vii.

[12] Cruickshank's Report, 17.

[13] However, Gezo may have had in mind expenditure incurred during the Customs, rather than an average over the whole year.

[14] Assuming the conventional equation of the French silver 5-franc piece to the dollar.

[15] Le Herissé (1911: 91). Another account estimates the king's income from the sale of palm produce c.1880 as 1,200,000 francs, or $240,000 (Djivo 2013, i: 151).

[16] Manning (1982: 300, n. 25).

[17] Lower taxes were indeed implicitly promised by the French at the time of their conquest of Dahomey in 1892 (Law 2004b: 276).

APPENDIX 3

SUPPLEMENTARY DOCUMENTS

1. King Gezo to Viscount Palmerston, Abomey, 7 September 1849[1]

I, Gezau, King of Dahomey beg to return my sincere thanks to the Queen of England, and Lord Palmerston, for presents sent to me by them through Mr Duncan, I beg also to thank Lord Palmerston for his good advice, respecting the trade of this country, and I do assure Lord Palmerston that the earliest opportunity will be taken of consulting my caboceers on the subject and at the next annual custom held here Mr Duncan shall be made acquainted with our decision. I have always a strong desire to cultivate a friendship with the people of England and to establish and increase a trade with that country, Englishmen were my Father's best friends, and he always told me to respect Englishmen, and look upon them in my heart as sincere in their promises and friendship, an Englishman's heart is big like a large calabash (gourd) that overflows with palm wine for those who are thirsty. I know that the Portuguese and Spaniards care nothing for me, their friendship and presents are all to serve their own purpose of obtaining slaves upon which they themselves derive the principal profit. I beg to thank Lord Palmerston for appointing my friend Mr Duncan, Vice Consul for my country and I promise to protect and assist him in performing the duties for which you have placed him here, and shall afford him the same protection when passing through my country as I did on his last journey in my Dominion. I have broken the Dassa country whose people went to war against Mr Duncan when passing their country,[2] I hold their chief a captive ever since 10 moons after Mr Duncan's visit to their country, and have kept him in my house, that Mr Duncan might see his enemies in captivity before he die, he has now seen him and my heart rejoiceth, and so shall fall every one who shall molest an Englishman while under my protection.

I am much pleased with the proposal of cultivating cotton in my country and have already planted the seeds given to me by Mr Duncan. Mayo has also planted some. I beg to assure the Queen of England, and also Lord Palmerston, of my sincere friendship and gratitude.

Signed (Mayo holding the tip of the pen) on behalf of Gezau, King of Dahomey,
Mayo Ladyetto, Prime Minister[3]

Read over three times, at the request of the King.

---

[1] TNA, FO84/775, ff. 75–6; also printed in HCPP, *Slave Trade*, 1849/50, Class B, incl. 1 in no. 6. Responding to Palmerston's letter of 29 May 1849, delivered by Vice-Consul Duncan.
[2] Dassa, a Yoruba town north of Dahomey, destroyed in 1846/7. Duncan, in passing through Dassa territory in 1845, was, according to his own account, cursed and threatened (but not actually attacked) by the inhabitants (1847, ii: 197–9).
[3] 'Ladyetto' is presumably the Mewu's personal name; but Dahomian tradition names Gezo's Mewu as Voglosu (Bay 1998: 177, 264).

2. King Gezo to Commodore Fanshawe, Abomey, 18 October 1849[4]

The King in answer to the Commander in chief's letter, has to state that at this moment he is alone in his capital and unprepared for a final answer to his letter.

At the Customs which take place in the early part of March he will be surrounded by his cabooceers and be ready to give a direct answer to the Commander in chief's request, concerning a Treaty for the abolition of the Foreign Slavery.

The King is much pleased with the assurances of the good will of Her Majesty the Queen of Great Britain towards himself and subjects, in return for which His Majesty will at all times afford protection to all British subjects, Missionaries or traders, or others visiting the kingdom.

The King requests that Lieutenant Forbes may be present at the Customs, and receive his final answer.

The King begs to state that originally the French were the first whites in Whydah, but after his Grandfather made war with that country,[5] the English were the first who settled here, and became his friends, and since then they have been the first.

That in the mean time he hopes the Commander in chief will not allow slave vessels to be taken in the roads of Whydah, as being under his protection.[6]

Given under my hands

Signed   Gezo, King of Dahomey
Drawn up by me at the King's dictation,
Signed   F.E. Forbes
                    Lieutenant Commanding Her Majesty's ship 'Bonetta'

Witness to having heard the above dictation, and to the King's holding the pen while his name was written.

Signed   John Duncan
                                    Vice Consul

3. Viscount Palmerston to Consul Beecroft, 25 February 1850 [giving instructions for the projected mission to Dahomey][7]

Lieutenant Forbes, of Her Majesty's navy, and the late Mr Duncan, who had been appointed Vice-Consul for Dahomey, went up in October last from Whydah upon a mission from Her Majesty's Government to the King of Dahomey. The object of their mission was to induce that African chief to put an end to the Slave Trade in and through his dominions, and Mr Duncan delivered to him two letters, of which the inclosed are copies, urging him to do so, and setting forth arguments to show that by doing so he would promote, instead of injuring, his own interest and those of his subjects.[8]

You will be furnished with copies of the dispatches from Lieutenant Forbes and from Mr Duncan, giving an account of their proceedings while employed on this

---

[4] TNA, FO84/785, ff. 477–9; also printed in HCPP, *Slave Trade*, 1849/50, Class B, incl. 8 in no. 9. Responding to Fanshawe's letter of 10 Sept. 1849, delivered by Lieutenant Forbes.

[5] Agaja, the conqueror of Ouidah (in 1727), was actually Gezo's great-great-grandfather, but the Fon term *tógbó*, 'grandfather', can also mean 'ancestor'.

[6] The kings of Dahomey objected to the capture of slave ships at Ouidah, because they traditionally asserted the neutrality of the roadstead, in which hostilities among Europeans were prohibited (Law 2010a: 155–7).

[7] HCPP, *Slave Trade*, 1849/50, Class B, no. 14; original draft in TNA, FO84/816, ff. 14–21v.

[8] I.e. letters from Palmerston (29 May 1849) and Commodore Fanshawe (10 Sept. 1849).

service, and of what passed between them and the King of Dahomey; and I have to request that you will make yourself acquainted with their contents.

You will see by these dispatches that Lieutenant Forbes and Mr Duncan were most kindly and hospitably received by the Dahomey Chief, and that they were assured by him of his sincere and anxious desire to secure for himself the friendship and good-will of the Queen of England, by following as far as it is possible for him to do so, any advice which Her Majesty's Government might give him; but he said that the profits which he derived from the Slave Trade constituted a considerable part of his revenue, and to put an end to that Traffic would be to sacrifice a material portion of his income. He said that, therefore, he must have time for full consideration and mature deliberation before he could answer the letter which Mr Duncan had delivered to him; but that if Lieutenant Forbes and Mr Duncan would come back to him, as he requested they would, at the next annual custom in March of this year, he would then be prepared to give his answer to Her Majesty's Government.

As Mr Duncan has been unfortunately lost to Her Majesty's service, I have to instruct you to accompany Lieutenant Forbes on his return to Dahomey, being satisfied that your judgement and discretion, together with your practical knowledge of the character and habits of the African races, peculiarly fit you for the performance of this duty. You will therefore proceed on the 24th of this month [*sic*], in Her Majesty's ship 'Sphinx',[9] which will convey you direct to Whydah, where it is probable that you will find Lieutenant Forbes; but if he should not be there he will be sent for, and you will await his arrival, which should not be long delayed, and you will in any case immediately on your landing at Whydah send up to the King of Dahomey to inform him of your arrival on the coast and of your intended visit to Dahomey.

You will proceed to Dahomey as soon as Lieutenant Forbes and yourself can set out for that place together.

If on your arrival at Dahomey, the King should declare himself ready to enter into the engagement which was proposed to him for the abolition of the Slave Trade in and through his dominions, you will, of course, at once proceed to conclude with him a Treaty to that effect, somewhat in the terms of the short and simple form of which I inclose a draft.[10] But the likelihood is that he will hold to you about the Slave Trade the same sort of language which he held on that subject last October to Lieutenant Forbes and Mr Duncan: that he will profess his anxious desire to comply with the wishes of Her Majesty's Government, but will plead financial considerations as reasons why it is impossible for him to do so.

In that case you will endeavour to explain to the Chief that the profits which he derives from the Slave Trade are precarious in their nature and limited in their extent. That they mainly depend upon the presents which the slave-dealers on the coast may be able to make to him, or upon duties paid to him on the passage of slaves through his territory, or on the price which he may obtain for captives taken in those warlike expeditions, the cost of which must in some measure absorb the profit which he may make by selling his prisoners. That the continued measures of various kinds, which the British Government are taking with a view to suppress the Slave Trade tend every year more and more to hamper the transactions of the slave-traders established on the coasts of his territory, and thus to diminish progressively the means of those

[9] The date is evidently wrong: the draft version has '1st of next month', but the *Sphinx* actually sailed from Plymouth on 2 March 1850 (Shadwell 1851: 561).
[10] Doc. 4 in this appendix.

slave-traders to make him presents or to pay duty on the passage of slaves through his dominions, or even to purchase the prisoners of war whom he may wish to sell. That, on the other hand, his territories abound with resources for legitimate trade, and that if he was to employ his great power and authority for the encouragement of legitimate commerce, as a substitute for the Slave Trade, he would very soon find that he would derive from moderate and reasonable customs duties a much greater and far more certain revenue than he at present receives from the Traffic in Slaves. Such legitimate commerce the British Government would use every proper endeavour to encourage and protect, and the interest of the King of Dahomey in regard to such trade would be identical with that of the British Government; and the States of Dahomey, and Great Britain, instead of being as now, kept in some degree on different courses, in regard to their supposed interests, in consequence of their different views and opinions with respect to the Slave Trade, would be drawn together in close bonds of union by their common feelings and mutual interests in regard to the protection, encouragement, and extension of legitimate commerce.

The foreign merchants established at Whydah are already beginning to see the great advantages which are to be derived from legitimate commerce; and whereas some years ago they were almost all of them engaged, chiefly if not entirely, in the Slave Trade, it appears that now they almost all of them have dealings in the palm-oil trade nearly as extensive as the dealings which they have in the Slave Trade.[11]

But palm-oil though a commodity much valued and wanted in Europe, and the exportation of which from Africa to Europe has been yearly increasing, is not the only produce of that part of Africa which could be the subject matter of extensive and profitable commerce between Dahomey and Great Britain. Cotton of excellent quality might be produced in almost any quantity within the territories of Dahomey, and any quantity of cotton there produced would find a ready and profitable market in the manufacturing districts of the United Kingdom. The cotton so sent to Europe would of course be paid for by such European commodities as might suit the wants and tastes of the people of Dahomey, and moderate customs duties levied upon the importation of such commodities would soon afford a considerable and increasing revenue to the King.

But the King of Dahomey might probably object that the loss which he would sustain by the suppression of the Slave Trade would be certain and immediate, while the profit which might accrue to him from import duties on legitimate trade would be uncertain, and at all events not arising until after some lapse of time.

To obviate this objection, if made, you are authorized to say that if the King of Dahomey would immediately and entirely put an end to the Slave Trade in and through his dominions, the British Government would engage to make him for a limited time, say three years, an annual present as a compensation for the loss which he would during that period sustain, it being reasonably to be expected that by the end of such a time legitimate commerce would have afforded him an income which would fully make up to him for the loss incurred by the cessation of the Slave Trade. Her Majesty's Government must leave it to your discretion to make with the Chief the best arrangement which you can on this head, and you are authorized, in case of necessity to promise an annual present,[12] either in money or goods, at the option of the King, to be continued for three years.

[11] As reported in HCPP, *Slave Trade*, 1849/50, Class B, no. 4, Duncan to Palmerston, 17 Aug. 1849.
[12] The draft here adds 'of three thousand pounds', and adds at the end of this sentence, 'but of course you will engage for a less amount if a less amount would satisfy the Dahomey chief'.

If you can conclude a satisfactory arrangement on this principle, you will draw up and sign with the King a treaty to that effect.[13]

You will express to the King of Dahomey the deep concern felt by Her Majesty's Government at the death of the late Mr Duncan, a concern which they are convinced is fully shared by the King whose kind and friendly conduct towards Mr Duncan afforded Her Majesty's Government the highest gratification; and you will say that Her Majesty's Government hope to be able to appoint some fit and proper person to be Vice-Consul in Dahomey in the place of Mr Duncan.

You will of course transmit to me a full report of all your proceedings in the execution of these instructions ...

4. Treaty to be proposed to the King of Dahomey[14]

Her Majesty the Queen of the United Kingdom of Great Britain and Ireland, and the King of Dahomey, being desirous of concluding a Treaty for the abolition of the barbarous practice of transporting natives of Africa across the sea for the purpose of consigning them to slavery in foreign countries, Her Majesty has for this purpose named as her Plenipotentiaries, John Beecroft, Esquire, her Consul to the native Chiefs of Africa whose territories lie between Cape St Paul and Cape St John, and Frederick Edwin [*sic* = Edwyn] Forbes, a Lieutenant in Her Majesty's Naval Service, and Commander of her ship of war the 'Bonetta'.

And they, Her Majesty's Plenipotentiaries, for and on behalf of Her Majesty, her heirs and successors, and His Majesty Gizo, King of Dahomey, for himself, his heirs and successors, have agreed upon and concluded the following Articles and Conditions:–

ARTICLE I

The exportation of slaves to foreign countries is for ever abolished in the territories of the King of Dahomey, and the King of Dahomey engages to make and proclaim a law prohibiting any of his subjects or any person within his jurisdiction from selling or assisting the sale of any slave for transportation to a foreign country; and the King of Dahomey promises to inflict a severe punishment on any person who shall break this law.

ARTICLE II

No European or other person whatever shall be permitted to reside within the territory of the King of Dahomey for the purpose of carrying on in any way the Traffic in Slaves; and no houses, stores, barracoons, or other buildings of any kind whatever shall be erected for the purpose of the Slave Trade within the territory of the King of Dahomey; and if any such houses, stores, barracoons or other buildings shall at any future time be erected within the territory of the King of Dahomey, and the King of Dahomey shall fail or be unable to destroy them, they may be destroyed by any British officers employed for the suppression of the Slave Trade.

ARTICLE III

If at any time it shall appear that the Slave Trade has been carried on through or from the territory of the King of Dahomey, such Slave Trade may be put down in that

---

[13] The draft here adds a section relating to the possible military reoccupation of the British fort at Ouidah. Since no reference was made to this in Beecroft's interview with Gezo on 4 July 1850, presumably it was omitted from the final version of the instructions.

[14] HCPP, *Slave Trade*, 1849/50, Class B, incl. 6 in no. 14; original draft in TNA, FO84/816, ff. 23–7v.

territory by Great Britain by force, and British officers may seize any boats of Daho-mey found anywhere carrying on the Slave Trade.

ARTICLE IV

The slaves now held for exportation in Dahomey shall be delivered up at Whydah to the senior officer of Her Britannic Majesty's naval forces in the Bight of Benin, for the purpose of being carried to a British colony, to be there set free; and all the imple-ments of the Slave Trade and the barracoons or buildings exclusively used in the Slave Trade shall be forthwith destroyed.

ARTICLE V

Europeans or other persons who may be found to be engaged in the Slave Trade in the territory of Dahomey, are to be expelled from the country; the houses, stores, or build-ings hitherto employed as slave-factories, if not converted to lawful purposes within three months from the conclusion of this Treaty, are to be destroyed.

ARTICLE VI

The subjects of Her Britannic Majesty may always trade freely with the people of Dahomey in every article which they may wish to buy or sell in all the places and ports and rivers within the territories of the King of Dahomey, and throughout the whole of his dominions; and the King of Dahomey pledges himself to show no favour and to give no privilege to the ships and traders of other countries, which he does not or will not show to those of England.

ARTICLE VII

In consideration of the above-mentioned concessions on the part of the King of Dahomey, and in full compensation for the temporary loss of revenue to which His Majesty may be subject therefrom, Her Majesty the Queen of the United Kingdom of Great Britain and Ireland engages to make to the King of Dahomey yearly for three years a present of either £   sterling, or of goods to that value, at the option of the King. But this annual present is to cease if Slave Trade should again be carried on within the territory of Dahomey.

ARTICLE VIII

This Treaty shall have full force and effect from the   day of   1850.

In faith whereof the above-named Plenipotentiaries of Her Britannic Majesty and His Majesty the King of Dahomey have signed the same, and have affixed thereto their respective seals.
Done at Abomey, the   day of   , 1850.

5. Extract from Viscount Palmerston to Consul Beecroft, 25 February 1850 [giving instructions for his projected mission to Abeokuta]:[15]
With respect to any aggressive intentions of the King of Dahomey towards the Yoruba people,[16] you will have an opportunity, during your visit to Abomey, to bring that subject under the notice of the King; you will represent to him that the people who

[15] HCPP, *Slave Trade*, 1849/50, Class B, no. 15; original draft in TNA, FO84/816, ff. 39–40.
[16] Here referring to Abeokuta.

dwell in the Yoruba and Popoe countries[17] are the friends of England, and that the British Government takes a great interest in their welfare, and would see with much concern and displeasure any acts of violence or oppression committed against them; that, moreover, there are dwelling among those tribes many liberated Africans and British-born subjects whom Her Majesty's Government are bound to protect from injury.

It is to be hoped that such representations as these, enforced by whatever influence you and Lieutenant Forbes may have acquired over the King in the course of your negotiations upon other matters, may induce the King to make a formal promise to abstain from future aggressions against the people of Yoruba and Popoe, and from molesting in any way the liberated Africans or Europeans who reside in Abbeokuta and Badagry, or who frequent the countries adjoining the territories of Dahomey.

6. Viscount Palmerston to King Gezo, 25 February 1850[18]

The Queen of Great Britain and Ireland, my Sovereign, has commanded me to inform you that she has been graciously pleased to grant a commission appointing John Beecroft, Esq, to be Her Majesty's Consul to the several chiefs of Africa whose territories lie between Cape St Paul, at the western extremity of the Bight of Benin, and Cape St John, at the southern extremity of the Bight of Biafra.

It will be an important part of Mr Beecroft's duties to endeavour to prevent misunderstandings from arising between the chiefs of that part of Africa, or their dependents, and Her Majesty's subjects, either residing in or resorting to those parts for the purpose of lawful commerce.

Mr Beecroft will be accompanied in his visit to you by Lieutenant Forbes, with whom you are already acquainted, and they are instructed to propose to you a formal Treaty for the abolition of Slave Trade within your dominions; and to explain to you the advantages which you and your territories would derive from the increase of lawful trade, and further to assure you of the earnest desire of the Queen and her Government to contribute in every way to your welfare and prosperity.

Mr Beecroft will reside at the Island of Fernando Po: and he will make periodical visits, as occasion may require, to the territories of the several chiefs to whom he is accredited. He is further instructed to take charge of and to forward to Her Majesty, or to Her Majesty's Government, any communications which you may have to make to them. He will confer with you as to the best means of developing the resources of your country and of increasing the lawful commerce of your dominions, and of thus adding to the wealth and comforts of yourself and your people.

The Queen trusts that you will receive Mr Beecroft with the respect due to his character and rank, that you will put entire faith in what he shall state to you in her name, and that you will extend to him your protection, while within the limits of your dominions.

7. King Gezo to Queen Victoria, Abomey, 4 July 1850[19]

Being desirous that the Slave Trade should be stopped in the minor ports, prior to my entering into a treaty, I have to request that you will endeavour to blockade the slave

---

[17] I.e. Abeokuta and Badagry. 'Popo' was used by the Yoruba as a name for the people of Badagry and Porto-Novo, who call themselves Gun.

[18] HCPP, *Slave Trade*, 1849/50, Class B, incl. in no. 16; original draft in TNA, FO84/818, ff. 5–8v.

[19] HCPP, *Slave Trade*, 1850/1, Class B, incl. in no. 9: original not traced, but the text is copied into Forbes' Journal (see p. 194) and another copy is in TNA, CO96/20, incl. to H.U. Addington to H. Merivale, 11 Oct. 1850.

ports between Quittah[20] and Lagos, and then I can endeavour to enter into an agreement for the stoppage of the Slave Trade in my own country.

At present, my people are a warlike people, and unaccustomed to agricultural pursuits. I should not be enabled to keep up my revenue, were I at once to stop the Slave Trade.

I am always desirous of being at peace with Great Britain.

I am anxious that some person should be sent as Governor of the British fort at Whydah, and having known him, should wish for Lieutenant Forbes, R.N.

(Signed)   GEZO, King of Dahomey
his X mark

Witness to the royal mark:

(Signed)   JOHN BEECROFT,
Her Majesty's Consul,
Bights of Benin and Biafra
F.E. FORBES, Lieutenant Commanding
Her Majesty's Ship 'Bonetta'

P.S.—Some years ago I entrusted two boys and a girl to the care of Mr Freeman, I am anxious they should be returned.

I am anxious that missionaries should settle at Whydah.

8. Consul Beecroft to Viscount Palmerston, Prince's Island,[21] 22 July 1850[22]

I have the honour to communicate to your Lordship my proceedings since my last, dated the 4th of May.

I sailed from Fernando Po on the 5th and arrived at Whydah on the 10th in Her Majesty's steamer Phoenix, and landed on the 14th of May, accompanied by Commander Forbes, left with the Presents for the King of Dahomey on the 21st, and arrived at Abomey on the 26th and was Graciously received by His Majesty, he told us that he would give us a day's respite to rest after our Journey, our next interview was on the 28th. I handed to the King Her Majesty's Letter,[23] he received it very cordially and pressed it to his Forehead, and then handed it to me to read, the conference relative to the Treaty for the suppression of the Foreign Slave Trade was postponed until his Majesty's first Custom was over, which would last about six weeks, we then should have witnessed the most extensive and expensive part of his Annual Customs.

The Presents from Her Majesty's Government were given over next day to the Mayo-gau, His Majesty's Prime Minister, after which I was anxious to have a day appointed to confer on this momentous question, after a great deal of Procrastination the 4th of July was the day appointed. It commenced with heavy rain, and continued without intermission until one o'clock, when it partially cleared away; we then set off for the Palace; we of course were courteously received by His Majesty.

[20] Keta, on the coast west of Little Popo, in what is today south-eastern Ghana.
[21] The island of Príncipe, at this time a Portuguese colony (nowadays part of the independent state of São Tomé and Príncipe).
[22] TNA, FO84/816, ff. 148–52; also printed, with some omissions, in HCPP, *Slave Trade*, 1850/1, Class B, no. 9.
[23] I.e. Palmerston's letter to the King (see doc. 6).

After a few complimentary remarks from the King, relative to our not remaining to see the whole of the annual customs, and so forth.

I told him that it would be five or six months ere the whole of his Customs were finally finished; that would be too long to stop, he said yes and did not wish it, His Majesty then desired us to proceed with our statement, we then laid before him the subsidy that Her Majesty's Government authorized us to offer to His Majesty the King of Dahomey, annually for five years, instead of three, subject to ratification. His Majesty made no reply, he was silent on the matter, he did not once refer to the amount, whether it was too small or otherwise, although with his own permission it was read to him a second time.

He commenced to state in detail, the friendship that had existed between His Majesty's Grandfather, and the King of England, and stated that the Country of Dahomey had not changed but remained the same to this day.

We endeavoured to expostulate, and explain to His Majesty, the advantages that he must ultimately reap from agriculture, growing of cotton as well as cultivating the Palm-oil Tree.

In reply the King stated that they were a warlike people the Dahomians, and of course unaccustomed to agricultural pursuits; that he would not be able to keep up his Revenue, was he at once to stop the Slave Trade. Being desirous that it should be stopped, in the minor Ports, Prior to his entering into a Treaty, requests that Her Majesty's Government will endeavour to Blockade between Quitta and Lagos, and then he would endeavour, to enter into an agreement for the suppression of the Slave Trade in His Majesty's own country, he asked if we had seen any Farms between the swamp and Abomey, he could not disgrace himself, and subject himself to be laughed at, by sending the women from his Palace yard to Plant, and cultivate cotton.

He also stated that he had taken and destroyed all the countries that formerly cultivated cotton.

We endeavoured to impress on His Majesty that if he employed the prisoners, that were captured, instead of selling them out of the country, he might grow as much cotton as he pleased, and furthermore England, would buy it all from him, and his people, however, he did not appear desirous to listen to any further discussions on agriculture.

His Majesty then requested us to address a Letter to Her Majesty the Queen of England his friend, that she would allow Whydah to become a Free-Port, stating that he had five agents, mentioning at the same time their names, viz., Isidore, Ignacio, & Antonio, three Bastards of the late De Souza, also Domingo Martins, and Joachim Antonio. His Majesty's simple request was to have Papers, and Flags, to allow them to pass without hinderance, or molestation from Her Majesty's cruisers, our reply was, that it was impossible, he appeared much perplexed, and harped upon the same theme for some time, at last His Majesty said surely my Friend, the Queen of England, will allow Papers and Colours, for one vessel for myself to go free from the men-a-war, his pride must have fallen when the great King of Dahomey, condescended to ask for one vessel, on similar terms as the five, when he found it impossible to induce us to change our theme, and write such unholy balderdash in the Queen of England's dispatch, he felt much chagrined, and his countenance changed, and became a shade lighter.

We then told him that as he had declined the Queen of England's liberal offer that there was only the last resource, to go on the old plan, and take his chance, that it was not within the range of possibility, that any favors, can be shown His Majesty's vessels, beyond the minor Ports.

I then found that our mission was drawing to a close, and being determined to draw his attention to Abbeokutta, I asked his permission to allow us to read the Earl of Chichester's letter from the Queen to Sagbua, chief of the abovementioned Town, finding the Queen's expressions of kindness to the chief so strong, with thanks for his kindness, and protection to the missionaries, &c, His Majesty appeared to be greatly excited, and jealous, and said that he was going to war with that place, they were bad people, that the white men and Ladies must be removed, I then told him that I was going to visit it as soon as the dry season set in that would be about December, he then said you must take the Englishmen away from that place.

Mayo-gau His Majesty's Prime Minister made a very harsh remark, and said, what right have the white men to go and teach those fellows, Book Palaver.

His Majesty then said, that when Freeman, from Cape Coast, visited Abomey, when he left he promised to send a white Teacher but he has not done so, neither had he heard any more on that matter.

He was then asked if a white missionary were sent to Abomey, would His Majesty afford him protection, and give him a grant of land to build a House, he replied in the affirmative, but he must reside at Whydah, it appears that he is averse to them residing at Abomey, but, I really believe he was prompted by his minister in a whisper to make that reply relative to the missionary residing at Whydah instead of Abomey.

I had another important Request to lay before His Majesty with his permission, which was granted. I then stated that Mrs McCarthy, wife of John McCarthy, liberated Africans from Siereleon, late [of] Ahguay, and residents of Whydah, the said Mrs McCarthy complained to me that her husband John McCarthy was confined as a Prisoner in His Majesty's court yard, that he had been seized between Ah-taa-Pam and Popoo on his route from the former to the latter, not any person knew anything about the matter, I told the Cabooceer of Whydah, that he must know her, but he denied it. The King ordered the Mayo-gau to enquire into the affair, after which the Queen's dispatch was read, and he made his mark we witnessed it,[24] He had not any more to say, only that he would communicate with me at Fernando Po, either by Letter or a messenger, by any vessel that may be going that route from Whydah, It rained we continued a short time, but no appearance of dry weather, we asked permission to depart, he said we must taste with him before we leave we went through the ceremony, he conducted us outside of the Porch, shook hands, with his respects & best wishes for our safe arrivals at our different destinations, we left the Palace of Abomey, for our own Domicile, it rained the remainder of the day.

Next morning it was fine and dry King sent our Presents for the road, of cowries, cloth, rum, &c also a little girl each, after which we entered our house, and held a short conference[,] present the Mayo-gau, Eh-ah-voo-gan and Nawhey relative to Mr McCarthy, his wife was presented with her child, the Mayo said he would send her with a messenger to the home of the Cam-baa-dee, and they should both return here during the day, they asked when we intended to leave, we told them on the morrow, if we received a decisive answer about the man McCarthy, they said that it was a small Palaver, and would soon be settled, they took their leave.

Next morning early the same party came, we had to sit and hear the salutes fired, 21 Guns for the Queen, and thirteen for each of us, which took full two hours, after which the McCarthy question was again mooted, stating that they did not make their appearance yesterday as you all particularly the Mayo-gau promised, the latter said he sent her to the King yesterday, and that he sent her to the Cam-baa-dee's, to see if her husband was there. I then told him that, I know from good authority, that she is also a Prisoner, but not with her husband; it is a farce, you are making fools of us.

---

[24] I.e. Gezo's letter to the Queen, doc. 7.

Commander Forbes, expressed himself very warmly and told them that he was going to England, and would report to the Queen, that two British subjects were detained as Prisoners, in Abomey, at the same time threw his memorandum Book on the Table, they looked at him seriously and said we hope you are not vexed, if so we must tell our master the King, rose and shook hands and left us to take our Breakfast before we started, odd to state that the day before I got an attack of Gout, prevented me from walking, a few Packages being left detained us, Commander Forbes kindly offered to remain and start them off before him, and recommended me to leave for Cana, I left at 10 o'clock and arrived at noon, half an hour afterwards Forbes joined, he remained to get a hammock and carriers for a sick man, I went on and arrived at Zoobodoo at 2.20 pm. Commander Forbes did not arrive until 5 o'clock, during his detention a messenger arrived in post haste bringing with him McCarthy and his wife.

I presume they must have communicated the warm debate on the matter this morning, it shows a dread of the King's meeting the displeasure of Her Majesty's Government.

We started at 5 o'clock next morning, crossed the swamp of which we had thirteen hours before we arrived at our halting place, ultimately arrived at Whydah on the 9th found HM sloop Bonetta. Gladiator and Jackal arrived on the 11th we succeeded in embarking through the surf on the 12th, and communicated with Captain Adams the Senior Officer, and stated that, I was anxious that my Journal should go by HM Sloop Bonetta, but it would take me ten days to prepare it. he advised me to go to Princes with the Bonetta, where she [was] ordered to join the Commodore, and he would order the Jackal HM St to touch there and take me to Fernando Po, the matter was arranged and sailed the same evening anchored at West Bay Princes on the 16th Commodore Fanshawe arrived in Her Majesty's Steam Frigate Centaur, he very kindly allowed me two or three days to prepare my Journal, I trust your Lordship will forgive grammatical errors, for it was written in a very hurried state. I will amend it at Fernando Po in Duplicate and detail more fully my opinion on the Slave Trade at Whydah, trusting that my proceedings will meet with your full approbation.

I trust that it will be proved on the Perusal of the Journal, that this great Despot the King of Dahomey has been awfully exaggerated as to his wealth and Power. I am perfectly satisfied that he is under the control and opinion of several of his principal officers, and it is too obvious, that he has not the slightest desire to abandon the abominable Traffic.

The only effectual means to bring him to a full sense of his error, if international Law will admit of it, is to take his own advice and Blockade Whydah.[25] Hutton's agent has not much Property there. The French House would of course be a great obstacle,[26] nevertheless it would be Political to hold out a threat that if he should attack Abbeokutta, Her Majesty's Government would Blockade and stop all Trade at Whydah.[27] Lagos is another point. If the legitimate King could be seen and communicated with, so as to make a treaty with him for the suppression of the Foreign Slave Trade and place him at Lagos, his former seat of Government it would release the people of Abbeokutta from the jeopardy that they are continually in of the fear of the King of Dahomey.

[25] Since blockade was legally an act of war, there was in fact no basis in international law for its use to force Dahomey to accept abolition of the slave trade (Law 2010a: 157–8).

[26] I.e. the firm of Régis, which occupied the French fort at Ouidah.

[27] Although this is offered as a suggestion for Palmerston's consideration, in fact this was preempted by Commodore Fanshawe, who issued such a threat on the following day (doc. 9).

My Lord I have presumed to give my opinion perhaps too freely which I trust you will pardon should I have done so.

I beg leave to state that Mr Hastie agent to Mr Hutton at Whydah has been remarkably kind and attentive during the whole of residence at Abomey and Whydah, but still think there is room for an amendment.

I beg to state that the walls of the Fort are out of repair and, I presume it would take 2000 £s to get it in order, leaving the Guns out of the account they are honey combed and useless.

HM Steamer Gladiator has captured two empty slavers.[28] HM Steamer Hecla two with slaves lately from Lagos;[29] I believe they have been trying it hard there latterly.

HM Brig Wolverine took a Felucca, two or three days ago.[30] Other particulars will be gleaned from my Journal.

I can only state that I have been greatly disappointed at the King of Dahomey's power and wealth. As reported, he has 18,000 Amazons as a body Guard[31]—we have only seen and counted 3000 and about the same number of men, at a Grand review he stated himself the same day that we did not see all his warriors, he had a great body guarding his frontiers. I estimate his army at twenty or twenty five thousand.

His Majesty's account of his total expenditure of cowries for the year is only 42,000 [heads], his first account 32,000; about $^2/_3$ more than we could account for.

I was anxious to get a just estimate of the number of Tons of Palm oil shipped from Whydah &c, but I could not get any but exaggerated accounts, so I have declined making any statement at present, until my next visit at latter end of the year.

[PS] I transmit to your Lordship an original letter, dated the 4th instant, addressed by the King of Dahomey to Her Majesty.[32]

9. Commodore Fanshawe to King Gezo, 'Centaur', Prince's Island, 23 July 1850[33]

I have learned with extreme regret, from Lieutenant Forbes, the officer of Her Majesty the Queen of England, my Sovereign, whom I sent to your capital of Abomey, that you have refused the proposals made to you by the directions of the Queen, to abandon the traffic in slaves in your Dominions, and that you proposed making war on Abbeokuta, in the Yoruba country, for the object of obtaining more slaves for sale.[34]

It becomes my duty, therefore, to apprize you that the people of Yoruba are the friends of Her Majesty the Queen of England, and that Her Majesty's Government will see with much displeasure any act of violence or oppression committed against

[28] I.e. the *Bom Fim* (see Beecroft's Journal, pp. 85–6 and note 407) and the *Juliana* (Forbes' Journal, p. 191 and note 94).

[29] I.e. the *Flor de Maria* and the *Caramaru*, taken respectively on 8 and 11 June 1850: HCPP, *Slave Trade*, 1851/2, Class A, incl. in no. 147: List of vessels captured or detained by Her Majesty's squadron ... between March 1, 1850, & Feb. 28, 1851 (TASTD, nos 4015–16).

[30] Unnamed vessel, taken on 8 [*sic*] July 1850: ibid. (TASTD, no. 4018). A *felucca* is a small coasting vessel.

[31] No earlier source giving this figure has been traced: possibly it is an imprecise recollection of Duncan (1847, i: 231), who recorded seeing 8,000 female soldiers in a procession, or else refers to oral reports.

[32] Doc. 7.

[33] TNA, FO84/828, ff. 44–5; also printed in HCPP, *Slave Trade*, 1850/1, Class A, incl. in no. 225.

[34] This statement of motive seems unwarranted by anything recorded by Beecroft and Forbes at Abomey.

them, and also that there are dwelling at Abbeokuta, and in the Yoruba country, many British-born subjects, and liberated Africans, whom they are bound to protect from injury, and that if they receive any from your hands, it will be considered an act of hostility against the Queen and the English people, and will cause the coast of your Majesty's Dominions to be immediately invested and blockaded by Her Majesty's ships under my command, and all trade stopped.

I hope your Majesty will come to some wiser conclusion, and that God may so dispose you.

10. Viscount Palmerston to King Gezo, 11 October 1850[35]

I am commanded by Her Majesty to acknowledge the receipt of the letter which you addressed to her on the 4th of July last;[36] and I have in the first place to beg you to accept the best thanks of the British Government for the very hospitable manner in which you received Mr Beecroft and Commander Forbes, during their late visit to your Majesty's capital of Abomey; and I beg to assure you, Sir, that this friendly conduct on your part has still more increased the earnest desire of the British Government to cultivate the most intimate relations between the Kingdoms of Great Britain and of Dahomey.

But as nothing more contributes to the maintenance of friendship than a frank explanation of mutual feelings and opinions, I deem it of importance to advert to the statement which you made to Mr Beecroft, that you intended to make war upon the chiefs of Abeokuta, and I feel It right to inform you that the Queen of England takes a great interest in favour of that city and its people, and that if you value the friendship of England you will abstain from any attack upon and from any hostility against that town and people.

The British Government would be sorry that you should make such an attack, 1st, because Her Majesty's Government would deeply regret that any evil should happen to the people of Abbeokuta; and, 2ndly, because Her Majesty's Government would feel much concern if anything should be done by your Majesty which would lead to an interruption of the friendly relations between yourself and the Government of England.

With respect to what you have written about the Slave Trade, the British Government is much disappointed at your answer, for they had hoped and expected that you would have complied with their very reasonable request, accompanied as it was by a handsome offer of full compensation for any temporary loss which you might sustain by putting an end to the Slave Trade. But as you have declined to consent to what the British Government has asked you to do, the British Government will be obliged to employ its own means to accomplish its purpose, and as England is sure to succeed in any object it is determined to attain, the result will be, that the Slave Trade from Dahomey will be put an end to by British cruisers, and thus you will sustain the loss of revenue without receiving the offered compensation.

But it is at least a satisfaction to Her Majesty's Government to think that your loss of revenue will only be felt by you for a short time, and that the profits which will arise from legal commerce will very soon amply repay you for any deficiency of revenue caused by the cessation of the Slave Trade.

[35] HCPP, *Slave Trade*, 1850/1, Class B, incl. in no. 10; original draft in TNA, FO84/819, ff. 4–6v. Delivered to Gezo by Vice-Consul Fraser in August 1851.
[36] Doc. 7.

ENDNOTE 1

THE 'ANNUAL CUSTOMS'

One of the main purposes of the mission of 1850 was to attend and witness the King's 'Annual Customs'—this term translates the Fon *hwenùwá*, 'annual performance', which was recorded by Forbes as 'Hwae-noo-ee-wha'.[1] Although there was a series of 'customs' held through the year (as is noted in the journals of Beecroft and Forbes),[2] the term 'Annual Customs' was normally used to refer to one ceremony (or rather, set of ceremonies) in particular, which was regarded as the most important. The principal ceremony involved the public sacrifice of human victims, who were thrown from a platform, before being killed.

In the eighteenth century, the Annual Customs normally began in late December/ early January.[3] By 1850, however, they were held later in the year, normally beginning in March.[4] This change was presumably due to the insertion of an additional 'Custom', performed at Kana, preceding the main Customs at Abomey.[5] The ceremonial cycle was linked to the Dahomian year, which was regarded as beginning with the onset of the main dry season, that is, in December.[6] The new year thus began with the launching of the annual military campaign, normally conducted during this dry season. The annual cycle of Customs began on the return home of the army, and insofar as this might vary, the precise dating of the Customs was also variable.

The Annual Customs of 1850 were originally scheduled to begin on 13 March.[7] But their performance was delayed by the late return of the Dahomian army from its campaign against Atakpamé. Forbes, on arrival at Ouidah in February 1850, found that the army was still in the field, so that the Customs had been deferred. The return home of the army was reported to Ouidah only on 11 March, and Forbes was subsequently informed that the Customs would now begin on 15 May.[8] However, they in fact began two weeks later still. When Beecroft and Forbes met King Gezo for the first time, on 28 May, he told them that he had finished the Kana Custom, and 'was just

---

[1] Forbes' Journal, pp. 157, 190.

[2] See their Journals, pp. 145–6, 191–2.

[3] Pruneau de Pommegorge (1789: 178–9) ('vers Noël'); but Dalzel (1793: xx), says that the governors of the European forts at Ouidah received invitations to attend 'soon after Christmas', which implies that the Customs actually began a few days later.

[4] Forbes (1851, i: 17).

[5] Burton says that the Kana Custom was initiated by King Gezo to commemorate his victory over Oyo in 1823 (1864, i: 198–9). However, the rescheduling of the main Customs to March/ April seems already to have been operative during 1803–11: see Nicolau Parés (2016: 200–2). Perhaps commemoration of the Oyo war was a feature added to the Kana Custom subsequently.

[6] For the Dahomian calendar, see Le Herissé (1911: 355–7).

[7] HCPP, *Slave Trade*, 1849/50, Class B, incl. 1 in no. 9, Lieutenant Forbes to Commodore Fanshawe, 5 Nov. 1849.

[8] HCPP, *Slave Trade*, 1850/1, Class A, incl.1 in no. 198: Forbes to Fanshawe, 2 April 1850, journal entries for 27 Feb., 11 and 16 March 1850.

now going to commence' the main Customs.[9] Beecroft and Forbes then witnessed ceremonies over the next three and a half weeks, with the 'Platform Custom' occurring on 31 May and the final ceremony on 22 June.

The accounts of the Annual Customs of 1850 by Beecroft and Forbes represent the first (and indeed, only) complete descriptions of these ceremonies. Earlier eyewitness accounts, for example by the English trader Robert Norris (between 5–16 February 1772), cover only part of the ceremonies.[10] The only other comparably detailed accounts are those by Consul Richard Burton, of ceremonies performed in December–January 1863/4, and the entomologist J.A. Skertchly, in September–December 1871.[11] Strictly, however, the Customs witnessed by Burton and Skertchly were not the same as those attended by Beecroft and Forbes in 1850, but corresponded rather to what Beecroft's informants called the 'small customs', which occurred later in the cycle (in fact at the very end of it), immediately preceding the departure of the army on its annual campaign.[12] It seems that under Gezo's successor, Glele, the Customs which preceded the annual campaign were now regarded as the principal ones, while those which followed it were demoted in status.[13] The particular form of Customs which Burton witnessed also differed from those seen by Beecroft and Forbes in 1850, called the 'So-sin' (Horse-tying), because it began with the confiscation of horses owned by the Dahomian officials, which were released on payment of a fine. At this date, the 'So-sin' Custom and a version of the 'Platform' ceremony were performed on alternate years.[14] Although some ceremonies were common to both forms of Customs, there were significant differences: in particular, all the human sacrifices witnessed or reported by Beecroft and Forbes were decapitated, whereas some of those seen by Burton had been clubbed to death and their bodies exhibited entire, on poles or gibbets.[15] Skertchly in 1871 claims to have seen both the 'So-sin' Custom and the 'Platform Custom', though it is implied that only the 'So-sin' was originally scheduled, the King having allegedly ordered the performance of the 'Platform Custom' also, so that Skertchly could witness and write about both.[16] The status of Skertchly's account, however, is problematic, since much of its detail seems to be plagiarised from the earlier account of Burton, though he also offers a fair amount of original information, presumably based on his own observation.

---

[9] Beecroft's Journal, p. 28.

[10] Norris (1789: 93–112, 121–6). John Duncan seems also to have witnessed part of the Annual Customs, between 11 and 20 June 1845, but his account is frustratingly vague and uninformative (1847, i: 224–56).

[11] Burton (1864, i: 348–86; ii, 1–128); Skertchly (1874: 186–299, 338–431).

[12] Beecroft's Journal, p. 146. The name given by Burton for these ceremonies, 'Khwe-ta-nun', i.e. *hwetanú*, 'Year-head-thing', refers to their being held at the end ('head') of the year (1864, i: 345); cf. Segurola & Rassinoux (2000: 321), s.v. *xwetanù*.

[13] See Le Herissé (1911: 182–92), whose informants referred to the ceremonies which preceded the annual military campaign as the '*grandes coutumes*', and those which followed it as a 'repetition [*reprise*]' of them.

[14] Burton (1864, i: 346–7; ii: 170).

[15] Note that Norris in 1772 saw both severed heads and complete bodies on gibbets exhibited—which suggests that the distinction between the 'So-sin' and 'Platform' Customs involved the separation of rituals which had previously been combined (cf. Nicolau Parés 2016: 208).

[16] Skertchly (1874: 303).

The schedule of ceremonies

In the eighteenth century, the Annual Customs are stated to have lasted 'about a month' and to have been structured around the Dahomian 'week' of four days, with 'some public exhibition every fourth, or market day; the intermediate days being employed in preparations'.[17] Norris' observations in 1772 confirm this latter feature, with major ceremonies on 8, 12 and 16 February.

The Customs of 1850 occupied slightly less than a month at 25 days (29 May–22 June). In fact, the contrast with earlier practice is even greater than this, since the term of 'about a month' given earlier clearly refers to the major public ceremonies only, not including subsequent rites at the shrines of deceased kings inside the palace, which Europeans did not normally witness. In 1850 the initial public ceremonies occupied only six days (29 May–3 June). The ceremonies also no longer followed a strict four-day cycle, for much of the time occurring almost daily, although there was a gap of four days between the conclusion of the main public ceremonies (on 3 June) and the first royal funerary rites (7 June), as well as between these and the next two of the latter (11 and 15 June), and in the case of one ceremony which was performed twice—a procession of the King's wives displaying his wealth—there was again a four-day interval between them (30 May and 3 June). The abandonment of the 'weekly' format may have been due, again, to the need to fit additional ceremonies into the available time.

The nature of the successive ceremonies reported in 1850 is set out below in tabular form, including their local names (as reported by Forbes) and proposed interpretations of these in the Fon language.

---

[17] Dalzel (1793: xx–xxii).

Date	Nature of ceremony	Location	Indigenous name (+ Forbes' explanation)	Fon interpretation
29 May	singing of praise songs by 'minstrels' (or 'troubadours') and their payment by the King[18]	courtyard inside palace	*Eh nah ek beh*, 'Day of giving'[19]	= *nǎ gbè*, 'day of giving'[20]
29/30 May (overnight)	victims beheaded at palace gate	severed heads displayed in Singbodji Square[21]	(not given)[22]	
30 May	display of royal wealth[23]	procession from inside palace to Adjahi market	*Ak-bah-tong-ek-beh*, 'Carrying goods to market'[24]	= *agbàn tòn gbè*, 'day of displaying goods'
31 May	throwing of gifts and human sacrifices from a platform[25]	Adjahi	*Ek-que-noo-ah-toh*, or *Ek-que-noo-ah-toh-me*, 'Throwing away cowries from Ahtoh (= platform)', or 'throwing presents from the Ah-toh'	= *hwe nú atò, hwe nú atòmé* 'yearly platform thing', 'yearly thing at platform'
1 June	parades of soldiers	Adjahi	*Eh-dah-soh-ek-beh*, 'firing guns'	= *dǎ sò gbè*, 'day of firing guns'
2 June	(none)			
2/3 June (overnight)	victims beheaded	heads displayed in Singbodji Square	see 30 May	see 30 May
3 June	display of royal wealth, repeated	procession from palace to Adjahi	see 30 May	
(evening)	meal[26]	Adjahi	*Ee doo beh pah meh*, 'Go to Pah meh to eat'	= *yì dù gbè kpámè*, 'go be joyful [lit. 'eat life']'[27] at the *kpámè* [= enclosure]

4 June	distribution of cowries to male soldiers		
5–6 June	(none)		
7 June	commemorative rites at 'tombs' of unnamed king(s) (= Agonglo?)	Adanjloakode section of the palace	*Sequeahee*, 'throwing water', or 'watering the graves' = *sin kòn ny'àyĭ*, 'pouring water on the earth'
	+ distribution of royal bounty to officers & traders[28]		
8–10 June	(none)		
11 June	rites for King Dakodonu etc. (+ Kings Wegbaja and Akaba?)	Dahomey palace	See 7 June
	+ 'war palaver', discussing the recent campaign and the object of the next		
12 June	(none)		
13 June	parade of female soldiers, swearing oath for next campaign[29]	Adjahi	
14 June	'sham fight' (simulation of attack on a village)[30]	Adjahi	
15 June	commemorative rites for King Agaja (+ Tegbesu and Kpengla?)	Agringomè section of the palace	See 7 June

(Continued)

Date	Nature of ceremony	Location	Indigenous name (+ Forbes' explanation)	Fon interpretation
16 June	rites for Agaja (and/or Tegbesu and Kpengla?)[31]	Agringomè	See 7 June	
17 June	rites for Adono, mother of King Agaja	courtyard entered through Adono's gate, western side of palace	See 7 June	
	+ distribution of royal bounty to officers and traders			
	+ 'trial' of an officer for cowardice in the recent war			
18 June	rites for Hwanjile, mother of King Tegbesu	courtyard entered by Hwanjile's gate, western side of palace	See 7 June	
	+ conclusion of 'trial' and degrading of officer accused of cowardice			
19 June	rites for Chai, mother of King Kpengla	courtyard entered by Chai's gate, western side of palace	See 7 June	
	+ swearing of oath by male soldiers			
20 June	(none)			

21 June	rites for Senunme, mother of King Agonglo	courtyard entered by Senunme's gate, western side of palace	See 7 June
22 June	rites for Agotime, mother of King Gezo[32]	courtyard entered by Agotime's gate, western side of palace	See 7 June

[18] Dalzel noted that one of the festival days was 'set apart for singing and dancing', including by 'professed singers' who sang 'in praise of the Monarch and his exploits' and were 'rewarded on the spot' (ibid., xxii).

[19] In his book (1851, ii: 1), Forbes elaborates this into 'Paying the Troubadours'.

[20] This is clearly a generic term, rather than the name of this specific ceremony: there were other such distributions of gifts on 4, 7 and 17 June.

[21] Norris in 1772 saw severed heads from overnight sacrifices at the palace entrance on three days (1789: 94, 106, 111).

[22] Burton later reported that overnight sacrifices were referred to as zān nyanya, 'evil night' (1864, ii: 18).

[23] Norris witnessed this 'display of the king's furniture and trinkets', on 12 February 1772 (1789: 111–12); cf. also Pruneau de Pommegorge (1789: 189–90).

[24] In Forbes' book (1851, ii: 33), this becomes 'Display of the King's wealth'.

[25] Norris describes this ceremony (from hearsay, rather than from his own observation), on 16 February 1772 (1789: 124-6). He calls it 'the last day of the Annual Customs', but this evidently means the last public ceremony, in distinction from subsequent ceremonies inside the palace. It is also described by Dalzel (1793: xxiii–xxiv); Pruneau de Pommegorge (1789: 190-4).

[26] Norris participated in a dinner, on 8 February 1772, but at a different point in the cycle of ceremonies (before the 'Platform' Custom), at a different location (inside the Dahomey palace), and in the daytime rather than the evening (1789: 102–5; cf. also Dalzel (1793: xxii–xxiii); Pruneau de Pommegorge (1789: 186–9).

[27] For the idiom 'eating life' in this context, cf. Le Herissé (1911: 187–8).

[28] In his book, Forbes calls this ceremony 'Paying the Ministers' (1851, ii: 74–8).

[29] Duncan on 11 June 1845 witnessed a parade of female soldiers, who 'declare[d] their fidelity' to the King (1847, i: 224–7).

[30] Duncan witnessed this ceremony of a simulated attack on a village, on 12 June 1845 (ibid., i: 231–3).

[31] The ceremonies involved the sacrifice of four victims, including one each by the Mewu and the Yovogan. Duncan, on 14 June 1845, witnessed the decapitation inside the palace of four men, two of whom were killed by the Mewu, which probably refers to the same ceremony (ibid., i: 249–53).

[32] During this day the King's 'mother' and other women danced while carrying skulls: the same ceremony seems to have been witnessed by Duncan on 20 June 1845 (ibid., i: 253–4).

2 The numbers sacrificed

A prominent feature of the Annual Customs was the offering of human sacrifices. The numbers sacrificed became an issue of concern to the British, in part due to King Gezo's claim that he had reduced the scale of the practice.[33] The question is difficult to resolve, because many of the estimates of numbers sacrificed offered in contemporary European sources (in hundreds, or even thousands) seem to be based on hearsay and to be greatly exaggerated. Eyewitness accounts generally offer more modest numbers. A British official who attended three successive Annual Customs in the early nineteenth century, for example, never counted more than 65 victims on any one occasion, though this figure probably relates only to public sacrifices and does not include those killed in the subsequent 'watering' of the royal graves inside the palace, which Europeans did not normally witness.[34] The numbers sacrificed may, however, have increased under King Gezo in the early part of his reign as a consequence of his military successes, which yielded large numbers of war captives, who were available for sacrifice as well as for sale overseas. A witness of the Annual Customs in May 1843 claimed to have seen no fewer than 64 severed heads of victims killed overnight at the palace gate (by comparison with only 6 each on two occasions in 1850), and estimated the total number of those killed (improbably) at over 1,000.[35]

In 1850 Isidoro de Souza, in a conversation recorded in Beecroft's journal (on 18 May), stated that at the forthcoming Customs the King would decapitate 250 victims.[36] Forbes, in his book, suggested that this account was 'exaggerated'.[37] Nevertheless, he himself gave a similar figure, 240, as the number of those who had been sacrificed in the Annual Customs in the previous year, 1849.[38] Since Forbes had not himself witnessed these earlier Customs, this figure must derive from hearsay, and indeed very likely from Isodoro's statement, imperfectly (or at least differently) heard or remembered.

However, at the Customs which he and Beecroft witnessed in May–June 1850, Forbes counted a total of only 32 victims, which he interpreted as indicating that the sacrifices had been 'much diminished in numbers' from the previous year.[39] Forbes' figure comprised the following:

> **29 May**: Forbes saw, in a courtyard inside the palace, a 'newly formed heap' of earth, which he understood to cover the head of a victim sacrificed the previous night—this is not mentioned by Beecroft.
> **30 May**: in Singbodji Square, both Forbes and Beecroft saw six severed heads of victims killed the previous night.
> **31 May**: in the 'Platform Custom' in Adjahi market, Forbes and Beecroft witnessed the sacrifice of 11 victims, who were thrown from a platform and decapitated.

---

[33] See Introduction, p. xxxii.
[34] M'Leod (1820: 60) (reported in 1803).
[35] Brue (1845: 66–7).
[36] Beecroft's Journal, p. 12.
[37] Forbes (1851, ii: 6).
[38] Forbes (1851, i: 33), which interprets 'last year' as 1848, presumably through misguided editorial intervention.
[39] Forbes (1851, i: 33).

3 June: Forbes again saw six severed heads of victims sacrificed the previous night—Beecroft records seeing five (*sic*) prospective victims paraded on 1 June, but not seeing their heads subsequently.

11 June: in the 'watering' of the 'grave' of King Dakodonu, inside the Dahomey palace, Forbes and Beecroft both understood that four victims were sacrificed (after they themselves had left).

16 June: in the 'watering' of the 'grave' of King Agaja (and/or perhaps, those of some of his successor kings), inside the main palace, Forbes and Beecroft again understood that four victims were sacrificed (again, after they had left).[40]

However, Forbes himself stressed that 32 was only the number of sacrifices 'of which we were aware', and that 'he had no doubt that many more victims were sacrificed'.[41] Logically, indeed, it might expected that there would also have been sacrifices at the other ceremonies of 'watering the graves' of kings or royal 'mothers' (Kpojito) reported as held on seven other days: on 7 June (for a king or kings unnamed) and 15 June (for King Agaja), and on 17–19 and 21–22 June (for the Kpojito of Agaja and the four Dahomian kings who preceded Gezo). Forbes himself observed that, although he knew directly of human sacrifices at only two of the 'watering' customs, 'I much doubt if every day, inside or outside [the palace], one or more victims were not offered', and again that 'I much fear that sacrifices of female prisoners took place in the evenings', although he had been told that King Gezo had 'discontinued' such sacrifices.[42] Beecroft in fact understood that an unspecified number of 'victims to be sacrificed in the evening' were held ready in the ceremonies on 15 June, which are not mentioned in Forbes' account.[43] If we assume that the victims on this occasion also numbered 4, this would bring the total number those killed up to 36. If we further assume that 4 persons were sacrificed at each of the other 'watering' ceremonies, this would add a further 24 to the tally of victims, giving a grand total of 60.

This, however, is a hazardous assumption, since it is possible that sacrifices were not in fact offered on every occasion, or more precisely that sacrificial 'victims' were sometimes not actually killed. Burton later observed that 'at times the King exposes without slaying his victims', and more specifically that at a ceremony of 'watering the grave' of the late King Gezo of which he heard report (on 31 January 1864), 'two [victims], a youth and a maiden, were offered up (officially)' but in fact 'kept alive to sweep King Gezo's grave'.[44] In the Annual Customs of 1850, in the 'watering' ceremony for Chai, the Kpojito of King Kpengla, on 19 June, both Forbes and Beecroft mention that the King presented eight boys taken prisoner in the recent Atakpamé war 'to be kept, in his Grandfather's [i.e. Kpengla's] courtyard, in commemoration of the event of that war'.[45] It seems likely that this was in lieu of sacrificing them. This

---

[40] Forbes' Journal mentions only two victims (p. 183), but in his book (1851, ii: 134) he adds that two others were also sacrificed, making four in all, which is confirmed by Beecroft (Journal, p. 110).

[41] Forbes (1851, ii: 171).

[42] Forbes (1851, ii: 128, n. 152). The wording is ambiguous, but what Gezo had reportedly 'discontinued' was probably the sacrifice specifically of female victims.

[43] Beecroft's Journal, p. 107.

[44] Burton (1864, i: 350; ii: 24n.). Vice-Consul Fraser in September 1851 likewise saw a woman and two boys paraded as prospective sacrificial victims, but understood that they in fact 'escaped' this fate (2012: 103–5).

[45] See pp. 125–6, 187.

might be interpreted—assuming that nobody was sacrificed on 19 June, but allowing 4 victims each at some or all of the other 5 'watering' ceremonies—to indicate a total of between 36 and 56 for the victims of the Annual Customs of 1850.

However, this was not the total of those sacrificed during the year, since other customs of the annual cycle also involved human sacrifices. The Kana Custom which preceded the main Annual Customs included human sacrifices: when they were performed in May 1863, the bodies of 11 victims were exhibited.[46] The 'ship' Custom which followed the main Annual Customs, as performed on 18 August 1850, according to the eyewitness testimony of the French agent Blanchely, involved the parading of six prospective victims (although he did not actually witness their killing).[47] The Custom of 'firing to Whydah', as reported by Vice-Consul Fraser in the following year, November 1851, is said to have included a ceremony of 'watering the graves' of deceased kings, which may also have included human sacrifices.[48] The Customs at the end of the year also involved human sacrifices, at least in the upgraded version witnessed by Burton in 1863/4, who counted a total of 39 victims in the public ceremonies, plus an uncertain number of others at 'watering' ceremonies for the deceased kings which followed, which he did not himself witness.[49] Burton thought that the total number killed in all ceremonies through the year might have been as high as 500, though this is evidently only speculative and perhaps an exaggeration.[50] Skertchly in 1871 estimated the annual toll more modestly at 'not less than 200'.[51] The scale of sacrifices in the 1860s, however, had probably increased since 1850.[52]

---

[46] Burton (1864, i: 199). A French naval officer who visited Kana in 1851 (but did not actually witness the Kana Custom), says that 'a large number' of human victims were sacrificed (Bouet 1852: 42).

[47] Blanchely (1891: 575–6).

[48] Fraser (2012: 126).

[49] Burton (1864, ii: 102, 173–6).

[50] Burton (1864, ii: 24–5). Burton thought that his own count of 39 victims at the So-sin Custom should be doubled, on the assumption that a corresponding number of female victims were sacrificed inside the palace (ii: 22)—for which there seems little supporting evidence.

[51] Skertchly (1874: 239).

[52] Sixteen of the 39 victims seen by Burton were sacrificed for the 'Bush King', a second identity for the King which required the performance of some ceremonies for a second time (Bay 1998: 215–22). This practice is not mentioned by Beecroft and Forbes in 1850, so had presumably been introduced only later.

ENDNOTE 2

WHAT DID GEZO SAY ON 4 JULY 1850?

The extent and nature of differences between the reportage of Beecroft and Forbes are here illustrated by their different accounts of what King Gezo said in their final audience with him on 4 July 1850. There are, in fact, four rather than only two versions, since Beecroft included an account of Gezo's statements in the letter which he wrote to the Foreign Office written on 22 July 1850, as well as in his journal, while Forbes reworked the account in his original journal in his subsequently published book. There are discrepancies, not only between Beecroft and Forbes, but between the successive versions of each of them. The four versions are presented here in tabular form, in order to facilitate comparison, although this is not straightforward, since there are differences in the ordering of the material as well as in wording among the various versions; moreover it is not always clear whether passages with similar content should be regarded as different renderings of the same statements—especially since the King appears to have repeated himself on at least a couple of occasions. It may be noted that both Beecroft and Forbes include material omitted by the other; both also add material in their second versions which does not appear in their first text, although in Beecroft's case the additional material is recycled from the letter which Gezo dictated during the interview (reproduced in Appendix 3, doc. 7).

	Version 1: Beecroft's journal	Version 2: Beecroft's letter	Version 3: Forbes' journal	Version 4: Forbes' book
1	He commenced in detail to relate the state of Abomey a century back	He commenced to state in detail the friendship that had existed between His Majesty's grandfather and the King of England	His Majesty gave us a history of the foreign trade of Dahomey from its earliest dates, and the continued good feeling that had always existed between his ancestors and former Kings of Great Britain	The king gave a history of the trade, from its earliest commencement in Whydah and Dahomey, down to the present date
2	It is just the same at this day	The country of Dahomey had not changed, but remained the same to this day	Throughout, the Dahomans had sold slaves	See §8
3	The French was the first nation at one time, but after they conquered Whydah			First, the French came to Whydah before Dahomey conquered it
4				War put a stop to trade for many years. The white man left Whydah in A-dah-hoon-zar's time[1]
5	the English became the first and most confidential friend of the King of Dahomey, not any other nation knew the extent of their friendship			The English traders were the first who landed there, and bought slaves.

No.				
6				*His father had impressed him with the belief that the English were the first of white men: he believed so himself, and desired much to be at peace with them.*
7	*It continued so, and two of his grandfather's children were sent to England to be educated*			
8	*See §2*	*See §2*	*See §2*	*Time had passed, but the Dahomians had never given up slave-dealing*
9	*He very soon expressed himself, that he could not leave off the awful traffic in slaves*	*See §19*		
10	*We ought to commence with those inferior places, Popoo, Aghwey, Porto Novo, Badagry and Lagos, then come to him and talk the palaver, he would then try. He expressed a strong desire that Her Majesty's Government should blockade all these above mentioned places*	*See §19*	*See §19*	*See §19*

(Continued)

	Version 1: Beecroft's journal	Version 2: Beecroft's letter	Version 3: Forbes' journal	Version 4: Forbes' book
11	*for they were not like him, liberal and munificent, they kept it all from their people.*		See §18	See §18
12	*His Majesty's desire was that Whydah was to be a free port, for he acknowledged that he had five men to attend to his merchants in Whydah &c mentioning at the same time their names, Isadore, the Cha-Cha of Whydah, Ignatio, Caboceer, and Antonio, King's Friend, three bastards to the late De Souza's, Domingo Martins, and Joachim Antonio, he wanted papers and colours for five ships to pass without hindrance, or molestation, from Her Majesty's cruisers*	See §24	See §24	
13	*He then ardently requested that we would mention in the letter to the Queen to allow himself one ship to pass without molestation. The Queen of England his friend surely could not object to that, allow him papers with a flag for one*	See §26	See §26	

solitary ship … he certainly thought it very hard that his friend could not allow one vessel to pass, to bring articles for himself and his people				
14 His people were a warlike people, unaccustomed to the agricultural pursuits		They were a warlike people, the Dahomians, and of course unaccustomed to agricultural pursuits	My people are a military people male and Female	His people were soldiers
15 He could not attempt to send his people to plant and cultivate cotton, and make farms, that they were warriors, and he did not wish to be laughed at by other nations	See §22	Cf. §28?		
16 He would not be able to keep up his revenues, was he at once to stop the slave trade²	See §21	My revenue is the proceeds of the sale of prisoners of war		His revenue [was] the proceeds of the slave trade (or the sale of prisoners of war)
17 See §21		Did you, after you passed the swamp, except in the neighbourhood of towns, meet any farms?		Do we not observe the absence of agriculture?
18 See §11		Other nations deal in slaves, but not like me, they keep all the proceeds to themselves, I give mine to the people		Other nations deal in slaves, but not like me: they keep no customs, make no general disbursement

(Continued)

	Version 1: Beecroft's journal	Version 2: Beecroft's letter	Version 3: Forbes' journal	Version 4: Forbes' book
19	See §10	Being desirous that it should be stopped in the minor ports prior to his entering into a treaty, requests that Her Majesty's Government will endeavour to blockade between Quittah and Lagos; and then he would endeavour to enter into an agreement for the suppression of the slave trade in his own country[3]	I would wish the ports of Little Popoe, Argwee, Great Popoe, Porto Novo and Lagos to be forced to stop the slave trade, before I could treat	The slave-trade of these states must be stopped before I can treat
20	All the nations that had planted and sold cotton he had conquered, so there is very little cotton for sale	See §23	Cf. §30	
21	He asked us, from the swamp to Abomey did you see any farms?	He asked if we had seen any farms between the swamp and Abomey?	See §17	See §17
22	See §15	He could not disgrace himself and subject himself to being laughed at by sending the women from his palace-yard to plant and cultivate cotton	Cf. §28?	

23	See §20	*He also stated that he had taken and destroyed all the countries that formerly cultivated cotton*	Cf. §30
24	See §12	*His Majesty then requested us to address a letter to Her Majesty the Queen of England, his friend, that she would allow Whydah to become a free port; stating that he had five agents, mentioning at the same time their names, viz., Isidore, Ignacio, and Antonio three sons of the late de Souza, also Domingo Martins and Joaquim Antonio. His Majesty's simple request was to have papers and flags to allow them to pass without hindrance or molestation from Her Majesty's cruisers*	*In the meantime let the port of Whydah be thrown open to my slave trade, not to all the merchants there but to my agents, Cha Cha, Domingo José Martins, Joaquim Antonio, Ignatio and Antonio Da Souza, let the ships belonging to these 5 pass free*
25			*Cha Cha has given me one Ship—Domingo and Joaquim also one each, make a Letter to the Queen to grant me a flag and protection for these three*

(Continued)

	Version 1: Beecroft's journal	Version 2: Beecroft's letter	Version 3: Forbes' journal	Version 4: Forbes' book
26	See §13	*Surely my friend, the Queen of England, will allow papers and colours for one vessel for myself to go free from the men-of-war?*	*Write to the Queen and ask her to direct her Men of War to allow one ship to pass in my name to the Brazils, to carry a cargo of slaves and bring back goods for me*	
27			*If I stop the slave trade how can the Miegan, the Mayo &c, each of whom and the merchants—Narwhey, Ah-joo-bee, Quenung &c, who pay me 5,000 dollars annually …duties and presents afford to pay their customs?*	
28	*I cannot take my women to plant farms* [repetition of §15?]		*I cannot send my women to cultivate the soil—it would kill them*[4]	
29			*My people cannot in a short space of time become an agricultural people*	
30		Cf. §20	*War has destroyed all the neighbouring countries and my people have far to go for food*	

All my nation, all are soldiers,
and the slave trade feeds them

[repetition of §14?]

---

[1] The name resembles 'Adahoonzou', given in contemporary sources (including Dalzel 1793) to the king known to tradition as Kpengla (r. 1774–89), and rendered as 'Ada Hoonzoo' in Forbes (1851, ii: 88). But the reference here must be to Gezo's immediate predecessor Adandozan, during whose reign (1797–1818) the European forts at Ouidah were abandoned.

[2] Wording taken from Gezo's letter.

[3] Wording from Gezo's letter.

[4] This looks like a variant of Beecroft's statement of not wishing to be 'laughed at', which occurs earlier (see §§ 15, 22). See further Introduction, pp. xlvi–xlvii.

SOURCES AND BIBLIOGRAPHY

Archival Sources

Church Missionary Society Archives, University of Birmingham:
C/A2/085: Letters and Papers of Rev. Henry Townsend, 1845–80.

The National Archives (TNA), Kew, London:

Colonial Office records:
CO96/2–4, 6, 8, 11, 13, 20: Gold Coast, Dispatches, 1843–8, 1850.

Foreign Office records:
FO2/7: General Correspondence, Consular, Domestic, 1852.
FO84/775, 816: Slave Trade Department, Africa (West Coast), Consular, 1849–50.
FO84/785, 826–8: Slave Trade Department, Admiralty, Letters: 1849–50.
FO84/818–19: Slave Trade Department, Foreign, Various, 1850.

United Kingdom Hydrographic Office, Taunton:
OD 9A: Ferdinand Struvé, 'Report on the Results Obtained by the Expedition … to Survey and Explore the Coast Lagoon between the River Benin to the Eastward and the River Volta to the Westward, in the Bight of Benin, West Africa; the Present Portion of the Survey Having Extended from Whydah to Adjudo [1848–9]', n.d.

Wesleyan Methodist Missionary Society Archives, School of Oriental and African Studies, London:
Box 262: Correspondence, Gold Coast, 1855–7.

House of Commons Parliamentary Papers (HCPP)

Copy of Dispatches from the Lieutenant-Governor of the Gold Coast, Giving an Account of Missions to the Kings of Ashantee and Dohomey (1849).

Correspondence Relating to the Slave Trade, Class A (from British Commissioners, Vice-Admiralty Courts and Naval Officers) and Class B (with British Ministers and Agents in Foreign Countries and Foreign Ministers in England) 1849/50–1855/6.

Papers Relative to the Reduction of Lagos by Her Majesty's Forces (1852).

Report from the Select Committee on the West Coast of Africa (1842).

Report from the Select Committee on the Slave Trade (1848).

Published Sources

Allen, William, and Thomson, T.R.H., 1848: *Narrative of the Expedition to the River Niger in 1841*, 2 vols (London: Richard Bentley).

Baikie, William Balfour, 1856: *Narrative of an Exploring Voyage up the Rivers Kwóra and Binue (Commonly Known as the Niger and Tsadda) in 1854* (London: John Murray).

Barth, Heinrich, 1857: *Travels and Discoveries in North and Central Africa*, 3 vols (London: Longman, Brown, Green, Longmans & Roberts).

Be[e]croft, Captain [John], 1841: 'On Benin and the Upper Course of the River Quorra, or Niger', *Journal of the Royal Geographical Society*, 11: 184–92.

Blanchely, 1891: 'Au Dahomey', *Les Missions Catholiques*, 23: 534–7, 545–8, 562–4, 575–6, 587–8.

Bouet, Auguste, 1852: 'Le royaume de Dahomey', *L'Illustration*, 20: 31–42, 58–62, 71–4.

Brue, [Blaise], 1845: 'Voyage fait en 1843, dans le royaume de Dahomey', *Revue coloniale*, 7: 55–68.

Burton, Richard F., 1864: *A Mission to Gelele, King of Dahome*, 2 vols (London: Tinsley Brothers).

Buxton, Thomas Fowell, 1840: *The African Slave Trade and its Remedy* (London: Richard Bentley).

Clapperton, Hugh, 1829: *Journal of a Second Expedition into the Interior of Africa* (London: John Murray).

Coates, Tim (ed.), 2001: *King Guezo of Dahomey, 1850–52: The Abolition of the Slave Trade on the West Coast of Africa* (London: The Stationery Office).

Crooks, J.J. (ed.), 1923: *Records relating to the Gold Coast Settlements from 1750 to 1874* (Dublin: Browne & Nolan).

Crowther, Samuel, 1855: *Journal of an Expedition up the Niger and Tshadda Rivers* (London: Church Missionary Society House).

Dalzel, Archibald, 1793: *The History of Dahomy, an Inland Kingdom of Africa* (London: The Author).

Duncan, John, 1847: *Travels in Western Africa in 1845 and 1846, Comprising a Journey from Whydah, through the Kingdom of Dahomey, to Adofoodia in the Interior*, 2 vols (London: Richard Bentley).

Forbes, Lieutenant F[rederick] E., 1848: *Five Years in China; from 1842 to 1847: With an Account of the Occupation of the Islands of Labuan and Borneo by Her Majesty's Forces* (London: Richard Bentley).

Forbes, Lieutenant [Frederick E.], 1849: *Six Months' Service in the African Blockade, from April to October, 1848, in Command of H.M.S. Bonetta* (London: Richard Bentley).

Forbes, Lieutenant F[rederick] E., n.d. [1850]: *Despatch Communicating the Discovery of a Native Written Character at Bohmar, on the Western Coast of Africa, near Liberia, Accompanied by a Vocabulary of the Vahie or Vei Tongue [Read before the Royal Geographical Society of London, on the 23rd of April 1849]* (London: William Clowes & Sons).

Forbes, [Lieutenant] Frederick E., 1851: *Dahomey and the Dahomans, being the Journals of Two Missions to the King of Dahomey in the Years 1849 and 1850*, 2 vols (London: Longman, Brown, Green & Longmans).

Fraser, Louis, 2012: *Dahomey and the Ending of the Trans-Atlantic Slave Trade: The Journals and Correspondence of Vice-Consul Louis Fraser 1851–1852*, ed. Robin Law (Oxford: Oxford University Press, for the British Academy).

Freeman, Rev. Thomas B., 1844: *Journal of Various Visits to the Kingdoms of Ashanti, Aku and Dahomi in West Africa* (London: John Mason).

Hazoumé, Paul, 1978 [1938]: *Doguicimi*, 2nd edn (Paris: G.-P. Maisonneuve et Larose).

Koelle, Rev. S.W., 1849: *Narrative of an Expedition into the Vy Country of West Africa, and the Discovery of a System of Syllabic Writing Recently Invented by the Natives of the Vy Tribe* (London: Seeley, Hatchards, & J. Nisbet).

Laird, MacGregor, and Oldfield, R.A.K., 1837: *Narrative of an Expedition into the Interior of Africa*, 2 vols (London: Richard Bentley).

Le Herissé, A., 1911: *L'Ancien royaume du Dahomey: moeurs, religion, histoire* (Paris: E. Larose).

M'Leod, John, 1820: *A Voyage to Africa, with some Account of the Manners and Customs of the Dahomian People* (London: John Murray).

Mouléro, Abbé Th[omas], 1965: 'Guézo ou Guédizo Massigbé', *Études dahoméennes*, ns 4: 51–9.

Norris, Robert, 1789: *Memoirs of the Reign of Bossa Ahadee, King of Dahomy* (London: W. Lowndes).

P[runeau] de P[ommegorge], [Antoine-Edmé], 1789: *Description de la Nigritie* (Paris: Maradan).

Ridgway, Archibald R., 1847: 'Journal of a Visit to Dahomey, or the Snake Kingdom, in the Months of March and April 1847', *New Monthly Magazine*, 81: 187–98, 299–309, 406–14.

Robertson, G.A., 1819: *Notes on Africa, Particularly those Parts which are Situated between Cape Verd and the River Congo* (London: Sherwood, Neely, & Sons).

Shadwell, Commander C.F.A, 1851: 'Proceedings of H.M.S. Sphinx: Extracts from the Remark Book of Com. C.F.A. Shadwell', in *The Nautical Magazine and Naval Chronicle for 1851* (London: Simpkin, Marshall & Co.): 561–9, 624–33.

Skertchly, J.A., 1874: *Dahomey as It Is* (London: Chapman & Hill).

Vallon, A., 1860/1: 'Le royaume de Dahomey', *Revue maritime et coloniale*, 2 parts, 1: 332–63; 2: 329–53.

Vattel, Emer de, 1797: *The Law of Nations*, revised edn (London: G.G. & J. Robinson).

Secondary Literature

Adandé, Alexandre, 1962: *Les Récades des rois du Dahomey* (Dakar: Institut Français d'Afrique Noire).

Adeyinka, Augustus A., 1974: 'King Gezo of Dahomey, 1818–1858: A Reassessment of a West African Monarch in the Nineteenth Century', *African Studies Review*, 17/3: 541–8.

Akinjogbin, I.A., 1967: *Dahomey and its Neighbours 1708–1818* (Cambridge: Cambridge University Press).

Alpern, Stanley B., 1998: *Amazons of Black Sparta: The Women Warriors of Dahomey* (New York: New York University Press).

Bassett, Thomas J., and Porter, Philip W., 1991: '"From the Best Authorities": The Mountains of Kong in the Cartography of West Africa', *Journal of African History*, 32/3: 367–431.

Bay, Edna G., 1998: *Wives of the Leopard: Gender, Politics and Culture in the Kingdom of Dahomey* (Charlottesville: University Press of Virginia).

Bay, Edna G., 2008: *Asen, Ancestors and Vodun: Tracing Change in African Art* (Urbana: University of Illinois Press).

Biobaku, S.O., 1957: *The Egba and their Neighbours 1842–1872* (Oxford: Clarendon Press).

Coquery-Vidrovitch, Catherine, 1964: 'La fête des coutumes au Dahomey: historique et essai d'interprétation', *Annales ESC*, 19: 696–717.

Dike, K. O[nwuka], 1956a: 'John Beecroft (1790–1854): Her Britannic Majesty's Consul to the Bights of Benin and Biafra, 1849–1854', *Journal of the Historical Society of Nigeria*, 1/1: 5–14.

Dike, K. Onwuka, 1956b: *Trade and Politics in the Niger Delta 1830–1885: An Introduction to the Economic and Political History of Nigeria* (Oxford: Clarendon Press).

Djivo, Joseph Adrien, 1977: *Guézo: la rénovation du Dahomey* (Dakar: Nouvelles Éditions Africaines).

Djivo, Joseph Adrien, 2013: *Le refus de la colonisation dans l'ancien royaume de Danxomε 1875–1900: Gbεhanzin et Ago-li-Agbo*, 2 vols (Paris: L'Harmattan).

Dunglas, Édouard, 1957–8: 'Contribution à l'histoire du Moyen-Dahomey', *Études dahoméennes*, 19–21 (Special Issues).

Euba, O., 1982: 'Of Blue Beads and Red: The Role of Ife in the West African Trade in Kori Beads', *Journal of the Historical Society of Nigeria*, 21/1–2: 109–27.

Folayan, Kola, 1972: 'International Politics in a Frontier Zone: Egbado, 1833–63', *Odu: A Journal of West African Studies*, ns 8: 3–32.

Gallagher, J., 1950: 'Fowell Buxton and the New African Policy, 1838–1842', *Cambridge Historical Journal*, 10/1: 36–58.

Glélé, Maurice Ahanhanzo, 1974: *Le Danxomε: du pouvoir aja à la nation fon* (Paris: Nubia).

Jones, Adam, 1999: 'Little Popo and Agoué at the End of the Atlantic Slave Trade: Glimpses from the Lawson Correspondence and Other Sources', in *Ports of the Slave Trade (Bights of Benin and Biafra)*, ed. Robin Law and Silke Strickrodt (Stirling: Centre of Commonwealth Studies, University of Stirling): 122–34.

Law, Robin, 1977a: *The Oyo Empire, c. 1600–c. 1836: A West African Imperialism in the Era of the Atlantic Slave Trade* (Oxford: Clarendon Press).

Law, Robin, 1977b: 'Royal Monopoly and Private Enterprise in the Atlantic Trade: The Case of Dahomey', *Journal of African History*, 18/4: 555–77.

Law, Robin, 1980a: *The Horse in West African History: The Role of the Horse in the Societies of Pre-colonial West Africa* (Oxford: Oxford University Press, for International African Institute).

Law, Robin, 1980b: 'Wheeled Transport in Pre-colonial West Africa', *Africa*, 50/3: 249–62.

Law, Robin, 1985: 'Human Sacrifice in Pre-colonial West Africa', *African Affairs*, 84/344: 53–87.

Law, Robin, 1986: 'Islam in Dahomey: A Case Study of the Introduction and Influence of Islam in a Peripheral Area of West Africa', *Scottish Journal of Religious Studies*, 7/2: 95–1.

Law, Robin, 1989: '"My Head Belongs to the King": On the Political and Ritual Significance of Decapitation in Pre-colonial Dahomey', *Journal of African History*, 30/3: 399–415.

Law, Robin, 1991: *The Slave Coast of West Africa, 1550–1750: The Impact of the Atlantic Slave Trade on an African Society* (Oxford: Clarendon Press).

Law, Robin, 1993: 'The "Amazons" of Dahomey', *Paideuma*, 39: 23–44.

Law, Robin, 1994a: 'Cowries, Gold, and Dollars: Exchange Rate Instability and Domestic Price Inflation in Dahomey in the Eighteenth and Nineteenth Centuries', in *Money Matters: Instability, Values and Social Payments in the Modern History of West African Communities*, ed. Jane Guyer (Portsmouth, NH: Heinemann): 53–73.

Law, Robin, 1994b: 'Dahomey and the North-West', *Cahiers du Centre de Recherches Africaines: Spécial Togo-Bénin*, 8 (Special Issue): 149–67.

Law, Robin, 1995a: 'An African Response to Abolition: Anglo-Dahomian Negotiations on Ending the Slave Trade, 1838–77', *Slavery & Abolition*, 16/3: 281–310.

Law, Robin, 1995b: '"Legitimate" Trade and Gender Relations in Yorubaland and Dahomey', in *From Slave Trade to 'Legitimate' Commerce: The Commercial Transition in Nineteenth-Century West Africa*, ed. Robin Law (Cambridge: Cambridge University Press): 195–214.

Law, Robin, 1997a: 'Ethnicity and the Slave Trade: "Lucumi" and "Nago" as Ethnonyms in West Africa', *History in Africa*, 24: 205–19.

Law, Robin, 1997b: 'The Politics of Commercial Transition: Factional Conflict in Dahomey in the Context of the Ending of the Atlantic Slave Trade', *Journal of African History*, 38/2: 213–33.

Law, Robin, 1999: 'Finance and Credit in Pre-colonial Dahomey', in *Credit, Currencies and Culture: African Financial Institutions in Historical Perspective*, ed. Endre Stiansen and Jane I. Guyer (Uppsala: Nordiska Afrikainstitutet): 15–37.

Law, Robin, 2004a: 'Francisco Felix de Souza in West Africa, 1820–1849', in *Enslaving Connections: Changing Cultures of Africa and Brazil during the Era of Slavery*, ed. José C. Curto and Paul E. Lovejoy (New York: Humanities Books): 187–211.

Law, Robin, 2004b: *Ouidah: The Social History of a West African Slaving 'Port', 1727–1892* (Oxford: James Currey).

Law, Robin, 2010a: 'Abolition and Imperialism: International Law and the British Suppression of the Atlantic Slave Trade', in *Abolition and Imperialism in Britain, Africa and the Atlantic*, ed. Derek R. Peterson (Athens, OH: Ohio University Press): 150–74.

Law, Robin, 2010b: 'Madiki Lemon, the "English Captain" at Ouidah, 1843–1852: An Exploration in Biography', *History in Africa*, 37: 107–23.

Law, Robin, 2016: 'The English Interpreters in Dahomey, 1843–52', *Journal of Imperial & Commonwealth History*, 44/5: 730–51.

Lynn, Martin, 1984: 'Commerce, Christianity and the Origins of the "Creoles" of Fernando Po', *Journal of African History*, 25/3: 257–78.

Lynn, Martin, 1992: 'Consul and Kings: "The Man on the Spot" and the Seizure of Lagos, 1851', *Journal of Imperial & Commonwealth History*, 10/2: 150–67.

Lynn, Martin, 1997: *Commerce and Economic Change in West Africa: The Palm Oil Trade in the Nineteenth Century* (Cambridge: Cambridge University Press).

Manning, Patrick, 1982: *Slavery, Colonialism and Economic Growth in Dahomey, 1640–1960* (Cambridge: Cambridge University Press).

Mercier, Paul, 1952: *Les Asẽ du Musée d'Abomey* (Dakar: Institut Français d'Afrique Noire).

Mercier, P[aul], and Lombard, J[acques], 1959: *Guide du Musée d'Abomey* (Porto-Novo: Institut Français d'Afrique Noire).

Monroe, J. Cameron, 2014: *The Precolonial State in West Africa: Building Power in Dahomey* (New York: Cambridge University Press).

Myers, Walter Dean, 1999: *At Her Majesty's Request: An African Princess in Victorian England* (New York: Scholastic Press).

Newbury, C.W., 1961: *The Western Slave Coast and its Rulers: European Trade and Administration among the Yoruba and Aja-Speaking Peoples of South-Western Nigeria, Southern Dahomey and Togo* (Oxford: Clarendon Press).

Nicolau Parés, Luis, 2016: *O rei, o pai e a morte: A religião vodum na antiga Costa dos Escravos na África Ocidental* (São Paulo: Companhia das Letras).

O'Connor, Derek, 2006: *The King's Stranger: A Biography of John Duncan, Scotland's Forgotten Explorer* (USA: Long Rider's Guild Press).

Palau Marti, Montserrat, 1992: *L'Histoire de Sàbé et de ses rois (République du Bénin)* (Paris: Maisonneuve et Larose).

Picton, John, and Mack, John, 1979: *African Textiles: Looms, Weaving and Design* (London: British Museum Publications).

Randsborg, Klavs, and Merkyte, Inge, with Niels Algreen Møller and Søren Albek, 2009: *Bénin Archaeology: The Ancient Kingdoms*, 2 vols (Oxford: Wiley-Blackwell).

Ratcliffe, Barrie, 1982: 'Cotton Imperialism: Manchester Merchants and Cotton Cultivation in West Africa in the Mid-Nineteenth Century', *African Economic History*, 11: 88–113.

Ross, David A., 1965: 'The Career of Domingo Martinez in the Bight of Benin, 1833–64', *Journal of African History*, 6/1: 79–90.

Ross, David A., 1969: 'The First Chacha of Whydah, Francisco Felix de Souza', *Odu: A Journal of West African Studies*, ns 2: 19–28.

Segurola, B., and Rassinoux, J., 2000: *Dictionnaire fon-français* (Madrid: Société des Missions Africaines).

Smith, Robert S., 1978: *The Lagos Consulate 1851–1861* (London: Macmillan).

Sorensen-Gilmour, Caroline, 1999: 'Slave-Trading along the Lagoons of South-West Nigeria: The Case of Badagry', in *Ports of the Slave Trade (Bights of Benin and Biafra)*, ed. Robin Law and Silke Strickrodt (Stirling: Centre of Commonwealth Studies, University of Stirling): 84–95.

Soumonni, E.A., 1980: 'Dahomean Economic Policy under Ghezo, 1818–1858', *Journal of the Historical Society of Nigeria*, 10/2: 1–11.

Soumonni, E.A., 1995: 'The Compatibility of the Slave and Palm Oil Trades in Dahomey, 1818–1858', in *From Slave Trade to 'Legitimate' Commerce: The Commercial Transition in Nineteenth-Century West Africa*, ed. Robin Law (Cambridge: Cambridge University Press): 78–92.

Strickrodt, Silke, 2015: *Afro-European Trade in the Atlantic World: The Western Slave Coast c.1550–c.1885* (Woodbridge: James Currey).

Videgla, Michel, 1999: 'Le royaume de Porto-Novo face à la politique abolitionniste des nations européennes de 1848 à 1882', in *Ports of the Slave Trade (Bights of Benin and Biafra)*, ed. Robin Law and Silke Strickrodt (Stirling: Centre of Commonwealth Studies, University of Stirling): 135–52.

Waterlot, Em. G., 1926: *Les Bas-Reliefs des Bâtiments royaux d'Abomey (Dahomey)* (Paris: Institut d'Ethnologie).

Yoder, John C., 1974: 'Fly and Elephant Parties: Political Polarization in Dahomey 1840–70', *Journal of African History*, 15/3: 417–32.

Unpublished Items

Reid, John, 1986: 'Warrior Aristocrats in Crisis: The Political Effects of the Transition from the Slave Trade to Palm Oil Commerce in the Nineteenth-Century Kingdom of Dahomey' (PhD thesis, University of Stirling).

Ross, David A., 1967: 'The Autonomous Kingdom of Dahomey, 1818–1894' (PhD thesis, University of London).

Sorensen-Gilmour, Caroline, 1995: 'Badagry 1784–1863: The Political and Commercial History of a Pre-colonial Lagoonside Community in South-West Nigeria' (PhD thesis, University of Stirling).

Soumonni, E.A., 1983: 'Trade and Politics in Dahomey, with Particular Reference to the House of Régis, 1841–1892' (PhD thesis, University of Ife).

Internet Source

Trans-Atlantic Slave Trade Database (TASTD), http://www.slavevoyages.org/

INDEX